Joan Collins

Second Act

Joan Collins

Second Act

BOXTREE

First published in Great Britain in 1996 by Boxtree Limited, Broadwall
House, 21 Broadwall, London SE1 9PL

1 3 5 7 9 10 9 6 4 2

ISBN 0 7522 1698 8

Designed by Hammond Hammond
Typeset by SX Composing DTP, Rayleigh, Essex
Extract from Suzy's Column courtesy of *Women's Wear Daily*

Printed and bound in Great Britain by The Bath Press, Bath, Avon

A CIP catalogue entry for this book is available from the British Library

In loving memory of my mother Elsa Collins

ACKNOWLEDGEMENTS

My sincere thanks to Michael Alcock, the best editor one could have, who encouraged me through the dark days and into the light; to Paul Keylock, for his help in collating many of the photographs; and, of course, to Robin.

Contents

I am not afraid
of tomorrow,
For I have seen yesterday
And I love today.

William White

CHAPTER ONE

In the beginning

'From birth to eighteen, a girl needs good parents, from eighteen to twenty-five she needs good looks, from thirty-five to fifty-five she needs a good personality, and from fifty-five onwards a girl needs good cash.'

Sophie Tucker came up with that little gem, and I believe the old girl was right – especially about the parents. Few of us are born with the proverbial silver spoon at our lips, so those who are blessed with intelligent and loving mothers and fathers are the fortunate ones.

I was more than lucky with mine, so if you want to read a sorry saga of parental ill-treatment, childhood deprivation or drug and alcohol abuse, this book is not for you. My life has been favoured with much good fortune and some tragedy but, on the whole, it has been richly fulfilling – and much of that is due to my family, and the heritage they have passed on to me.

There was never any question that I would become an actress for, long before I was born, my path had been more or less laid out.

My paternal grandfather, Will Collins, was an impresario and a showman, his wife, Henrietta, was a variety star, as were three of her sisters, my father was a theatrical agent, my aunts musical-comedy actresses and my mother a dancer. They had embraced both sides of the footlights with passion, so acting was in my genes.

The roots of my family saga go back to a winter's day in 1875 when my eighteen-year-old great-grandmother, Julia Phillips, married twenty-one-year-old Zeusman Hart in the Great Synagogue Chamber in London. It looked as though this young couple would live happily ever after, but pretty Julia was no ordinary Victorian bride. She had a mind of her own and the iron will to follow it. She was flirtatious and flighty, had had several boyfriends before her marriage and continued to see other men afterwards – a shocking state of affairs for those moral times.

One of Mrs Hart's beaux was William Connell, a handsome twenty-three-year-old Protestant Irishman, who lived in Camden Town where he ran a cab-hire business with his father. William and Julia had a passionate affair, in which she allowed her heart to rule her head – with devastating consequences. Sixteen months after her marriage, she gave birth to a son, and although Zeusman Hart was recorded as the baby's father, it was doubtful that he truly believed he was. However, he kept his mouth firmly shut on the subject, as any breath of scandal could have meant banishment for Julia, and, besides, the Hart family honour was at stake. The eldest son of a Jewish family was often called by his father's first name, but this baby was named Isaac, after Julia's father.

Shortly after Isaac's birth, Julia and Zeusman decided amicably to part, and she and baby Isaac went to live with her father, a small shopkeeper. It wasn't long before she began another affair, with a man called Gilbert, and in 1878 she gave birth to her second son, Joseph Gilbert.

William Connell married someone else and Julia didn't see him for several years, but in 1890, after his wife died, the charismatic, green-eyed Irishman came striding back into her life. They married and went to live in Oakley Street, Chelsea, where their son Isaac was eventually told of his true paternal origins.

Isaac Hart grew into a handsome young man, with the same dark curly hair and flashing Irish eyes as his father. His first job was driving hansom cabs around London with his father, often to and from the thriving variety theatres and music-halls. He became obsessed with the theatre and, like his granddaughter many years later, started collecting the stars' autographs. He was fifteen when he became smitten with the young soubrette Lottie Collins, whom he saw make her sensational début at the Tivoli theatre. Wearing an enormous feathered Gainsborough hat perched on her auburn curls, a short red dress over copious frilly petticoats, and sexy high-heeled boots, Lottie danced and sang her famous song, 'Tar-ra-ra-boom-de-ay', while entrancing the audience with the saucy, provocative glances for which she became famous. Isaac idolized Lottie to such an extent that he adopted her surname, then – in honour of his father – he changed his first name to William, which he soon shortened to Will.

Towards the end of the century Will Collins, like many young men of that time, decided to seek his fortune in South Africa, and sailed for Cape Town with his vivacious sixteen-year-old girlfriend, Henrietta Assenheim. My grandmother came from a close-knit East End family of nineteen children who had all the humour and *joie de vivre* that so many true East Enders still have today.

Henrietta, the daughter of Joseph and Leah Assenheim, was half Jewish, as was Will. Although she had no professional stage training, she possessed style and charisma. She loved performing, and had already played Principal Girl in *Aladdin* at the Theatre Royal, Bristol. But Will thought 'Henrietta Assenheim' a clumsy name for an actress and persuaded her, even though they weren't yet married, to change her name to the more conventional Hettie Collins.

In South Africa Hettie quickly became popular, topping the bill in revue at the Alhambra Palace of Varieties in Cape Town, playing Fifi in the new musical comedy *A Chinese Honeymoon* at the Empire theatre, and receiving excellent reviews:

> Hettie Collins is a thundering favourite, a most charming little lady, who takes the bun for dancing and singing and in fact everything she does.

> Miss Collins is a dashing, dauntless, daring dancer, and a comely, cooing, kicking comedienne.

Will became the business manager of a theatrical company, staging concerts and variety shows that toured all over South Africa – undaunted by the Boer War and the Siege of Mafeking. He posted his show bills everywhere and his audiences came from both sides of the warring factions. His celebrity even reached London, where the theatrical newspaper *The Encore* reported:

Mr Will Collins is a most obliging gentleman who will get up a show to suit all the classes in South Africa. He is on friendly terms with both the Boers and the Britons, and also *persona grata* among the Zulus, the Basutos, the Matabele and other dusky gentry who are now our friends and allies but who were once arrayed in war panoply against us.

The Boer War created a tremendous demand for entertainment for the troops and, just as the likes of Bob Hope and Marlene Dietrich entertained the GIs in the Second World War, Hettie Collins and her company regaled thousands of homesick young Englishmen with song and *divertissement*. The troupe travelled across the veldt in a bullock wagon in the wake of the soldiers, but Hettie, still a feisty teenager, seldom complained. She adored playing to the troops and became their pin-up girl, handing out seductive pictures of herself with her legs high in the air and a saucy smile on her face.

On 17 May 1900, Hettie was appearing in Kimberley when – in the middle of her number – the company manager rushed on to the stage to announce that Mafeking had been relieved. 'Let us raise our voices to cheer the gallant cavalry hero, Colonel Baden-Powell,' cried Hettie. The audience cheered themselves hoarse and she led them in several rousing choruses of 'God Save the Queen'.

Will and Hettie finally reached Cape Town where they married in January 1901, and on 4 November 1902, six months after the Boer War had ended, my father, Joseph William Collins, was born.

Unhampered by a new baby, ambitious Hettie was determined to improve her act, and brought over two of her sisters, Annie and Bessie, from England. Billing themselves as The Three Cape Girls, they 'blacked up' – Black and White Minstrels were a popular music-hall tradition – and, outrageously costumed, performed their novelty routines with zest and style.

The fun-loving girls would often make their quick changes on stage in two tents, in one of which was hidden baby Joe and also Bessie's favourite tipple, a large bottle of Guinness. One night, Bessie had a quick swig, then inadvertently dropped the Guinness on the sleeping infant's head. Joe's yells made the audience hoot with laughter and The Three Cape Girls were so convulsed that they could barely finish the act. Will, though, was *not* amused. At the ripe old age of twenty-eight he was becoming a strict disciplinarian, and less than enthusiastic that his wife was enjoying herself onstage so much. Like many men of his generation, he believed that Hettie's place was as 'a proper wife and mother', so he decided to put a stop to 'all this theatrical nonsense'. The Three Cape Girls were disbanded and everyone sailed back to England. Joe was eighteen months old when he won the prize for being the most beautiful baby on board.

Although only twenty-one, Hettie was devastated to quit the theatrical life she loved. Will installed her in a London flat where she awaited the birth of her second child, Lalla, and became a good Edwardian wife who obeyed her husband.

Will's first job in London was assistant manager of Sir Oswald Stoll's Holloway Empire. He did so well that he was soon promoted to manage Stoll's newest and most modern theatre, the Ardwick Empire in Manchester, a glamorous red plush and gilt palace, which boasted the *dernier cri* in new technology – chandeliers powered by electricity instead of gas. A short time later, Will was moved on again, this time to become circuit manager of all of Sir Oswald's London variety and music-hall theatres.

In 1907, a second daughter, Pauline, was born, and the Collins family moved to a much grander house with a large garden in Goldhawk Road. As an affluent young theatrical manager, Will Collins's world had become one of elegance and grandeur. Every day he would go to his office in the Shepherd's Bush Empire, returning home for lunch and a nap. Then in the evening, in white tie, a black scarlet-lined cape and shiny top hat, he would sally forth to one of his theatres, often taking Hettie, who loved to parade herself in one of her luxurious gowns. Sometimes little Joe would accompany them, dressed up in a blue velvet suit with a white silk collar.

Joe was drawn to show business from an early age, and was often allowed to go to rehearsals. He would follow his father through the winding alleyways behind the theatres, then sit spellbound in the auditorium, watching the gorgeously-gowned showgirls, actresses, singers and soubrettes who all fussed over him. Occasionally he would be allowed to sit in the orchestra pit, pretending to conduct with a little stick. He attracted everyone's attention, and soon became rather spoilt, a trait that remained with him for the rest of his life.

As Will became more prosperous, his constantly repeated edict to his son was: 'You've got to *push* hard and have *get up and go* to get ahead in this world, my boy. And don't expect anyone to do anything for you – you've *got* to do it all yourself.'

Will was well ahead of his times. He was one of the earliest theatrical impresarios to realize the value of publicity, even employing a new and strange breed called a press agent. He was also one of the first to have a telephone installed in his office and a pianola in the front parlour, which might be considered the equivalent of today's video player. He quickly lost interest in this curious instrument, however, when the motor car suddenly became the grand passion of every young Englishman who could afford one. Every weekend the Collins family piled into their current vehicle and off they would venture for long drives, usually finishing up at that most fashionable of watering-places – Brighton.

Will Collins remained a stern disciplinarian, and woe betide anyone in his productions who stepped out of line. One night at the Shepherd's Bush Empire, a dancer was being twirled around the stage by her partner and husband, Larry Sebelus, when her belt fell off. Instinctively she stopped to pick it up while the orchestra continued to play, and her partner waited. Will, with the quick temper he'd inherited from Julia – which he in turn passed on to his son, Joe – stormed backstage and tore into the hapless girl. Sebelus was furious to hear his wife spoken to like this, and raised his fist at Will, only to be socked first by his employer. Sebelus stared at him angrily, then kicked him viciously on the ankle and stormed off to his dressing room.

Unfortunately this kick caused a blood clot to form in Will's leg and his doctor told him to rest for a fortnight. But tragedy struck. While listening to a bawdy anecdote, told by the music-hall comedian S. W. Wyndham, the unfortunate Will laughed so much that the clot went to his brain and he died on 7 June 1915 at the age of thirty-nine.

Now, at thirteen, Joe had to become the man of the family, but he soon realized that without his father's income the family could no longer afford to live in the high style to which they had become accustomed, with several servants, a motor car and all the other luxuries of modern living.

To economize, Hettie moved to a small house on the Brighton seafront, next to the Grand Hotel. But no money was coming in and Lalla and Pauline, who were spoiled, ambitious little girls, anxious to become stars, both cost a great deal in tap-dancing, ballet and elocution lessons. Reluctantly their mother decided that, to make ends meet, she must take in lodgers.

Hettie's paying guests, however, were by no means ordinary: some of the biggest names in vaudeville came to stay at her home. Marie Lloyd, known as the Queen of British music-hall, was almost as famous as Queen Victoria. She had performed with Hettie during the Boer War and they had remained close friends. In her forties, bawdy Marie was married to a handsome jockey eighteen years her junior – and was terrified of losing her looks and her young husband. One of her youth-enhancing tricks was to smooth out the wrinkles on her belly with a warm iron, which Grandma used to watch her do with horror.

Another lodger who stayed in the little boarding house was a young Jack Buchanan, the urbane, sophisticated matinée idol.

In his own effort to help the dwindling family finances, Joe announced he was leaving school. At fourteen, he had been offered a job as office boy at the Moss Empire offices in London. Tall and precocious for his age, he was determined to take it. There were sixty music halls and variety palaces in Greater London alone, still flourishing in spite of the burgeoning popularity of cinema, which was still in relative infancy.

While Joe was on the way to becoming an impresario, Lalla and Pauline started to blossom into bright young things. They couldn't have been more different. Lalla, petite, blonde, and exquisitely dressed, was possessed of rather affected airs and graces. Although to keep her figure she hardly ate, as soon as she landed her first stage job she started each day with a rejuvenating glass of champagne. She was the prototype of the frivolous, sparkling flapper and swathed in furs, dripping with diamonds, a regular *femme fatale*, she would dance until the wee hours in all the most fashionable night-clubs.

Pauline was more of the saucy soubrette type. Also petite but dark-haired, she featured in some of André Charlot's popular revues and was, like Lalla, one of Charles Cochrane's Young Ladies. Pauline was more daring than Lalla and, in some publicity photographs, she appeared topless. This is probably why, of all my family, she was the most delighted when I posed for *Playboy* in 1983. I suppose she was considered 'fast', as she was outspoken and 'did her own thing'.

Eventually Joe went into business with another agent, Jack French, to run theatres, budget shows, and to manage touring companies. They took an office in Shaftesbury Avenue and initially the business was small, but Joe was enterprising and determined. He found good acts and set about booking them. One of his first clients was Lew Grade, a twenty-four-year-old hoofer who billed himself as 'The Dancer with the Humorous Feet'. Neither handsome nor a brilliant song-and-dance man, he nevertheless had a whole heap of chutzpa and soon developed a faithful following.

Lew's *pièce de résistance* was an athletic tap-dance-cum-Charleston on a table top, which presented a problem when he had to play three different dates on the same night. He couldn't perform on just *any* old table, he had to have his own special one. Ever the shrewd businessman, Joe agreed to ferry him between engagements, as Lew didn't have a car, if Lew paid for the petrol. Joe took 10 per cent of his earnings, and when he became a popular cabaret act, money started to roll in.

Meanwhile, Lalla had gone to New York to appear in André Charlot's *Revue of 1924* with two future screen stars, Jessie Matthews and Anna Neagle. Jack Buchanan was the star and Lalla was one of his leading ladies.

Jack was then, arguably, England's most popular leading man. Elegant and debonair, he epitomized the top-hat-and-tails atmosphere of twenties and thirties musical theatre. He played in musical comedies, in revue, on stage and in films as an actor/producer/director and was a true heart-throb. Handsome, generous and utterly professional, he was also a well-known Lothario, and it wasn't long before he and Lalla began an affair. Their correspondence was copious and in 1930 when Lalla left by boat for New York, Jack inundated her with daily cables, all proclaiming his undying love.

Elsa Bessant was a beautiful slim young blonde in her mid-twenties when she met Joe Collins. One of eleven children, she and her family still lived in a large Georgian house in South London. They were simple working-class people, kind-hearted, unpretentious, hard-working and moral. Elsa's father, William, was a tram driver while her mother, Ada, ran the household.

Ada was stout and jolly, and her passion was keeping her house immaculate. Every day she would polish and wax the furniture in her pristine parlour, although family life usually centred around the kitchen. Keeping a well-run house entailed an enormous amount of cleaning, scrubbing, cooking, shopping, drawing water, even making the children's clothes. All of Ada's children were scrupulously clean and immaculately dressed. Elsa, in particular, was always elegant and well groomed. It was second nature to her.

Daddy told me that when he first met Mummie she looked exceptionally glamorous, in a flame-coloured chiffon dress with flowers pinned to her shoulders, her golden hair in soft waves around her lovely face. A gold medallist in dance, she was working as an instructress at a Regent Street night-club. Although he had no interest in ballroom dancing, the moment Joe saw Elsa he felt an instant attraction and asked her to give him a lesson. He was a terrible dancer with no rhythm at all, and although Elsa tried hard, coaching him in the intricacies of the latest craze, the Tiger Rag, he trod on her feet and seemed far more interested in asking for a date than mastering dance steps. He also took the time to ingratiate himself with the booking manager at the club, who arranged for some of his acts to appear there – among them Lew Grade.

Elsa's family was entirely different from Joe's: they were calm, happy and even-tempered. There was never any shouting, few arguments or emotional outbursts: in the thirties correct behaviour and manners were still extremely important. Joe's effervescent family, which consisted of Hettie – she had married Jack French, who was even more quick-tempered than Will had been – and his wild sisters, were showbiz incarnate:

excitable, capricious and passionate. Elsa's gentle sweetness appealed greatly to the volatile Joe and, after several months of courtship, they were married at Paddington registry office. My favourite photograph of my parents was taken on their honeymoon. Wrapped in terry-cloth robes, dark, tousle-haired Joe and the elegant, high-cheekboned fair Elsa are smiling blissfully, cuddled close together and leaning against an open-topped car. This picture epitomizes the happiness I truly believe my parents shared for the almost thirty years they spent together before my mother's tragic and untimely death in 1962.

Quite unlike Daddy, Mummie had no burning desire for a career. Like most girls of her generation, her only ambition was to meet a nice young man, settle down and raise a family. She was feminine and home-loving, liked cooking and domestic chores, and was the type of woman whom today the ultra-feminist brigade would despise. But she found the secret of a happy marriage.

My father ruled the roost with a rod of iron and nobody dared raise their voice to him, but Mummie never needed to. Her serenity worked miracles on my frequently quick-tempered father, and even though his anger often scared the hell out of me, Mummie seemed to take it all in her stride.

Elsa's bright, outgoing and sociable personality perfectly comple-mented Joe's pursuit of show business success, which he had started to achieve. Our flat resounded with the laughter and gaiety of many a strolling troubadour, comedian or soubrette. He and Lew Grade had formed the highly successful Collins and Grade Theatrical Agency, but when he married Mummie, she was earning more as a dance instructress than he was as an agent. Consequently, when they moved into their first flat in Castellain Mansions, Maida Vale, not only did she pay the first month's rent but she also bought most of the furniture. Most of Joe's money went into pampering his motor of the moment.

In their Regent Street offices, Daddy and Lew ran a virtual job-centre for singers, dancers, comedians, acrobats, ventriloquists, jugglers and conjurors. The early thirties saw the zenith of music-hall and variety mania, and even though most people had radios, they still loved to see their favourites in the flesh.

One of Daddy's early ventures, however, was a freak show, in which people with terrible disabilities were displayed for the curious to gape at in horror. Back in the thirties, this was thought of as just another form of entertainment and authentic Siamese twins, one-legged men, giants with misshapen heads, midgets, bearded and grossly fat women were all able to earn a reasonable living.

One popular act Collins and Grade booked was Max Miller, the original Cheeky Chappie. Famous for his loud checked suits, garish kipper ties and jaunty 'titfer-tats', Max originated the insult school of comedy, for which he became universally loved. They also booked Flanagan and Allen, who started the legendary Crazy Gang. Their theme songs were 'Underneath the Arches' and 'Run, Rabbit, Run', which was one of the first songs I learned to sing. Collins and Grade's other popular acts included Henry Hall and His Band, Jack Hylton, the Kit-Kat Saxophone Band, Nat Gonella the trumpeter, Django Reinhardt the guitarist, and Stéphane Grappelli the jazz violinist. They also had the innovative idea of booking well-known radio performers into the music-halls, starting with Elsie and Doris Waters, who played the two famous charladies, Gert and Daisy.

Towards the end of the thirties, Daddy and Lew came up with the whimsical plan to open a night-club. The most famous and elegant night-club in the world was El Morocco in New York, so they called theirs El Morocco too. London's El Morocco was in the basement of a building in the heart of the West End. Patrons liked the anticipation of descending into 'dives', so whenever possible night-clubs were below street level. El Morocco, with its inky velvet ceiling scattered with electric 'stars', attracted some of the most glamorous people of the day, and to be glamorous was every woman's aim then. No stylish woman would have considered going out at night unless properly dressed in a flowing silk or satin gown, fur cape, gloves and jewels, her escort either in the casual black tie made popular by the Prince of Wales or preferably in white tie. Nothing is more flattering to a man than white tie and tails.

Joan Henrietta Collins was born on a warm May morning in a Bayswater nursing-home, weighing in at almost eight pounds. When Joe viewed his first-born, mewling in Elsa's arms, he looked nonplussed at the red-faced, squalling creature, then joked, 'She looks like half a pound of scrag end.' My father was never one for the effusive compliment. But I soon became the apple of my family's eye. Modesty aside, I was considered a gorgeous baby. I had big green eyes, fine black hair and Cupid's bow lips. Mummie thought I was so irresistible that she took every precaution to protect me from the wicked world. Unbelievably germ-conscious she couldn't bear strangers to come near me, so she pinned a sign to the front of my pram warning, 'Please do not kiss me.'

Although I had several nannies, Mummie insisted on doing every-thing for me herself. While I slept, she constantly checked to reassure herself that I was still breathing. She even put my ice-cream in the oven to take the chill off.

I was just a few months old when I had the first of several close encounters with death. Returning with Mummie one Sunday in Daddy's favourite car, having visited Grandma Hettie in Brighton, I was frac-tiously cutting my first teeth in the back seat. As the flat hove into view, Mummie saw several fire engines outside and, standing in the street, our young nanny in floods of tears. 'I'm sorry, I don't know how it happened, but I was smoking a cigarette and I dropped it into the baby's cot. I don't know why, I must have fallen asleep or something,' she sobbed.

Legend has it that Mummie fired the girl on the spot, thinking her precious little darling could have been consumed by the flames.

Both grandmothers adored me too, so I soon became quite a little madam and keen to show off my singing and dancing at the drop of a hat.

I danced with wild abandon to the radio sounds of Henry Hall or Victor Sylvester, and Mummie would play gramophone records for me of Al Jolson, Bing Crosby and the Andrews Sisters. I sang along with all of them. It wasn't long before Mummie, encouraged by Hettie and my aunts – who believed that all this talent should be nurtured – insisted that I should be enrolled in a dancing class.

My first professional appearance – well, amateur, really – was in a school musical called *Why the Fairies Cried*, and naturally I played a fairy, to rave reviews from Grandma. It was a particular favourite of amateur drama teachers and many future thespians had appeared in it, even Noël

Coward. So complete with tutu and ballet slippers, this precocious three-year-old teetered around the stage on plump wobbly legs to thunderous applause from all the members of our large family.

Daddy didn't have time to indulge his Gemini child by watching her début stage performances. Interestingly enough, many years later, he still preferred *Coronation Street* to *Dynasty*. I've often wondered if this masculine Edwardian attitude of not allowing your children to believe that they're anything special had to do with Daddy's character or with the strict moralistic age into which he was born. I certainly received plenty of approval, compliments and love from the women of my family, but my father always remained rather reserved. Perhaps he felt that to show overt affection was to show weakness, and I rarely saw him demonstrative even towards Mummie. But there was no doubt that my mother and father were deeply in love, and although I rarely witnessed visible displays of affection between them, I knew instinctively that they cared tremendously about each other.

Hettie was mad about her first granddaughter. Since most of her sisters weren't married they had no grandchildren, so I was a most popular little person. On many a Sunday we arranged ourselves on Brighton beach, sitting on those hard pebbles, me in a sun-bonnet and a scowl, being passed around like a bag of sweets between Grandma, Auntie Hannah, Auntie Sadie, Auntie Minnie, Auntie Bessie and Auntie Annie, all dressed in their bombazine Sunday best.

Hettie was convinced that I would be the one to carry on the Collins show business tradition and would one day become a star. She taught me dance routines, songs, sketches, tricks and 'bits of business' and actively encouraged my dream to tread the boards. She even taught me to do the splits, with which she herself had created a sensation at the turn of the century. With my chubby baby legs it wasn't hard, particularly since I was double-jointed, but Grandma could still do them until she was seventy.

I had a privileged middle-class upbringing in a family with traditional values, including stiff-upper-lip behaviour, respect for your elders and high moral standards. Plenty of toys, lovely flats with roomy nurseries, pretty clothes, lots of ice-cream and sweets, and the occasional kitten or puppy, with which I soon became bored. I have never been known for my love of our four-legged friends.

Neither have I been known for my love of swimming and to this day I loathe putting my head under water. This can be traced back to Betty, a young nanny who took me, aged four, into the sea at Brighton and attempted to teach me to swim.

'Now you must be *very* careful not to let your head get under the water,' Betty admonished me seriously.

'Why?' I asked. 'Lots of the other children do. Why can't I?'

'Because,' Betty said darkly, 'if you put your head under the sea you could swallow a piece of octopus egg. It's invisible and deadly dangerous. I know a little girl who swallowed a bit of octopus egg. The baby octopus grew and grew inside her tummy, until all its tentacles burst out of her body and she had to go round like that for the rest of her life.'

I screamed my lungs out, rushed back to shore, and didn't venture back into the sea for a very long time. For years I had nightmares about that little girl, with the huge octopus growing inside her.

Some months later Mummie and Auntie Renee took me to the open-air swimming pool at Roehampton. Renee, her glamorous, slightly wild youngest sister, was my mother's favourite and her best friend. It was a boiling hot September day and the pool was full of frolicking jollity. Mummie was deep in conversation with Auntie Renee so I paddled off to what I thought was the shallow end and suddenly found myself under-water. I still couldn't swim so I hadn't a clue how to get back up to the surface. All I could see was a mass of waving legs and floating bodies. I tried to attract attention by screaming but swallowed so much water it's a miracle I didn't drown. Eventually I tugged weakly at a hairy leg and a man hoisted me out. Gasping for air like a landed trout, I lay on my back, arms akimbo.

'Little girl, you're out of your depth,' the man said kindly. 'That was nearly the end of you.'

Mummie and Renee came rushing over in hysterics and I was forbidden to go near the water again until after I'd taken proper swimming lessons.

However much I might have hated water, though, I adored dressing up, and my mother's, aunts' and grandmothers' wardrobes and trunks were a treasure trove of glorious things in which to parade around and generally show off. Pearls and feather boas, lace fans and cobweb gloves, garnet earrings and silk-flowered hats, all were scattered in profusion around these ladies' boudoirs. For this was a time when women revelled in their femininity. I can still smell the rosewater with which Grandma doused herself, and the Coty face powder that Mummie always used. Most women enjoyed the grooming ritual, painting, powdering and perfuming themselves, and weren't self-conscious then about doing it as some are today. I enjoyed being a girl and couldn't wait to grow up and become a big girl.

For my fifth birthday, I was given my first fur coat, a gorgeous creation made of white rabbit fur. Mummie took me to the local photographer's where I posed in it – turned-up nose in the air, with patent shoes, frilly white socks, a white satin hair ribbon, white gloves and holding a tiny beaded purse. Look out, Shirley Temple, here I come, I thought. I imagined I was fashion and glamour incarnate and ready for anything the theatre could offer me. In reality, though, I was in grave danger of becoming a regular spoilt brat.

One day, Mummie, Auntie Renee and I were roaming through Selfridges toy department when I spotted a doll that I fancied. I asked if I could have it.

'No,' said my mother firmly, grabbing me by the hand. 'You've got too many dolls, and you've already got one almost exactly like that.'

'But I want *this* one,' I insisted. 'She's so pretty. She looks just like Shirley Temple. Please let me have her, Mummie, *please*.'

'Absolutely not,' said Mummie. 'You had lots of dolls on your birthday last week. You *can't* have her.'

My five-year-old lungs let out a deafening scream of rage, and to the horror of Mummie and Renee, and much to the disdainful amusement of the other shoppers, I threw myself on to the ground in a paroxysm of temper.

'I'm leaving you here,' Mummie hissed at me, scarlet with embarrassment. 'I'm leaving you *right* there on the carpet and I will *never* speak to you again.'

This was so unlike my mother that I didn't believe her. But then she and Renee walked away, leaving me rolling around on the floor, kicking my little legs in the air like a distressed beetle. I looked up to see myself surrounded by a derisive group of older children and some disapproving adults. After a few seconds of astonishing histrionics, terror overcame me. I was in this huge place, alone, and where was Mummie? I stopped crying instantly, sat up, and the horrible truth dawned that Mummie and Auntie had abandoned their precious little girl. Unaware that they were watching me from behind a pillar, and now weeping genuine tears, I tore madly around the toy department. 'Mummie,' I wailed, 'Mummie, please come and find me. I promise I'll never be naughty again.' After a short interval, my mother thought I'd been suitably punished, and came to claim me. After that I behaved reasonably well for at least a week.

With the advent of a new sister (Jacqueline Jill Collins who was born on a cold October day in a nursing home near our flat in Maida Vale), attention was temporarily deflected from me.

My singing and dancing skills were being honed by regular sessions after school and Saturday morning lessons at Madame Vacani's dancing academy for young ladies. So I wasn't at all thrilled when Daddy, with commendable foresight, suddenly decided to uproot our little family to the safety of Bognor Regis, down on the Sussex coast, because of the imminence of war.

CHAPTER TWO

'Oh, what a lovely war!'

During the war years I was never worried about anything. Little children are usually fearless about events that petrify their parents and which they don't understand. Being woken in the middle of the night during air-raids, rushed to the shelter by panicking parents, and hiding under school desks while the Blitz raged all around us just seemed like one huge adventure.

But the war seemed to last for ever: to a child five years seems a lifetime. The war years were indeed hard, and everyone needed to be tough to survive. When the bombing became particularly heavy, Daddy stayed in London while the rest of us only returned when things calmed down.

At the beginning of the war we stayed in Bognor with Mummie's mother, Ada Bessant. In her old age she had lost her jolliness and had become an intransigent old lady, who usually dressed Victorian-style in starched black ankle-length bombazine, her grey hair pulled severely back into a tight bun. Her habitual expression was grim, akin to that of Grandma in a Giles cartoon.

Grandma Bessant, whom we all called 'Nana', was a strict disciplinarian, uncompromising and stubborn as a monkey. Since her husband had died in an accident, she had become the ruling matriarch and her word was law. She was the complete opposite of Hettie, Daddy's mother, who was gregarious and fun-loving.

I wasn't happy to move from Alexandra Court, our spacious second-floor flat in London, to a house crowded with relations stuck in the middle of the countryside with not even a view of the sea. I was even less happy to have to share a bedroom with my cousin Yvonne, my age and the daughter of Mummie's sister Pat. Some of Mummie's other sisters stayed with us too. Norah, the typical spinster aunt, was fortyish, lived with Nana and rushed to do her every bidding. She had sacrificed love and marriage to take care of her grumpy old mother and was thus pitied by one and all.

Renee, the youngest of the Bessant sisters, had long black curly hair, a vivacious personality and bore a passing resemblance to Paulette Goddard, a popular film favourite with our family. Renee's husband George had already been drafted overseas. (I suspect that Renee and Elsa, two pretty young women alone in Bognor, acted as a magnet for the few men still about.)

Also living in Nana's tiny house were Renee's toddler, George, my only male cousin, and my mother's friend Hilda Burns with her two sons, Geoffrey and Robin. They were slightly older than me – loud, naughty boys, always getting into mischief, bringing home mud, tadpoles and trouble. In such a female-oriented household, I quickly adapted to their tomboy mode. I liked changing my personality and could go from sweet-little-girl to Tomboy Sal in a trice, furiously playing ball games or racing Geoffrey across the field at the back of the house.

At the other end of this field was the local newsagent's and sweet shop, where on a Sunday morning, 3 September 1939, to be exact, Geoffrey and I went to spend our pocket money on our weekly fix of sherbet and liquorice allsorts. Outside the shop we saw a huge newspaper hoarding proclaiming, 'War Declared!'

Geoffrey and I gazed open-mouthed at the sign, then, squealing with delight, raced back across the field to impart this exciting news to the rest of the family.

I beat Geoffrey and arrived to announce breathlessly to the assembled adults and squawking babies: 'War's arrived! I must be only about the third person in the whole world to find out about it, but it's *true*! We're at war, Mummie.' I was puffed up with self-importance.

Of course, the grown-ups had already heard it on the radio, and must have been waiting many nail-biting months for this day, but to me it was thrilling. WAR! The very word spelled excitement.

When lunch was ready, the children were admonished by Nana, as usual, to 'Finish everything on your plate, because the children are starving in India and now they'll be starving in Germany too.' The logic of this went over our heads, but when the meal was over Nana solemnly produced a small box of Cadbury's Milk Tray, took a sharp knife and cut one chocolate into several pieces. Then she announced, in her raspy old voice, 'These are for you, but you mustn't eat them all at once, because this box must last you for the whole of the war.'

Nana handed a slice to each of us, saying, 'This is your chocolate ration for the week.'

The week! I, who habitually gorged myself on jelly babies and chocolate bars, had to make this tiny scrap last a *week*? Impossible. Over-excited after the dash from the newsagent with my world exclusive, I burst into tears and was thus sent straight to bed.

We stayed in Bognor for a few months, during which *Gone with the Wind* played at the local Odeon. Mummie and her sisters saw it several times, extolling the beauty and talent of Vivien Leigh. I begged to be allowed to see this legendary film but alas I was considered too young. As a consolation, however, I was taken to see *The Wizard of Oz* with Judy Garland, which I thought was simply the greatest picture ever. I believed that a yellow brick road really existed (still do) and spent hours singing, 'We're off to see the Wizard' and practising the dance steps of Dorothy, the Tin Man and the Cowardly Lion.

Auntie Renee had heard the villagers muttering darkly about Hitler's latest evil plan. They said he'd threatened that whenever German bombers flew over the Sussex coast towards London they would shoot as many women and children walking on the promenade as they could. This rumour quickly gathered momentum, and genuine panic ensued.

Mummie managed to get word to Daddy, who summoned us immediately back to the temporary safety of London, where no bombs as yet had fallen. We didn't go back to central London, however, but to a tiny rented flat near Maidenhead. Daddy was a fishing fanatic and I suspect that his selection of this location stemmed less from a desire to be with us than from the urge to spend weekends with his rod at the ready. We weren't there for long because, for some reason I have never fathomed, at the height of the 1940 Blitz, when bombs were falling on London like raindrops, we moved back to the Maida Vale flat.

With all this moving about, I couldn't keep a schoolfriend for long and whenever I attempted to keep a pet – a black rabbit in Maidenhead, a black and white kitten in Maida Vale – I soon had to get rid of it.

Back in Alexandra Court, in the nursery, surrounded by toys and games, I was in my element. I had a wonderful doll's house meticulously furnished with pre-war, exquisitely made miniature furniture, some of which I'd been given, some of which I'd found in junk shops in Bognor. When it became impossible to find toys, I started to make tiny furniture out of conkers, pins and bits of old fabric.

My favourite game consisted of turning the blue wooden nursery table upside down, covering it with a heavy rug and furnishing it with a radio, assorted dolls, cushions and stuffed animals. I would then set forth on thrilling imaginary voyages around the world.

I was perfectly happy playing alone with only my dolls for company, all of whom I talked to as if they were my closest friends. I spent hours on these journeys, visiting foreign places I never thought I would ever actually visit. India, China, Africa, Japan, they all sounded so exotic. My life-long curiosity to discover new places was born right under that blue wooden table.

Although the Blitz had suddenly become more ferocious, we stayed on in London, probably because Mummie didn't want to leave Daddy again. He was then about thirty-seven, handsome and, no doubt, catnip to the show business dollies who habitually surrounded him.

Mummie decided we should spend the nights at Daddy's sister Pauline's flat in nearby Marble Arch, which had a proper air-raid shelter in the basement. There we could sleep soundly, ignoring the crash of bombs, the moan of low-flying enemy aircraft and the almost constant explosions. We always carried our gas masks in a cardboard box. They smelt disgustingly of old rubber, and I dreaded to think that one day we might actually have to wear them for real.

One night the block of flats next to us took a direct hit. The whole building looked like a sheet of flame hundreds of feet high, and dozens of firemen tried ineffectually to put out the inferno. I felt my first real stab of wartime fear and developed my lifelong dread of fire.

During the short time we stayed with Auntie Pauline, I went to a school in Gloucester Place. This was my first mixed school, and, apart from Geoffrey, Robin and cousin Georgie, I hadn't been around boys much.

These boys were a rowdy lot, but then so were we girls. These were tough, dangerous times and we lived with the constant threat that we might die in the very next air-raid.

We often had competitions at school as to who could draw the most hideous caricature of Adolf Hitler. Although he was universally hated, we didn't really understand why. He just represented Germany which, in turn, represented the enemy. He was more of a joke figure to us, as was the scrawny Goebbels, the swollen-bellied Goering and the posturing Mussolini, along with a new arrival, Stalin, whom we didn't know much about except that he had plenty of hair, a bushy moustache and a chest-ful of medals. To us, Hitler was just like the Big Bad Wolf in *The Tale of the Three Little Pigs*, all huffing and puffing and not much else. My caricature often won the competition: mad, staring eyes, black scruffy hair flopped over one eye in a greasy half fringe, a soppy toothbrush moustache, a potato nose and an evil leer.

Because there were no air-raid shelters at school, when the inevitable sirens went off, we had to crawl under our wooden desks. While we crouched there, pretending not to be scared even though we could clearly hear the whine of the bombs and the crisp sound of anti-aircraft gunfire, the boys would tease the girls relentlessly.

One of their sayings which had us falling about in hysterics was: 'A blob on your knob could cause your demob.' None of us had a clue what this meant. We knew what a blob was, and a demob, but what was a knob? I asked my mother and quoted the saying to her. She blushed. 'Ask your father, darling,' she snapped. 'Don't ask me.'

I never did ask Daddy. I felt it probably had hidden meanings that I knew he wouldn't divulge.

Sometimes we'd all bravely sing that famous little ditty to the tune of Colonel Bogey:

Hitler has only got one ball
Goering has two but they are small
Himmler is somewhat similar
And Doctor Goebbels has no balls at all

We would then all screech with laughter, although only the boys knew what we were laughing about. Another song we used to sing in the playground was ''Oo's this geezer 'Itler, 'Oo does 'e fink 'e is?' We would march around, pretending to be the Führer, scraping our hair over our foreheads, goose-stepping and with two fingers above our upper lip to imitate his moustache. It was unimaginable to us that this buffoon might actually be a real threat.

One morning, when the comforting wailing of the all-clear sounded, we left Auntie Pauline's shelter and picked our way gingerly towards our own flat up the Edgware Road, which was littered with the debris from several bombed-out buildings. I dashed excitedly about picking up bits of shrapnel, which I collected in an old cigar box and swapped at school with the other children.

When we arrived at Alexandra Court we found that our flat no longer existed. The building had suffered a direct hit, and although the façade was still intact our bedrooms, including the nursery and my beloved blue table, had been destroyed.

'That's it,' Mummie despairingly announced to Daddy. 'I can't stand it here any more. I'm taking these children away from London.'

This time we set off for Devon, on the estuary of the Bristol Channel, to an idyllic seaside resort called Ilfracombe. Daddy's little Ford was loaded with the pathetic remnants of our clothes and toys, and with blankets and bed linen, pots and pans stuffed into every available crevice of the car, we probably resembled a band of roving tinkers. Mummie was crying, the baby was wailing, I was sniffling, and gloom pervaded the car.

When we finally arrived at our new home, a tiny flat on the seafront, we spotted straightaway that it was above – what bliss – a sweet shop.

Auntie Lalla was living nearby with her husband Godfrey, as was my old playmate Geoffrey Burns with his mother and brother Robin.

I loved Ilfracombe, which was far enough away from the Blitz to remain a thriving holiday resort, despite it being wartime. I started yet another new school down there and quickly made some new friends. Every Saturday a group of very old and very young musicians played their brass instruments on the bandstand, and everyone would lie back in deck-chairs and listen contentedly. All except me, of course. I could never keep still so I skipped around on the periphery of the deck-chair group, marching, dancing and twirling about, dreaming of a possible future as a drum majorette (I'd just seen *Yankee Doodle Dandy*).

By dint of judicious black marketeering, which practically everyone who could afford it indulged in, Daddy was able to buy enough petrol to visit us every couple of weeks. In the meantime, Mummie, Hilda and Lalla had opened a little drinking club, frequented by American and Canadian soldiers, called the Odd Spot. There was a US Air Force base nearby and a jolly corporal called Ted soon befriended us. He was a good-looking, gregarious man who remained in touch with us for several years after the war. I liked him, especially because he brought us all manner of goodies, including chocolate – we'd long since finished the Cadbury's Milk Tray – chewing gum, candy (the Yankee term for boiled sweets), cigarettes for Daddy and nylons for the ladies.

I'm sure no impropriety really went on between Ted and the married women – even in wartime most women stayed true to their men but, of course, there were always exceptions. One day in Barnstaple High Street Mummie pointed out to me a stringy-haired, pimply, skinny woman with shiny lipstick and stockings, wearing an obviously new pair of court shoes. She was 'no better than she should be,' my mother hissed. Why was this ordinary-looking girl the target of my mother's rare disapproval? I asked her but she wouldn't tell me. It makes sense in retrospect, though, because my mother's Victorian mother lived her life by the strict codes of behaviour of that era, which in turn became my mother's. Although

Mummie adored dancing, parties and fun, she would never have *dreamed* of being unfaithful to Daddy.

I wish I could say the same about my father, but double standards were rife, and he was still heavily involved in show business. He was surrounded by temptation, and I'm sure, once in a while, succumbed to it. He must have had considerable sex-appeal, because even today I occasionally bump into some sweet old lady, and a glazed expression will cross her face, as she recalls my father in his prime. But whatever Daddy did, it didn't in anyway debase his love for my mother, to whom he remained devoted until her death.

My parents were always telling me horror stories of what was happening in Europe. I knew about the occupation of France, Poland, Belgium and Holland, but to me, as a child, these places might as well have been Outer Mongolia. I'd never been out of England, and it seemed as though none of those awful things could happen *here*. Besides we were invincible, weren't we? We were British and proud of it, every man, woman and child of us. We were the greatest nation on earth.

This optimistic patriotism was not just wartime conditioning – everyone *believed* it. We saw the newspaper photographs of King George and Queen Elizabeth standing in the rubble of the East End shaking hands sympathetically with survivors. We listened on the radio to the comforting tones of Winston Churchill, whom most people thought of as the greatest living Englishman; and we cheered the newspaper reports of General Montgomery and his brave troops – among them Uncle George – defeating the enemy in faraway lands.

For adults the war was horrible, but for me it was a sort of real-life, sometimes scary fairy-tale from the pen of Hans Christian Andersen or the Brothers Grimm. I knew it *had* to have a happy ending. There could be no other way. And with the confidence of childhood, I knew for sure that nothing was going to happen to us. No bomb would demolish our flat again, no wicked enemy would destroy our little family. Uncle George sent heavily censored letters from Burma, but while the bombs continued to fall and the Germans renewed their threats against England, the Collins family had enough to eat, warm beds and a loving environment.

What else could a war baby have possibly wanted?

Perhaps a bit more chocolate?

We spent the last couple of years of the war living in a sunny fifth-floor flat, next to the clock tower in Brighton, because Daddy wanted us to be near Hettie. The Blitz was still devastating London and the new doodle-bugs were falling here, there and everywhere.

Our flat was on the seafront, with a tiny balcony and a restricted view of the shingle on the beach. I remembered gazing at the sea through the thick tangles of barbed wire. We were told it was to stop the Germans invading, and that the beach was terribly dangerous, a trap filled with land-mines which could blow you into a thousand pieces. I would stare sadly out of the window at the choppy grey waves, longing to paddle in them as we had in Ilfracombe.

Meanwhile I attended a rather up-tight all-girls' school, called St Wilfred's, started studying drama, and started to realize that I wanted to become an actress rather than a singer or dancer. A visit to the theatre or cinema turned into almost a religious experience and our block of flats was next door to a small cinema, which showed an eclectic selection of movies: *Jane Eyre, Great Expectations, Bambi* and *Mrs Miniver* were just a few of the dozens of films we saw. Mummie did not look unlike Greer Garson, the star of *Mrs Miniver*, with her soft blonde curls, warm blue eyes and high, sculpted cheekbones. For a few months Mummie featured the Greer Garson look, which I much preferred to the Betty Grable image she had adopted when we were living in Ilfracombe. (Betty Grable was flavour-of-the-month all over the world, in those days, with her tight white bathing-suit, come-hither over-the-shoulder grin, and piled-high blonde hair.) Later, Mummie metamorphosed again, this time into a more refined version of Lana Turner.

Mummie had terrific legs, often wore shorts and her skirts as short as fashion permitted. Her nickname among many of her friends was Marlene.

In Brighton my happiest times were visiting Grandma. Hettie, then in her early seventies, was still a bright spark, with the zest and vitality of a woman half her age. Although she painted me a dazzling picture of a performer's on-stage glory, with adoring audiences rising in clamorous applause, stage-door Johnnies bearing prodigious gifts, she never mentioned the dirty, cramped dressing rooms, or endless waits on draughty stations. She never warned me either about the bitchiness, the rivalry, the jealousies and tantrums, the clashes of ego, and the backstage piranhas in suits. She made the theatre sound like a glorious fairy-tale, of which I desperately wanted to be a part.

So, encouraged by my glamorous grandma, I learned my song-and-dance routines, entrancing our Christmas guests with exuberant twirly dances and cutesy-pie renditions of 'Run Little Raindrop Run' and 'There are Fairies at the Bottom of my Garden'. I diligently attended all the extra dance, ballet and elocution lessons, and, whenever I could, it was off to the movies – perferably starring Betty Grable, John Payne, Carmen Miranda, Danny Kaye, Judy Garland and Gene Kelly. Movies were my life before the theatre took hold, and I revelled in that magical screen, its spellbinding stories and extravagant musical numbers. I also listened voraciously to the radio, our lifeline to the outside world.

By 1944 it seemed as if the war had been going on all my life. Richard Dimbleby and Wynford Vaughan-Thomas, the BBC news commentators, vividly described the horrors of the fighting, but as the year came to an end, the light of victory grew brighter.

Once a week we would be glued to the hilarious antics of Tommy Handley, the most popular radio comedian in Britain, on *ITMA*, and I saw some terrific comedians in the music-halls and variety theatres where Daddy sometimes took me when we were in London. The Crazy Gang were zanier than anyone I'd ever seen, and I loved Arthur Askey, horse-faced Tommy Trinder and that Cheeky Chappie, Max Miller.

One of my favourite comic papers was *Radio Fun*, which featured cartoon characters from all the current radio favourites. One was Old Mother Riley and her lovely daughter Kitty. Old Mother Riley was played by a man and Kitty by his shrewish real-life wife. Daddy used to book them and said that they drove each other mad, with their screaming matches and endless infidelities.

I was a staunch fan of the Forces Network, listening avidly to *Bandwagon*, Gracie Fields and Richard 'Stinker' Murdoch. My hero, though, was Winston Churchill, and I would sometimes be allowed to stay up and listen to some of his speeches on the Nine o'Clock News just before bedtime.

Alvar Lidell and Bruce Belfrage would read the news every night and Mummie and my aunts would listen as if their lives depended on it. As for me, I preferred *Music While You Work, Workers' Playtime* and even Victor Sylvester and his Ballroom Orchestra, when I was able to glide around in my gingham school dress and sensible brown shoes, imagining myself to be Rita Hayworth or Betty Grable. The importance of radio during the war can't be exaggerated: Mrs Mopp on *ITMA*, and her 'Can I do you now, sir?' catchphrase, brought everybody to the verge of hysteria – but maybe we were already there because of the seemingly endless strain of war.

Another gateway to the outside world was *Picture Post*, which was always filled with front-line photos, human-interest stories and current events. I discovered the film magazines *Picture Show* and *Picturegoer*, which were crammed with gorgeous snaps of all my current favourites. I would painstakingly cut these out and paste them into a huge album, which I still have. I also wrote to film stars. Oh, the thrill of receiving that buff envelope with the US air-mail stamp on it, and pulling out a signed photograph of Frank Sinatra, Gene Kelly, or Hedy Lamarr.

In 1944, during another brief lull in the bombing we came back to London, this time to a big flat in Great Portland Street, which had a warm, safe air-raid shelter in the basement. Everybody believed this would keep us safe from a direct hit on our block by a doodle-bug or a V1 bomb, a new horror the Germans had recently launched against us. Every night Nanny or Mummie would wake me from a deep sleep, help me into my siren suit and pixie bonnet, and fling my gas mask around my neck. Then, clutching either a teddy bear or my favourite pre-war Shirley Temple doll – complete with porcelain face and real golden hair – I would stagger sleepily down to the shelter. This shelter had one of the most convivial atmospheres I've ever known. Even with the fear of imminent death, everybody seemed incredibly jolly. Everyone had a Thermos of tea, greaseproof-paper packages of sandwiches – Spam or chopped-up boiled eggs, and even the occasional bit of lettuce or tomato. Biscuits would suddenly appear out of nowhere, along with slabs of hard-to-get chocolate. Some of the men had mouth-organs or accordions, and sing-songs would often keep up our spirits during those long nights. There was plenty of laughter, but often screaming too, when the ominous buzz of a doodle-bug suddenly stopped and we all thought that at any second it would crash down on top of us.

Then towards dawn we would hear the glorious sound of the all-clear, and wearily the grown-ups would help the children and the old people upstairs to snatch an hour or two of sleep before it was time to totter off to school or work.

All the young men were now at war but my father, over forty and con-sidered too old, had joined the Home Guard. One day he proudly demonstrated the beauty of his ancient bayonet to us. When he unsheathed it, we were horrified to see that the blade still had traces of what looked like dried blood on it, which we believed was probably from some poor soul in the First World War, but was only rust.

Of course, there was no television, but at the cinema there were twice-weekly newsreels which featured reports of wartime activity. We usually went in the afternoon because of the blackout. It was pitch dark outside at night, the few cars around without headlights, and even if Mummie would occasionally agree to switch on her tiny torch of very low wattage, more often than not an air-raid warden would yell, 'Put that bloody thing out!'

Because we had so little sleep, I often used to nod off during lessons, along with most of the other pupils. But we were never allowed to com-plain. We had to eat everything on our plates, and grin and bear it. Everybody's energy went into beating Hitler, and due to the unbreakable spirit of our hero Winston Churchill, the cheerful, portly figure with the Homburg, bow tie and cane, the whole country pulled as one in the same direction.

And then, miraculously, it was all over. 8 May 1945, was celebrated as Victory in Europe Day. Daddy managed to fill the car with petrol, so we clambered aboard and drove into the West End to join in the festivities. Thousands of Union Jacks had appeared in Regent Street, and people were grinning joyously, rushing about and dancing riotiously. They even climbed over the car, cheering, full of exuberance. Daddy started cursing, of course, Mummie as usual calming him down. It was all unbelievably thrilling. Everyone wanted to have fun, to share in the excitement and joy. As we approached Piccadilly Circus, the crowds were so dense that the car could barely move through them.

Eros was still boarded up but the Bisto sign was twinkling again and dozens of people had joined into a ragged conga-line, dancing and singing. We managed to drive into Trafalgar Square where the sights were even more unbelievable. Hundreds of servicemen and young men and women were dunking themselves in the fountains, shrieking and laughing. Against some of the bronze lions, what my mother called hanky-panky was enthusiastically taking place and a couple of times she had to turn my inquisitive face away from some X-rated episode. People were literally intoxicated with happiness, and high on atmosphere and booze. Everyone, it seemed, had a bottle of wine or beer in their hand. Then suddenly the first fireworks I'd ever seen burst in huge clusters in the spring evening sky. The sky was red with the glow of thousands of bonfires all over London and the world itself seemed ablaze with euphoria.

Young and old, servicemen and women, American, Canadian, Polish, Czech, every nationality mingled together with gusto. When we reached the Victoria Memorial, in front of Buckingham Palace, Daddy had to stop the car. I stood on the roof until, in the distance, I saw the King, Queen Elizabeth, and the two young princesses, Elizabeth and Margaret Rose, step out on to the balcony. A deafening cheer went up from the thousands gathered there, and the rush to get closer to the Royal Family almost overturned the car.

'Well, it's over,' my father said pragmatically. 'About bloody time. Come on, Elsa, let's go home. I feel like a cup of tea.'

CHAPTER THREE

Starting out

At the ripe old age of twelve I joined the fashionable theatrical school Cone-Ripman, for children who were 'born to perform'. In the morning we took the three Rs, as well as the other usual subjects, and after lunch we would give vent to our pent-up performing talents. We were taught drama, ballet, tap and ballroom dancing, classical movement, mime, elocution, singing and fencing. All of us were in our element, as we all fancied ourselves as future Judy Garlands, Mickey Rooneys or Vivien Leighs. We would slump over boring history and geography each morning, to be transformed into bright-eyed dancing dervishes in the afternoon. I learnt how to do folk dances, the sailors' hornpipe, even the Gay Gordons. Grandma Hettie was delighted to be asked to coach me at home in the Dutch clog dance, with which she'd had huge success in Cape Town some fifty years earlier. Although the dancing lessons often put us into close proximity with the opposite sex, this didn't cause the slightest flutter in my pre-pubescent heart. I called boys 'the other enemy' and they were of no interest to me: as far as I was concerned they were from an alien planet and could happily all stay there.

Shortly after I started at the school, Judith Bennet and I were chosen by director John Fernald, after a gruelling audition, to play Jenny Laird's sons in a London production of Ibsen's *A Doll's House*. Fernald believed girls were less trouble than boys, which is why we played boys' parts. How wrong we proved him to be.

We squealed with delight when we were cast, and, in the charming way of children, crowed and bragged to the other green-eyed students about how we were both going to wow the West End critics.

The tiny Arts Theatre is tucked away in a street behind Charing Cross Road. Although it was not strictly West End, it had a first-class reputation for staging not only avant-garde plays, but also excellent productions of the classics.

Opening night was a triumph of family solidarity. Mine practically took over the second and third rows. Mummie and Daddy, Lalla and Pauline and the collective aunts Bessie, Minnie, Hannah, Renee, Norah and Pat, with their various husbands and consorts, were all there, the ladies wearing enough powder, paint and perfume to have supplied the entire chorus-line of the Windmill Theatre.

My part was small, only two entrances with Judith. I came on once in the first act, dressed in a fetching white sailor suit, my short hair pinned into a bob, and once in the last act, wearing a boy's sensible serge suit. In between, Judith and I sat in our minuscule dressing room bored to tears. We amused ourselves by playing cards or reading *Girls' Crystal*, a fabulous magazine for young girls. On the third night, I was so engrossed in reading a story aloud to an enthralled Judith that we completely missed our final cue and our careers as juveniles came to an abrupt end.

John Fernald burst in and screamed 'I will *never* have children in my plays again. You're a pair of unprofessional idiots who don't deserve to become actresses, and don't have the talent or intelligence to even do so.'

We burst into floods of tears and, for the rest of the run, were made to sit in the wings throughout each performance. I became somewhat disheartened. Perhaps I wasn't cut out for the theatre, after all. All that waiting around made me catatonic with boredom.

Then, several months later with another friend, Fiona, I saw the most extraordinary movie of my life. It was called *The Red Shoes* and starred a luminous, ravishing flame-haired ballerina called Moira Shearer.

When I saw the dazzling, innovative dance sequences performed by Miss Shearer with Robert Helpmann and the gorgeous Ludmilla Tcherina, whose waist couldn't have been more than fourteen inches, I changed my mind about acting. I was going to become a ballerina. However, because of *The Red Shoes* thousands of other young English girls suddenly had the same idea and ballet schools all over the country were swamped with applicants.

Although Fiona and I went to the Cone-Ripman day school, we both persuaded our parents to send us to their new country boarding school, which had recently opened up in Tring, Hertfordshire, in a house once owned by Lord Rothschild. Once I'd set my mind on anything it was usually difficult for my parents to dissuade me. I must have known instinctively that the squeaky wheel gets the oil because after months of relentless nagging my parents reluctantly gave in.

We set off with mixed feelings. Mummie was pregnant and emotional so she was in tears all the way. 'If you don't like it there, darling, you must let us know *immediately* and we'll bring you home at once,' she sobbed.

'Shut up, Elsa,' snapped Daddy, who was driving his smart racing-green Rover as usual with ill-concealed road rage.

'Joanie always gets her own way. If she doesn't like it she's bloody well going to have to stick it out this time.'

I couldn't stop fidgeting with delightful anticipation. 'Don't worry, you two,' I said, 'I *will* like it. I know I will. I'm almost a teenager so I know what I'm doing.'

Two pairs of parental eyebrows were simultaneously raised. Teenagehood was neither known about nor understood in the forties. The maxim for the young was: 'Children should be seen and not heard.' Discipline was strict and the 'Me-Generation' was yet to come. Respect for parents and authority was all-encompassing, childish rebellion practically unheard of.

I bade a blithe goodbye to my parents and entered the portals of this forbidding old country manor, which had only recently been transformed into a school – of sorts. There was no fence around the grounds and the rolling green fields seemed to go on for ever. To my dismay, Fiona and I were not in the same dormitory, and I was with a group of tough older girls with whom I soon fell out.

Having glimpsed my pregnant mother waving goodbye to me at the gate, that first night in the dormitory they took great delight in teasing me about my mother's condition. 'Do you know what your mother *did* to get a belly like that?' mocked a red-haired girl, whose father was a well-known, low-life comedian on the B music-hall circuit.

'No, and I don't want to,' I sobbed with tears of shame.

'She had to do dirty things with your father,' she jeered. 'Filthy *disgusting* things.'

All the girls cackled with laughter and then proceeded to tell me the so-called facts of life. This was the first time I'd heard about such dreadful things. Although I was twelve I knew as much about life as one of today's six-year-olds. I couldn't *believe* such vile things happened between men and women. I refused to listen and put my head under the pillow, fingers pushed firmly into my ears and cried myself to sleep.

Revenge came a few nights later. I'd always been good at imitations and I found that by making vomiting sounds, several girls would have to rush to the lavatory to be sick. There was only one loo for the four dormitories, so this caused an irate mistress to come storming in. Since it was an unspoken code not to snitch on one another, an uneasy truce was formed. The girls stopped talking about my mother's pregnancy and I stopped making them throw up.

Boarding school was tough, as were most of the girls, and neither Fiona nor I was happy there.

There was only one telephone between us all, which was usually out of order, and because a long queue waited every night to use it, I couldn't call my parents. Instead I sent impassioned letters to my fastidious mother in which I told her all the gory details about the chaotic way the school was run.

One night Matron told me to wash my hair with Vim, a bathroom scourer. 'Why Vim,' I wailed. 'Isn't there any shampoo?'

'If it's good enough for the other girls, it'll be good enough for you,' Matron said briskly. 'And when you've washed your hair, go straight to bed.'

'What about drying it?' I asked.

'No time for that,' said Matron brusquely. 'Just wash it and go to bed, it won't hurt you. You're all spoilt, you London girls, that's the trouble with you.'

She stalked off leaving me to wash my hair with the harsh dry powder. There were no showers so we rinsed our hair by pouring glasses of water over it. With my soaking wet hair wrapped in a frayed towel, I went to bed in tears once again.

Things came to a head in the fifth week. Every night we gathered in the draughty dining room for supper, which consisted of a thick slice of dry bread, on the stale side, an apple and a mug of watery cocoa or Ovaltine. This was always scooped out of a huge ten-quart milk canister with an iron ladle. That night, the girls who first sipped this lukewarm concoction looked disgusted. I was just raising my mug to my lips when the teacher who was doing the ladling let out a shriek. Hanging from the ladle was a man's large black sock which looked as if it was encrusted in cow-dung! With screams of horror everyone slammed down their mugs and stared accusingly at the teacher, who at least had the good grace to look embarrassed.

'All right, girls,' she said. 'You don't have to drink your cocoa tonight. There's obviously been some kind of mistake.'

Some kind of mistake? Someone's filthy sock in the milk canister. We all looked at each other with revulsion, and went to bed with our stomachs grumbling.

Shortly after I'd fallen asleep I woke to the sound of rat-like scrabbles at the dormitory window. A male face, illuminated by the moon, grinned in at me. I screamed, but one of the girls hissed, 'Shut up, Joan, it's only Harry.'

Only Harry? 'Who's Harry?' I whispered, but she was already off to open the window. The boy scrambled in, and promptly climbed into her bed and began doing things I sensed I shouldn't know anything about.

I started to protest but was again told firmly to shut up. These nightly fumblings had apparently been going on for a week. There was a cadets' training school across the open fields, and when the pupils of that establishment had met some of ours recently in the village, fraternization had begun.

That was it. That was *definitely* it. There was *no way* I was going to stay in this hell-hole of a boarding school a moment longer. I penned another despairing missive to my mother. Half-term was coming up the following weekend, and I was determined that my parents were going to take me home for good. Little Joan had made up her mind.

My broken-hearted-child act did the trick. My parents drove down to Tring, Mummie resplendent and bigger than ever as the birth was imminent. Without further ado I was packed into the back of the Rover and we drove back to London.

'That's what most theatricals are like,' said my father scornfully. 'They're vulgar, common and coarse, and if that's the profession you want to take up, you'll become just like them.'

'It's OK, Daddy,' I said. 'I've decided I don't want to be a ballerina, after all. I wasn't terribly good at ballet anyway. I'm going to be a detective.'

'A *detective*!' His tone would have done Edith Evans proud.

'Yes, a girl detective like Dick Barton Special Agent,' I sparkled. 'I've been working on my technique.'

Mummie sighed but gave me a happy smile, and I knew she was glad I was coming back to Great Portland Street and returning to the bosom of the family.

Top of the list of my parents' priorities now was my baby brother. William Richard Collins was born shortly after my ignominious return from boarding school, and immediately became the apple of everyone's eye. There's nothing like a baby for bringing families together, and Bill was adorable. I wasn't keen on nappy changing, though, so I applied myself diligently to my studies at my latest school, Francis Holland in Baker Street.

I had now identified several professions I was interested in pursuing, but on which should I concentrate? It became clear during my first term that I could become a journalist, because I did quite well at grammar, literature and composition. To this end, I launched and edited the fourth form magazine, calling it, rather unoriginally, *Much-Binding-in-the-Form* after the popular radio programme *Much-Binding-in-the-Marsh*. This phase lasted for a whole year, only to be overtaken by my urgent desire to become a dress designer, which stemmed from the flurry of excitement over Christian Dior's 'New Look', which he had just bestowed on a female population eager to get as far away as possible from post-war austerity clothes. I was thrilled by the New Look. It was so glamorous, so flattering, so dazzling. Every female over the age of thirteen had to have a New Look outfit, and no girl craved one more than I did.

C & A was the first department store to stock the full ankle-length skirts and the tiny bolero jackets. I saved my pocket money and bought a brown wool skirt and a yellow bolero for two pounds. Mummie helped me with my purchase, and I was convinced I looked like the famous model Barbara Goalen. My father thought I was far too young to wear such sophisticated clothes, and forbade me to wear lipstick or earrings, so I usually scuttled out of his way when I wore them.

By the time I turned fifteen, my mind was finally made up. Enough of this journalism, criminology and fashion design. I was made to be an actress, and that was what I was determined to become.

One day I came home from school to our Great Portland Street flat and heard a woman's high-pitched laugh, then the same voice yelling angrily at my father. I slipped in through the front door and saw, sitting in the hall, one of the most handsome men I'd ever seen in my life. I blushed, practically swooning, as he stood up, smiled his devastating smile at me, and said, 'How do you do? You must be Joan. I'm Roger Moore.'

I stuttered a few banalities, my ears tuned in to the cacophony of screeching coming from the living room, where Daddy seemed to be locked in mortal combat with a demented parakeet. Roger noticed my expression, smiled and said, 'Oh, don't take any notice of that. It's just my girlfriend discussing a deal with your father.'

'Your girlfriend?' I said. He seemed awfully boyish and looked about twenty-three. 'Who is she?' I asked boldly.

'Dorothy Squires.' He smiled again.

'Oh, yes, the singer, yes, I've heard of her.' I wondered what this gorgeous young man was doing with someone I considered rather elderly.

Suddenly the lady in question came bursting out of the living room followed by my father. They were shrieking at each other at the tops of their lungs. My father could bellow with the best, but Dorothy was in a league of her own. Her voice was so shrill it could shatter glass. She was wearing what was then called 'the lot' – peroxide hair piled high, a ton of blue eye-shadow, cyclamen lipstick, several rings, bracelets, dangling ear-rings, a necklace, a low-cut floral frock, ankle-strap shoes and a mink stole over her arm. Dorothy Squires was about ten years older than Roger

Moore, but in those days *any* woman over thirty was considered over the hill – my father had told me *that* enough times.

Then, to my surprise, Dorothy's tirade turned to howls of laughter and she turned to my father, kissed him full on the lips, which made me blush, and announced, 'All right, darling, you win. I'll take the bloody date.' With that she took her handsome boyfriend's arm and teetered out of the front door.

'What was all that about, Daddy?' I asked.

'Oh, it's just Dorothy being difficult as usual.' He snorted. 'I've just signed her for a tour. She wants this, she wants that, and then she wants the other. She always asks for the moon.'

'Why does she need the moon when she's got Roger Moore?' I asked.

'He's got some promise,' said Daddy. 'Maybe I'll sign him too. He could be good for films.'

'You're right,' I said fervently. 'I think he could be *wonderful.*'

For a short time my father did indeed represent Roger, and they remained close friends until Daddy's death.

'Daddy, I've just *got* to be an actress,' I pleaded.

'How many times must I tell you that's a *terrible* idea?' said my father. 'It's a perilous profession and all actresses have difficulty even *sustaining* a career, let alone getting a part. It's harsh, you have to take loads of rejection, and most people in the business are greedy and crooked or vulgar. I tell you, you'll be lucky to even *get* a job.'

Nothing if not stubborn, I finally persuaded him that I really believed it was my true calling. I *had* to act and I *had* to go to RADA.

Finally, and reluctantly, Daddy agreed that if I passed the stiff entrance exam, he would pay the fees. But he believed I should only pursue a career for a short while and then, like all good women, get married, settle down and become a mother. He added that if I didn't pass the exam, I would have to become his secretary. The thought of learning to type was too horrible to contemplate so I became more resolute than ever to get into RADA.

I wanted to wear my New Look outfit for the audition, but Mummie thought it might be too sophisticated. Instead she took me to John Lewis and bought me a pretty blue and white polka dot dress, which I called my lucky dress for years afterwards.

I thought long and hard about which pieces to do for my audition and finally chose the 'You are a funny old gentleman' speech from Shaw's *Caesar and Cleopatra*, and one of Emily's speeches from *Our Town*, Thornton Wilder's story of an American family.

The audition was a nightmare. I was in such a paroxysm of fear that I could barely speak. I couldn't move my hands, let alone do 'gestures' and my arms stayed glued to my sides. I was in such awe of the theatrical luminaries who were judging me that I shook like a jelly. Seated before me, smiling benevolently, was the illustrious Sir Kenneth Barnes, the large and avuncular head of RADA, Flora Robson, one of England's greatest actresses, John Gielgud, arguably the greatest actor of his generation, Godfrey Tearle and several other distinguished thespians, at whom I was too shy to look.

I did my best hamming but I was convinced I'd blown it and went off on holiday to Cannes with Lalla and Godfrey, feeling depressed at the idea of the secretarial school. But the Riviera soon cheered me up, with mornings spent on the beach topping up my tan in a sleek new black bikini and afternoons of window-shopping or browsing through Lalla's wardrobe of glamorous finery, baubles, bangles and beads.

Lalla was generous and gave me lots of her cast-offs, which became jolly useful. Clothes for young girls were still hideous, as teenagers were considered non-people – neither children nor adults. We were like the song said: 'Two old for toys and too young for boys – I'm just an in-between'.

The film *Scudda Hoo, Scudda Hay*, a youth-oriented Western in which all the young people, including a new starlet called Marilyn Monroe, wore tight-fitting jeans, captivated me. I coveted a pair of Western blue jeans which were not yet generally available in England. Eventually I discovered authentic imported American men's Levis in a discount store in Tottenham Court Road. They were far too big but I'd read in an American magazine how to shrink them. I bought the smallest pair, put them on, then lay for hours in a bathtub of water, as hot as I could bear, hoping that they would shrink. It worked! I was one of the first girls in

London to wear a pair of real American Levis that fitted perfectly, much to the envy of my friends. With them I wore a black polo-necked or scoop-necked sweater under a man's tartan shirt, ballet shoes and the gypsy earrings I couldn't wear in front of Daddy, who still disapproved of lipstick or jewellery even though I was now fifteen. The lipstick and earrings would be stuffed into my back pocket and put on just before I reached my destination, usually a jazz club or coffee bar.

When my letter of acceptance to RADA, the most distinguished dramatic school in the world, arrived I couldn't believe my luck. More than a thousand young hopefuls had applied for the audition, but only about two hundred had passed. I started in the autumn term. Situated in Gower Street, in the heart of London, from the outside RADA looked more like a shrine than a school. The rather grand white façade loomed behind a thick black-painted iron fence, and a pair of heraldic beasts flanked the imposing four-panelled door. Inside, the front hall was spartan, and the classrooms quite small.

I was terribly nervous on my first day, but I needn't have worried as everyone else felt just the same. Mummie had walked there with me, giving me a little pep talk.

'Are you nervous, darling?'

'Not at all,' I lied bravely. 'Let's face it, Mummie, I *do* have a show business background, which I'm sure most of the others don't, so I'm starting with an advantage, aren't I?'

Mummie nodded sagely at my childlike logic.

'Yes, darling, and I know you're going to succeed.'

I simply loved RADA and fitted into student life with a vengeance. Among my contemporaries were David McCallum, Diane Cilento, John Turner, Susan Stephen and Eileen Moore. Others, a few years older because they had done their National Service, were Gerald Harper, Ronald Lewis, David Conville, Michael Blakemore, Tenniel Evans, Trevor Baxter and Anthony Livesey, son of Roger and the first of my many RADA boyfriends.

We studied every aspect of our craft: voice production, elocution, movement, make-up, stage design, expressive dancing and fencing. During each term we dissected and rehearsed at least one classical play, Shakespeare, Pinero or Wilde, and one modern one – Coward, Lonsdale or Rattigan. These were performed at the end of term by each class in RADA's tiny theatre in front of Sir Kenneth, the teachers and the rest of the student body, most of whom were far more viciously hostile than the London critics. Since there were many more female students than male, the girls often had to play boys' roles.

At the end of each day, many of us made our headquarters at Olivelli's, a small Italian restaurant nearby. There, fuelled by coffee and wine – licensing laws permitting – and smoking like fiends, we would fantasize about our starry futures because we *all* believed we were going to make it and become the toast of Shaftesbury Avenue.

Having recently discovered the opposite sex, I suppose it is true to say that I became rather popular with the RADA boys, as did Susan and Eileen. The three of us formed a lethal trio, nicknamed Face, Figure and Personality. Eileen, who subsequently married George Cole, was Face, the classically beautifully English rose; Susan, with her short spiky blonde hair and bubbly personality, was Personality; and I, with my ubiquitous tight jeans and sweater and large bosom, was Figure. The three of us teased, giggled and flirted with all the boys, but none of us ever gave away our most prized possession – our virginity.

Once a week we'd queue for the gallery at one of the dozens of West End theatres. The seats cost two shillings and were so high up in the gods that the actors' faces were visible only through opera glasses. It was such a thrill to see Laurence Olivier, John Gielgud, Ralph Richardson, Pamela Brown, Edith Evans and Michael Redgrave in the flesh and at their peak.

John Gielgud and Pamela Brown were appearing at the Globe Theatre on Shaftesbury Avenue in *The Lady's Not For Burning*, which I saw from 'the gods' with my friend Adele and several fellow students. The Christopher Fry play, written in verse, is set in the Middle Ages, the story of a soldier back from the wars who wants to die, and a beautiful witch who wants to live. But I barely watched Gielgud and Brown as I was completely swept away by the mesmerizing presence of a young actor called Richard Burton. He was electrifying with an amazing voice, a faint but mellifluous Welsh accent, and piercing green eyes, which gave off a luminous glow visible even from where we sat. I'd had crushes on a long line of movie stars – John Payne, Gene Kelly, Richard Widmark, Montgomery Clift, Maxwell Reed and Danny Kaye – but Burton was my first flesh and blood passion and I couldn't take my eyes off him.

Adele and I waited excitedly outside the stage door, autograph books at the ready, until the idol himself came out. He scribbled his name and bestowed upon us a devastating matinée-idol smile. We almost fainted, then became convulsed in giggles, watching his hunched figure in a shabby overcoat striding off down Shaftesbury Avenue.

'He's so gorgeous,' I sighed. 'Simply gorgeous.'

'But did you see his skin?' Adele was ever pragmatic. 'It was covered in pock-marks.'

'Doesn't matter,' said I. 'That voice and those eyes make up for anything.'

The Lady's Not For Burning was a huge hit and ran for over a year – I saw it at least a dozen times and wrote to Burton for an autographed photograph. Sure enough, back came a five-by-seven black-and-white glossy, with the rather mundane inscription, 'To Joan. Thank you for your letter. Best Wishes. Richard Burton.' I still have it.

Less than seven years later this thespian god would be smouldering opposite me in *Sea Wife*.

The *Daily Graphic*, a popular newspaper, wanted to photograph and interview three RADA students on a typical day at the Academy. They chose me and two other girls and shot us taking ballet, fencing and acting classes. Also – joy of joys – not only did they take us to see *The Lady's Not For Burning* yet again but we were taken backstage afterwards and photographed with John Gielgud and Pamela Brown. Much to my disappointment, dreamboat Burton wasn't available for this photo-session – no doubt he had some pressing assignation with his current inamorata.

When this double-page tabloid spread appeared, Grandma and Mummie were almost more thrilled than I was. It was the second time my photograph had been printed in a newspaper, the first, at a dance, had appeared in William Hickey's gossip column the previous year.

Shortly afterwards *Picture Post* captured me with my current boyfriend, John Turner, on a river-boat shuffle. We wore matching Levis, plaid shirts and chic little scarves round our necks. I sported the regulation fringe and pony tail. We were described as 'the couple who dress *très jazz*' and thus achieved a brief celebrity at RADA. A river-boat shuffle was a momentous event for jazz aficionados like us. A boat would sail down the Thames two or three times during the summer, and Humphrey Lyttelton, Claude Luter or, if we were really lucky, the legendary Sidney Bechet would play, and we could jive to our hearts' content.

Then, suddenly, a fairy godfather appeared at my side, in the guise of none other than my father, who in a complete turn-about had decided to back me in my acting career.

With the help of Leslie Bloom, another agent with Collins and Grade, Daddy was putting together a repertory company, called the Eros Players, so that his darling daughter could be given the opportunity to learn her craft the hard way during the RADA summer break.

This was more than generous of Daddy and, naturally, I was enormously grateful. Real stage work in a real repertory company was more than any other fellow student had going for them during the holidays.

The Eros Players were based in Maidstone, Kent, and I was paid the gargantuan salary of three pounds ten shillings a week. My job was assistant-assistant stage manager, assistant prop-master, and all round utility in-fielder. I understudied the maid in *Private Lives*, the maid in *French Without Tears* and the maid in *Dangerous Corner*. Altogether I spent many an hour mastering strangulated Swedish, French and regional accents while only managing to tread the boards once, in *French Without Tears* – *naturellement* as the maid.

I stayed in dingy digs with two of the company, Christopher and Patricia. Five or six years older than me, they were racy theatrical types, the kind Daddy had warned me about. They smoked, they drank, they swore, and I suspect they did other things too, but these were still far from my mind. I had just turned sixteen and my eyes and head were still full of stardust. Possibly too full.

One of my jobs was to bring the curtain down at the end of the show. One night the company were doing J. B. Priestley's *Dangerous Corner*. I managed to pull the heavy old-fashioned rope down once then up again with all my strength. However, I was unable to bring it down a second time. The six actors stood in the full glare of the footlights, bristling with a mixture of embarrassment and fury at the dwindling applause of the audience and glaring at me in the wings, as I heaved ineffectually at the ancient rope.

'Get that effing curtain down *now*,' hissed Michael, our leading man. I tugged away madly, but the bloody thing wouldn't budge and the actors stood stock-still and stone-faced – you'd have thought at least the juvenile would have tried to help.

'I can't do it,' I cried, loud enough for half the audience to hear. Titters and whispers rippled through the audience, which then erupted into loud guffaws as my anxious pink face popped momentarily into view as I glanced desperately stage left for Chris, the stage manager.

The audience left, still laughing, and with muffled curses the actors shuffled off stage.

'You blockhead,' hissed the overly grand leading lady, as I cowered against a flat. 'You stupid little *fool*. Don't you even know how to bring a curtain down properly?'

'You'll never make it in this business, my dear. Not a bloody chance,' sneered the gruff character actor. 'No backbone, you young 'uns, no talent and no spine at all. Why in my day we were *trained* to do *everything*.'

They swept off and, trying hard not to cry, I went to find Chris and head for the nearest pub before it shut. I needed to drown my humiliation with a stiff gin. I'd wanted to begin at the bottom and I realized how lucky I was that Daddy had arranged this job for me – but I also realized that manual labour, just like housework and cookery, was *not* my forte.

The next day I trailed around Maidstone as prop-master, cajoling, borrowing and begging props for the following week's performance of *French Without Tears*. To my horror, I heard one of the shopkeepers sniggering about the lamentable débâcle at the Maidstone Theatre the previous night.

'It was all that young girl stage manager's fault.' He chortled. 'Some rich man's daughter, grew up with a silver spoon in 'er mouf and can't do a bleedin' thing!'

Utterly mortified I made a vow that, in the future, I would always try to get my jobs myself, without help from anyone.

A well-known photographer asked to see the ten most beautiful girls at RADA. Along with Susan Stephen, Eileen Moore and Yvonne Furneaux, I was chosen to parade in front of his beady professional eye. To my amazement he chose me as his ideal, and I was immediately thrust into a series of modelling engagements for short stories in women's magazines. I illustrated a story about a tense young girl threatened by a killer, and a teenager discovering she was pregnant.

I posed for teenage fashion layouts in hideous clothes – dowdy jumpers, long plaid skirts and baggy, unbecoming pedal-pushers. I was photographed sitting on a bike looking surly, lacing up ice-skates, licking an ice-cream cone, peeping round someone's door, and in most of the shots appeared awkward, plump and gawky.

My first magazine cover on *Good Taste* featured me in a bathing suit lying on some studio sand. With a plump face, big red lips and a total lack of eye make-up, I resembled nothing more than a startled mouse.

But modelling supplemented my allowance and, at roughly two pounds an hour, it was certainly lucrative.

Although Sir Kenneth was probably aware that I was moonlighting he didn't seem to mind, as long as it didn't interfere with classes. My tearful 'pregnant' photo in a yellow jumper in *Woman's Own* had been passed around the RADA canteen avidly, to a certain amount of admiration and jealousy.

Then Daddy decided that I should have a professional photograph taken by a theatrical photographer and placed it in *Spotlight*, the casting bible, under 'Juvenile Leads, Female', putting down his name as my agent. A few months after the second autumn term began, Bill Watts, a theatrical agent, called my father. 'I would be very interested in seeing your daughter for possible film roles,' he said. Although I wasn't interested in making movies, I was intrigued enough to make an appointment. So, with my father's approval, I set off to see Mr Watts at his tiny offices in Dover Street off Piccadilly.

An avuncular, plumpish man in his late forties with thinning hair, he was dressed in a smart grey suit with an expensive silk tie. The walls behind his desk were covered in framed photographs of pretty young pin-up girls, some of whom I recognized from cameo roles in films and photographs in the tabloids. Bill's wife, Cherry, worked as a receptionist, and in the foyer several other girls sat, long-legged, beautifully coiffed and well groomed.

I was wearing my 'serious actress' uniform, which consisted of a long black skirt, black ballet pumps, black sweater, gold earrings and bracelets, a fringe that hid my mascara-ed eyes and hair hanging past my shoulders. I thought I looked like the cat's pyjamas, a lookalike Juliette Greco, who was the current existentialist idol of the young. I thought Bill Watts must have thought so, too, for he wasted no time.

'You're a very pretty girl,' he said, 'but for films we need to clean you up.'

'Clean me up?' I gasped, à la Eliza Doolittle.

'Yes,' he said. 'Sidney Gilliat and Frank Launder are casting the lead in *Lady Godiva Rides Again*. It's about a beauty queen, and the girl who lands the main role will *definitely* become a star. They're testing next week at Elstree and I think you stand a chance. How old are you?'

'Seventeen,' I stammered, 'but – but – Mr Watts—'

'What?' he asked, flicking through a batch of my latest pictures and frowning.

'I don't want to be in films,' I faltered. 'I want to be on the stage.'

He laughed hoarsely. 'The stage? There's no money in the stage. There's no fame in the stage. It's hard bloody work. Wouldn't you like to be a film star?'

'No,' I bleated. 'I don't want to be a film star. Film stars can't act, they're just all fake glamour and make-up. I don't want to be like that.'

He looked at me, his eyes twinkling. 'So who do you want to be like? Vivien Leigh?' His sarcasm didn't escape me.

'As a matter of fact, yes, she's my favourite – and Pamela Brown as well. Then eventually I hope I'll become like Flora Robson.'

'How long have you been at RADA?' he asked.

'A year,' I replied, 'with another year to go.'

'What are you doing for money?' he asked. 'For clothes and the bits and pieces you girls like.'

'Well, I've been doing some modelling, I live at home, and I managed to save over twenty pounds doing ten weeks in rep this summer,' I said proudly.

'Twenty pounds, eh?' His eyebrows waggled jovially. 'You could make more than twenty a *day* in films, don't you realize that?'

'But won't it affect me being taken seriously as a stage actress?' I asked.

'No,' he said firmly, 'it certainly would not. Did it affect Vivien Leigh?'

I thought about this. Mr Watts was right. She'd certainly managed to combine stage and film work brilliantly.

'It'll bring you in some pin-money. Wouldn't you like that? Wouldn't you like to buy a few nice new clothes?' He looked disparagingly at my carefully chosen Bohemian outfit.

'I suppose so,' I said uncertainly. 'But I'll have to ask Sir Kenneth.'

'*Don't*, for *God's* sake, whatever you do, *don't* ask Sir Kenneth,' Bill Watts boomed. 'I know exactly what he'll say. He'll say no. I know I can get Launder and Gilliat to test you. But first we need to have some new glamour pictures taken of you. These are terrible.'

I sashayed off to one of the top glamour photographers in London, armed with my one black swimsuit, a chaste bikini, and two or three of Lalla's cast-off dresses. The photographer made me get into all manner of uncomfortable positions but I complied meekly. This was what Vivien Leigh and Margaret Lockwood must have had to do, after all, and twenty pounds a day sounded to me like a fortune.

With Joan Rice – who went on to star opposite Burt Lancaster in *The Crimson Pirate* – Jean Marsh, who became a household name later on for writing and starring in *Upstairs, Downstairs*, and several others, I tested for the title role in *Lady Godiva Rides Again*.

The tabloids had a field day: they made out that a search akin to that for Scarlett O'Hara was under way. The girl who would play the lead, they crowed, was going to become the biggest English star ever. It was the opportunity of a lifetime and every girl in Britain with acting pretensions sent in her photograph. Eventually Lady Godiva was played by Pauline Stroud who, unfortunately, was never heard of again. So much for overnight stardom. Others in the cast were Kay Kendall, Diana Dors, Ann Heywood, Stanley Holloway, John McCallum and me, playing the small, totally insignificant role of a beauty contestant.

Lady Godiva was nothing more than a jolly romp, shot mainly in and around Folkestone town hall. All we 'beauty contestants' had to do was hold in our stomachs and parade in hideously unflattering one-piece 'skirted' bathing suits, the type Princess Margaret still wears, and high-heeled black suede court shoes. This was by no means an elegant look, and we all looked as if we had short chunky legs and fat bellies.

My first appearance on celluloid did not lead to overnight stardom, but it did lead to my second movie. I'd just bagged the part of a Greek serving-wench in *The Woman's Angle*. It was a two-day role and I was seriously chuffed about it. Dressed to the nines, in what I considered the height of fifties chic, I strutted down Oxford Street for some Saturday-morning window-shopping, hoping to add to my burgeoning collection of audacious costumes. What I was wearing was pretty audacious already, though. My waist, cinched by a wide black-patent belt, was a gratifying but agonizing twenty inches. 'You must suffer to be beautiful': Mummie and Grandma had told me *that* often enough. My cleavage was displayed in an off-the-shoulder yellow Jane Russell mohair sweater, which left little to the imagination, and the rest of me was encased in a sausage tight calf-length slit skirt, so form-fitting that the only possible form of forward propulsion was a wiggle.

I had carefully studied photographs of Jean Simmons in a similar out-fit and was convinced I looked enough like her to be her younger sister. In fact, I thought myself the quintessence of grace and glamour, and bestowed on any lucky passer-by, who glanced at me approvingly, a shy smile.

'What *does* she think she looks like?' I heard a chorus of disapproval behind me, and turned to see the large and formidable Joanne Heyworth, a former classmate at Francis Holland, with her even fatter and more for-midable mamma.

Joanne and I chatted briefly but I was well aware of the sneering condemnation of my outfit visible in her mother's beady eyes, which became ever more probingly intense when I proudly announced that I was about to take on the small but telling role of a Greek girl in *The Woman's Angle* 'to be made at Elstree Studios'.

Mrs Heyworth's eyes gleamed. 'Is Stewart Granger in it?' she asked, a hint of lust spreading over her chubby features.

'No, Edward Underdown and Lois Maxwell are the stars, actually,' I said. 'They're quite important stars.'

'Never heard of either of 'em,' boomed Mrs Heyworth. 'Can't be much of a film, then. Come along Joanne, time to go, or we'll miss the train.'

They waddled off and I went into Bourne and Hollingsworth, but not before I heard the stiff county tones of Heyworth the Elder hiss: 'Silly little cow, *she*'ll never make it as an actress, not if she's going to go around in *those* tarty clothes.'

My face flamed but I tossed my fringe and, staring hard at a flat-eyed mannequin, muttered: 'Silly *old* cow. I'll bloody well show her.'

A decade later Lois Maxwell was playing Miss Moneypenny in the Bond films but that didn't help *The Woman's Angle*, which was a B pic through and through.

Filming was quite boring – 90 per cent of the work consisted of waiting around to go before the cameras – but the money was good. I earned the princely sum of fifty pounds for only two days' work, so I was able to buy two new blouses and more dangling earrings.

Then Bill Watts called me excitedly. 'They've seen *The Woman's Angle* and they want to make a test of you at Elstree for *The Red Beret*. You'll play the girlfriend of Alan Ladd. He's a great Hollywood star!'

I'd never heard Bill so enthusiastic. I wasn't a fan of Alan Ladd – he was a small boy's idea of a tough guy – and although a big star he was not so great height-wise. When I met him in person, I found a short, blondish chap with bags under his pale-blue eyes and receding hair, wearing a beige gabardine 'leisure jacket' and belted trousers which seemed to come up to his armpits. This, I imagined, was a failed attempt to make his little legs appear longer. I was about a quarter of a century younger than Mr Ladd, but this seemed not to matter. What *did* matter was that I was about three inches taller, so for our test a trench was dug in which I had to walk in flats while Ladd strode next to me on the raised part wearing lifts. This solved the height problem – now he towered over me – but it wasn't good enough. When the moguls saw the test they thought I looked far too young, with my round baby face and high voice, so they cast Susan Stephen, who bravely climbed down into the trench.

While I had been getting coiffed for this test the make-up man had gleefully told me a story. One day Alan Ladd was stopped by a friend on the Paramount lot who said, 'Hey, Alan, I hear your new picture starts Monday.'

'Yeah,' Ladd sighed, 'and I haven't even read the script yet, can you believe it?'

'That must be very disturbing for you,' sympathized the friend.

'Sure is,' said Ladd, looking peeved. 'I *still* don't know *what* I'm going to wear.' I giggled along with the make-up man, and realized then that Make-up and Hair were always first with the gossip.

Soon afterwards, I tested again, this time at Pinewood Studios with the 'idol of the Odeons', the gorgeous, sensitive Dirk Bogarde. We slithered around self-consciously on creamy satin sheets, I wearing a pink baby-doll nightgown, he a bemused expression. We attempted to look as though we were made for each other but we were seriously ill-matched and this time the part went to Brigitte Bardot.

But it was all good experience and I was a busy girl indeed. Between studying, socializing with my RADA pals, seeing as many plays and films as possible, cha-cha-cha-ing or jiving at jazz clubs all night, and the newly found delights of dating, I was totally involved in life. My mother dubbed me Miss Perpetual Motion, and informed me that 'You've never kept still, and have always had a genius for the unexpected.'

My first sizeable role, in *Judgement Deferred*, meant I had to spent time away from RADA. It was decision time.

'It's either RADA or "the films",' Sir Kenneth Barnes enunciated. 'You cannot do both, my dear.'

'But I'd like to come back after this film and continue my studies,' I said. 'I've only been at RADA just over a year and I know I've still a lot to learn.'

Sir Kenneth was appalled. 'Absolutely not. You simply cannot go into *films*. The Films! It's absolutely not on, my dear. You want to be a *serious* actress, don't you?'

'Yes, sir,' I mumbled.

'There are no *serious* actors in the films. They are just attractive faces who cannot act. Only in the theatre does one find *real* actors.'

I was faced with a tremendously difficult decision, and I agonized over it. I loved RADA, even though I was beginning to find it irritating that all the students had to conform to a specific way of speaking. No regional accents were allowed, and although I didn't have one, plenty of students did, and suffered torments trying to rid themselves of their Liverpudlian, Mancunian or Scottish burrs, sometimes to the mockery of the teachers. The main problem with my voice was its pitch, which was considered too high. In one of my report cards it was pointed out, some-what flatteringly, that 'If she doesn't watch her voice, it will be "the films" for Joan Collins, and that would be *such* a pity, as she does have a lot of talent.'

I discussed these problems endlessly with Mummie, Daddy and Bill Watts. My parents vacillated: Mummie wanted me to do what would make me happy; Daddy felt that I should spend another year at RADA, then get married and have children. It was Bill Watts who finally made the decision: 'If you don't take this part, Joanie, somebody else will. This is really a chance in a *million*. Do you realize how many girls would give their front teeth to get this role? You've *got* to do it.'

So, on the strength of Bill's persuasion, I accepted the part – but I didn't tell Sir Kenneth. For the duration of that film, in which I worked approximately twelve days over a five-week period, I pleaded a succes-sion of ailments that prevented me from going to my RADA studies and was thus able to have my cake and eat it too – one of my favourite things.

Judgement Deferred, shot at the old Southall Studios, starred Hugh Sinclair, and I played a 'once-beautiful young girl fallen on hard times through drink, drugs and deprivation'. Since I was only seventeen Make-up painted dark circles under my eyes, smeared my lipstick and gave me a generally debauched look that made me look all of eighteen.

It was around this time that the tabloids, gossip columnists and magazines began to notice me seriously, and made flattering comments about my looks, sex-appeal and potential. 'Britain's best bet since Jean Simmons,' blared the *Daily Mirror*. 'England's answer to Ava Gardner and Marilyn Monroe,' declared another. This was all strong stuff for a teenager, but my father did not allow it to go to my head. He constantly admonished me to 'Keep a level head on your shoulders', and 'You're only as good as other people think you are' (what a load of baloney *that* is) and other succinct aphorisms designed to cut me down to size. However, he was secretly proud of me and would brag to his cronies about my success while pulling out of his pocket a few of my latest press clippings.

Mummie and Grandma Hettie, of course, were in seventh heaven, collecting every cutting and all the photographs. Grandma even made a scrapbook, painstakingly pasting in every snippet of newsprint about her favourite granddaughter. It even contained the review from my first stage appearance, aged three, in *Why the Fairies Cried*: 'Joan Collins makes an entirely believable fairy.'

Then came the telephone call that sent my life into top gear. The Rank Organization was then the most important film company in England. It boasted a huge stable of stars, including Margaret Lockwood, Stewart Granger, James Mason, Patricia Roc, Susan Shaw, Maxwell Reed, Kieron Moore, Petula Clarke, Phyllis Calvert, Jean Kent, Anthony Steele and many others. Rank had also been famed for its Charm School, a feature they copied from the American studio system, which had been formed before the war, to which they would recruit pretty young girls and boys aged between sixteen and twenty-five and make them spend most of their time posing for pin-ups and learning deportment and elocution. They were taught to walk and talk properly, as many were literally pulled from behind the counter of Boots, Woolworths or petrol stations. When I arrived on the scene, the Charm School had been disbanded, and Rank weren't signing any new talent. But luckily they thought enough of me, on the strength of two more screen tests I'd made, to cast me as Renee, the juvenile lead in a hugely important film called *I Believe In You*.

The director, who was none other than the illustrious Basil Dearden, had previously made the *The Captive Heart*, a prisoner-of-war drama with Michael Redgrave, *Saraband for Dead Lovers* with Stewart Granger, and *Halfway House*. Michael Relph, our producer, had recently made *Kind Hearts and Coronets* with Alec Guinness, and both men were considered first-rate film-makers. My co-stars would include Celia Johnson, Cecil Parker, Laurence Harvey, Godfrey Tearle and a young Harry Fowler as my Cockney boyfriend.

When I found out that I'd been cast in this film, which would entail twelve weeks of shooting at Ealing Studios during RADA term time, I practically went down on my hands and knees to Sir Kenneth to ask for a leave of absence – which he refused absolutely. He had found out that I had made *Judgement Deferred* and was less than pleased.

'You have to choose,' he boomed. 'You either finish your year at RADA or you go into films. You simply cannot do both, my dear, I've told you before. And it's your decision alone.'

For a week I agonized again over my dilemma, but Bill Watts – about to make his 10 per cent on my three-hundred-pound salary for the film – was the real decision-maker. 'You've done over a year at the Academy,' he said brusquely. 'And you've done three months in rep. You've learned your craft, and now you've got this *huge* break. If you don't take it, some other girl is going to. Big breaks like this don't come along every day. You're going to have to give up RADA, dear.'

And that was the decision I made. I bade a sad farewell to the Academy, and to all my friends, and on a cold January day in 1952 started shooting *I Believe In You*.

To my surprise, making this film was a great experience. Ealing had always been my favourite British studio because of the consistently high quality of the films they turned out. I'd kept scrapbooks of photographs of all their productions and I was still sending off for autographed pictures of their stars.

I spent hours trudging around London's second-hand shops with the costume designer Anthony Mendleson in search of well-worn clothes and shoes for my character. To get the right down-at-heel look my hair was greased to hang in lank rat's tails, and my make-up – such as it was – carelessly applied.

To work with an actress of Celia Johnson's calibre was a great honour for me and I knew it. Several years earlier she had scored an enormous success in *Brief Encounter*, and she decided to impart to me an important tip about film acting: 'Forget most of what they taught you at RADA, dear,' she said, as we sat on the sound stage waiting for a call. 'Film acting is less about acting and more about *reacting*. *Always* listen to whatever the other actor is saying and only react to *that*. Film acting is totally different from stage acting, dear. It's much more subtle and understated.'

Laurence Harvey, who was playing one of my character's lovers, also gave me some advice – albeit rather cynical.

'Darling Joanie, in the great scheme of things actors aren't important – but plumbers are. The best film performers are children, because they have the secret of truth and honesty that no adult can possibly have.'

Although he sounded more English than Noël Coward, Larry was actually Lithuanian and had been born Larushke Skikne. Then in his twenties, he was flamboyant, eccentric and elegantly dressed, in a slightly louche way, in wide-shouldered suits and pastel shirts. He drank vodka as though it was about to be rationed and constantly smoked exotic cigarettes through a long holder. He valiantly tried to educate me in the ways of a glamorous *femme du monde*. 'To start with, my dear, your dress sense is *atrocious*,' he said, and took me off to the Rahvis sisters' couture. There, he insisted that I invest hundreds of pounds I didn't have on several suitably sparkling evening dresses. 'Borrow it, my dear, borrow it,' he said, wearily. 'You *must* try to look *soignée*.'

My parents adored Larry, and he beguiled people with his outrageous Wildean mannerisms and wit. We often dined at one of the most glamorous and sophisticated restaurants in London, the Caprice. Soft pink flattering lights, tinkling crystal chandeliers, sweeping red curtains and gorgeous women in strapless Hartnell and Dior gowns chatting grandly to each other, as I imagined Noël, Gertie and Vivien did.

Larry also took me to the splendid private club Les Ambassadeurs on Park Lane, where we dined on his favourite dish, caviar and baked potato, rhumba-ed the night away and smoked Luckies, till my lungs gave out. The cosmopolitan drinking club La Rue, in Curzon Street, was another of his haunts, although a more sinister element was present there among the clientele. One night I saw the notorious East End gangster Jack Spot at the centre of a laughing crowd. He looked me over with cold black eyes.

'Keep well away from him, darling,' warned my mentor. 'He's *big* trouble.'

I only wished Larry had warned me about Maxwell Reed, the devastatingly handsome Anglo-Irish movie actor to whom he introduced me at La Rue. To say that I was impressed is putting it mildly. Reed had been one of my film idols at school, his *Picturegoer* photograph taking pride of place inside my desk where I'd gaze longingly at his darkly brooding countenance. Now here he was in person – a real live movie star and, surprise, surprise, he seemed terribly interested in naïve, innocent, virginal little me! I became a tongue-tied ninny before this six-foot-four icon. Little wonder I was so flattered when he started to pursue me.

I was living life to the hilt, learning something new from Larry every day, and with Maxwell Reed's attentions I was now learning from him what my parents empemistically called 'the facts of life'.

I was still awestruck by everybody on *I Believe In You*, even calling the crew Mr or Mrs So-and-So. Respect for one's 'elders and betters' had been drilled into me by my parents, and at thirty-two to my eighteen, Max was certainly older, but not necessarily better.

When *I Believe In You* came out, I received some head-turning reviews. Jympson Harman, one of England's top critics, wrote, 'Joan Collins makes a tremendous impression as the wayward girl. She has a dark, luscious kind of beauty which puts her in the Jane Russell class, but Joan already seems to be an actress of greater ability. On the showing of this first big film part, she looks like the most impressive recruit to British films for many a moon.' And the *News of the World* raved, 'A dozen of my darkest red roses to Joan Collins. Fire and spirit in her acting and that odd combination of allure and mystery that spells eventual world stardom.'

The film was so successful that Rank signed me to an astronomical five-year contract, starting at one hundred pounds a week which would be increased to two hundred in the second year. Max, however, thought this was 'peanuts'. I was also concerned that Rank would keep me too

Left: Grandma and Great Aunt Bessie strut their stuff in 'black face' as part of their act, The Three Cape Girls, South Africa 1900.

(JOAN COLLINS)

Below: Grandma Henrietta performing one of her more patriotic numbers during the Boer War.

(JOAN COLLINS)

Right: Pauline, Lalla and Joe rehearsing for their music-hall debut, circa 1911.

(JOAN COLLINS)

Above: Grandma's *pièce de résistance* which she also taught me. The splits brought the house down in 1900.

(JOAN COLLINS)

Far left: Auntie Lalla playing the definitive flapper in the title role of *Sunny*.

(JOAN COLLINS)

Left: Auntie Pauline in revue as an extremely daring Charles Cochrane Young Lady.

(JOAN COLLINS)

Above: I love this picture of Mummie and Daddy on their honeymoon with car (of course) and laughing entourage. This picture epitomizes the happiness I truly believe my parents shared for the almost thirty years they spent together.

(JOAN COLLINS)

Right: Four generations of Collins women. Me aged two months (held by Grandma Hettie), Great Grandmama Leah and Mummie.

(JOAN COLLINS)

Left: Around this time
Mummie hung the
'Please do not kiss me'
sign on my pram.
(JOAN COLLINS)

Above: My favourite
photograph of Mummie.
(JOAN COLLINS)

Left: Daddy's girl aged two in Brighton.
(JOAN COLLINS)

Below: Grandma Hettie in Brighton with her favourite grandchild, done up in full Shirley Temple mode.
(JOAN COLLINS)

Below: Aged five, London.
(JOAN COLLINS)

Left: Proud to wear rabbit fur on my fifth birthday. A studio shot to give to doting grandparents.
(JOAN COLLINS)

Opposite: The Collins girls. Two future sisterly media stars.
(JOAN COLLINS)

Right: There are no small parts, only small actors. First appearance in Ibsen's *A Doll's House* with Judith Bennet, Jenny Laird and Edgar Norfolk, The Arts Theatre, London, 1946.
(JOAN COLLINS)

Below: Stars in my eyes at thirteen.
(JOAN COLLINS)

Right: With Jean Marsh, Violet Pretty, Simone Silva, Diana Dors, Madelaine Mono, Pauline Stroud et al in my first teeny role *Lady Godiva Rides Again*, in which I had but one line, 1951.
(BRITISH FILM INSTITUTE)

Below: Daddy signing Roger Moore to his agency. It was only a brief tenure for Roger, but he and Daddy remained close friends.
(JOAN COLLINS)

Opposite: My modelling career took off, but I didn't always get to wear teenaged trendsetting gear. I thought this awful plastic mac an abomination.

(TITBITS)

Right: *Do* put your daughter on the stage, Mrs Worthington. Three star-struck RADA students backstage at the Globe Theatre meet John Gielgud and Pamela Brown in *The Lady's Not For Burning* 1950.

(JOAN COLLINS)

Below: Preparing to be a wicked lady in *Turn The Key Softly*, 1952.

Above: This poster for *I Believe In You* went to town on Joan Collins but it didn't go to my head.

Right: Honeymooners but not for long. On location with Maxwell Reed who was starring as the villain in *Sea Devils* with Rock Hudson, 1952.

Right: Kenneth More, George Cole and Robertson Hare drawing straws for sleeping with Sadie and looking pretty glum about it in *Our Girl Friday*, Majorca, 1954.

(BRITISH FILM INSTITUTE)

Far right: Sydney Chaplin and I off set in Rome during *Land of the Pharaohs*.

(HULTON-DEUTSCH COLLECTION LTD)

Left: That damn ruby is about to pop out again! The perils of pizza during *Land of the Pharaohs*, Rome.

(HULTON-DEUTSCH COLLECTION LTD)

Below: Howard Hawks directing me not to eat so much in *Land of the Pharaohs*.

(HULTON-DEUTSCH COLLECTION LTD)

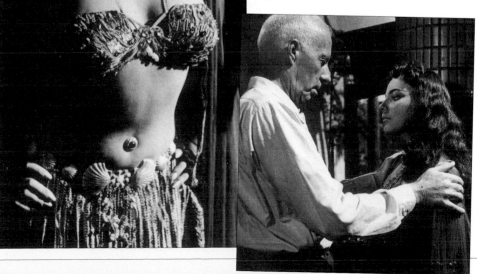

Above: Marlon Brando collects his Oscar for *On the Waterfront* and Bette Davis (then appearing in *The Virgin Queen*) looks like the cat who got the cream, Hollywood 1954.

Above: Robert Wagner and me testing for *Lord Vanity* which was never made. Was it because of my stomach rumbles picked up by the sound boom above us?

(20TH CENTURY-FOX)

Below. With Farley Granger in my first starring role at Fox, *The Girl in the Red Velvet Swing*, a lush cinemascope true-life epic, 1955.

(THE KOBAL COLLECTION)

Above: More stars in the audience than on the screen. Fox's private screening of *There's No Business Like Show Business*, 1954. Marilyn Monroe sits surrounded by Milton Greene, Irving Berlin, me, Bing Crosby, Olivia de Havilland, Mona Freeman, Judy Garland, Joseph Mankiewicz, Donald O'Connor and Ann Southern amongst others.

(JAMES HASPIEL)

Left: One of Fox's many stills taken in an attempt to glamorize me.

(20TH CENTURY-FOX)

Above: Off the set of *Sea Wife* with Richard Burton.
(BRITISH FILM INSTITUTE)

Above left: Richard Burton tries to sully the face of innocence in *Sea Wife*, Jamaica 1958.
(BRITISH FILM INSTITUTE)

Left: With John Justin, James Mason and the infamous Darryl F. Zanuck arriving in Barbados for *Island in the Sun*.
(PAUL KEYLOCK)

Left: Paul and I get down and dirty in *Rally Round the Flag, Boys* during our drunk scene, at 20th Century-Fox 1958.

(BRITISH FILM INSTITUTE)

Below: Joanne Woodward watching her husband watching my legs in *Rally Round the Flag, Boys*, Los Angeles 1958.

(20TH CENTURY-FOX)

Bottom: Joanne Woodward with her Oscar for *The Three Faces of Eve* wearing the dress she made herself, 1958.

(JOAN COLLINS)

Left: Dana Wynter, Angela Lansbury and me making fools of ourselves at the 1959 Oscar ceremony as we performed 'It's Bully Not To Be Nominated'.

(BRITISH FILM INSTITUTE)

Below: Cary Grant and I are equally fascinated by Marlon Brando at the opening of the Broadway production of *The Birthday Party*, 1960.

(UNITED PICTURES INTERNATIONAL)

Above: The poster for *The Wayward Bus*.

(20TH CENTURY-FOX)

Opposite: Orgasmic frenzy with Eli Wallach in Fox's *Seven Thieves*, 1960.

(HULTON-DEUTSCH COLLECTION LTD)

Above: Warren Beatty and I promote ourselves by feeding the ducks in Central Park for a movie magazine layout, New York 1961.

(Friedman-Abeles/Galaxy Pictures)

Left: Chatting to the siblings Shirley MacLaine and Warren Beatty on the set of *Can-Can*, Hollywood 1960.

(Bob Willoughby)

busy for any theatre work, but Bill Watts had cleverly put a clause in my contract that, if there were no immediate film plans for me, Rank would allow me to appear in a play, as long as it was only for a limited run.

When not filming much of my day was spent in the stills gallery with the brilliant photographer Cornel Lucas, who tried his damnedest to make me look sultry, glamorous and as much like a budding Ava Gardner as possible.

Theo Cowan, head of Rank publicity, was a famously humorous man – he needed to be as publicity was a funny business. Theo took me in hand, attempting to teach me how to deal with the press, and we became great friends.

Rank often used to make their contract stars attend film premières – even if we weren't in the picture we still had to appear. Since I was just a little starlet, whom Rank were trying to push, I needed to do as much publicity as possible. One night I was dispatched to a première in Birmingham with Anthony Steele, then a major star.

We left the cinema to ear-splitting screams from the fans for Anthony, but when we got into the limousine Theo, who was in the front seat, hissed, '*Smile, Joanie, smile* – not at me, at those fans, DAMMIT!'

'They're not calling for me, Theo, they want Tony,' I said. 'Anyway, I'm scared. They're all banging on the window and I think it's going to break.'

'Never mind that, bloody well SMILE. You're on display and you've *got* to smile. Your future public's out there,' he barked. 'Let them remember you looking pleasant for a change.' I smiled until my jaw ached as the car moved slowly through the throng of hysterical girls. Suddenly I spotted a woman near the car screaming her head off like the figure in the famous Munch painting. She looked totally terrified and the crowd were beating even more frantically on the car windows. Now, however, they looked angry, but mindful of Theo's instructions I carried on smiling, even though the crowd's faces resembled those of the mob running beside Marie-Antoinette's tumbril on her way to the guillotine. 'What on earth's going on?' I asked Theo.

'Beats me.' He shrugged. 'Doesn't matter – smile, dear. Go on *smile*.'

Suddenly I looked down and saw the same woman now being

dragged along the street almost under the car. The hem of her dress was caught on the bumper, and she was about to be run over.

The fixed smile instantly left my face, and I shrieked. Anthony Steele leapt up, hitting his head on the roof of the car, Theo cursed and the car screeched to a halt. To the relief of the crowd, and the delight of the photographers, the woman's skirt was released. Anthony then climbed out unruffled and plonked a smacker on her cheek to loud cheers from the onlookers. He milked the occasion for all it was worth, turning this way and that, flashing his perfect profile and his toothsome teeth while clutching the tearful woman to his breast. I watched, fascinated. 'He's an expert at this publicity stuff, isn't he, Theo?'

'Yes, dear, and, by the way, I didn't expect you to smile under *those* circumstances,' Theo said. 'But this is all *great* publicity! We'll make the Birmingham papers for certain – and the nationals, too, I bet.'

Which, of course, we did, proving that anything unseemly will usually put you into the papers.

Life at Rank was a constant round of being on display, parties, lunches, launches, garden fêtes and premières but, unfortunately, I didn't have enough of the right clothes. I had jeans, sweaters and skirts and a couple of Rahvis dresses I'd worn a good deal, but nothing chic, so Theo took me to Wardrobe.

'You've got to attend the *Photoplay* party next Friday,' he commanded. 'You *must* have something decent to wear, and try not to look like a gypsy for once.'

'Yes, Theo,' I said meekly.

Photoplay's annual Christmas party, which inexplicably took place in July, was one of the high points of a starlet's social calendar. Margaret Lockwood, James Mason and Stewart Granger would all be there, as would a host of other British stars. There was even a rumour that Lana Turner, the sweater girl herself who was filming in England with an unknown called Sean Connery, might possibly show up.

The stylist in Wardrobe said, 'We had a girl in a film here who's just gone off to Hollywood. She's about your size. Try this on. She wore it in *The Lavender Hill Mob*.' She then brought out the most beautiful yellow and white brocade dress, which I tried on but which didn't go near me.

This wasn't surprising: the girl it had been made for was the elfin Audrey Hepburn, and I was most definitely *not* elfin.

But Wardrobe performed their magic, and off I swanned in Audrey's dress to the *Photoplay* party at Ciro's club. There, I posed with David Tomlinson, Dinah Sheridan, Jean Simmons and many other stars to whom I'd been writing for autographs only a couple of years earlier.

After *I Believe In You*, the Rank Organization started to groom me in earnest. This was a glamorous time for actresses, who had to look sensational at all times. We were instructed not walk into the street without full slap applied, hair coiffed to a T and a band-box fresh elegant outfit. There was to be no dashing out to the grocery store in T-shirt and jeans. For an eighteen-year-old who fancied herself an existentialist this was a crashing bore. I wasn't at all glamorous, I was Bohemian and proud of it, with long, fringed hair and my own gypsyish style. But, reluctantly, I submitted myself to the inevitable.

All Rank actresses had to conform to a certain 'look' copied from Hollywood. My hair was cut short and permed, and I was taught to plaster my face with a heavy pan-stick base, crimson lipstick and black eyeliner, which had to be painted into the popular doe-eyed look. We had to wear pristine white gloves when we went out – at least mine covered the bitten fingernails – and to give us tiny waists, we cinched them in until we could hardly breathe with a wide leather belt or a Merry Widow, the basque-type undergarment popularized by Lana Turner, which was dreadfully uncomfortable. Skirts were mid-calf and either full and flowing or so tight it was hard to walk without waggling your bottom like an arthritic duck. Bosoms were pushed up and out, enhanced with an up-lift bra. At eighteen I looked thirty. Still a rebellious teenager, I hated being 'glamorized' but Mr Rank owned me and I had to conform, just like all his other contractees, to the exact way he wanted his stars to look. But when I wasn't, as Mummie said, 'on parade to my public', I reverted to jeans or capri pants and flats.

I still had time to appear in several plays, limited runs at the Q Theatre, Richmond, which included *The Seventh Veil*, a stage adaptation of the film, which had starred Ann Todd and James Mason, *Jassy*, another adaptation, this time from the Margaret Lockwood pot-boiler, which I did with

Maxwell Reed and *Claudia and David* with Donald Houston. My particular favourite was Thornton Wilder's American classic *The Skin of Our Teeth*, which I did with Max, in which I played Sabina, a vixenish minx of a temptress who represents Everywoman in the shape of Eve. Vivien Leigh had originally played my role in the West End and, although I hadn't seen her 1945 performance, I based my Sabina look exactly on hers by studying photographs of her in the role: a strapless, tightly boned, red-velvet bathing-suit costume with sexy white frills around the *décolleté* and hips, black net stockings, stiletto sandals laced to the knee, black elbow-length gloves, all topped off with a long chestnut wig and a wicked pout.

My excellent reviews made up for the acid comment on my RADA report card about my voice being too thin for the stage.

The play is an American classic. As the curtain rises, Sabina is discovered flicking a feather duster insouciantly around the furniture, declaiming petulantly, 'Oh, oh, *oh*, six o'clock and the master not home yet. Pray God nothing serious happens to him crossing the Hudson river.' She then starts to polish the silver in a desultory manner.

My American accent, a mélange of Scarlett O'Hara, Adelaide in *Guys and Dolls*, and strangulated RADA vowels left much to be desired, as indeed did my dusting. On opening night, my mother was so convulsed at seeing her daughter doing the only dusting she'd ever done in her life that she had to leave her seat in hysterics. Back stage afterwards, all Mummie could talk about was my housework, as tears of mirth ran down her cheeks.

'Don't get any ideas, Mummie.' I smiled. 'This doesn't mean I've turned into some kind of domestic slave, and if you ever find me doing a bit of Hoovering for pleasure, you'll know that either I've abandoned acting, or it's abandoned me.'

It was exciting to be young in the fifties and in London there were so many things to do. There were dozens of theatres, and the cinemas were showing fabulous movies like *A Place in the Sun, High Noon*, Chaplin's *Limelight, On the Waterfront, Roman Holiday, From Here to Eternity, The African Queen, A Streetcar Named Desire, An American in Paris, East of Eden, All About Eve* and *Sunset Boulevard*.

There were exciting night-clubs, jazz clubs, Latin-American clubs or just plain drinking clubs. The Café de Paris, 100 Oxford Street, the Stork Club and the Embassy were some of my hang-outs and Max introduced me to some less salubrious ones too – while Soho was a hot-bed of coffee-bars, dives, strip joints and fun. There was little traffic in the streets, relatively few private cars, and about a quarter as many buses as there are today. Practically everywhere the shells of bombed-out buildings were a grim reminder of the last decade. Young girls could happily go alone to the Soho clubs and walk freely round the West End without having to worry about being mugged or raped. Leicester Square, where one would have coffee after the cinema or theatre, was a beautiful square filled with flowers and trees, where the pigeons cooed, and with just the occasional busker, accordionist, or pavement artist around to make it interesting.

The fifties was also the golden age of family life, although, of course, teenagers used to moan about the tedium of having to spend weekends with their parents and grandparents, going for drives or just sharing Sunday lunch. The consumer society had been born and labour-saving gadgets were spilling into department stores. Our mothers were thrilled by the revolutionary new washing machines, fridges, electric kettles and toasters which had been practically unknown before the war. Mummie adored gadgets and our kitchen was a temple to John Lewis and Selfridges.

Everyone in Britain seemed content because the terrible war had ended and life was looking rosy for most of us. Although some foods were still rationed, like sugar and meat, everyone appreciated fresh fruit, ice-cream, Coca-Cola, milk-shakes and even frozen peas – most of which I never saw until well after the war. When young people left school or college there were plenty of jobs available. The shops were full of bright, cheap clothes – and mercifully clothing coupons were a thing of the past. People considered themselves fortunate indeed, and my parents constantly told us how lucky we were to be alive in the post-war world that was looking starry-eyed towards a bright and affluent future for everyone.

CHAPTER FOUR

Roman holiday

In the space of a year, I moved out of Harley House and married Maxwell Reed. Mummie had instilled in me the moral ignominy of 'giving myself' to a man outside of wedlock but, heedless of her advice, I had done the deed with Max, then paid the price in guilt. I knew that nice girls, if they 'did it', should get married, so when Max proposed, I took my first trip down the aisle. Sex with my husband was a non-event to be tolerated. Mummie had told me it was no big deal, and she proved absolutely right.

I made films non-stop. A slew of 'naughty girl' roles came my way. A thug's young girlfriend who becomes pregnant in *Cosh Boy* (a shocking predicament in those far-off days); a boxer's boozy girlfriend (the boxer being husband Max) in *The Square Ring*; a teenage prostitute fresh out of jail in *Turn the Key Softly*, complete with tight black satin slit skirt, fishnet stockings, suede ankle-strap shoes and three inches of make-up; and the spoiled and sulky rich girl marooned on a desert island with three lecherous men in *Our Girl Friday*, known in America as *The Adventures of Sadie*.

The press labelled me 'Britain's Bad Girl', 'A Vest Pocket Ava Gardner – Provocative, Sexy and Fascinating'. One magazine even called me 'The Three Esses Girl: "She's sultry! She's sexy!! She's a siren!!!"' My favourite epithet at the time was, 'The Coffee-bar Jezebel', which made Rank decide to photograph me sitting on a high stool in one of my old haunts with a sultry sulk, a straining sweater and a steaming cappuccino at my elbow.

Then, for a quick change of pace, I played a saintly role, Richard Baseheart's wife in *The Good Die Young*.

Although I was being publicized to the hilt, none of my movies was setting the world on fire, and I was becoming bored with being bad. The constant media criticism – that I was a 'naughty' girl like my film roles portrayed – was jarring to me and upsetting to my parents. Rank didn't really know what to do with me because I wasn't the archetypal English rose *à la* Susan Shaw or Virginia McKenna, who looked like prim and proper 'nice girls'. Then along came Signor Renato Castellani, an influential Italian film director who wanted to test me for the leading role in *Romeo and Juliet*.

'You have the face of innocence,' he crowed.

'You could have fooled me,' I mused, gazing at said face, which was looking distinctly spotty.

The suggestion that I might play Shakespeare's favourite 'girlie gone wrong' caused guffaws in the popular press. They couldn't imagine me as the tender, innocent Juliet, although in real life I was *still* practically as tender as a lamb. I, too, thought the idea crazy, and many people believed it was a publicity stunt, which it certainly was not. Signor Castellani didn't care which parts an actress had played before, his only interest was whether she would be suitable for whatever role he was casting, and he believed that I had the look he wanted for Shakespeare's heroine.

I made three thoroughly exhausting tests with Laurence Harvey, who would play Romeo, and soon came to realize what playing this part would entail.

Signor Castellani said that I mustn't use lipstick, even off-screen, because it would stain my lips. He wanted me to shave off my eyebrows and half an inch of my hairline, and finally insisted that I have all my front teeth capped. I had been toying with the idea of doing all of this, as Juliet was indeed a dream role, but the final request was that I should undergo cosmetic surgery to change my looks completely. Castellani wanted Juliet to have a Roman nose and he knew of a plastic surgeon who would make 'a perfect nose, a nose to be proud of – not a turned-up little thing like yours'.

'But, Signor Castellani,' I wailed, 'if I do all these improvements to my face and hair and nose, I won't look like *me* any more.'

'What's wrong with that?' he boomed. 'You'll look more like Silvana Mangano – *bellissima*.'

Then why the hell didn't he cast her, I wondered. Why did he want me when I didn't look in the least like the girl he envisaged? I knew how important the picture could be and that it was an acting plum, but all these cosmetic improvements were terrifying. Eventually, after agonizing for days, I flatly refused either to cap my teeth, shave my eyebrows or have a nose-job and Signor Castellani disdainfully passed me over.

Suddenly, although I was under contract, I had nothing whatsoever to do. None of Rank's current films had roles which suited me, so for six months I lived in a vacuum. I got up late, wandered around the shops, sometimes went to the cinema twice a day or watched television, which was so dull I usually fell asleep.

Whenever I complained, my father reminded me of his warnings: 'An actor's lot is to wait. They'll probably drop your contract at the end of the year,' he prophesied. 'Then you can stop this nonsense and you and Max can start a family.'

'A family!' I shuddered. 'I'm not ready for a family. I'm only just nineteen.' In fact, I had been barely ready for the marriage, and regretted it already.

Before my wedding day, I announced grandly to the *Daily Mirror*: 'I shall do no cooking or cleaning after my wedding. I must get up at five o'clock in the morning so why should I slave domestically? We pay a daily for that.'

Shock. Horror. I was castigated in the media for these avant-garde statements. 'Who is this terrible female? What a selfish cruel person she is. She can't be a *real* woman if she doesn't like cooking, cleaning or ironing. She doesn't want *children*! Who the hell does she think she is? *All women want children*.' The sob sisters had a field day, making me out to be some kind of creature from another planet. Criticism is always hard to take and I'd begun to see that as a pretty young actress with unconventional ideas I was going to be punished in print, and often. After I'd cried my eyes out I found the whole thing quite amusing.

But I wasn't selfish. I was impatient. I was nineteen, my husband was thirteen years older, and my life wasn't going according to plan. I hadn't worked for several months, I didn't want children yet, and I was beginning to understand that, in marrying so young, I'd made an awful mistake.

A glimmer of hope came when Bill Watts suggested that there might be a role for me in *My Kingdom for a Woman*, to be made in Paris. I didn't get the part but it was a turning point in my faltering career, because while I was in Paris, being interviewed, I was introduced to the famous Hollywood director Howard Hawks. I met him for five minutes in the bar of the Georges V Hotel. He seemed gruff, acerbic and uninterested in me, but those few brief minutes proved to have been among the most important of my professional life.

One of Maxwell Reed's more ridiculous credos was, 'A star should always behave like a star.'

'You gotta be difficult and temperamental, baby, because you get more "respect" that way.'

When I went on location for my first loan-out from Rank, *Our Girl Friday*, he sent me the following letter:

> . . . you are the star of this picture, so act like one, don't play the little girl, don't be too familiar with anyone, keep yourself to yourself and don't get pushed around by anyone. Remember familiarity breeds contempt. It's a lonely life that way but it pays big dividends in prestige and, in the end, money, baby. Don't forget to see that you get the respect and the treatment that a Star gets, and you should expect.
>
> *Insist* on a caravan to be on the location all the time for your use only (and no one else).
>
> Hire yourself a local girl to be your dresser and to fetch and carry for you, you will be able to get one very cheap out there. Insist on the make-up man and hairdresser being with you for *every* take with a mirror. Be the Star.'

I thought his advice was ludicrous, and it certainly hadn't done him any good for his own career was dying on its feet. This was sad as Max had been so spectacularly handsome – but if he'd had any common sense he'd have worked harder at his craft and tried to become a James Mason-type character actor instead of being completely influenced by the lightweight Lothario Stewart Granger, whom he hero-worshipped.

Our Girl Friday was my first real above-the-title starring role, and I was excited and nervous about going on location to Majorca. My three leading men were Kenneth More, George Cole and Robertson Hare, all of whom, particularly the latter, were considerably older than me, so it was a somewhat lonely life on the fabulous location. I spoke no Spanish, although I was anxious to learn and was constantly asking the English crew to translate words and phrases for me.

The prop and special-effects man was a twinkly-eyed prankster called Eddie Fowlie, who later worked on all of David Lean's productions including *The Bridge on the River Kwai*, becoming Lean's closest lifelong friend. In his early thirties, tall, dark and wiry, he was constantly cracking Cockney jokes, often in rhyming slang, and kept most of the crew in stitches with his cheeky asides. One day he had to construct a bra for me out of tropical flowers for a Christmas calendar the film company were sending out. I was deeply embarrassed as Eddie insisted on arranging every blossom of his creation on my *embonpoint*, bossily shooing the worried Wardrobe lady out of sight.

My costume in *Our Girl Friday* was skimpy to say the least – for the fifties, it was practically obscene, consisting of ragged dresses made to reveal as much leg as possible, and teeny-weeny bikini tops or halters.

One day, shooting on a new location, my 'local girl' had gone missing, so I asked Eddie where the 'honey-wagon' was. 'Honey-wagon' is the silly euphemism given to the portable loos that always accompany a location troup.

'Dunno where the ladies' is, luv,' said Eddie twinkling away as usual. 'Why don't you ask one of the dagoes?'

'But how do I say "Where's the lavatory?" in Spanish?' I asked.

Eddie paused. Then with a slight grin, he told me, 'Go and ask them that question.' He gestured to a grinning young group of 'sparks', lounging on their equipment at the top of the hill.

I sauntered up in my too-short shorts and skimpy bra and asked a nice-looking boy the Spanish phrase which Eddie had just taught me.

'Ah, *si, si, Señorita.*' The Spanish electrician became extremely over-excited. Smirking, he grabbed me around the waist and attempted a hug while his mates screamed with laughter. I managed to extricate myself, then hauled myself off and slapped him on the face, conscious that half the English crew were now looking at me and grinning away too. This was certainly not how a star should behave and I knew it.

Eddie rushed to my rescue, splitting his sides with laughter. 'S'okay, s'okay, luv. Don't worry – it's my fault.' He told the sparks to bugger off in Spanish then pointed me towards the honey-wagon.

'So what did you tell me to say to them?' I asked Eddie frostily, when I'd recovered.

'I'm sorry, luv.' Eddie had the grace to look abashed. 'I told you to ask him "Fancy a quickie, big boy?"'

We both howled with laughter. 'Forget prestige and respect.' I giggled. 'I'm much too young for it – I think I'll just wait till I'm older.'

On location in Majorca, I discovered much more about physical love than I'd ever dreamed possible, after my mother's dire prophecies. That side of life with Max was becoming abhorrent, particularly as he wanted to get his kicks from seeing me with other men, and was pressuring me to do so. That was a big 'no, no' in my book, so eventually I packed my bags and went home to Mummie. Our unfortunate marriage had lasted barely eighteen months, which seems par for the course if a virgin marries out of guilt.

In spite of Maxwell Reed's cynical advice, I always tried to get on with everyone on the set and it was only when I met Joan Crawford, some months later, that I discovered what he meant when he had said, 'A star should pull rank. A star must be bigger than life.'

I'd been invited to a 'Welcome to London' party at my favourite haunt, Les Ambassadeurs, for Miss Crawford, then married to Alfred Steel, chief executive officer and president of the Pepsi-Cola company. The newspapers had been full of her starry arrival at London Airport: a huge black limo was followed by three white Pepsi vans, on top of which was stacked Joan's massive amount of luggage, each piece emblazoned with a large J. C. The star took over the Oliver Messel suite at the

Dorchester for her press conference for *The Story of Esther Costello*, which she was making for my friend the producer James Woolf. He and his brother John ran the successful Romulus Films, which had produced *The Good Die Young*.

Jimmy had discovered Laurence Harvey, had groomed him into the elegant man about town, and some people thought he was in love with Larry, as they were exceptionally close friends. In his late thirties, Jimmy was witty, a profligate spender and adored luxurious living in a large flat in the Grosvenor House Hotel, where he entertained visiting Hollywood stars lavishly.

Joan Crawford was also an executive producer of *Esther Costello* and, ever-mindful of costs, Jimmy told me that she had reviewed her wardrobe budget and had lopped off thirty thousand dollars from the original seventy thousand by such drastic measures as leaving the sable and mink trims off the hem and sleeves of several dresses, and having a coat lined with velvet instead of seal. The ultimate sacrifice had been for her to wear the same pair of shoes several times in the movie.

I went to the *Esther Costello* party with Gordon White, a theatrical agent, popular man-about-London and, since I was now separated, an occasional date. Gordon was tall, dark and good looking. He was number one on the date list for all the visiting glamour queens, and he had wined and dined Rita Hayworth, Grace Kelly, Ava Gardner, Princess Margaret and Joan Fontaine, like a clever puppeteer managing to keep them all on a string at once.

Miss Crawford had suggested that all the women attending the party wore either ballerina length or long gowns, so I put on my best bib and tucker to mingle with such august persons as Laurence Olivier, Vivien Leigh, John Gielgud, Noël Coward, Marlene Dietrich, Edith Evans, Rita Hayworth and, of course, Laurence Harvey, who was starring opposite Joan in *Esther Costello*.

Miss Crawford was ensconced like a queen on a tall chair at one end of the triple banqueting rooms of the glamorous Les Ambassadeurs. A middle-aged, regal, but not terribly attractive, woman in a sea-green silk dress embroidered with sequins in the fashionable 'short in front and long in back' style. Her eyebrows were as thick and black as Groucho

Marx's, her lipstick and matching nail varnish were obviously 'Jungle Red', her black hair was done up in a curiously old-fashioned forties' style, which was echoed in her ankle-strapped, stiletto-heeled, platform-soled shoes. Carmen Miranda, eat your heart out. When each guest was brought over to greet her, she extended her hand graciously, giving a more than passable imitation of our own dear queen.

When Jimmy introduced me as 'one of England's newest and brightest young stars', Miss Crawford didn't take my outstretched hand. Her eyes swept me dismissively from top to toe, her lip curling disdainfully at my low-cut white organza top and full black and white tulle skirt. She obviously didn't like what she saw so didn't deign to speak to me, but chatted animatedly to Jimmy. I wanted to tell her that my mother, a great Crawford fan, had named me after her, but I didn't think she would have the stomach for such trivia.

When I returned to the main room Gordon was on the dance floor, deep in conversation with Rita Hayworth. Without make-up and with her long red tresses tumbling down her back, she looked *far* more glamorous than the hard, painted Crawford. Gordon asked if I minded him escorting Rita home. 'She's got an early call tomorrow on the film she's making at Elstree with Robert Mitchum.'

That was fine with me. Gordon and I were just friends, I was enjoying the party and didn't want to leave yet.

But the next day the tabloid newspapers were full of 'Rita Hayworth Steals Joan Collins' Boyfriend' stories. Gordon and I giggled over them. He adored his playboy reputation and played it to the hilt. But he got into really hot water with Joan Fontaine.

I was enjoying a holiday at the Hotel du Cap d'Antibes on the French Riviera. Gordon and his best friend James Hanson (who had been briefly engaged to Audrey Hepburn and was also tall and good-looking) were staying in Cannes at the Carlton and asked me to join them for dinner. James and Gordon were great company and we had a jolly evening, dining on the hotel terrace with the lights of the Côte d'Azur twinkling before us. Afterwards Gordon and I were ready to hit the clubs but James preferred to turn in.

'We'll go in my new car,' Gordon announced proudly. 'You'll love it.'

I certainly did when I saw the valet pull up in a gleaming silvery-grey Facel Vega.

'It's simply gorgeous. My little brother would adore a ride in this.' Bill, like Daddy, had already become a car fanatic.

We jumped in to a sudden barrage of flash-bulbs. A *paparazzo* had magically appeared from behind a palm tree and was snapping away at us. I smiled sweetly. I was almost divorced, Gordon wasn't married so there was no big deal about our date. The following day a glamorous photograph of Gordon and me in the Facel Vega appeared in the *Daily Express*. I thought nothing more of it until I bumped into Joan Fontaine a few weeks later at a party in London. I'd worked with her the previous year in Spain, on a flaccid Technicolor epic called *Decameron Nights* where I had discovered that she was not a lady to mince her words.

'What the *hell* were you doing with Gordie White in *my* car?' she bellowed accusingly.

'*Your* car?' I answered. 'I thought it was Gordon's.'

'Gordie! That rat! I *lent* him my car on the *express* condition that he only use it for himself. I didn't expect him to take *passengers*.' She shook her head contemptuously with a 'Men! They're all the same' look.

I laughed and apologized, although I didn't think I was at fault, then rang Gordon and asked him what was going on.

'Oh, that bloody Joan Fontaine! She *really* gave me hell,' he admitted. 'It was kind of her to lend me her damn Facel Vega, but what about *my* reputation? I'm a playboy. How the *hell* did she expect me *not* to drive any other female in it but her?'

I ran into a torrent of abuse after making a personal appearance at a provincial cinema for *Turn the Key Softly*. At home in the full-length mirror my low-cut white dress wasn't terribly daring – in fact, I thought I looked rather chic for once.

At the cinema a little girl presented me with a bouquet and the photographer asked me to hold the pose with her. I didn't realize that in bending down to the three-year-old, I had showed a vast expanse of cleavage. The photographs were followed by indignant letters both to the local newspaper and to me personally, from enraged mothers accusing me of being a loose woman, an immoral influence on their children and completely lacking in good taste. 'How dare you go around publicly half-naked?' remonstrated Disgusted of Devon.

I didn't *try* to upset people but I was always being accused of rebelliousness. My refusal to be a yes-woman and to take control of my life often got me into hot water. However, it has to be said that sometimes sheer devilment or boredom got the better of me.

During one of those mind-numbing personal appearances, which Theo Cowan insisted played such an important part in every starlet's training, it looked as though it would never stop raining. It was a wretched day for a garden party, and I was cold, depressed and in no mood to make polite conversation with one of the organizers, a stout, florid bore. We had little in common and, as he was groping for a subject, I tried to move on.

'I love horses, don't you?' he barked eagerly, his eyes on my chest.

Not even stopping to think, I retorted, 'No, I *don't*! I *hate* horses almost as much as I *hate* people – especially boring people.'

I knew that I was being rude – stupid and untruthful, too, as I do like people. But that remark, which had been overheard by a journalist, was quoted against me for years afterwards.

At another dull-as-dishwater film garden-party, Bill Watts introduced me to a well-known film director. After saying hello, I asked Bill if I could have some strawberries and cream.

Bill became agitated. 'In a minute,' he hissed in a sort of half-undertone and rolled his eyes towards the man. I ignored him, repeated my request and, with an aggrieved look, the director wandered off.

Bill glared at me. 'That,' he said, 'was a *very* important director who could have done you a lot of good.'

'I don't care who he is,' I retorted. 'He just seemed an awful bore to me, and I want some strawberries, please.'

I don't think Bill ever forgave me. A starlet was supposed to behave herself at *all* times and in *all* places and talk charmingly to *all* people – especially men. But something perverse would just bubble up inside me when I was expected to behave conventionally.

I'm sure that's why I was often described as 'difficult'. I've been told that I would have fared better in British films if I'd been less outspoken, and 'nicer', but I always fought against being thrown into the same stultifying mould that turned so many young actresses into carbon copies of each other – and I was, after all, still a teenager.

Howard Hawks was making the Warner Brothers film *Land of the Pharaohs*. In his late fifties, the legendary director was tough, outspoken, often disliked – but always respected. He was a man-about-town who loved parties, socializing, sharp talk, sharp clothes and sharp women. How he ever became involved with a turkey like *Pharaohs* is a mystery to me, because most of his films were brilliant.

Hawks was a true stylist, one of the few American directors who left his intellectual stamp on all his films. He had started in the 1920s in the tradition of the writer/director and had his initial success with *The Dawn Patrol*, starring Richard Barthelmess. Then, in the thirties, he produced *Scarface* with Paul Muni, an excellent cast and a splendid script by Ben Hecht, in which George Raft first did his memorable coin-flicking business. Hawks then made *Only Angels Have Wings*, with Jean Harlow, and *Ball of Fire*, one of my favourite movies, in which he satirized romance and destroyed Barbara Stanwyck's dignity. In his films, he always cast a certain kind of actress as heroine: tall, rangy and husky-voiced like Stanwyck, Katherine Hepburn, Lauren Bacall, Lizbeth Scott or Carole Lombard, all of whom had little in common with the post-adolescent, round, squeaky-voiced Joan Collins.

'He's looking for his ideal woman for this movie,' said my agent excitedly. 'This is your big chance, dear. If you make your mark in *this* movie then Hollywood's going to be your next stop.'

Hawks had initially cast Ivy Nicholson, a New York model, in the main female role of Nellifer, the wicked princess who brings down not only the Pharaoh but also herself. Some of Ivy's scenes had been shot but she was making imperious demands and giving Hawks a torturous time. He never stood for any nonsense from an actress so he fired Ivy, then found he had the difficult task of finding an *immediate* replacement. He remembered me from our brief meeting at the Georges V in Paris, and called Warner Brothers to hire me. Ivy was five foot ten and probably weighed considerably less than me, but minor details like that didn't bother Warner Brothers. They viewed some footage from *Our Girl Friday*, liked what they saw, and within three days had whisked me to Rome to play the evil Princess Nellifer. I didn't even have to test. It was just the sort of juicy part I'd longed for: dramatic, ultra-glamorous and unconventionally villainous. It was my first grown-up leading-lady role. What an incredible contrast to *I Believe In You*.

I'd been doing *Claudia* at the Q theatre, finished my last performance in it at eleven on Sunday night, then dashed home where several friends helped me pack practically all the clothes I possessed – I was going to be on location for nearly three months. After less than three hours' sleep, I caught the 7.30 a.m. Rome flight with a spring in my sling-backs and a heart full of hope.

Howard Hawks needed me and I couldn't wait to meet him once again and to become his latest 'ideal woman'.

Howard Hawks liked his women tall and lean, so no luck there, and for them to have low sexy voices, no luck there either. But he had concocted a plan to lower my voice: every morning I was to stand on the roof of Scalera Studios for half an hour and scream my lungs out.

'It'll crack your vocal chords, honey,' he told me sternly. 'It worked for Richard Burton. His voice is the secret of his success.'

I thought this was a terrible idea, but I fibbed shamelessly to him that I was screaming like a banshee while in my scenes I simply lowered my voice artificially. And artificial was exactly how I sounded. Whenever I see *Pharaohs*, I sound *so* ghastly that I cringe with embarrassment. I speak in this deep fake voice, almost as phoney as Tony Curtis when he said that immortal line in *The Black Shield of Falmouth*: 'And yonder is de castle of my fadder de king . . .'

The film, written by William Faulkner and Harry Kurnitz, two of the most respected screen-writers in the business, was a disaster, particularly in the dialogue department, some of which was beyond appalling.

In one unmemorable scene, Alexis Minotis, playing Pharaoh's sage adviser, addressed me in stern pontificating tones with this piece of deathless prose: 'I do not like you, Princess Nellifer.'

To which I must reply, with a curl of a carmine lip and a raised and painted brow, 'The feeling, *sir*, is mutual.'

Oh dear! Faulkner and Kurnitz must have had their minds on other things while they were penning this tripe. But at least it had a good cast. Jack Hawkins played Pharaoh, James Robertson Justice the architect of the Pyramid, Dewey Martin his son, Kerima Pharaoh's wife, and Sydney Chaplin was Trenah, the Captain of the Guard.

Apart from my voice problems I had the most incredible time in the Eternal City. After eighteen months of unhappily married life I was a free spirit for the first time. No longer under my parents' influence, a swinging bachelor girl at last, I adored every moment of that *dolce vita* summer.

While Sydney Chaplin and I played lovers on-screen, we also did so in real life. Charlie Chaplin's twenty-eight-year-old son was one of the funniest men I'd ever met, a true original, both in wit and attitude. He gave new meaning to the expression *bon viveur*, and if he wasn't working, playing golf or living it up, he loved nothing better than doing nothing. When we were not on call, our lazy afternoons were spent sipping drinks at Doney's *caffè* in the Via Veneto with a group of fellow actors or lazing about on the beach. Sydney had a nippy Aston Martin drop-head and when we zoomed off to Fregene beach, with the wind whipping my hair and the radio playing 'Fly me to the moon/And let me play among the stars', I thought I'd never be as happy again. Roman nights were for love, for food and for fun. To me, fresh from post-war Britain, the restaurants were gastronomic marvels while the dazzling bars and clubs made London's night-life seem like it was set in the Stone Age.

Young and fond of food, I loved to eat and carouse all night, but after several weeks of gorging another problem developed. My exotic scanty costumes consisted mainly of strapless 'Frederick's of Hollywood' cone-shaped bras made of jewelled mesh, diaphanous chiffon skirts, and ropes of gold, silver and pearls hanging from white gold belts slung around my hips. I wore laced-up silver sandals, solid golden chokers encrusted with jewels, bracelets all the way up my arms, and an enormously long, impossibly thick, modern dark brown wig, which hung down my back almost to my bottom. Between my midriff and hips I wore nothing but a 'ruby', the size of a grape, screwed into my navel. This jewel had to be applied

every day with false-eyelash glue and, being a somewhat ticklish individual, I squirmed and giggled while it was stuck on.

I was reasonably slim when shooting started and the ruby stayed in
place, but with all the merry-making my weight soon shot up so that when
I breathed too hard the damned ruby would pop out. This usually happened during a dramatic scene, and a treasure-hunt would ensue all over
the set to recapture it. After a few days of this Hawks took a long hard
look at me.

'*Look* at the size of that belly. You must have gained seven pounds
this week,' he scoffed, to my mortification, in front of the whole crew.

'It's not true, Mr Hawks,' I was still at the Mr stage, 'I'm the same
weight as when we started.' I sucked in my stomach hard and the ruby
popped out yet again, this time to disappear under an arc lamp. The crew
muffled their giggles. I was humiliated but I was having far too much fun
to quit my *dolce vita* life in spite of Hawks's threats to recast again.

'He'll never do it,' Syd comforted me. 'They've shot too much of you
already.'

Nevertheless I dutifully quit pasta and took up grilled veggies for a
while.

I'd rented a tiny apartment in Ostia, a small seaside town outside
Rome. Mummie came to stay with me, sometimes bringing brother Bill.
On my days off I'd sit on the beach, with a couple of girlfriends,
astounded by the loutish behaviour of some of the Italian youths. Except
for the ubiquitous shouts of '*Bella – bella ragazza*' wherever we went, they
were usually so polite. But not here. Dozens came to sit in a large ring
around our group.

Bikinis were relatively new in Italy and most 'nice' Italian girls still
wore one-pieces, so these lads would feast their eyes endlessly on our
nubile tanned flesh. To get to the sea, we had to step over their inert
bodies, which was when they tried to brush their hands or some other
part of their bodies against our bare skin.

An Italian magazine had recently printed a ridiculous story about me
saying that I was known as 'The Kiss Girl': 'Joan Collins *always* kisses
men on the lips when she's introduced to them, whether she's met them
or not.' The boys had read the article, recognized me and went crazy.

They would wander across, their tumescent excitement quite obvious, and stammer, 'Hey, *cara*, how about giving us one of those kisses you're so famous for?' One boy even came up to me while I was sunbathing, eyes closed, and planted a smacker right on my lips. I screamed blue murder, and slapped his face, and Mummie, who had witnessed the event from afar, was so furious that she insisted we move back into the centre of Rome. 'You'll be safer there, darling.'

Fat chance of *that*, I thought. Roman men were as lecherously libidinous as Italian beach boys. They just wore more clothes.

Italy was at the height of fashion. Dozens of movies were being made in Rome and a fascinating group of people was living and working there. Sitting in the bar of the Hôtel de la Ville one night, the only girl surrounded by a group of men, which included Roger Vadim, Sydney Chaplin and Christian Marquand, I was enjoying being the centre of attention. Suddenly the dazzling Brigitte Bardot appeared and sauntered up to the bar. My age, but taller, curvier, with a pouting come-get-me-into-bed look, she wore a daringly *décolleté*, but somehow virginal, pink and white gingham dress, which had a stunningly erotic effect on all the men in the vicinity. A mixture of Alice-in-Wonderland innocence and Marilyn Monroe come-hither, Brigitte was a consummate flirt. Her eyes swept the bar coquettishly, which attracted the men at our table like a magnet, and instantly several flocked over to where she was coolly holding court from a bar stool. Sydney – no fool he – remained by my side.

Bardot dealt with her drooling admirers with practised skill, and I suddenly understood what real in-your-face sex-appeal was. It was said in private life Marilyn Monroe didn't have it, but Bardot most certainly did – and positively basked in the effect she had on the opposite sex.

After *Pharaohs* finished Sydney and I moved to Paris, living together at the Hôtel Tremoille. We spent lazy autumn mornings recovering from hangovers, listening to Sinatra records or drinking cappuccino at the café below while watching the world go by. Later, we met up with a core group of friends for long, loud and boisterous lunches: the illustrious, iconoclastic director Anatole 'Tola' Litvak at fifty-three was the oldest, had been Oscar-nominated for *The Snake Pit*, and had an admirable reputation as a maker of star-driven vehicles; set-designer Alexander Trauner; Bettina Graziani, a beautiful red-haired model, the Linda Evangelista of her day, and the current girlfriend of Aly Khan; Christian Marquand, the handsome charismatic French actor, and intimate friend of Marlon Brandon; Noel Howerd, an American writer; Harry Kurnitz, the screenwriter; and the hysterically funny Adolph Green, one half of the Comden and Green musical comedy writing team.

Our favourite lunch venue was Moustache where the owner, magnificently hirsute and brimming with bonhomie and benevolence, would frequently waive the bill. We would stay till about four, when those who weren't working – which was usually the majority – would repair to a nearby bar for more liquid refreshment and several rowdy games of pinball. Syd's afternoons were often spent playing cards or golf, while I explored the exquisite charms of Paris, and its museums and boutiques. By night we would hit the city's fleshpots, making whoopee with unbridled enthusiasm.

This voluptuary's existence, a continuation of my Roman summer, was thankfully short-lived – neither my complexion nor my waistline could have withstood this dawn-to-dusk lifestyle for much longer. Reality hit with a vengeance when we were invited by Sydney's father, Charlie, to spend a pre-Christmas weekend with the Chaplin clan in their Swiss villa.

Their enormous house was set in extensive grounds by a beautiful lake just outside the tiny and exclusive village of Vevey. Pushing seventy, Charlie Chaplin was both autocratic and charming at the same time, with a strong streak of irascibility. He ruled his brood of children with a patriarchal iron rod, and his beautiful, patient wife Oona – thirty-five years his junior – catered to him with an almost geisha-like deference.

Although Charlie had earned his living as a comedian, in life he was extremely serious, verging on pompous. Around him Sydney's wacky humour had to be toned down and he carefully watched his Ps and Qs.

Charlie was not particularly generous with his offspring and Sydney's allowance was almost penurious, considering the size of the old man's fortune. Sydney believed that if he didn't behave himself, Dad might cut him off, so he struggled to be on his best behaviour – which was a huge effort for him as he was virtually irrepressible – but he had a genuine respect for his father, and one evening I found out why.

Adolph Green, Sydney and I had been in a frivolous mood all day. We had escaped to the village after the family lunch and had spent the afternoon playing pin-ball and drinking a particularly potent brand of schnapps.

For pre-prandial drinks the family congregated in the enormous chintz and mahogany living room, which looked out on to sparkling snowy-capped mountains. Squashy sofas, rows of shelves packed with books, and a roaring fire, almost too hot, helped everyone relax.

I sat by the fire in my crushed velvet skirt and Tyrolean blouse, enjoying the familiar family atmosphere as well as my hot toddy. Adolph was telling a hilarious anecdote about Hitler and, flushed with the fire and the afternoon's fire-water, I was giggling away.

This seemed to irritate the elder Chaplin who kept glaring at me *sans* amusement.

Syd nudged me a couple of times to shut up but Adolph – pleased with his appreciative audience – continued to embellish his tale.

A shadow loomed over us: Charlie Chaplin, all five foot six of him.

'Please share the joke,' he asked pleasantly.

'Oh – er – it's not *that* funny,' said Adolph.

'Oh, but it *is*.' I giggled again. 'Everything about Hitler is hysterical.'

'You really think so?' Charlie's voice was low and cold. I didn't notice the ice in his tone, even though Syd was now pinching my arm so hard that it almost bled.

'Oh, *yes*,' I continued blithely. 'At school during the war we'd all make up jokes about Hitler and sing silly songs.'

I laughed, then noticed everyone looking at me with pained expressions.

'So, you think Hitler is funny, do you?' asked Charlie, and marched over to the bookshelf from which he removed a large volume.

'Take a look at *this*, my dear, and see if you think Herr Hitler is *quite* so funny.'

I looked at the title: *Auschwitz – photographies de l'Holocauste 1945*. My face dropped. 'Oh – er – no thanks. I don't think I want to see these.'

'Oh, but I *insist* that you *do*,' said Charlie, who sat down next to me on the sofa and opened the book. 'This has just been published in France,' he explained. 'These pictures have never been seen before.'

I could understand why. I was appalled by the ghastly images before my eyes. Media censorship still existed, and few people could have actually imagined what the inmates of concentration camps had suffered at the hands of the Nazis.

Chaplin made me look closely at page after page of photographs. Starving, beaten, skeletal bodies, pictures of mass graves full of corpses, of emaciated children with terror-stricken faces, and brutal SS officers' faces grinning at it all.

Eventually I could bear it no longer. I covered my eyes with my hands. 'I can't look any more. I don't *believe* this could have happened.'

'*Believe it*,' Chaplin barked. 'And now maybe you'll realize how extremely *un*funny Adolf Hitler was.'

'Hey, Dad, quit it, will ya.' Sydney was worried by my distress.

'Shut up, Sydney,' said his father. 'It's time everyone started to understand about that monster Hitler and the monstrosities he committed against mankind, Jews in particular. He's no joke, I assure you.'

Then Oona broke the atmosphere by clapping her hands lightly and announcing that dinner was served. I started to rise but Chaplin pressed the book hard on to my lap. 'Finish looking at these pictures, my dear girl,' he said, 'and learn from them. You were *all* at fault. All of you English.'

I couldn't imagine how I, a little English schoolgirl during the war, could possibly have been to blame for Hitler's perversities. But then Chaplin said bitterly, 'Did you know your bloody Duke of Windsor *encouraged* Hitler? He *wanted* him to conquer Britain so that he could return to be king. Go on, go *on*, look at some more.' He turned to an even more horrific picture and I started to weep.

'That's *enough*, Charlie,' said Oona, in her calm she-who-must-be-obeyed voice. 'It's time for dinner.'

Charlie stared at me, bent over his book, my tears spattering down on to the terrible images. Then he relented. 'Right. Right. All right.' He beamed benevolently at the assembled family and a dumbstruck Sydney. 'That's enough for now. Let's have dinner. I'm starving.'

Needless to say, I was unable to eat a morsel and was haunted by nightmares for weeks. The following day Sydney and I left for Paris and from that day to this I have seldom enjoyed any Charlie Chaplin movies.

While I was still shooting *Land of the Pharaohs*, Darryl Zanuck, boss of Twentieth Century-Fox, had seen the rushes in Jack Warner's projection room and became interested in signing me. Zanuck was a movie legend: diminutive, moustachioed, cigar-chomping, he was the archetypal Hollywood mogul. He had founded Twentieth Century Productions in 1933, merged with Fox two years later and had run the studio ever since. He had produced many wonderful films, including *The Grapes of Wrath, Gentlemen's Agreement* and *All About Eve*, and his autobiography was entitled *Don't Say Yes Until I've Finished Talking*, perhaps one of his most-quoted lines.

Zanuck adored women and, although married to the long-suffering Virginia, his extra-curricular activities with big stars and busty starlets were scandalous and legendary. He usually kept an official mistress, whom he would try to turn into a star – living proof that the casting couch sometimes paid dividends. Bella Darvi (Zunuck even gave her her name: a combination of Darryl and Virginia), a Polish-Jewish actress with minimal talent but on whom Zanuck lavished millions, was just one of his paramours, and he starred her in several pseudo-Biblical epics, deter-mined to make her big. He didn't succeed, which proved that talent *is* important, after all.

He also had a liaison with my current idol Juliette Greco, and cast her in several of his films. I couldn't understand what Greco, the definitive existentialist Bohemian, could see in the capitalist Zanuck, who repre-sented everything she professed to despise, but they were together for several years.

In spite of his wife and his mistresses, Zanuck still regularly invited young actresses to his office to attempt to seduce them. One of the many stories then circulating about him was that he had summoned a pretty, well-stacked new contract girl to his office for a meeting. Then, as was his custom, cigar clamped in mouth, he proceeded to chase her around his desk. The starlet finally escaped, and at the door, chest heaving, she put her hand down her blouse, pulled out a large pair of falsies and threw them in his direction. 'Here, Mr Zanuck,' she said. 'I think these are what you're after.'

Shortly afterwards her contract was dropped.

But Zanuck was undeterred by rejection and his ego was even bigger than his cigar, so after seeing the *Pharaohs* rushes he wanted Joan Collins in his stable – and was determined to get her.

As Daddy had always maintained, and as by now I had learnt, 90 per cent of an actor's life is spent waiting. You wait for a job, for the phone to ring, and for your agent to express interest from a producer or direc-tor. When it happens, you don't hear another peep from *anyone* for days, weeks or, often, months. When you're lucky enough to land a job you spend three-quarters of the time in your dressing room waiting to be called to the set. Frustrating it may be, but you either learn to live with it or get out of the business.

However, when the *studios* want something or someone, they want them *now* and *everything* goes into top gear to get whatever or whoever it is.

Within days Fox, and the compelling Mr Zanuck, had persuaded J. Arthur Rank to sell me to them. I didn't have a hell of a lot of say in it but I did insist that my new MCA agent, John 'Goulash' Shepbridge, made sure I received the princely sum of $1250 a week which, for a twenty-one-year-old, was a *vast* amount of money. The usual salary was $75 to $200 a week. If the contracted artiste didn't 'click' instantly with the audiences *and* the powers that be, they were quietly dropped and replaced by a new crop who were constantly being discovered. Fresh faces were a dime a dozen in Hollywood, so my gut instinct told me that to have any chance of success, I needed to get Fox to pay me enough to appreciate my worth. For once, it wasn't hard to hold out for what I wanted because I was so crazy about Sydney that I couldn't bear to leave him.

However, the deal was done and, although grief-stricken, I felt pleased with myself as I bade tearful farewells to my lover in Paris and my family in London, and flew off on the series of planes which would whisk me to Hollywood, the golden land where dreams came true – supposedly.

CHAPTER FIVE

Hooray for Hollywood

I arrived in Tinseltown at the end of the golden age of cinema when the gold was just beginning to tarnish, but I didn't yet know that.

In the mid-fifties it took nearly twenty-four hours to fly from London to Los Angeles. My first stop was New York, where I waited six hours, then changed to another plane which stopped in Chicago before arriving, some ten hours later, in LA.

I'd been warned I'd be met in Hollywood by the press, so during the flight I'd been mentally rehearsing how to entrance them. When I finally arrived in LA I was so nervous that, when asked that oh-so-original question, 'What do you think about America?' I could only stammer, 'It's c-c-cool, crazy and jolly good.'

This sophomoric line was quoted extensively in all my future publicity. How I was expected to know what America was like, having just arrived from England, beats me, but I soon found out that asking your opinion of their country was a favourite American conversational gambit.

My first impression of Hollywood was of driving through drizzle down an endless grey and dreary freeway, then arriving in a bleak hotel room to be greeted by an enormous television set on which that curious creature Liberace was showing an inordinate amount of teeth while playing a grand piano the size of a villa.

Liberace was the biggest star on American television, a brilliant businessman who knew what the punters wanted. He was camp before it became fashionable, kitsch before much of the world even knew what it meant. If he's the biggest star, I wondered, what can the lesser ones be like?

As he tickled the ivories, his dentures flashed as brightly as the keys while he sang in a cracked falsetto voice. Resplendent in a sequinned satin dinner suit, complete with eighteenth-century-style lace cravat, he made Shirley Temple seem butch. There were rich tapestries on the walls of his set, furs on the floor, and a gigantic six-pronged silver candelabrum on top of his white concert grand.

English television was dull – only politics, sport and the occasional ballet or play – but here it was non-stop variety and soap-operas all day and I became addicted. I was lonely and homesick, and missed Sydney, my parents and friends, but luckily Emile, the make-up man from *Pharaohs*, and his wife took me in hand. It wasn't long before I started to get calls from all sorts of glamorous people, mainly men, was invited to lots of parties, and my social life took off with a vengeance.

Any new pretty face in Hollywood was catnip to the sophisticated predatory bachelors. If a 'great chick' was rumoured to be arriving sometimes they even greeted the plane.

Nicky Hilton, who had been married to Elizabeth Taylor, Gregg Bautzer, the foremost attorney in town, Bob Neal, a rich playboy, Arthur Loew Jnr, the grandson of the founder of MGM, and even Howard Hughes all telephoned me. Some sent flowers and candy and I dated a couple, although Sydney still remained my official boyfriend.

On my first day at the studio I lunched, saucer-eyed, in the fabled Fox commissary with the Shirley Temple murals on the walls, and spied Lana Turner sitting in one corner looking incredibly glamorous. Richard Burton, Susan Hayward, Joanne Woodward and Robert Wagner were scattered about the room looking like perfectly normal people. In fact, everywhere I looked I saw a household face.

A week after my arrival, Fox publicity invited me to an exclusive preview at the studio screening room of their latest blockbuster, *There's No Business Like Show Business*. Suddenly I was sitting with the *crème de la crème* of Hollywood and I felt so deliciously 'in' that I almost swooned.

What bliss! I was so impressed by Charles Le Maire's costume for Marilyn in her 'I'm Lazy' number that, three years later when he was designing for *Rally Round the Flag, Boys*, I asked him to create an almost identical one for me. Only the colour of the sash was different.

My first Fox film was to be *The Virgin Queen*, starring Richard Todd, who played Walter Raleigh, and the utterly terrifying Bette Davis who was playing Queen Elizabeth. Every morning the famous make-up expert Perc Westmore shaved her hairline back two inches and she strolled like that around the Fox lot covered in thick white face-paint not giving a damn, chain-smoking and blowing the fumes into everyone's faces. As the embittered and idiosyncratic old spinster Queen, Bette, at forty-seven, was a decade or more younger than Elizabeth had been, but she seemed really old to me.

I played one of her six handmaidens, Lady Beth Throckmorton, who was madly in love with Sir Walter Raleigh and vice versa. Unfortunately the Queen was also in love with Sir Walter so there was conflict and plenty of it. Bette scared the hell not only out of me but out of the other ladies-in-waiting and most of the crew. Charles Le Maire and Mary Wills, the costume designers, insisted on the utmost authenticity for her costumes which must have been terribly uncomfortable. Rigid steel-corseted bodices and wired lace collars so high that she could hardly move her head added to her ill-temper.

By contrast most of my costumes, although fairly constricting, were more modern in style, with lifted and shaped bodices that were strictly fifties-style. My hair and make-up were also contemporary, which was apparent in the bedchamber scene. For this Bette had to wear a 'bald' wig, a thin rubber head-piece covering all her hair but for a few strands attached to the back of it. The contrast between the two of us couldn't have been more striking: she hairless, with harsh white make-up and wrinkled skin, I young and heavily glamorized in a soft blue gown with a curved bodice, my hair upswept in spit curls with a feathery fringe. Bette's hairdresser confided to me that Bette was insecure about her looks and hated her face.

Several years later I was fascinated to watch Bette Davis on Johnny Carson's *Tonight* show and heard her say: 'When I was younger and was making *All About Eve* I loathed the way I looked. I thought I looked old and tired. Now when I see that film I think, Darling, you were gorgeous!'

Bette didn't particularly like young actresses, and made no attempt to hide her feelings. One day, during a difficult scene as I knelt at her feet, trying to lace up a satin bow on her shoe, she showed me exactly what she thought of me. I was wearing a wimple and a ruff, with a tight corset under a huge velvet skirt and I could barely move my arms as my sleeves were so tight.

Bette had been ratty with everybody that morning, particularly with her 'ladies-in-waiting', and after she had snapped viciously at one starlet for chewing gum, we all congregated in a corner to giggle nervously. 'What's happened to your manners, girls?' she barked. 'You're supposed to behave like ladies-in-waiting, not like a pack of tarty schoolgirls.' This made us squeak even more, and she glared over at us, basilisk-style, muttering another insult to the Hungarian director Henry Koster.

I wasn't looking forward to the shoe-tying scene and the first time I attempted the bow my fingers trembled so much that I couldn't do it up. Bette kicked out at me crossly, and I went flying across the set, petticoats over my head, much to the crew's amusement.

'Cut,' called Henry Koster. 'OK, Bette, OK, Joan. Let's all calm down and we'll go again.' A certain weary sympathy was in his tone.

Bette was furious with me. 'Don't you even know how do up a *shoe*?' she snarled. 'Don't they teach you *anything* at those English drama schools? How can you *possibly* think that you could ever succeed as an *actress*, you little fool?'

'Shit, damn, hell,' I hissed to the 'wrecking crew', as they tried to pull me together again. 'Why does she always pick on *me*?'

'Because you're prettier than she is,' whispered Helen, the sympathetic hairdresser.

'*Anyone*'s prettier than she is,' I snapped, my father's hot temper springing to the fore.

When the assistant director summoned me back to the set, I was in combative mod as we began take two, but Miss Davis's foot suddenly developed a life of its own. It jumped, wiggled and twitched and I couldn't even hold the bow this time, let alone tie it – to Henry's irritation and to Bette's sly amusement.

'*Cut*! – What the *hell*'s the matter? – Can't you tie a goddamned bow?' Henry asked exasperatedly. I sidled up to him and whispered that the great thespian's foot had developed St Vitus' Dance. He shrugged dismissively. 'Grab her by the ankle,' he growled. 'She's a tough old broad – bit of pain won't do her any harm.'

On take three, I grabbed the Oscar-winner's ankle with both hands, jammed it between my velvet-covered knees and clenched them together so tightly that she couldn't move her foot.

Bette shot vicious glances at me while she uttered her lines and I managed to yelp mine back at her. She was trying deliberately to unnerve me, but it was a contest of wills. The other ladies-in-waiting watched admiringly, twittering behind the camera, and when Henry yelled, 'Cut! OK, that's a print,' they gave a suppressed cheer. After that incident, when I had actually stood up to her, Bette acquired a grudging respect for me, and was never rude to me again. But I kept well out of her way for the rest of the picture.

She did, however, speak rudely about one of my idols, Laurence Olivier. I was sitting next to her one morning in Make-up, studying lines, while Whitey did his stuff and heard her say, 'Laurence Oliver shouldn't *dare* call himself an actor. He's just a chamelon who prances about wearing too much make-up and disguised in overdone costumes.' I raised my eyebrows as she continued her tirade: 'Half the time you can't even recognize him. A *true* actor is one whose personality always shines through the performance, whatever they're playing.'

That was *certainly* true of Bette Davis. Her dominant personality showed through in all her roles and, even as red-wigged Queen Elizabeth, it was unmistakably she.

I saw Bette Davis again in New York, some thirty years later, backstage at *Night of 100 Stars*. Every major star who could still walk, from James Cagney, who was actually in a wheelchair, and Lillian Gish to Grace Kelly and Paul Newman, was performing and since there were so many of us, everyone had to share dressing rooms. My heart sank when I entered mine. Bette Davis was sitting in a big low-backed chair, wearing an over-decorated blue satin dress, a forbidding expression and, naturally, cigarette in hand. Several other actresses were in there too, among them Jane Russell, Jean Simmons, and Alice Faye, and the atmosphere was friendly and convivial – except for the black cloud that seemed to envelop Bette. Nolan Miller had made me a revealing backless gold lamé dress. It was cut to the sternum for maximum cleavage, and the skirt was split to the top of my thighs. It was the full mid-eighties *Dynasty* dress, totally over the top but right for the occasion. Bette stared coolly at me for a long time, blowing smoke-rings. Then, with a sly foxy grin, she said, 'You *almost* have that dress on, my dear.'

'Thank you, Miss Davis,' I said, thinking, No thanks, Miss Davis, I *don't* want to get into another ruckus with you. But I smiled sweetly and said, 'Yes, and I think it just needs a little adjusting. Would you mind terribly pulling down my hem, please, Bette dear?'

Bette glowered, seemingly at an unusual loss for words. Then, sticking her cigarette in her mouth, she bent over, grabbed the gold lamé hem – and wordlessly yanked down hard on my skirt. The other actresses looked at the tableau with astonishment. Bette Davis bowing down in front of Joan Collins? Whatever next?

Bette grumbled to Nolan the following day, 'How the *hell* can you let that girl go out in a dress as low-cut as that? It's disgusting. You could see everything she's got.'

'That's the whole point,' he answered calmly. 'If you've got it these days, Bette dear, you *have* to flaunt it.'

'Huh,' sniffed Bette, 'never in *my* day, dear,' and hung up on him.

I was sitting with the witty Henry Koster and some others at lunch in the commissary half-way through shooting *Virgin Queen*. He had made many successful films for Fox but was having a difficult time with one of the young starlets playing a lady-in-waiting. A writer at the table said, 'I've heard you're having a hard time with Miss X.'

'That's because I'm making two pictures with her at the same time,' Koster growled, 'her first and her last.'

'But I heard she graduated with honours in drama from UCLA,' said the writer.

'Huh,' sniffed Koster. 'Dramatic art, in *her* opinion, is knowing how to fill a sweater.'

Another time he was doing take after take on my close-up. Eventually I bleated, 'Mr Koster, it's one thirty and I'm starving – can't we break for lunch?'

'Miss Collins,' he said briskly, 'we are photographing your *face*, not your stomach.'

What I wasn't aware of was that all the studios, particularly Twentieth Century-Fox, were in the midst of a major crisis. Television was mesmerizing American movie-goers and millions were transfixed by the crazy antics of Milton Berle and the clowning of Lucille Ball. The cinema business was losing out and the economy-minded studios realized they could no longer afford their expensive lists of contract players, writers, directors and producers. Workers were being laid off all round and that I had just been signed to a lucrative contract was a lucky omen indeed. Another menace to Hollywood's well-being was runaway overseas production. Local government subsidies, tax benefits, inexpensive labour and exotic scenery had lured a third of American film-making to Europe.

Studio bosses were tearing out what remained of their hair to tempt the fickle public back to the movie houses. The ingredients they could offer their audiences, which television couldn't, were sex – albeit the coyly titillating variety – and violence.

Fox had spent seven years promoting their number-one star, Marilyn Monroe, into the reigning sex-symbol of the world. She was now of mythical status but rebellious, wanting to spread her wings in more substantial material than *Gentlemen Prefer Blondes* and *How to Marry a Millionaire*. Consequently she had turned down the lead in Fox's forthcoming costume drama *The Girl in the Red Velvet Swing* and had jetted off to New York and the Actors' Studio to become a 'serious' actress. Although she was at the pinnacle of her stardom, Fox immediately put her on suspension, which prohibited her from working anywhere else.

Marilyn had been on suspension several times since making *There's No Business Like Show Business*, and had gone off on trips with her new husband Joe DiMaggio. Even though the studio had just given her a lucrative new seven-year contract she soon broke it by turning down the lead in a movie called *Pink Tights*, which Fox gave to Sophia Loren.

Fox desperately needed a sexy creature to take over the lead in their hoped-for blockbuster *The Girl in the Red Velvet Swing*, and they were thinking of replacing Marilyn with me.

When the British press heard about this, they went wild with proud hyperbole. Headlines screamed, 'Our Joanie's a Contender for the Monroe Throne', 'Our own Joan   Princess to Topple Queen of Fox?'.

Fox were the innovators of Cinemascope, the trade-name for an anamorphic system of lenses that allowed wide-screen filming projection but used standard film stock. Their first Cinemascope release had been *The Robe* in 1953 with Richard Burton, Jean Simmons and a cast of thousands. Other studios quickly followed suit with Panavision and Technoscope, but Cinemascope was the public's favourite and *The Girl in the Red Velvet Swing* was to be made in it.

The studio believed that the story of the seventeen-year-old chorus girl Evelyn Nesbitt would have enough sex and violence to entice audiences back into the cinema in droves. Nesbitt, the original Gibson Girl, had been abused and corrupted by a much older man who was then subsequently murdered by her jealous aristocratic husband.

Fox had always relied heavily on their female stars: in the thirties Shirley Temple's movies had helped them through the depression, then later, Janet Gaynor, Loretta Young, Anne Baxter, Susan Hayward, Sonja Henie, Jeanne Crain, June Haver, Betty Grable, and Alice Faye had become big stars.

But they hadn't been so lucky with their leading men. With the exception of Tyrone Power, their current weak male roster consisted of Don Ameche, Macdonald Carey, John Payne, Victor Mature and, more recently, Robert Wagner and Jeff Hunter.

Betty Grable had reigned as Queen of the Fox lot during the war years and had recently starred with Monroe in *How to Marry a Millionaire*. She was philosophical about pushing forty, and knew that her tenure as a sex queen was coming to an end. Monroe was her natural successor. But Monroe was in New York and the studio didn't have a current contract blonde with the necessary attributes. They had an over-the-top oomphy blonde – both in bust measurement and personality – in Jayne Mansfield, the brassy, sassy, sharp blonde in Sheree North, and the intelligent girl-next-door blonde in Joanne Woodward, but they needed a sexy blonde bombshell. This, the head office decided, would be me. I was the right age and height, and had all the right measurements. Apparently I also possessed that exact combination of innocence and worldliness that appealed to male movie-goers. It didn't matter that I wasn't blonde. Evelyn Nesbitt had been a brunette, and after filming on *Red Velvet Swing* finished, Publicity informed me that 'It'll be the peroxide bottle for you, kiddo.'

'Over my dead body,' I vowed.

In late August, while Monroe was in New York shooting *The Seven Year Itch* for Billy Wilder, I was in Rome finishing *Land of the Pharaohs* and being discussed by Zanuck as Marilyn's replacement.

In an interview about Monroe and her problems, Darryl Zanuck had said, 'She's not very fit. Wave a script in her face and she's apt to catch cold from the draught. Sure, we gave her the publicity build-up at the beginning but now it's gone too far. We've gotta stop it before the public gets sick of her so I've put a temporary ban on all studio publicity about her. Publicity can be more damaging than helpful. It can help you grow but you have to fight to control it.'

When asked in the same interview about Joan Collins he said, 'I think the girl has possibilities. I've seen her once or twice in English movies and she always seems better than her parts. I'm signing her to a long-term contract, but we won't do anything with her until we've tested her exhaustively and found out what's best for her.'

This was how the studio system worked when Zanuck ran Fox. In spite of his sexual eccentricities, he was a brilliant man who knew the movie business inside out. He kept an enormous chart in his office, which showed what all the contract stars, directors, producers, even art directors and composers were working on. A Fox producer could easily cast his entire picture from Zanuck's extensive chart, and the studios were turning out at least two features a week.

Zanuck was influential in every movie made at Fox and put his personal stamp on everything. He was a great supervisor and checked all the rushes every night. Often after he'd viewed a film, he would make slight – or major – changes, which usually guaranteed that the picture would succeed.

He was one of the first executives to have his own steam-room and gym connected to his office, and he usually smoked his ubiquitous cigar during workouts. His tough, macho image was vitally important to him, probably because of his short stature.

I'd heard all the rumours about Zanuck so I was determined to make it clear to him that I wasn't about to be 'got' by him. However, soon after I arrived, he tracked me down one day and chased me along a corridor outside the executive offices, finally trapping me against a wall. 'You haven't had anyone till you've had me.' He wheezed cigar-fetid breath into my face and his straggly grey moustache brushed my cheek. 'I've got the biggest and the best and I can go all night!'

Utterly unable to come up with a witty riposte I squawked, wriggled free of his muscular arms and dashed down the corridor to the sanctuary of Publicity.

Convinced I'd be fired I gloomily reflected on the after-effects of the pass he had made at an older and wiser contract starlet, one of my fellow ladies-in-waiting in *The Virgin Queen*. 'Ha,' she had laughed. 'I gave it to Darryl *good* when he propositioned me last week. He said, "Y'know, doll, I'm the best in the business," so I told him, "You'd better be, sweetie, 'cos you're only five foot two!"'

She didn't laugh for long: her jobs started to drop off dramatically and shortly thereafter she was released from her contract. Perhaps it was fortuitous that I was at a loss for clever insults to the great and fearsome Mr Z, because I remained under contract for six years without having to resort to the casting-couch – his or anyone else's.

A famous story about Zanuck's casting-couch propensities concerned Joan Crawford, who was not contracted to Fox but was a star of huge magnitude. One day, swathed in furs, ankle-straps and white turban, she swept into Zanuck's office suite for a story conference on a movie she wanted to make there. Immediately she was ushered into his sanctum Zanuck opened a drawer and produced the famous solid-gold casting of his genitals.

'Whaddya think of this?' he asked proudly, waving it before her. 'Impressive, huh?'

What Crawford said would have made a trucker blush. She stalked out of his office never to work at Twentieth Century-Fox again.

How many hapless starlets had been asked to view this bizarre piece of modern art?

George Jessel, the old time vaudevillian and comedian told me another Zanuck anecdote when we worked on *Hieronymus Merkin*. He was a great crony of Zanuck and one night was discovered lying in the gutter in front of Mocambo night club, the centre of a laughing crowd. The doorman went over to him and asked, 'Hey buddy, what are you doing here? Are you sick?'

'Run along, man, run along,' said Jessel breezily. 'I'm just saving Mr Darryl Zanuck a parking space.'

One day, *en route* to the stills gallery, an eclectic group was walking towards me. Marilyn Monroe was sashaying along, surrounded by a motley crew of hairdressers, make-up artists, costumiers, publicists and agents, who were all trying to talk to her. She wasn't paying attention to any of them.

There had been enormous excitement about her return to the Fox lot where, after so long at Lee Strasberg's Actors' Studio, she was shooting *Bus Stop*. She looked like a bird of superb plumage. Her blonde hair, swept up in tiny tendrils, was like spun sugar, and she wore a little bathing-suit creation of shimmering green brocade. The bodice was almost transparent net with bits of silvery-gold thread hanging from it, her fishnet tights had big holes in them, and a rather shabby-looking robe flopped open over the whole ensemble.

As we passed she gave me a faint smile and I smiled back. I was desperate to talk to her, but much too shy. In the columns I was painted as this be-bop madcap vamp when, in reality, I often felt out of place and, to add to my insecurity, wherever I went I was always the youngest.

Some weeks later, at a party at Gene Kelly's, I wandered into the barroom where a blonde girl sat alone forlornly sipping a vodka martini. 'Hi, I'm Marilyn,' she murmured.

'Hi,' I said, 'I'm Joan.'

I gulped and sat down beside her. Yes, it was she – but far removed from the glorious butterfly flitting around the Fox lot, whose skin had looked finer than porcelain powder and whose enormous azure eyes seemed to have been lit up from the inside. This girl, for indeed she did seem girlish although she must have been thirty, was simply, even carelessly, dressed in a pink, slightly grubby mohair sweater and a black pencil skirt. She had a dazzling figure and bare white legs but her face, almost devoid of make-up, seemed ordinary and rather pug-nosed. She wore no jewellery – and no bra. It was an altogether unlikely look for the sex bomb of the age.

We started to chat and discovered that we were both Geminis. Gemini is the butterfly sign of the zodiac. Multi-faceted, diverse and childlike, Geminis often look younger than their years and can be fragmented, fickle and pleasure-loving. Marilyn and I possessed many of these qualities. She asked how I was getting on at Fox and I said it was all so new and strange after what I'd been used to. America's golden girl said in her breathy little-girl-lost voice: 'Yeah, I guess it must be hard.' Then with a Gemini quick change of subject, she remarked, 'Gee, I love your hair. It's so different from the way the studio makes us all look.'

'The studio *hate* my hair,' I said. I had grown out the Rank perm and it was long and straight again, with a fringe that almost covered my eyes. 'They're trying to make me cut it.'

'I guess they think you look like a beatnik.' She giggled.

Marilyn's short hair was yellow blonde, rather messy and showing dark roots. She looked as though she hadn't really bothered, which was somehow appealing in an age when everyone cared tremendously how they looked. I studied her carefully, in awe, for this was the woman I was supposed to replace in *Red Velvet Swing*. Mission impossible?

'I need some advice,' I said hesitantly. 'I'm a bit scared about what's happening to me. Fox seems to be taking over my life.'

'Don't let the studio guys dictate to you,' she warned, in her tiny voice. 'They want to take you over completely – mould you – make you do everything *they* want. Don't buy into it.'

As she talked she became more animated and relaxed. She was not classically beautiful: her face was that of a sensual Cupid, erotic, innocent yet sexy, with the quality of a frightened child.

Her eyes were gorgeous – blue, expressive, and set wide apart. They were sketchily outlined in black, the fashionable doe-eyed look which turned up at the corners, and her upper lids were several shades lighter than her complexion, which gave her the famous half-lidded look. She wore little foundation or rouge and her lipstick was shiny pink – and wearing off. A male friend, not unsusceptible to feminine charms, wandered over from the poker game. I introduced him to Marilyn and as they spoke, I watched the 'Monroe Magic' switch itself on – almost palpable, despite the timidity and careless grooming.

After he had left we started talking again. She knew I was English, and cooed, 'Oh, I'd *love* to go to London. I *adore* your theatre and all your actors, especially Laurence Olivier and John Gielgud. Have you met them?'

I told her how I'd met Gielgud when I was a student after a matinée of *The Lady's Not For Burning*, which impressed her. Then, glowing with pride, Marilyn told me of her own hopes – to study at the Actors' Studio and maybe appear on Broadway.

'Hollywood is all crap,' she said simply, with an edge of contempt. 'You're just a piece of meat to the studio – we all are. They're always looking for new girls, and the public is *so* fickle. They want fresh faces all the time – they're never satisfied and their appetite is huge.'

However, she didn't seem bitter, and I sensed in her a determination to break away from the restrictive mould that Hollywood had made for her – mindless cutie with a great body. And in spite of her massive worldwide popularity, that, indeed, was what the Fox bosses thought of Monroe: that she was a difficult, loose-moralled flavour-of-the-decade, whom the public adored in films like *The Seven Year Itch* and *Gentlemen Prefer Blondes*, but who was getting ideas far above her station in wanting to become a serious actress.

Monroe and her sisters in sex-appeal – Jane Russell, Betty Grable, Rita Hayworth and Jayne Mansfield – were cast mainly in fluff. But fluff could be major box office, as demonstrated by the success of their movies. Marilyn was firmly typecast in that frivolous niche and it would be hard, if not impossible, for her to escape it.

She was wise in the ways of Hollywood and tried to warn me of the pitfalls. 'Don't let them push you around,' she said. 'They tried to push me around, even when I was the biggest star on the lot, and I didn't believe in myself enough so I made a lot of crappy movies.'

I disagreed about her films but she interrupted, 'No, no, it's true. They said I could never be thought of as a proper actress, not with these.' She gestured contemptuously to her bosom, then to mine. 'You, too, honey, it'll be tough for you as well. Any gal who looks like she's hot stuff in the sack will *never* be taken seriously in this town.'

I sipped my martini and ruminated on this sad fact.

Then she confided that when she had first gone under contract to Fox, in 1949, her salary had been at subsistence level: 'I spent my time hanging around the publicity department in a tight sweater, and posing for photographs in the stills gallery dressed up as a turkey, or Santa Claus, sometimes even dressed in a sack. I was always cutting ribbons at super-markets, opening stores. Boy, did they make me earn my keep. Fox are a heartless bunch, and they'll drop you in a second if you don't do things their way. Honey, you better look out for yourself with the top guns. The Fox hierarchy are more dangerous than at any other studio.'

'What do you mean?' I asked naïvely.

'Wolves,' mouthed Marilyn, looking nervously over her shoulder as if expecting one to jump out from behind a sofa. 'There's a whole bunch of big bad wolves at Fox.'

'I can handle *wolves*,' I scoffed.

'Not these wolves, honey. They're the power bosses, and they just *love* to push us girls around. Particularly look out for Darryl Zanuck,' she whispered. 'If he doesn't get what he wants, honey, he won't have *any* scruples about dropping your contract. It's happened to lots of starlets.'

'But Zanuck brought me here from England, and I ran away from him the other day, but I'm still here.'

Marilyn snorted derisively. 'Sure, honey, but if the first picture in which you're above the title doesn't make big bucks, Zanuck won't hesi-tate to chuck you like a used toothbrush.'

We had had another drink, and were becoming quite mellow, when

Marilyn said that her closest confidant was the make-up man whom she'd had since the beginning, Allan 'Whitey' Snyder. 'He's been making me up for my tests,' I said.

'You can trust him *totally*,' said Marilyn. 'He's one of the few on the lot you can, he's real wise.'

She giggled then told me that she'd once been voted Miss Cheesecake by the Army newspaper *Stars and Stripes*.

'Something else we have in common,' I said. 'In England I was voted Miss Press Clippings. It was *so* embarrassing.'

'No, honey, that's great. Y'know, your fans are *real* important, even if they are fickle. I owe a lot to those boys in Korea. Fox sent thousands of pin-ups of me to the troops and my fan mail got so immense that the studio *had* to put me in some kinda movie.'

(The something that they'd put her in was *Don't Bother to Knock*, a *film noir* in which she played her first major dramatic role and finally started to excite hard-core cineastes.)

'I've had enormous financial and creative battles with the studio. They never really appreciated me. I mean, I've come a long way from the orphanage, you'd think they'd give me credit for that.' She shook her blonde curls. 'But, of course, they don't.'

Marilyn seemed so sweet-natured and down to earth that it was hard to believe that she was not only the biggest female star in the world but, in retrospect, the greatest sex-goddess of the century.

'How did you feel the first time you saw yourself on the screen?' I asked, relishing our new-found intimacy.

'Gee, it was an extraordinary feeling. I realized I didn't have to be insecure, unhappy and scared little Norma Jean any more. I was Marilyn Monroe, gorgeous, happy and confident up there, and nobody would *ever* believe that inside I was still that little brown mouse.' She sounded a touch woozy after another vodka martini. 'So whenever I got depressed I'd disguise myself and sneak into a movie-house and watch that radiant creature up there and she somehow seemed separate from me. She was fifteen feet tall and I felt real good just watching her. She was just gorgeous.' Marilyn wasn't bragging – it was a simple fact. 'Whitey said it was because the camera loved me. He said the camera loves some people –

"It's like you're born with the magic," Whitey says.'

Leaning closer, Marilyn lit a cigarette and became even more confiding. 'Have you ever met Bette Davis?' she whispered.

'Oh, yes,' I said, 'I'm working with her now. Why?'

She launched into a tirade about the legendary star with whom she'd worked on *All About Eve*. 'That woman hates every female who can walk.' She shuddered. 'She made me feel *so* nervous. She didn't talk to me at all, just sort of swept around the set, nose and cigarette in the air. I guess it was because I was only a bit-part player and she was the big star.'

I shrugged sympathetically. 'Yes, I had problems with her too. She did give me one interesting piece of advice, though.'

'I'm surprised she gave you anything,' said Marilyn. 'She's a mean old broad.'

'She told me that if I wanted to stay the course in this business I should become tougher, but she warned that it would make many people dislike me because, she said, "When a man is outspoken people think he's forthright, but when a woman speaks her mind people think she's a bitch."'

'*That*'s for sure,' said Marilyn, vehemently. 'There's only three categories of female in this town. Bitches, broads – and by that I mean whores – and virgins, whether they're the real thing or just faking it. It's a man's town, honey, and you'll be finding that out soon enough.'

Then Marilyn turned, blue eyes wide, and said simply, 'And it's *not* true blondes have more fun either. Most men in this town think that blondes are just toys, and if you're a blonde with a bosom, watch *out*. Do you know what everyone said about me my first year at Fox?' I was spellbound by these true-life confessions. 'They said that when I got started I was handed around guys in the business like hors d'oeuvres. All of 'em, from grips and gaffers to the big-shots. Can you *believe* it?'

'No.' I stared at her, as she gave me her tentative smile, and understood why movie audiences all over the world were bedazzled by Marilyn Monroe.

'But I guess those sons-of-bitches are all laughing on the other side of their faces now, aren't they?' giggled Marilyn. A few minutes later Marilyn bade me a breathy goodbye and left. I watched her shimmy through Gene Kelly's living room. She really did have the most astonishing walk – as Jack Lemmon squawked in *Some Like It Hot*, 'That's Jello on springs.'

I never saw Marilyn Monroe again, but when I was in Rome in 1962 and heard the news of her death, I must confess I wept for her, and for all of her pain.

Fox started pulling out all the stops to make me the current flavour-of-the-month with the American movie public, and I made a variety of tests for a variety of roles. The script still wasn't ready for *The Girl in the Red Velvet Swing* so in the meantime I just tested and tested.

The first one was with Fox's current heart-throb, Robert Wagner. At twenty-five he was boyishly handsome with engaging blue eyes and thick light-brown floppy hair. RJ, as everyone called him, was rightly considered one of the most charming and personable young men in Hollywood. He possessed enormous warmth and wonderful manners, and I thought him devastatingly attractive but, like me, rather shy.

We were to test for an eighteenth-century epic called *Lord Vanity*, and I was thrilled to wear the gorgeous, tightly corseted brocade costumes and white powdered wigs. But on the first day I was understandably nervous as I tottered on to Sound Stage 7 on Louis heels, balancing an industrial-sized wig on my hot head. It was a boiling California winter day, the sky a pure azure blue, no wind and no smog. To protect my wig I was driven to the set by a gum-chewing teamster in a little white cart.

Technicians bustled around. There seemed far more of them to make this test than there had been on any British films. RJ came over, looking dashing in powder-blue satin breeches and lace cravat, but I didn't think his white wig did him any favours. He was, if anything, more self-conscious than I was.

'How're you doing, JC?' he asked, coining the nickname by which he still calls me.

'Fine.' I puffed at a Lucky Strike, my mouth dry as a bone. 'A bit nervous, though.'

'Don't be,' said RJ. 'But if you are, use it. Spence always told me to do that.'

RJ had recently finished filming *The Mountain* with Spencer Tracy, whom he idolized, and Tracy had taken the young actor under his wing, treating him like a son.

'You know the best bit of acting advice Spence gave me?' RJ said.

'No, but I hope you're going to tell me.'

'First he always said acting's no big deal. It's just about hitting your mark and not blowing your lines. Then he said that if the audience *catch* you acting, you're not doing it right. They actually have to *believe* you're the character you're playing.'

'Let's go, let's go.' The assistant director bustled up, an imposing figure in a red and black tartan shirt, black gabardine trousers, with a black silk scarf slung insouciantly, Gilbert Roland fashion, around his shrivelled neck. All the crew seemed impossibly well dressed. The continuity girl was wearing a crisp blue gingham shirt-waist, shiny patent shoes and neat pearl earrings. The director, a formidable figure in his sixties, was festooned as if he was about to attend a costume ball as Cecil B. De Mille: buff and khaki from head to toe, in his jodhpurs, polished riding boots and fingerless leather gloves, he was a study in elegant, sophisticated casualness. I was used to the laid-back scruffiness of English units – ancient jumpers unravelling at the cuff, baggy grey flannels sagging at the knees, and the ubiquitous cloth caps. Everyone in LA seemed glamorous and groomed to the teeth.

RJ and I had rehearsed alone the previous day, but rehearsals are never the same as when you are done up to the nines in an eighteenth-century fairy frock and a two-ton wig that looks as if it's made of candy floss. Bits of it kept coming loose and clinging to my lip-gloss and eyelashes. Whitey, the make-up maestro, had given me a 'natural' look, but as this was Hollywood this included pencilled eyebrows, false lashes, sky-blue eyeshadow, glossed lips outlined in light vermilion, and peach rouge. RJ wore a similar *maquillage*, minus the lip gloss and eyelashes, I think.

My stomach was rumbling – I hadn't eaten breakfast and my body was telling me to do something about it. But there was no time for that. 'Gilbert Roland' told us to hit our marks and we started rehearsing.

The scene was simple enough, ending in a passionate kiss, but to save our make-up we only rehearsed dialogue. Each time we got to the point where our lips had to meet, the director yelled, 'Cut, cut! OK, kids, let's save the smooch for the takes.'

'What's that funny noise?' asked the sound engineer, looking puzzled.

I went scarlet beneath my panstick. Could he possibly hear my stomach?

I glanced at RJ, who gave me a conspiratorial wink and handed me a piece of chewing gum. 'Don't worry, JC, it happens to everyone,' he whispered. 'Give you a little tip. Always have breakfast before you shoot. Saves the sound guy's ears and your embarrassment.'

I cursed myself. In London, I was used to tea and bacon rolls in the morning and in Rome it had been croissants and cappuccino. I hadn't fancied cereal or cheese Danish here so far but I figured that I was going to have to put up with it in future.

'It's better than coming out the *other* end,' whispered RJ. 'I worked with a leading lady once who couldn't stop farting. The sound guys used to go crazy.' He rolled his eyes and I corpsed. I had to leave the set to giggle by myself in a corner where Whitey gave me a Danish, which I stuffed down quickly.

'OK, kids, c'mon, c'mon, we're ready for a take,' called 'Cecil B. De Mille'. 'Aaand – action.'

My heart was thumping so loudly that I felt sure Sound would hear that, too, and complain again. Then RJ moved in for the kiss. Being such a gentleman, he was a little anxious about smudging my lipstick so his lips missed mine by about three inches.

'Shit! Cut, cut, cut, cut, cut!' The director, who to my amazement was suddenly brandishing a riding crop, rushed up excitedly. 'You gotta kiss her like you *mean* it, RJ. None of this faggoty on-the-cheek stuff. Grab her and buss her properly, man.'

He stalked back to his director's chair and Whitey came up, patted my sweating brow and needlessly perfected the untouched lip-gloss.

'Don't worry, hon, you're doing fine,' he said. I wanted to ask him if Marilyn had ever had problems with her stomach rumbling but there wasn't time.

'OK, *aaand* ACTION,' yelled the director. This time there was no faking it. RJ and I kissed deeply and properly, our lips writhing around each other's for what seemed like an hour. If the director wanted passion we were going to supply it. He had been told by his bosses in the white concrete bunker up the hill to 'Make 'em look sexy', but it's hard to be sexy when you're laced into a constricting corset with a man you've only recently met and pieces of his wig falling into your mouth. It's even harder to be sexy when the actor you're kissing is wearing almost as much make-up as you are and only a minimally smaller hairdo. I wanted to laugh again but was saved by Cecil B. yelling, '*Aaand* cut! – OK, cut, kids.'

Gingerly we moved apart and found to our embarrassed dismay that we were still connected at the lip by a long line of saliva. We stared at each other in horror, hoping it would just disappear. It didn't, so RJ put up his finger and snapped it. I almost passed out with shame.

'Don't worry. It must be because our mouths are so dry,' RJ muttered reassuringly.

'OK, kids, we're going again,' said De Mille, wearily.

'Oh, my God, *No*! I can't face it.' I staggered to the make-up table where Whitey and his team slapped more paint on my flushed face.

We endured three more agonizing takes which all ended with a washing-line of saliva hanging between our mouths. The director, sadistic beast, seemed to take a perverse pleasure in it. Finally, when lunch was called, he took me aside and whispered with a smirk, 'I guess you two kids really dig each other, huh?'

I looked at him in amazement. Were all of Fox's directors like this caricature? Speechless I rushed to the commissary for lunch with RJ, where we attempted to laugh off the whole fiasco.

'You do realize, JC, that there's no *possible* chance of either of us ever playing the leads in this movie,' said RJ wisely. And he was right, for *Lord Vanity* was never made.

Although RJ and I didn't work together for three years, we became close friends, and I had learned my first important lessons about movie making: whatever happens, whatever's going on, whatever the tantrums of your director or fellow actors, don't let it throw you. Keep on shooting, keep that dialogue going, never give up – and, most importantly, *never* lose your sense of humour.

Fox Publicity consisted of several enormous interconnecting rooms, which took up an entire floor in the administration building. There, I met an army of press agents and publicists, three in particular who would be guiding my life and career in more ways than six. Roy Craft, middle-aged, clever and formerly of *Life* magazine, was the man responsible for seeing that Fox's stars and starlets received enough media coverage, and he hustled magazine editors and newspapers for it relentlessly. Johnny Cook, young, wisecracking and good-looking, was personally responsible for showing me the ropes and watching over me in in interviews to see that I didn't put my foot in my mouth.

And then there was 'The Boss', the fearsome, fiftyish publicity genius Harry Brand, who ruled the roost and was known as the only man in Hollywood who had the ear of both Hedda Hopper *and* Louella Parsons. It was rumoured that it was he who had coined many of the suggestively witty *bons mots* uttered by Marilyn Monroe. Brand, who had been at Fox since the mid-thirties, had the unenviable task of damage control to the stars. When a star did something wrong – for example, posed for a nude calendar *à la* Marilyn, or was found dead drunk in a bar, as a few of Hollywood's male stars were wont to be, or discovered *in flagrante* with someone else's wife – Brand was able either to turn the scandal into an asset, as he did with Marilyn's calendar, or make sure it *never* hit the newspapers and that the public didn't get to hear about it. He knew many powerful people in high places. Fox protected its stars, as did the other studios, to such an extent that at industry parties and premières when photographers were present, a publicity delegate from each studio made certain that none of their stars was ever caught with either a cigarette, a drink or someone else's spouse in their hand. Magazines and newspapers accorded the stars great respect and scandal sheets like the *National Enquirer* didn't yet exist.

Brand was also Darryl Zanuck's closest confidant and had probably soothed things countless times for his indiscreet employer. He had been quoted as saying, 'When I die there's just one more thing I can do for Darryl. I'll have my ashes scattered on his driveway so his tyres won't skid.'

I told Roy Craft the short story of my life, which he wrote up into a long bio, then suggested that I make myself eighteen years old instead of twenty-one. When I demurred, he said: 'Aw, heck, honey, everyone does *that*. You'd be surprised at how much older some of our stars *really* are as opposed to their official publicity ages.'

I thought it stupid to try to make out I was three years younger so I put my foot down and forbade them to lop years off – which I've since occasionally regretted!

Johnny, who had been assigned to make the world take notice of me, said confidently, 'This film factory here is gonna turn you into one large-scale lollipop, hon.' He became a close friend and taught me a great deal.

I asked him the difference between all the different titles Fox producers had. 'It's unbelievably confusing. What's the difference between a producer, an associate producer, and an assistant producer?'

'It's easy,' said Johnny. 'The producer is the executive whose assistant wears a worried look on his face, the associate producer is the only one who would associate with the producer, and an assistant producer is just a mouse studying to be a rat.' He went on, 'You wanna know *all* the juicy stories about Hollywood, hon?'

'Oh, yes. I know a few but tell me more. I want to know *everything*.'

Johnny was quite a raconteur and we sat in his office on many an afternoon while he regaled me with fascinating Tinseltown tit-bits of gossip about the stars. Some of his *bon mots* were, 'Hollywood's where a guy can get stabbed in the back while climbing up the ladder, where everyone's a genius until they've lost their job, where they put you under contract instead of under observation. And that's the end of today's lesson, hon.'

One day he remarked, 'Vic was in here last week. Now he *really* knows some great stories.'

'Mature?' I asked.

'Yup,' said Johnny. 'He told me a new one. He said, "Hollywood's a place where you twinkle till you wrinkle."' I laughed. Then Johnny asked, 'Hey, d'ya need a new TV set?'

'I don't even own an old one yet,' I said. 'I'm still staying at the Beverly Glen.'

'Well, when you wanna buy one, Vic's the guy,' said Johnny. 'He's got this great new TV and appliance shop on Pico. Bought it with his kiss-off money from Fox.'

'Really?' I couldn't believe that Victor Mature, Fox's dashing star of *Samson and Delilah, The Robe, Demetrius and the Gladiators* and *Androcles and the Lion*, whom Fox's publicity machine had called 'a beautiful hunk of man', was now selling appliances for a living.

'Sure is,' said Johnny. 'And he's more contented than he's ever been. Wanna go to his store one day?'

'Sure.' I was adapting easily to the slangy California talk. 'Soon as I move into my new apartment I'd love to.'

A week later Johnny took me to Victor Mature's store, where the movie idol himself served me. In his late thirties, he still looked pretty good, with jet black hair, thick sensual lips and a laid back heavy-lidded charm – the Sylvester Stallone of his day.

I asked him, rather boldly I thought, why he'd quit movies.

'I got bored with all those parts where I just wore a skirt and a scowl. I'm much happier now.' He gave me a lazy smile and winked. 'D'ya wanna buy a radio too, kid?' He had a nice line in radios and toasters so I bought several gadgets, which he promised to have delivered the next day. He waved us a sleepy-eyed goodbye, and in the car I told Johnny how nice and normal Mature had seemed.

'Yeah, he's a great guy,' said Johnny. 'Self-deprecating too – something few of the rest of the loons are. He loves golf and he recently applied for membership in the LA country club.'

'Isn't that the club that won't admit actors?'

'Right,' said Johnny. 'You're learning. Vic was turned down 'cos of that ruling, so he protested to the board and said, "Hell, *I*'m no actor, and I've got twenty-five pictures to prove it."'

With the announcement that I was to play Evelyn Nesbitt, the most beautiful girl in New York, in *The Girl in the Red Velvet Swing* Fox needed to get my face known to the American public fast, so when I wasn't filming my days were even more filled with sessions in publicity and endless interviews with everyone from the *Podunk Iowa Chronicle* to those terrifying *grandes dames* and empresses of gossip, Hedda Hopper and Louella Parsons.

I'd been warned about these two old bats, the snoop sisters, who, such was their power and influence, practically ran Hollywood. If either woman rang Darryl Zanuck, Harry Cohn, Jack Warner or any other studio head, he would get back to them within the hour.

When I met the fabled Miss Hopper for tea at her English-style country house in the heart of Bel-Air, I was surprised at how British she attempted to appear. Her over decorated hat made her look as if she was off to Ladies' Day at Ascot, her house was furnished in chintzy olde-English style, and she sported a fake British accent as she served Earl Grey tea and cucumber sandwiches from a Wedgwood tea-set. Other than reporting to her twenty million readers the following week that I was 'cute and polite, and looked like she combed her hair with an egg beater', she imparted to me one astute piece of advice: 'Don't ever use the casting-couch to get ahead, dear. It's a one-way ticket to nowhere.'

'I wouldn't dream of such a thing,' I retorted huffily. 'The *thought* of it – ugh.'

'I believe you.' She stared through me with cold marble eyes. 'You look too clever for that. But sometimes you'll find that you'll lose roles to girls who *have* given their favours. Just remember, dear, don't give in, and *don't* let the bastards get you down.'

Hedda had been a minor Hollywood actress for years until she started her column, so I realized she knew her onions in this town. I also realized that casting-couch propositions probably hadn't come her way too often. Maybe that was why she was so venomous about people in the industry. Even if you don't want to do it, it's always nice to be asked.

Louella Parsons talked in a high, coarse voice, was short, squat, unbelievably ugly and totally devoid of charm. She had wielded immense power through her four hundred newspaper columns in the thirties and forties, but now that power was on the wane. Although she was still invited to the A-list parties, sometimes three or four a night, and received extravagant Christmas gifts from the most influential people in Hollywood, she had grown bitter, and was hitting the bottle with a vengeance. She was also incontinent, and needed to wear rubber-backed pants, which was a huge source of merriment in Hollywood.

She was married to a doctor, whom she referred to as Dockie. He specialized in the treatment of venereal diseases, and through him she gained much of her inside information on some Hollywood stars, which she would ruthlessly use to blackmail studios and actors into giving her exclusive information.

The only thing these two dangerous dowagers ever agreed on was the depth of their hatred for each other.

Between them, Hedda and Louella had seventy-five million readers a day, and if they didn't like you they could destroy your career in an instant. They would finish you off first in print, then follow it up with sly calls to studio heads, suggesting that a particular individual be 'let go'. They were the keepers of the moral flame in Hollywood, venting their disapproval freely, and had successfully destroyed the careers of several stars, among them Ingrid Bergman when she had become pregnant by Roberto Rossellini. But there were many other stories that everyone knew which never hit their columns, such as the Spencer Tracy–Katherine Hepburn liaison, which had lasted for years, the Cary Grant–Randolph Scott love-nest, and the illegitimate daughter of Clark Gable and Loretta Young. Hollywood shut its doors firmly on these and many other scandals, and God knows what pay-offs went to Hedda and Louella to keep it that way.

At the other end of Hollywood's moral spectrum were the outrageous practical jokers and bizarre nonconformists of which, thankfully, there were many. One day, while shooting a crowd scene for *The Girl in the Red Velvet Swing* on the Madison Square Garden set, I saw an elderly extra surrounded by a group who were laughing hysterically.

'Who's that?' I asked Ray Milland.

'*That*, my dear, is the legendary OK Freddie,' said the suave Mr Milland, and proceeded to tell me this tale.

'OK Freddie is a Hollywood extra much in demand by some of our raunchier and jokier leading men. One of the reasons he works so much is because supposedly he has the most enormous cock in town. Whenever he was on set and was summoned by Clark Gable, Cary Grant, David Niven or Errol Flynn to "C'mon, Freddie, show us your cock," he would always chirp, "OK," quite happily, and out it would come to gasps of amazement and amusement.'

'But he looks so ordinary,' I said, glancing at the funny-looking wizened old guy.

'Ah, my dear, it's what's known as a surprise package.' Milland winked.

'Good Lord,' I said. 'It must be.'

By the time I came to Hollywood Freddie rarely worked, having been put out to pasture or wherever it was that old extras go to when they can no longer cut it, but rumour and legend still abounded about the size of his equipment.

This, however, is my favourite story about Freddie. At an extremely elegant garden-party, given by one of those *grande dame* actresses of the late forties, the guests mingled glamorously on the emerald-green lawn, the men impeccable in white flannels, ascots and blazers, the women gorgeous in gauzy chiffons and big white hats.

A trio of roguish actors – apparently one was Errol Flynn, another David Niven – decided to play a joke on some of the more uptight females. They arranged to have Freddie come along dressed as a waiter. He was given a large silver tray, on which was arranged every kind of delicacy. Smoked salmon, quails' eggs, tiny sausages on sticks, caviar on biscuits and, in the centre, the *pièce de résistance*, a large pork sausage somewhat bigger than an Italian salami. It was decorated with paper thin slices of raw beef and baby prawns. Freddie's tray was held somewhat lower than those of the other waiters, but the guests were so engrossed in their gossip that few noticed.

Freddie, who had a lugubrious Buster Keaton-type face, mingled with the guests, all of whom took a little egg or a taste of caviar. Nobody attempted to slice the sausage. Nobody, that is, until a distinguished matron of advancing years decided to put on her lorgnette for a closer look. The three naughty box-office icons stood behind a tree, by now helpless with laughter.

'My goodness, that's a *very* big sausage,' said the matron, and plunged her fork into the middle of it. There was a howl of agony from Freddie and all hell broke loose as the tray was dropped and the sausage was revealed as Freddie's gigantic member. The three hysterical actors almost had to be carried out on stretchers, but their venerable hostess was *not* amused.

Gene Kelly's Rodeo Drive house attracted some of the most interesting people in Hollywood – and not just pretty faces: some of them were considered to be intellectual giants. The regulars included Stanley Donen, a young producer/director who had already directed some of MGM's starriest musicals, Adolph Green and Betty Comden, musical-comedy writers whose many Broadway smash hits included *Bells Are Ringing* and *On the Town*, screenwriter and wit Harry Kurnitz, from *Land of the Pharaohs*, who was always amusing, in stark contrast to the turgid dialogue he'd whipped up for that picture, handsome producer George Englund and his actress wife Cloris Leachman, Arthur Loew Jnr, Frank Sinatra with various dates, one of whom was Lauren Bacall, and, of course, Sydney Chaplin. Sydney was trying, rather unsuccessfully, to resurrect his career so between auditions we spent a lot of time at Gene's, particularly at weekends. His volleyball court was a Mecca for all those who managed to penetrate this élite and inner circle. Volleyball was the game of the day, but they also excelled at card games and charades, and the sparkling conversation was always witty and erudite.

I'd admired Gene Kelly since seeing him first in the musical *For Me and My Gal* with Judy Garland. He was utterly charming with a zany sense of humour and tremendous energy and vitality. Highly competitive, he played vicious games of tennis with the leading Beverly Hills pro, Jack Cushingham, who also gave me lessons. The Beverly Hills Tennis Club became another of my major hang-outs, and since the courts were thronged with the most attractive and seductive men in Hollywood, it was a great place to play tennis – and to get one's ego massaged.

The Girl in the Red Velvet Swing, my second Fox movie, was set at the turn of the century. It was beautifully mounted, with gorgeous sets and ravishing costumes by Charles Le Maire, Fox's finest costume designer.

It was during the making of this film that I started to develop my passion for beautiful clothes, and I also learned from the make-up and wardrobe people more about beautification and glamour in one month than I'd learned during my entire three years in British films.

I had no idea how a dress was made until I wandered into the back rooms of the vast wardrobe department, and watched the seamstresses at their painstaking work. Every garment was made of fabulous fabrics and exquisitely finished. All the period bodices were authentically boned with stiff whalebone and the inside of each dress was as beautifully finished as the outside. I regret that I didn't keep one of those ravishing works of art.

There are few couturiers today who know how to design clothes of such superb quality, and few remain of the women who actually made the gowns. These expert dressmakers knew their craft inside out, and, curiously, were all either Romanian, Bulgarian or French. The Fox wardrobe department even employed a Russian girl who specialized in smocking.

Wardrobe for a picture was of vital importance, and no producer or director underestimated it. For instance, if a leading lady wore a red dress, nobody else in the scene would be allowed to wear the same colour. Nothing must be allowed to detract from the star.

The main problem Fox had with me was my accent. It was too British and some of the executives said they couldn't understand me. To ensure that I spoke correctly for *The Girl in the Red Velvet Swing* I was instructed in American by Jeffrey Hunter. The studio insisted that I lose my accent in real life too and when I went back to London the following year Mummie could barely understand me. I continued to speak with a slight American accent until I returned to England in the sixties, but it still sometimes creeps up on me.

When Johnny Cook breezed on to the *Swing* set one day looking like the cat who'd swallowed Tweety-pie I knew something was up.

Barely able to control his excitement he announced nonchalantly, 'We've got you a *Life* cover for the fall, honey.'

I couldn't believe my good fortune. I'd been in Hollywood just nine months and one of the highest publicity scoops was about to be mine. Shooting a cover for *Life* magazine wasn't just any old shoot. The photographer demanded a whole day of my time, plus Ray Milland and Farley Granger thrown in for good measure, and complete run of all the sets.

We hadn't yet shot the controversial scene of Evelyn on the swing, but *Life* insisted that the set be ready for them in a week. Teams of set-designers, painters and carpenters worked overtime to ensure that everything would be ready for the prestigious magazine.

When the set was finished it looked enchanting: a windowless panelled room, with silken drapes, in the middle of which hung a swing with red velvet ropes strung with green leaves supporting the seat. On the ceiling a large silver moon was suspended for Evelyn to reach for as she swung.

The photographer didn't think my movie dresses were sexy enough for the shots on the swing, so he persuaded Charles Le Maire to design a more girlie dress, all pink ruffles, and flouncy frills with a Chanel-type camellia pinned to the neckline.

Evelyn Nesbitt was a naughty young chorine of seventeen, and Stanford White was a dirty old man who loved to sit his inamorata on this glass-bottomed swing *sans* knickers and push her harder and harder until she kicked her feet through the *papier-mâché* moon to a crescendo of music.

We shot for *Life* magazine all day, until I never wanted to see another damn swing in my life, and although I thought I looked chunky and pudding-faced on the *Life* cover, the Fox brass were pleased.

'You've arrived,' said a jubilant Johnny. 'You're gonna be a star now, hon.'

But sadly, though, it wasn't as easy as that. Although the notices were good for *The Girl in the Red Velvet Swing*, which was gratifying, this lovely movie did not do well at the box office. *C'est la vie.*

It was certainly refreshing to read that 'Joan Collins is startlingly beautiful and sexy as Evelyn, and displays more acting talent than during previous appearances before the cameras.' Another said, 'Joan Collins takes this opportunity and grabs it with both hands.' Even the London papers got on the band-wagon. The *Daily Sketch* reported, 'A young woman of almost disturbing beauty, technically accomplished, perfectly poised, stylish from the top of her head to the turn of her ankle. She possesses the capacity to express an eager eroticism beneath the appearance of virginal innocence and gives a performance as sweet and intelligent as any we have reason to expect.' Robert Ottoway wrote, 'Joan was the most mishandled actress that ever belonged to the Rank Organization. Now she's set fair to join the ranks of top-grade international stars.'

The American media described me with more exotic epithets: 'She's a torrid baggage,' said one. 'Her face exudes the simple allure of the old-time sirens,' said another. *Variety* called me 'a captivating bundle of sex-appeal'. Heady stuff, perhaps, but I was determined not to let it go to my head. I was learning my craft, living my life and loving everything about Hollywood.

CHAPTER SIX

A foxy lot

Romanoff's was the most elegant and glamorous restaurant I'd ever been to. The food even more delicious than at the Caprice or Les Ambassadeurs. Situated in the centre of fashionable Rodeo Drive, below the Beverly Wilshire Hotel, it was a Mecca for every reigning star and producer of the day. The Hollywood wit Oscar Levant had told me that Romanoff's was 'so swanky that they served pigs' feet with the shoe trees still in them'.

The first time I went with one of my richer dates, the proprietor greeted us effusively. A tiny man, no taller than five foot four, with a full head of pepper-and-salt hair, wearing an incredibly loud Savile Row checked suit, which on him managed to look elegant, he carried a silver-topped cane with startling panache. His full title, so he claimed, was His Imperial Highness Prince Michael Alexandrovich Dmitri Romanoff. However, rumours circulated constantly that his real name was Harry Gurgerson, and that he was a poor New Yorker from Brooklyn. Nevertheless, he had the most impeccable English manners and the accent to match.

On entering Romanoff's, one looked down four wide, red-carpeted steps from which everyone sitting in the semi-circular, low backed red leather banquettes was visible. Here, one could see and be seen and freely turn to chat with friends at other tables.

I immediately spotted Lauren Bacall, Humphrey Bogart and Billy and Audrey Wilder dining with the diminutive, dynamic agent Irving Lazar. Rosalind Russell was over in one corner, Ava Gardner in another, not to mention half a dozen of Hollywood's top directors and producers.

I was stunned by the gorgeous clothes. All the women looked groomed and *soignée* and even though I'd pulled out all the stops, I felt like that little brown mouse in such a roomful of haute couture.

The fifties was the zenith of Hollywood's glamour period. In a few short years it would die a slow agonizing death as mini-skirts, jeans, and the un-made-up look took over. It's hard to imagine today (other than at private parties) the effort and care that people took with their appearance. If manners maketh man then clothes maketh the woman, and every woman at Romanoff's oozed the confidence which comes from looking fabulous.

But Romanoff's also let in the tourists. I was sitting in a booth one night when a woman rushed over and gushed, 'Susie Powell! My, how you've changed! You used to be so overweight and now you've got such a great figure. How did you *do* that, Susie?'

She babbled on, and when she finally paused for breath I said, 'Sorry, you've made a mistake. I'm not your friend Susie.' She interrupted, 'Hey, Susie! You used to be taller too. Howja do it?'

Another of my favourite restaurants was Chasen's, on Beverly Boulevard. Owned and run by Dave Chasen and his wife Maude, this was a more conservative watering-hole than Romanoff's, and was frequented by an older group of stars and executives. Chasen's famous *chilli con carne* and corned beef hash were the greatest. Sadly it closed its doors for the last time recently, and glamorous Romanoff's didn't even survive the sixties. Nor did my other favourites, La Rue, L'Escoffier, Villa Capri, the Villa Nova and the Cock and Bull. Both Chasen's and Romanoff's had enormous banqueting rooms at the back where glittering industry parties were held regularly.

Every Friday and Saturday night, the jewels and gowns came out and the revels began – if not in a restaurant then in a private house. The most profligate of party-givers were Jack Warner and his wife Ann; the agent and famous wheeler-dealer Charlie Feldman; Ray and Fran Stark, he a prestigious mini-sized producer, she the daughter of the Broadway star Fanny Brice; Connie and Jerry Wald, a Fox producer; and last, but not least, the writer Francis Lederer and his wife.

As the newest pretty young starlet in town I found myself invited to many of them. At one party given by Buddy Adler, the head of Fox, and his glamorous wife, Anita Louise, I saw Lana Turner wearing a low-cut gown with a tiny gold and diamond aeroplane hanging on a chain between her breasts. Charles Brackett, the producer of *The Girl in the Red Velvet Swing*, was chatting to Mike Romanoff and me. Mike glanced at Lana, then asked, 'What do think of Lana's aeroplane?'

'It's delightful,' said Charles, in his charming old-fashioned way, 'and *what* a delicious landing field!'

Charlie Brackett was warmth and old-world charm personified, a great producer and writer. He had collaborated with Billy Wilder on many movies and had recently started producing on his own. He was distinguished-looking with a thick head of snow-white hair, matching moustache, twinkling blue eyes, and always dressed in impeccably tailored suits – from Savile Row, of course.

Anglo-mania had hit Hollywood in the late twenties, when everyone aspired to the genteel English taste in home-decoration and gardening. The Hollywood set strove to imitate the elegance of English society and its aristocracy, and many of the more conservative still do so today. All things English were embraced wholeheartedly from huge coal fires – even when it was eighty degrees outside – Chippendale furniture and afternoon tea, to croquet and Sunday cricket games on the lawn. Some of them were brash carpet-baggers who'd started the motion-picture industry in Hollywood and believed that having an English lifestyle made them instantly acceptable. 'Genteel' was the buzz word. *Le style anglais* reigned in the fifties, and many of the houses I went to – those of Jules and Doris Stein, Bill and Edie Goetz, the two leading socialite couples in town, and Edie and Lew Wasserman, the head honcho at Universal Studios and one of the most influential men in moviedom, Jack Warner and Ray and Frank Stark – were all furnished in the distinctive chintzy style of Sybil Colefax and Nancy Lancaster.

However, behind the Matisses and the Picassos in the enormous drawing rooms you would usually find a huge movie screen and at the back of the room a projector lay hidden behind another masterpiece.

After dinner, which always started *promptly* at seven or seven thirty, the guests would adjourn to the drawing room for coffee and the evening's entertainment.

The status-symbol painting was electronically raised, the lights were dimmed and the audience would watch Fox's, Metro's or Warner's latest hit – or flop. Scathing or bawdy comments would often be addressed to the screen because there's nothing a movie mogul enjoys more than slagging off a rival.

Oscar Levant, the town wit, always kept up an acid running commentary on lesser cinematic works, which sometimes meant that the hosts would have second thoughts about inviting him, but he was so amusing, with his scowling, surly-little-boy charm, that they couldn't resist making him part of the group.

I was often invited to Oscar and June's and, as I was usually the youngest, I dressed in the skimpiest of clothing as befits a starlet. I came in for much teasing from Oscar. 'I've now seen every part of your anatomy except your forehead,' he boomed at me one night, as I sat at his feet, lapping up his wit and wisdom, while I gazed up at him through my long fringe.

Dean and Jeanne Martin used to give riotously entertaining and wild parties in their sprawling Holmby Hills house. They had tons of kids and Dean always pretended to be much more drunk than he was and clowned outrageously.

Sammy Davis Jnr was a regular guest there and he and Dean would banter and insult each other until everyone's face ached from laughing. Sammy, too, was a prolific entertainer at home, and his parties usually lasted till dawn. His cast list often included Judy Garland and Frank Sinatra, Johnny Mathis, Shirley MacLaine and the Swedish actress Mai Britt, a Fox contractee whom Sammy later married.

One night a group of us were at the Sands Hotel, Las Vegas, watching the Martin and Lewis show at a ringside table, which was close to the stage and about eight inches lower than it. The act was hilarious. Dean was pushing forty, Jerry a few years younger and their act had become a showbiz legend. Dean, who fully admitted he had copied Bing Crosby's lazy style of singing, was a natural comedian and excellent straight man to the bedlam Jerry created. They weren't witty but their personalities and delivery made their dialogue hilarious.

Dean: 'Did ya take a bath this morning?'

Jerry: 'Why? Has one gone missing?'

Devastatingly handsome Dean, a family man with a roving eye for the ladies, was a brilliant foil for Jerry. As always he was performing rather tipsily but ever cool, a tumbler of Scotch in one hand, a cigarette in the other. Jerry, who was strangely attractive when he wasn't stalking knock-kneed about the stage talking in his crazy high-pitched manic voice and making ridiculous faces, looked over at our table crossly as we were screaming with laughter at them.

I'd put my feet up on the edge of the stage and was laughing hilariously. Sporting my usual vampy look and low-cut dress, I thought myself quite the cat's miaow that night – until Jerry burst my bubble. He strutted over, kicked at my feet and screamed, 'Don't bruise the stage, girlie. You keep those feet up there any longer and we'll get you up here to join us. Can you sing, girlie? Can you dance? Hey, c'mon, show this audience what you can do, girl.'

He made a grab for me. Hastily I removed my feet and, scarlet-faced, vehemently shook my head. But, undeterred, Jerry kept on, kidding and yelling at me, which amused the audience but mortified me. The more he jokingly insulted me, the worse I felt until Dean, who had recognized me, pulled him back in his sleepy good-natured way and threw a lazy wink in my direction.

Later that night he knocked insistently at my hotel-room door, beseeching me charmingly to 'C'mon, baby, let's have a drink. I just wanna have a little talk. Hey, baby, you owe me one.'

Well, charming as he was, I didn't feel Dean had to be rewarded for rescuing me, and my door remained firmly locked.

After the show our group had had dinner with Dean and Jerry and they were almost more outrageous and funnier than they had been on stage.

I asked Jerry how he was able to be so uninhibited on stage and he answered: 'There's twenty thousand actors who can play Hamlet, but only a handful who can be funny. Comedy is tough – real tough – and the reason we get paid so much is that to be a good comedian you also have to be a *great* actor, and, with due modesty, girlie, *that* I am!'

I murmured in agreement, then said, 'My drama teacher loved telling us the story of Edmund Kean on his death-bed. A young actor knelt at his side and whispered earnestly, "Sir, what is dying like?" To which the old actor replied, "My boy, dying is easy. *Comedy* is difficult."'

Jerry laughed. 'Yeah, that's a great exit line, but John Barrymore's was the best. When he was on his death-bed a young nurse came to ask if he was comfortable. Barrymore turned over, looked at her, winked and said, "OK, honey, hop in!"' Then he said seriously, 'But to be a good dramatic actor you *don't* have to be a great comedian – get it?'

Jerry was an extremely astute, intelligent man whom I've always believed was a great talent, underrated in his country but appreciated in France where they consider him equal to Chaplin.

By the late fifties the Martin and Lewis partnership was on rocky ground. They boys had a love-hate relationship and although they'd made several movies together they wanted to go their separate ways.

One night I went to the 'Share Party', held by an important charity that raised money for handicapped children. It was organized by some of the most influential women in Hollywood, including Audrey Wilder, Gloria Cahn – Sammy's wife – and Debbie Reynolds. Every year they put on a huge benefit and coerced the biggest stars to perform: Barbra Streisand, Sammy Davis, Frank Sinatra, Jack Benny, George Burns and Tony Martin would work for nothing and often joined in the chorus, which some unkind wit referred to as the Menopause Ballet. Rosalind Russell, Lucille Ball, Marge Champion, Jeanne Martin   Dean's wife – and Ruth Berle – Milton's wife – all performed. The theme of this year's party was Cowboys and Cowgals and I went with Warren Beatty.

Jeanne had persuaded Dean to MC but he developed a terrible case of stage-fright. He wasn't used to 'doing a single' and had been working in Jerry's shadow for so long that suddenly he didn't have confidence in his own ability. He asked Jerry to co-host with him but Jerry had refused. Jeanne was ministering to Dean backstage, as was his best friend Mort Viner, but he was still knocking back the Jack Daniels with a vengeance and Jeanne had to push him on stage. He strolled on, Scotch in hand, looking totally relaxed. Then, just as he started to speak, Jerry came bouncing on from the other side of the stage, stamping his feet, waving his hands and screaming, 'You can't do that! You can't *do* this without me, you stupid *putz*, you don't know how to work without me.' They fell into each other's arms then proceeded to perform a brilliantly funny off-the-cuff act.

Jerry Lewis was a tireless organizer for a muscular dystrophy charity. Every year he hosted a telethon and would cajole as many stars as he could to take part. He raised millions of dollars for this cause and was justifiably proud: one year he took a full page ad in the trade papers, which showed a photo of him with his arm around a seriously handicapped child and a banner headline saying, 'Thanks, Jerry Lewis.'

Everybody was moved by his dedication except for Dino who grumbled: 'He only does it for publicity. He doesn't really give a hoot about the kids.'

It was one of the few times I saw Dean's bitter side. He used to pretend he didn't like work, that he would rather be on the golf course or knocking back booze, but I think he loved it. He hit the bottle with a vengeance when the offers stopped coming, which is what finally, and sadly, destroyed him.

The Opposite Sex, a remake of the successful 1930s movie *The Women*, by Claire Booth Luce, was feline jungle warfare in the drawing rooms, boudoirs and beauty salons of New York café society. A Technicolor extravaganza, it glorified all women's worst excesses: gossip, shopping, bitchiness and husband-stealing. The original had starred Norma Shearer, Rosalind Russell, and Joan Crawford as the arch-bitch Crystal Allen. This was to be my third Hollywood film, and MGM had borrowed me from Fox to play that role. I was thrilled to be working at Metro, as it had always been the greatest movie studio of them all.

Joan Crawford had been the quintessential Hollywood glamour queen. A bold, bad broad, whom men desired yet who filled them with terror, and whom women were convinced would ensnare their men with her charms. Crawford had been about thirty-five when she played Crystal, had been a star for years, had married three times, made dozens of films and was a cinematic force to be reckoned with as the embodiment of glamour, steely strength and sensual sexuality. I was twenty-one, had been married merely once, and was still naïve in the ways of the world. My cheeks were chubby with puppy fat, although my figure was considered good. As the predatory show-girl Crystal, I had some sensational Helen Rose costumes, ravishing, tiny-waisted, boned to a T but hellish to wear. (Years later New York designer Isaac Mizrahi told me that he'd taken inspiration for some of his evening gowns from watching *The Opposite Sex*. This movie is shown on television with monotonous regularity and I cringe when I see how moon-faced I looked, and how slim my waist was.)

The producers were determined that this remake would have a similarly illustrious cast, and June Allyson, America's favourite girl-next-door, played Norma Shearer's role, Ann Sheridan, the original 'oomph' girl, was the broad with a heart, alongside Agnes Moorehead, Dolores Gray and Ann Miller, MGM's favourite resident tap dancer. Hollywood's joke about Annie was that she wore so much lacquer, that if she ever fell over her hair would break.

An unknown Leslie Nielsen played June's philandering husband, over whom she and I had to fight. He was a laid-back, rather ordinary-looking thirty-year-old, who seemed an odd choice for this coveted role. He was supposed to be sexually ensnared by the cunning Crystal yet in our scenes together he behaved with complete indifference.

I performed a couple of production numbers, one with comedian Dick Shawn, in which I mainly swung my hips around in a white crystal-beaded sheath and slinked my way down the stairs looking as *baaad* as possible – watched with jealous eyes by June. In her mid-thirties, June had been an MGM star for many years, and still featured the short girlie hair-cut and innocent-looking Peter Pan-collared frocks for which she had always been known. Hers was the antithesis of my part, which was the first of the contemporary evil vixens that I have played.

June had been in a terrible state about having to slap me when her character discovers that mine is bonking Steven, her husband. The scene takes place backstage in Crystal's dressing room as I am wriggling out of my beaded number to reveal a black lace low-cut Merry Widow.

'If you're dressing for Steven I wouldn't wear anything *quite* so obvious,' she sneers.

To which I retort pointedly, 'When Steven doesn't like what I wear –
I take it off.' Here, June was supposed to smack my face hard, and every
time she said the line I tensed for the blow but in each take she stopped
before the slap and wailed, 'I can't *do* it. I just *can't* hit Joan. I'm scared
I'll hurt her.'

'For Christ's *sake*, June,' barked our irascible director David Miller,
who was not known for his patience, 'go ahead and *slug* her. She can take
it, she's tough, aren't you, honey?'

I nodded tentatively. I loathed physical violence and I'd never been
hit by anyone, but this was acting and there was no way I could call for a
stunt double. Four times we shot it and four times June stopped short of
belting me. Then, on the fifth take, Miss Goody Two-Shoes hauled back
her tiny fist and socked it to me baby. I felt like I'd been hit by a two-ton
truck. I staggered backwards and, hearing my earrings clank to the floor,
I was half convinced they were my two front teeth. My face felt as though
a brick shit-house had fallen on it from a great height and I collapsed into
a chair and burst into tears. June, too, burst into tears, her voice rising to
a crescendo as she looked at my swelling cheek. 'Look at her face! I've
destroyed it,' she howled, then collapsed into her chair while sympathetic
minions clucked around her.

Ice-water was applied to my rapidly swelling cheek, but within five
minutes half of my face looked as though I had done five rounds with Joe
Louis.

The studio doctor announced I had a minor trauma to the left cheek
and I was whisked home to spend three days recovering.

During the making of this movie Sydney Chaplin and I came to an
amicable parting of the ways. His passion for cards and golf had eclipsed
his passion for me.

Carolyn Jones, who played Crystal's best friend, was a cute, perky
New York comedienne, who found greater fame a decade later playing
Morticia in the TV series *The Addams Family*. She was living with a slight
aspiring actor called Aaron Spelling. He had recently done his Army
service, but loathed air-travel and could never understand why I was so
keen on planes. I was always gaily flying somewhere – London, Las Vegas,
New York or Acapulco – jet-set was my middle name, 'Come Fly With

Me' my favourite song. Whenever I was with Carolyn and Aaron at their Sunset Boulevard apartment and mentioned that I was off on an other trip, Aaron would shiver and look scared.

'Why does Aaron worry about flying?' I asked Carolyn.

'He has vowed he will never travel by air again,' she said.

'Why?' I asked.

'When he was in the Army, the plane he was supposed to go on manoeuvres with crashed, killing everyone on board. Ever since then he's refused to fly.'

I could understand his phobia – and twenty-five years later when we were making *Dynasty*, he still had the same problem, and hadn't been on an aeroplane since his Army days.

When Roberto Rossellini, the distinguished Italian director and infamous lover of Ingrid Bergman, chose me to be his 'Face of Innocence' for *Sea Wife*, no one was more astonished than I. Signor Castellani had wanted me for the virgin Juliet, and now Signor Rossellini wanted me for a virgin nun. Italian directors, it seemed, saw a quality in me that English and American couldn't.

I felt some trepidation at the prospect of making this story of a young novice, wrecked on a desert island with three men – the main reason being that Biscuit, the potential lover of the nun, was to be played by Richard Burton.

I'd followed his career, worshipping at his shrine, since seeing him in *The Lady's Not For Burning*. I admired his talent, charisma and undeniable sex-appeal. He was a real 'comer', considered the natural successor to Laurence Olivier, although some sceptics were beginning to comment that he was spending too much time churning out corny Cinemascope epics and not enough time on the stage. But there was a motive in this. Burton, financially astute, was one of the first movie actors to become a Swiss resident, thus saving his salary from the clutches of the British Inland Revenue. The top rate of British tax at that time was horrendous – nineteen shillings and sixpence in the pound.

I'd just been voted the Star of Tomorrow by both *Photoplay* magazine and the Cinema Exhibitors of America, so Twentieth Century-Fox were delighted that Rossellini had chosen me. They were still giving me a big publicity build-up even though *The Virgin Queen* and *The Girl in the Red Velvet Swing* hadn't broken any box-office records.

I prepared for *Sea Wife* with zealous enthusiasm, visiting London convents and interviewing novice nuns, curious to discover how they had discovered their vocation. I studied the script, chopped off my hair and waited in London for the call that would whisk me off to Jamaica.

To my dismay, however, when the British press heard that I was playing this saint-like role, much hilarity ensued in the pages of the tabloids.

'Face of Innocence?' jeered one. 'More like the Face of the Coffee-bar Jezebel.'

When I first set foot in Jamaica it took my breath away. Gently waving palm trees, lapis-lazuli-coloured water, fine white sand and charming local inhabitants. I met Mr Burton, who was coolly charming as we sat in our hotel rooms waiting for our call to start filming. And there we waited and waited and waited. Shortly thereafter we discovered that a major impasse had arisen. In the script Sea Wife is supposed to fall in love with Biscuit, and a tender love scene naturally ensues. But when the puritanical American censors read this passage, they screamed bloody murder. 'This goes against all the moral mores of a civilized society; a nun would *never* succumb to sexual feelings. No way.'

'Then I will *not* make the film,' roared Signor Rossellini in return. Ensconced in his hotel reworking his version of the script, he was adamant. 'We *must* have the love scene. It's pivotal to the story.'

'Absolutely not,' insisted the censor.

Soon Fox's heavy brigade in suits descended on the island by the planeload to try to cajole Rossellini. But to no avail.

'If we do not have at least one kiss between Burton and Collins I will *not* direct *Sea Wife*.' Rossellini stamped a well-shod foot. 'Do you think a young girl trapped on an island with an attractive man for months on end is going to resist him – particularly if he looks like Burton?'

The Fox brass agreed among themselves, but they had to kow-tow to the omnipotent censor or the movie would not be released.

Every night in the bar at the Jamaica Inn a 'mole' gave us a blow-by-blow report of that day's dramas. Neither side would give in – and there were big bucks at stake. Meanwhile I had tons of fun with various young and jolly camera-crew members, and Mr Burton had tons of fun with various and sundry local ladies.

I'd been warned about Burton's reputation, and especially his boast that he'd bedded every one of his leading ladies. When he offered me a similar proposition I turned him down, smiling sweetly, saying, 'Sorry, darling, but I don't want to be just another notch on that well-punched belt of yours.'

Not only was he married but he was potential trouble – the sort of man who loves 'em and leaves 'em, and I've never been keen on going up *that* alley. Surprisingly, Burton was annoyed, and remained cool towards me throughout shooting.

Actually, Richard Burton didn't look nearly as good in life as he did on stage and screen. His voice, of course, was one of the greatest this century, but his complexion was pitted and pock-marked, his lined features rather coarse, and his light brown hair thinning, but the camera does love certain people, and Burton was one of them.

Rossellini stuck to his guns, and was soon on a plane back to Rome. The 'suits' went back to LA, leaving us with a new unknown director. This, his first and last film, did *not* set the world on fire and the best thing that came out of it for me was that Burton taught me how to play a ferocious game of Scrabble.

Alec Waugh's book *Island in the Sun* was one of Darryl Zanuck's pet projects. Everyone thought interracial romance very daring in the fifties, and particularly so on the big screen. All kinds of rules and regulations had been laid down by the ever-vigilant censor as to how this touchy issue should be handled, but eventually I went off again to shoot in the West Indies, this time to Barbados.

To say that this movie fell flat would be an understatement. As Jocelyn Fleury, a rich young Barbadian girl who falls in love with a titled aristocrat, then finds out that a sixteenth of her blood is 'coloured', I was adequate – deeply tanned and fetchingly dressed by Charles Le Maire once again.

It was a starry ensemble cast: Harry Belafonte, Joan Fontaine, James

Mason, Steven Boyd, Michael Rennie, Dorothy Dandridge and John Justin wandered in and out of the movie looking as if they'd all rather be in another one. There were no big parts, and we all spent a lot of time hoping our scenes would end quickly so that we could sample more of the sun and fun of the island.

Diana Wynyard, the ladylike English actress and an Oscar nominee for *Cavalcade*, played my mother, who had a seedy secret past, Steven Boyd, the handsome Irish actor, my lover, and James Mason was my brother. He was terribly civilised, with perfect manners. Quintessentially English, he was also a little intimidating. He had played glamorous yet sinister leading men in dozens of British pictures, and his slightly villainous image shrouded him, somehow, like an aura.

However, he *was* only human, as we found out when the company was travelling one day from Trinidad to Barbados in a small propeller plane through such turbulence that everyone's breakfast was threatening to come up. We were all nervous, even the flight attendants, so I was slinging back rum punches with Steven, who considered himself a pretty good drinker and a real tough guy. He was rattled, but refused to admit it, so he and I were getting plastered to kill the fear.

James sat, unperturbed, in an aisle seat calmly reading his *Times*.

'James,' I said, 'aren't you terrified? It's so bumpy we could *crash*!'

Without glancing up James said, in his dark brown reassuring voice, 'Oh, no, my dear, I'm never frightened in planes. I fly so much, what is there to be anxious about? They're perfectly safe.' He went back to his paper, which I suddenly spotted was upside-down.

Steven and I collapsed with giggles and had to move to other seats. James's eyes were riveted to the same page throughout the whole bumpy ride and his hands were clutching it so tightly that his knuckles were ivory white.

I fell totally in love with Barbados – so much so that, when it was time to leave, the production manager had literally to drag me out of the sea at dawn after an all-night party. On the plane I wept all the way back to New York, thinking I could never adore anywhere again as much as I loved that beautiful island.

Stopover Tokyo was yet another Cinemascope clinker for Twentieth Century-Fox. It was based on one of John P. Marquand's successful Mr Moto novels, and although it retained the plot, the Japanese sleuth was replaced by a couple of American private eyes straight out of a TV crime series played by Robert Wagner and Edmund O'Brien. It was a real B picture. B for boring, that is. The characters were stolid, the direction and action half-baked, so RJ and I nicknamed it *Stopover Acting*. To me, the most interesting thing about visiting Japan was that I could observe at first hand the immense cultural abyss between the Japanese and Westerners. I know that it has changed tremendously since then, but, at the time, I found the excessive male dominance and the female deference towards them quite alarming.

Fox were planning a comedy called *Rally Round the Flag, Boys*, to be directed by Leo McCarey. The studio wanted Jayne Mansfield to play Angela the vamp, but my great friends Paul Newman and Joanne Woodward wanted me. They petitioned Darryl Zanuck, Spyros Skouras and Buddy Adler but Adler was adamant. 'No way. Joan Collins is a brunette and brunettes aren't funny. Jayne Mansfield is a blonde and they *are*.'

His logic was beyond me but Paul and Joanne wouldn't give up. 'Joan *is* funny,' they argued. 'She's very amusing. You should see her at parties.' The Newmans were so insistent that eventually Fox capitulated and reluctantly gave me the part.

One day Paul and I played a scene in which we both had to appear roaring drunk. 'Jimmy would've gotten completely loaded for this.' Paul was referring to James Dean, a staunch Method actor. 'He did in *Giant*.' But since Paul and I weren't actually of the Stanislavsky School in which an actor actually *gets* drunk if the character is supposed to be, we faked it. We hung from the chandeliers, screaming with drunken laughter, our faces stuck in rictus grins. At one point when we'd collapsed on to the carpet, I raised myself on hands and knees so that my bottom was almost in his face. Paul shrieked: 'Why Angela, I'd know that face anywhere!' We collapsed in genuine laughter, which we couldn't control until Leo McCarey barked at us: 'Shape up, kids, and stop all this laughing crap. We're makin' a *comedy* here, for Chrissakes!'

When we finally lurched off the set, hiccuping and hysterical, some of the crew whispered that we actually *had* been hitting the bottle. So much for all that Method nonsense. The drunk scene turned out rather well and I was happy with my performance and the movie.

Rally Round the Flag, Boys was one of Leo McCarey's last films. I always seemed to work with old-time directors – Howard Hawks, Henry Kosher, Henry Hathaway and others, on their last films, but it was terrific working with the Newmans, who were, and still are, one of the happiest married couples I know. I don't think, immodestly, that Jayne Mansfield could have played my part any better.

In 1958 I was excited to be asked to present the Oscar for Best Cinematography. I went with Paul and Joanne and Arthur Loew Jnr. Joanne had been nominated for best performance by an actress in *The Three Faces of Eve* but as she was quite a frugal gal she'd decided that instead of buying a new dress she would make her own. She beavered away at it between takes and it turned out to be quite a work of art. She was proud of her dark green velvet dress and looked great in it when, to our immense joy, she won the Oscar. The following week, a museum in her home town asked its first native Oscar winner to donate the gown to its collection. Joanne adamantly refused, saying, 'I spent over a hundred dollars on the material and designed and made it all myself. I'm almost as proud of that dress as I am of the Oscar so I'm keeping them both, thank you very much.'

But that arch-bitch Joan Crawford couldn't wait to get in her snipe the following day: 'By making her own clothes Joanne Woodward sets the cause of Hollywood glamour back twenty years.'

I must confess that I didn't actually make my dress for that night, although I had designed the pale pink strapless taffeta with a huge 'bell' skirt shorter in front than at the back. It was so pretty it landed me on the cover of several European magazines.

One of the highlights of the previous year's Oscar evening had been Burt Lancaster and Kirk Douglas singing a tongue-in-cheek speciality 'point' number, written by Sammy Cahn and Jimmy van Heusen, called 'It's Great Not To Be Nominated'. The lyrics poked fun at some of that year's male nominees:

> There's Marlon Brando. Hi, y'all.
> How *about* that corny Southern drawl?'

Brando, in the audience with his 'date' George Englund, found this hilarious and waved good-naturedly at them. But Anthony Franciosa wasn't nearly as sanguine when Burt and Kirk sang,

> Anthony Franciosa, you've got our vote.
> If *he* wins I'll cut my throat.

He was escorted by his wife, Shelley Winters, who chewed a fingernail and screeched with laughter.

There were a few weak rhyming jokes about Charles Laughton, Anthony Quinn and Alec Guinness and the curtain came down to wild applause. It went up again as Lancaster and Douglas did a spectacular stunt. Kirk did a handstand over Lancaster who then held him aloft in his arms while dancing off-stage with seeming ease.

The audience loved the cheeky number so much that the following year I was asked to perform a female version of it with Dana Wynter and Angela Lansbury.

Jerry Lewis introduced us and on we strutted to sing 'It's Bully Not To Be Nominated'.

Never have three women looked so out of place. Angela was in strapless satin, as was Dana, and I wore slinky gold lamé. We *looked* glamorous but the crass amateurish lyrics that we had to sing and the reactions from the actresses on the receiving end were hideously embarrassing.

The first dreadful ditty, sung by Angela, to Susan Hayward ran:

> *She* didn't let Walter Wanger down.
> I didn't even know *she* was back in town.

Susan was in the audience, smiling faintly but seeming on the verge of tears. Then Dana and I chirped:

Shirley MacLaine, a talent that's rare . . .
If you like juvenile delinquent hair.

Shirley had the grace to smile and crinkle up her nose.
Of Elizabeth Taylor, Angela had to squawk the first line, while Dana and I, not exactly the Andrews Sisters, warbled the last:

Tell me, darling, what's *she* got?
Are you kidding? what d'ya think made the roof so hot?

Taylor wasn't there but I'm sure she would have seen the appalling jokes and lyrics for what they were, good clean fun in really bad taste.
Then lastly it was poor Rosalind Russell's turn:

Roz Russell, what a *marvellous* brain,
Your *mother* could have scored as Auntie Mame!

Miss Russell looked furious and glowered at the camera. Who could blame her? Ageist jokes didn't sit well with actresses over forty in Hollywood – still don't.
We finally finished the abysmal number, sweat pouring down our satin-clad backs, and performed a sort of ghastly two-step hurly-burly-girly grind as we tottered off the stage to minimal applause. It was seriously awful material, which we shouldn't have done, but as Fox con-tractees, Dana and I had been ordered to. I can't think why Angela Lansbury agreed to do it.
For the grand finale Mitzi Gaynor pranced on singing, 'There's No Business Like Show Business'. As she launched into the second chorus, the curtain behind her rose to reveal the winners and presenters standing and joining in enthusiastically. To be singing along with Cary Grant, Ingrid Bergman, Natalie Wood, Robert Wagner, Eve Marie Saint, Maurice Chevalier, Rosalind Russell, Bob Hope, Sophia Loren and Dean Martin was exhilarating. It didn't seem *quite* so jolly when Jerry Wald sig-nalled desperately to Jerry Lewis from the wings that the show was twenty minutes short and 'to keep 'em all singing!' Jerry turned to us yelling

'Another twenty choruses, kids.' Then he grabbed Sophia Loren and started dancing with her. 'C'mon everybody *dance!*' he shrieked and obediently we each hung on to the nearest partner and got going. Some stars, like Cary Grant and Eve Marie Saint, wouldn't join in but Jerry became even more manic, clutching the microphone and screeching to the fidgety audience:

'We'd *love* to sing another three choruses, folks, so stick around 'cos we might *have* to!' Then he pushed some of the more recalcitrant celebrities into each other's arms. They shuffled round half-heartedly, looking like refugees from an Arthur Murray dance class.

The audience were so fed up by now with this boring fiasco that many started to walk out, but NBC kept the cameras rolling, trying desperately to fill the remaining minutes.

'Now we'll have a test pattern for the next hour,' said Jerry, grabbing Lionel Newman's baton and pretending to conduct the orchestra, yelling, 'I may get a bar mitzvah date out of this!'

Some stars began to slink offstage, but as I tried to edge into the wings Jerry whirled me around and began a mad tango across the stage. By this time NBC had thrown in the towel and decided that the viewers must have had enough of the dancing celebrities and put on the closing credits fifteen minutes early.

The critics, who were usually scathing about every Oscar show, panned this one unmercifully. Jerry Lewis received the worst reviews for his handling of the celebrities' dance-a-thon. One paper jeered that his behaviour was so amateur that 'it had the sweaty aroma of a combination, Lawrence Welk and Dick Clark free-for-all'.

At the post-Oscar party I breezed over to congratulate the best actor winner, my friend David Niven, and the next day was accused of sucking up to somebody more famous than myself. I was becoming accustomed to the inventions of the press, but, as Johnny Cook said next day, 'Like all publicity in Hollywood, it doesn't matter if it's good or it's bad as long as they spell your name right. They *loved* your gown so much, they're gonna put your Oscar picture on the cover of *Gente*. Coverage, kid, coverage. That's all that counts.'

With nothing better for me to do, Fox tested me three times for their epic *Cleopatra*, set to shoot in England and Rome, with Steven Boyd as Mark Antony. I knew, of course, that there was one certainty by which I could secure this plum part – the dreaded casting-couch – but I was not about to take that demeaning route. My work credo had always been to sink or swim on my own merits.

During my tests for *Cleopatra* the studio supplied me with three different actors to play Mark Antony, each one worse than the last. 'To say that he's wooden is being unkind to trees,' I remarked wearily to Whitey as he removed my extravagant Egyptian eye-paint after one particularly ghastly test. 'I'll *never* get this part, I know it.'

I worked with Jayne Mansfield the following year in *The Wayward Bus*, based on a gritty John Steinbeck novel. For some unknown reason, the studio had put an obscure French director, Victor Vicas, at the helm of this all-American movie. I played a drunken slut who runs a sleazy diner. With bags under my eyes, unkempt hair and no make-up I looked suitably ravaged, and my big solo drunk scene wasn't so bad.

Both on and off screen, Jayne Mansfield was the archetypal blonde bimbo, who knew exactly how to pout, pose and toss off a provocative remark with the saucy innuendo that guaranteed her miles of column inches. She had the kind of naughty but nice image that, in the fifties, turned men on in droves. She was actually a brunette but had been shrewd enough to realize that the addition of platinum hair to her huge bosom and tiny waist could make her a fortune.

Jayne's discovery had been as spectacular as her chest measurement. In 1952 she had upstaged Jane Russell, the current sex-symbol, by arriving at Russell's press conference beside a swimming pool. Wearing just a tiny red bikini and high heels Mansfield dived into the pool, where she cunningly ditched her bra, and surfaced topless and grinning to the hoots, whistles and applause of all the photographers. The next day Jayne's forty-inch naked bosom was plastered all over American newspapers with a 'censored' band across it. Shortly thereafter she was crowned Miss Photoflash of 1952, Miss Tomato, Miss Fire-Alarm, Miss 100% Pure and Miss Négligée.

Her films thus far had been comedies that appealed to mainly working-class audiences – *The Girl Can't Help It* and *Will Success Spoil Rock Hunter?* – so for her, too, *The Wayward Bus* was a radical change of pace. She had announced in many interviews that she was about to become a 'serious' actress, and in this film she was playing the vamp – what else? – who befriends the trucker's sluttish wife: me.

Johnny Cook wasn't a Mansfield fan. 'She's a vacuum with nipples,' he sniffed, and passed her on to one of the other publicity boys.

Shooting started on Valentine's Day and as I wanted to run through the lines for our scene I knocked on her trailer door. A chirpy voice called: 'Come on in.'

I pushed open the door to be confronted by an astounding sight: Jayne, wearing nothing but a big smile and a small bra stood in the middle of her trailer, legs akimbo, one foot on a chair. Kneeling before her, a sheepish grin on his face and a razor in his hand, was Whitey's make-up assistant, who had been liberally applying shaving foam to Jayne's crotch.

'Oh – sorry,' I stammered, and tried to back out. She looked at me impishly. 'Don't be silly, hon, why are you so shocked?'

'I didn't mean to interrupt.' I felt my face go as red as the make-up man's.

'Gee, you English, you're all *so* inhibited.' She emitted her famous tinkling, high-pitched giggle and continued to chat as though nothing was happening down south. 'Dick here is just getting me ready for a swimming-pool shoot tomorrow. Can't have those tell-tale blackies sprouting out from my teeny-weeny white bikini, can we?' She giggled again and glanced down roguishly at the flame-faced make-up man.

'I'll come back later and run lines,' I mumbled.

'I don't mind doing them now,' she beamed. 'And I'm sure Dick won't.'

'No, that's OK. No – I'll come back later,' I burbled.

'OK.' She grinned, putting down one leg and raising the other on to the chair. She was probably the most uninhibited and open person I'd ever encountered.

Before I managed to get out of the door, Jayne asked chummily, 'By the way, didja know it's Valentine's Day? How are you celebrating it tonight?'

'Oh,' I stammered, 'I don't know yet. Probably going to some party. What are you doing?'

'The usual.' She smiled sexily and licked her lips. 'Dick's trimming things into a heart-shape down there, aren't you, Dick? Mickey can't get enough of it. We both want lots more kids.'

Since I knew she already had several I wondered how much longer she was going to keep her eighteen-inch waist but then, glancing at her again, I realized that it wasn't *that* small. A tight Merry Widow had obviously done wonders for her.

'Great. Well, good for you and Mickey. OK, I'll see you later.' I backed out of the trailer and almost fell down the steps as I heard Jayne say, giggling, to Dick, 'Gee you'd've thought Joanie would be different from the rest of the British, but she's just like 'em – real uptight.'

Shooting on *Bus* was going reasonably well until one day Jayne called in sick. The assistant director rang to say that I would have to work on my day off. Jayne, he said, had fallen foul of poison ivy while doing a photographic shoot in some bushes. In fact she was shooting a layout for *Look* magazine, with the legendary photographer Milton Green, who had taken fabulous pictures of Marilyn Monroe. Since the shots were needed urgently, Jayne had decided that publicity was more important than *The Wayward Bus*, thus the outlandish excuse.

Buddy Adler was furious and rumours rumbled across the lot that Jayne would be fired, but because her last movie had done well enough at the box-office, she was kept on for a few more years as the hot blonde – if only to keep Marilyn in line.

I first met Marlon Brando at a party at Arthur Loew Jnr's hilltop house on Miller Drive. The group who bonded together at that time consisted of Paul Newman, Joanne Woodward, James Dean, Sal Mineo, Dennis Hopper, Judy and Jay Kantor – Marlon's agent – Stewart Stern, the writer of *Rebel Without a Cause*, George Englund, John Foreman, a publicist at Rogers and Cowan, and, of course, Marlon and his girlfriend of the moment. Marlon's flings lasted months, years, or sometimes minutes. He was currently involved with Rita Moreno – a fiery Puerto Rican actress who, many were convinced, would lay down her life for him – and several other actresses, including Frances Nuyen, Katy Jurado and Pier Angeli. It was easy to work out what they saw in him: he was glorious to look at and riveting to talk to. Looking at photographs of the greatest-looking film actors ever, there isn't one – with the possible exception of Cary Grant – who has ever come close to Brando's physical perfection.

Marlon did nothing to enhance his handsomeness and dressed as slobbishly as possible. It was he who started the craze for blue jeans and black leather jackets when he wore them in *The Wild One*. (This film was considered so shocking that the English censors slapped it with an X-certificate. Seeing it today it is laughable to imagine that this movie was ever thought shocking.) His torn T-shirts in *Streetcar* had started a trend, which has never ended.

Marlon's brooding, sensual looks mesmerized everyone. James Dean, nine years Marlon's junior, worshipped him to the point of adulation and every young actor in Hollywood was influenced in some way by his mystique. He was, and remains, a lord of language and his seduction techniques were unparalleled. When he had his prey within his sights he was unstoppable and irresistible.

At a party at Arthur's one night, I watched Marlon zero in on a shy teenager, new in town and evidently a virgin. Within an hour he had seduced her with his eyes, his charm, his magnificent voice, and his fund of anecdotes. Shortly thereafter he gently led her by the hand upstairs to the master bedroom, while the rest of us stared at them goggle-eyed.

The women whom Marlon conquered, and there were many, never seemed to get over him and he left behind a trail of broken hearts but also many magical memories. To be loved, even for one night, by Brando must have been an unforgettable experience, and was one that I managed to avoid – although I found him extraordinarily attractive. But men like Brando and Burton have an invisible 'Caution – proceed at your own risk' sign hanging around their necks, and although I was more than partial to a handsome face, I wasn't about to plunge in where even archangels feared to tread.

In any case, I had done that inadvertently a year later when I started a raging love affair with Marlon's closest friend, George Englund. He emulated so many of Marlon's mannerisms and expressions, and his unique way with words was so magnetic that for the first time I dropped my vow never to get involved with a married man and fell hook, line and sinker for George. I threw myself totally into the relationship. Because Marlon's current 'main-squeeze' was 'getting too heavy' he preferred to hang out with George and me and the three of us had enormous fun together. Sometimes George and Marlon would come to my tiny one-bedroom apartment on Shoreham Drive, and I'd listen to them exchange views on everything from the state of the nation to Paramount's latest stacked starlet – who was then Ursula Andress. George was twenty-eight and an up-and-coming director-producer who had recently separated from his wife Cloris. He and Marlon were planning to film *The Ugly American* and were always bouncing ideas off each other.

Marlon was an ice-cream freak, so I made sure there were always plenty of different varieties in the freezer for when he visited. Though I never saw him eating it, he'd go into the kitchen and devour several cartons of chocolate chip then return to the living room to talk. And when Marlon talked all you wanted to do was listen. His astonishing ideas were brilliant, sometimes revolutionary and always original. He had scant respect for the acting profession. 'Acting is just an expression of one person's neurotic impulse. It's a bum's life. Actors get paid for doing nothing, and it *means* nothing. It's fundamentally a childish thing to do. The actors who quit acting, *they*'re the ones who've really evolved as people.'

I asked him why, if he hated acting so much, he lived and worked in Hollywood and why he didn't go back to the New York stage. He smiled his slow, dazzling, mischievous smile and answered enigmatically, 'Money, doll, money.'

When Marlon visited my apartment, he rarely stood still. He'd wander around looking at my pictures, which were about as interesting as a five-cent stamp – since it was rented, the only decoration on the walls were some Mexican bullfight posters and family snaps – sniffing at the dried flowers, fingering the silver ashtrays from Tijuana, picking up the dime-store cushions and examining them as though they were Aubusson, and looking outside at the Sunset Boulevard traffic as he paced about, talking of everything under the sun. George and I would sit spellbound.

Marlon was an expert on practically every subject, a voracious reader with the knack of remembering everything that he'd ever read. One day I told him about the brutal rape of a girl in the Olive Drive apartment I'd recently vacated. 'That could have been me.' I shuddered. He replied jokingly, 'Rape is just an assault with a friendly weapon.' One never knew whether Marlon was serious or not, but he could certainly have been described as a cynic.

He dismissed the magazine interviewers to which Fox publicity made me commit so much time and effort as 'scavengers and slime balls', and 'our libel laws give you no protection against them. There's too much money made from gossip columns and movie magazines. It's a multi-million-dollar industrial complex and if you don't kow-tow, if you don't call them up every time you have an attack of gastro-enteritis or if you don't describe the most intimate details of your personal life, the press think you're their enemy. The bottom line is that they don't want to discuss your work, only your private life.'

Brando had recently been considered by Sam Spiegel for the title role in *Lawrence of Arabia* but as Spiegel wanted a new face, Peter O'Toole had landed this plum. Spiegel was then quoted as saying, 'When you make a star, you make a monster.' Marlon agreed with him. 'We're all monsters, of course, some of us worse than others,' he said with a huge grin.

Even though Marlon had few positive things to say about our profession, that didn't stop him beaming happily the night he accepted an Oscar from Bette Davis for his performance in *On the Waterfront*. Still growing her hair from *The Virgin Queen*, she wore a sort of jewelled space-helmet and was wreathed in smiles. She, too, succumbed to Brando's charms, for later she cooed to the press: 'Mr Brando and I have so much in common. We are both perfectionists and we have both made enemies because of it.'

That's for sure, I thought.

Brando was in excellent humour on Oscar night, clowning around with Bob Hope who pretended to wrestle the statuette away from him.

One evening the three of us were sitting on my bed, eating chocolates – to which Marlon, like me, was addicted – and watching TV. Bob Hope was entertaining the troops, as was his wont, but Marlon didn't like him one bit, and gave free vent to his feelings, even blowing a raspberry or two. He was probably one of the few Americans who felt this way, since Hope was considered a national treasure.

'Why do you dislike him so much?' I asked.

'Because he's another of what I hate most about actors, an applause junkie, and he's got to keep on filling himself up. He'd go to the opening of a phone booth in a gas station in Anaheim provided they got a camera and four people to watch him,' he sneered.

Occasionally my phone would ring late at night and some tearful voice would ask, 'Is Marlon there?' He'd shake his head *no*. The girls must have all known about each other because the columns kept tabs on his every move as, arguably, he was America's most eligible bachelor. He was finally caught by the Anglo-Indian actress Anna Kashfi and eventually married her, with Jay and Judy Kantor as best man and matron-of-honour. A few weeks later Marlon threw a party at his home on Mulholland Drive to introduce his new bride to his friends.

His Japanese-type house was furnished sparsely but eclectically in Bohemian style, and had a spectacular view of the San Fernando Valley to the north and the winking lights of Benedict Canyon to the south. American-Indian artefacts and rugs hung on the whitewashed walls; candles stood on bare natural oak tables, large multi-coloured cushions were strewn on the polished wooden floors. It was simple yet stylish. Standing around, looking slightly uncomfortable, were such luminaries as Gregory Peck, Humphrey Bogart and Merle Oberon, along with Marlon's usual cronies, Wally Cox, Christian Marquand, Sam Gilman and, of course, George Englund.

Even though she was swathed in a sari, I thought Anna Kashfi seemed like a nice English girl although she was dark and exotic. A few weeks later, though, the tabloids screamed that this dusky maiden was, in fact, an Irish colleen and not Indian at all. Marlon was far from pleased at having been so hood-winked and, not surprisingly, their marriage hit the rocks shortly afterwards.

Marlon and George both escorted me to the Broadway opening of

Harold Pinter's *The Birthday Party*. When we arrived at the theatre, the photographers went bananas, for Marlon was the biggest male movie star in the world and I was considered up and coming. Cary Grant, sitting in front of us, seemed almost as fascinated by Brando as the rest of the auditorium of sophisticated New York first-nighters who gawped at both of them. Marlon was in one of his slim phases, looking good, and when he looked good, no one looked better.

I saw Marlon a few times at various parties during the sixties and seventies but eventually we lost touch, although we've both remained close friends of George. I last saw him a few years ago at Jay Kantor's birthday party at his Beverly Hills house. I was sitting at the bar talking to John Foreman. The immediate area around us was empty as most of the guests were on the dance floor. From the corner of my eye I glimpsed a massive figure dressed in a plain grey business suit amble up to the other end of the bar and ask for a drink. There was no mistaking that voice. It was Brando, but almost unrecognizable as the gorgeous young Apollo in jeans and T-shirt who had played the bongos so wildly in my apartment. I felt embarrassed and continued talking, but soon felt Marlon's powerful gaze boring into me. Finally I glanced at him. He gave a lop-sided grin. 'Trying to pretend you don't recognize me, Joanie?' he asked endearingly, hitting the nail right on the head as usual.

'Of course not,' I lied.

He lumbered over and we hugged. 'It's good to see you, Marlon,' I said, and I meant it.

'It's good to see you too, Joanie.' He held me at arm's length, his face wreathed in a dazzling sexy smile that evoked his sunshine years. 'You looked real good on your *Playboy* cover.'

We reminisced for a while until Jay came and whisked him away. I stared sadly after his retreating bulk. Even though he must have weighed at least three hundred pounds he remained charm personified – and still had the most astonishing charisma and undeniable sex-appeal.

During my Fox years I had a series of boyfriends, of whom George was the most significant. I was mad about him – he was tall, dark, handsome and clever, but not clever enough to stop vacillating about leaving Cloris permanently. Constant reconciliations were the order of their day, and our relationship was tempestuous, to put it mildly.

After George's latest rapprochement with the wife and kiddies, I begged the studio to send me on location – anywhere. I needed to get out of town, away from LA, and get Mr Englund out of my system for good.

I knew that Fox were casting a western, *The Bravados*, which Susan Hayward had apparently turned down, so I threw on my old jeans, mussed my hair and scurried down to casting to show 'em how All-American, home-on-the-range I could look.

I was totally wrong for the role of a tough frontiers-woman whose life was only complete when she was roping a horse or striding the dusty plains but, even though horses and I are like oil and water, I still wanted to do it.

To my amazement I was cast and was told to report to Wardrobe at nine o'clock the next morning. Gregory Peck would be the leading man, and some of the other actors, Steven Boyd, Henry Silva and Albert Salmi, were already chums. Susan Hayward's costumes from her last film were altered to fit me, and we were all dispatched to the dusty Mexican location, the tiny one-horse village of Moralia. The most significant thing that happened to me on *The Bravados* was that Greg made me ride a horse, even though I was terrified of them and issued frantic protests.

My fear of the four-legged memories was exacerbated by our handler, Chuck, a weather-beaten old cowboy, who constantly assured me, 'Horses ain't never gonna hurt ya, honey. They behave real good unless they see y'all scared, then they like to show ya who's the boss.'

Well, I already *knew* who was the boss – the black stallion with the giant yellow teeth who rolled his eyes in anticipatory pleasure whenever I wandered into his sightline. I informed Henry King – another elder statesman of the cinema – that I would only do my close-up sitting on said stallion if Chuck and the other handlers would hold on tight to his hoofs. He agreed reluctantly, muttering something about 'Temperamental English hot-house roses are a friggin' pain in the ass.'

Chuck and three tobacco-chewing stalwarts each clutched a hoof, looking bored while I emoted in close-up.

'OK, cut!' yelled Henry, and I dismounted gratefully, helped by a gallant Chuck. Then, walking to my trailer, I heard a stifled yelp.

'Shit!' screamed Chuck, hopping around on one foot, face scarlet with rage. 'Shit! This motherfuckin' nag's done broke my leg.'

In spite of Chuck's agony I couldn't help falling about with laughter. The horse had kicked him on the shin which had snapped like a dried twig. So much for four-legged friendship.

I left Moralia after three months with two things out of my system for ever. Horses and George Englund.

Soon afterwards I became involved, in spite of the disapproval of some of my friends, with Shirley MacLaine's kid brother, an out-of-work young actor called Warren Beatty. Cappy Yordan, my best friend and mentor, who later married Andrea Badrutt, the owner of the Palace Hotel in St Moritz, was particularly horrified.

'Broke – no job prospects – younger than you – and SPOTS!'

But I took no notice. This was my life and it was up to me to date whom I chose. I was never bothered by a man not having any money – in fact, I preferred them not to be stinking rich, as I believed that if they could buy anything they wanted, it usually meant they thought they could buy me too.

Seven Thieves was a clumsy sixties attempt at a French *cinéma-noir* thriller. I played a stripper, spending many an entertaining hour emulating my teacher, one of the world's most famous strip-tease artistes, Candy Barr. From this fabulous blonde I learned the intricacies of how to slide off a glove or a silk stocking with tantalising allure, how to entice an audience with just the subtlest shrug of a bare shoulder and a minimal twist of the hips, and how to look sexy while wriggling out of a tight dress with panache. We rehearsed every day for hours on Fox's Stage 5, which suddenly became the male employees' favourite short-cut. Grips, gaffers, assistant directors, actors and even high-ranking producers would take a ramble through the stage to watch us strut our stuff.

I enjoyed mastering this strange, erotic art and Candy said, 'You're beginning to become quite professional at it. You could make a good living at one of Hollywood's strip-joints if you wanted to, honey.'

'No thanks, Candy,' I demurred, 'I think I'll stick to acting.'

The *Seven Thieves* strip sequences are fairly tame because most of the sexy stripping had to be cut. I started both scenes fully clothed, seductively removing a satin dress, letting down my hair, lasciviously sliding off sheer black stockings, and finally peeling off the long silk gloves. But Mr Censor decided it was much too much, and could corrupt impressionable young minds, so most of my erotic stuff was dumped on the cutting-room floor. This left me to perform just a weird tribal twist-type dance dressed in a scanty bathing suit-type costume with lace and fringe in strategic places while writhing around Eli Wallach, my partner in the 'act', playing his phallic trombone. The overt suggestiveness of me going down on his instrument seemed to have been lost on the censor. Eli was a distinguished Broadway actor, and he played his trombone with a high degree of orgiastic excitement as I bumped and ground to a frenzied climax while he sank, panting to his knees, trombone firmly clenched to his lips.

Director Henry Hathaway behaved like a Tartar to almost everyone on the set but underneath his bluster he had a marshmallow heart. Many people were frightened of him although his bark was much worse than his bite. In his sixties, tall, tough and grizzled, he'd developed a reputation for getting his films finished on time and under budget.

One day, dolled up in Charles Le Maire's slinky beaded gown, bee-hive hairdo, and a ton of fake diamonds, I was having tremendous difficulty for some reason, with my relatively simple dialogue. My co-star Rod Steiger and I were on the steps of a casino, supposedly in the South of France, and we had to play the scene in front of dozens of extras. But they always seemed to be milling about in my eyeline or looking straight at me and I was becoming flustered. Strangers' eyes when they stare can be extremely off-putting, and one of the cardinal rules of film-making is *never* make eye-contact with an actor while he's shooting unless you're doing the scene with him.

Henry wasn't thrilled with my performance so he insisted I stand behind the camera and watch him while he demonstrated how he wanted me to play it. He put one hand on his hip, tossed his head archly and minced up the Casino steps spouting my dialogue in a high but simultaneously gruff voice. It was so hilarious that the crew had to stuff their fists in their mouths.

'Right. You got that, kid?' Henry barked. '*That's* how I want it.'

'Yes, sir,' I said, and dutifully did the next take exactly as he had performed it, swaying my hips like Mae West.

He stopped me in mid-take yelling, 'Cut! *Cut*! CUT! For *Christ's* sake, cut. That was *terrible* – absolutely terrible.'

'But I did it exactly the way you showed me, Henry,' I said, wide-eyed. 'Every flounce, every nuance, even my hand on my hip like yours was.'

'For Christ's sake,' fumed Hathaway, 'I'm no *actress*!'

He could also be very caustic. While blocking a sequence in the strip-club I was supposed to greet Steiger and Edward G. Robinson at their table. I asked Henry if I could sit down in the scene.

'Why?' he growled. 'Are you tired?'

Another day during a crowd scene in the casino when the noise level was getting higher and higher, Hathaway clapped his hands and yelled:

'QUIET – and if you can't keep quiet, *shut up!*'

Edward G. Robinson was sixty-seven, a delightful man of Romanian descent. He had made an enormous impact in the thirties, playing the title role in *Little Caesar*, and had become famous and successful for his many gangster roles. He was actually gentle and kind, and loved talking about his collection of post-impressionist paintings. He was justifiably proud that he was one of the first Hollywood actors to have become interested in great art, and he was incredibly knowledgeable about it, buying and selling with acumen. He had to sell his entire collection in the early sixties due to his acrimonious divorce. The Greek shipping billionaire Stavros Niarchos bought it, including many masterpieces, among them *The Black Clock* by Cézanne, for the then unheard-of price of around three million dollars.

At thirty-five Rod Steiger was not a glamorous leading man, but he had created some unforgettable characters, particularly as Marlon Brando's corrupt brother in *On the Waterfront*. He had also given a brilliant performance as the conniving loner Judd in *Oklahoma*, and was looking forward to playing Napoleon, for which physically he was eminently suited. Short and bullish-looking, he took himself very seriously indeed and was uncomfortable playing the romantic lead in such a blatant piece of commercialism, as this was far from a 'stretch' role for him.

Rod was one of the few people I knew who could cry at the drop of a hat. Sometimes I'd tell him some tragic story that I'd read, and his eyes would fill with big fat tears that would course down his cheeks. If I made the story *really* emotional he'd almost start sobbing. He has perfected this technique to such a pitch that on TV interviews, when he has to recall his childhood or any tragedy in his life, he always starts blubbing.

I spent most of my time with a group consisting of Warren Beatty, Paul and Joanne Newman, Peter and Linda Bren, Cappy and her then husband Philip Yordan, Mort and Barbara Viner, Shirley MacLaine, Natalie Wood and Robert Wagner, Warren Cowan and Barbara Rush, Judy and Jay Kantor and John and Linda Foreman. We'd party at Minna Wallis's, Charlie Feldman's and Pamela Mason's, or we'd rave the night away at La Scala, the Luau, the Coconut Grove, Ciro's and Mocambo. One of the best parts of going to night-clubs was looking at what the other girls were wearing.

The Mocambo, my favourite, was the ultimate of glamour and sophistication. Stars were a dime a dozen and along one wall was an enormous wire-fronted cage full of hundreds of yellow canaries. They always seemed chirpy and full of life and we often wondered how they managed to survive the noisy, smoke-filled atmosphere. One night I saw a canary drop off its perch and land on the floor of the cage. Within seconds a uniformed minder appeared with a shovel to remove the tiny corpse. The canary turnover at Mocambo must have been enormous.

CHAPTER SEVEN

Joan of Arc lights

In September 1959 a prestigious event was held by Twentieth Century-Fox. It took weeks to organize and the whole studio was suffused with excitement at the forthcoming arrival of the dignitary. The man to be honoured was no less than President Nikita Khrushchev of the USSR, who was on a goodwill tour of America. Now that the Cold War seemed to be briefly thawing, Khrushchev had expressed a strong desire to see a real Hollywood studio at work so, naturally, there had been intense competition between the majors to entertain the great man.

Fox pulled out every stop to make the gala a success and, on that smoggy, sunny afternoon, practically every major star in Hollywood arrived in their Sunday best to celebrate, to see and to be seen. Even Marilyn Monroe had flown back from the Actors' Studio for this auspicious occasion. She turned up punctually, pale, wistful yet eternally sexy, wearing what, for her, was a discreetly conservative suit, with a black lace bodice over nude-coloured net, black silk skirt and jacket, slung casually over pale powdered shoulders. She whispered to a friend, 'Don't call me a has-been, I'm studying to be a serious actress.' I overheard Billy Wilder telling Jack Lemmon, 'Obviously the best way to get Marilyn to the set on time would be to hire Khrushchev as director.' My date, again, was Warren.

Just before President Khrushchev arrived everyone trooped into a theatre that had been specially constructed on one of the sound stages. There we were to see several numbers from *Can-Can*, which was currently in production. The Khrushchev party sat in a tiny gilded box, which hung precariously almost on to the stage, and watched as Shirley MacLaine,

Juliet Prowse and Barrie Chase performed a risqué but highly energetic can-can. But Warren and I were far more fascinated in watching Mr Khrushchev than the dance. His broad, Slavic face, glistening with sweat,was stretched in a lascivious, wolfish grin, as the girls threw themselves around the stage with gusto, whipping their skirts over their heads and revealing frilly white knickers. Mrs Khrushchev's reaction to this Western depravity was to stare po-faced at Shirley and co, her lumpy peasant features totally out of place in this milieu. When the girls got on their backs with their legs up in the air and opened them wide, right in front of Mr and Mrs Khrushchev, I thought that the old girl would get up and leave but the President grinned even more hugely despite the glowers of his consort.

Also in the box were Fox President Spyros Skouros, Henry Cabot Lodge, Eric Johnson, Buddy Adler and his wife, former actress Anita Louise. It looked so rickety that I thought it was going to collapse at any moment on top of the dancers.

Then Frank Sinatra sang and Mrs Khrushchev finally allowed herself a thin smile while her husband stifled a yawn. At the end of the show, all the stars of *Can-Can* lined up to be introduced – Maurice Chevalier, Louis Jourdan, Shirley and Sinatra, along with a select few of Fox's more stellar performers. Khrushchev had a few words with Shirley, who told Warren and me later that she had asked him what he thought of the can-can. He had said to her in Russian – simultaneously translated – in a shocked low voice, 'Humanity's face is more beautiful than its backside.'

We all howled with laughter. 'The old goat looked like he wanted to eat you up,' I said.

But the star whom Khrushchev spent most time chatting up was, not surprisingly, Marilyn Monroe. His face literally shone as he leered at her while she adopted her most alluring little-girl-lost expression.

For the lunch, five-hundred-plus stars, producers, cameramen, directors and writers gathered on the sound stage, which was decorated with the hammer and sickle, the American flag and table centre-pieces of red, white and blue flowers. Since America had only recently come out of her most serious anti-Communist phase, it seemed extraordinary that we were embracing so wholeheartedly the leader of her old adversary.

Then, as the company assembled, a voice screeched over the loud-speaker: 'Please do not touch your food until Premier Khrushchev and his party are seated.' Then in strutted Khrushchev and the band struck up 'The Star-Spangled Banner', to which everyone sang along patriotically. Then we heard the Russian national anthem, to which no one sang except the Khrushchev party and Spyros Skouros.

Mrs Khrushchev sat between Bob Hope and Skouros and managed to look as though she was enjoying herself. After lunch, Khrushchev made an animated, obviously political speech in Russian, which no one except Natalie Wood, who spoke fluent Russian, could understand. He kept banging his fist on the table and some of the guests at his table looked concerned. 'This might start the Cold War all over again,' I whispered to Warren.

Then Skouros took the microphone and announced that Walt Disney had informed him that he didn't think it was safe for Mr Khrushchev to take his family to Disneyland that afternoon as unfortunately he couldn't guarantee their safety!

As coffee was being served, Skouros toasted our guests. 'Look at me, sir. I was once a poor Greek shepherd, and now I'm the boss of thirty-five thousand employees. That's America, Mr Khrushchev.'

Not to be outdone, Khrushchev stood and raised his glass. 'I was once a poor Ukrainian shepherd,' he boomed, 'and today I'm the boss of two hundred million citizens. That's the USSR, Mr Skouros!'

Afterwards there was great speculation as to what Marilyn had said to Khrushchev. Later, Whitey told me that before lunch Marilyn had asked Natalie Wood to teach her a couple of words of Russian. They had been well chosen, and, in that breathy little-girl whisper, they must have made the old man's trip worthwhile: 'We, the workers at Twentieth Century-Fox, rejoice that you have come to visit our studio and our great country. Thank you, Mr Khrushchev.'

I'd occasionally dated Gardner McKay, an actor whom *Life* magazine had recently voted 'the handsomest man in the world'. He wanted me to do an episode of the television series in which he was starring, but when I asked Lew Shrieber, the head of talent, for permission he shrieked,

'TV? You must be kidding – you're a movie star, kid, you *can't* do TV. It'll *kill* you in the business.'

'But why?' I asked. 'In England an actor's considered an actor, whether he does stage, films or radio.'

'Listen, kid.' Lew adopted the patronizing avuncular manner he used with recalcitrant contract artists. 'TV is just a flash in the pan. Yeah, I *know* it's been around a while, but in the final analysis the public knows what it wants and they want *movies* and movie stars – Gable, Turner, Monroe. You don't see *them* in everyone's living room, for Christ's sake. And you're *not* going to see one of Fox's stars on that shitty little screen – *ever.*'

I bowed to his superior knowledge, bade goodbye to my TV career and went back to being a good little contractee again.

I'd now been on suspension several times because I had become disenchanted with the roles I'd been playing, and at the beginning of 1960 Fox gave me yet another script that I thought was dire. However, I couldn't afford another suspension, so I hit on a rather cunning plan.

Big River, Big Man was a turn-of-the-century Western epic, in which I would play another plain-talking frontiers-woman, all scrubbed face, simple peasant clothes, artlessly coiffed and made-up. But, of course, this was still the age of glamour so my character was supposed to look ravishing and slender as well. The studio were so keen for their stars to be svelte that they employed a specialist diet doctor who would prescribe sinister green and white pills which would have killed even King Kong's appetite. When I first arrived at Fox I was about nine stone and they insisted I lose seven pounds *immediately* as the camera adds at least that much. Although I didn't eat a lot, Siegel prescribed a course of dexedrine and, within two weeks, I was the required one hundred and eighteen pounds, my perfect weight, apparently, for the camera.

My wardrobe, make-up and costume tests for *Big River, Big Man* were coming up in two weeks, so I proceeded to go on a mad eating jag. Dolores' Drive-in on Wilshire Boulevard, where they made the most delicious triple cheeseburgers in the world, was everyone's favourite hangout. With the assistance of their legendary 'Special Zee Sauce' and double-thick chocolate milkshakes I started bingeing there twice a day in between meals. I also hit the chocolate bars in a big way, which wasn't difficult as I've always been a confirmed chocoholic. By the time Lee Garmes, the cameraman, came to shoot my test, I was pushing ten stone. My stomach and upper arms were huge, my eyes had disappeared into pads of fat, and my face had turned into a balloon. Michelin woman had nothing on me.

When Fox saw how bloated and awful I looked in the test, they gave the part to Dolores Hart who eventually gave up show business to become a nun. Did she know something I didn't?

The studio's head honcho admonished me to diet and said that if I didn't pull myself together and become more disciplined about my looks, I would be fast approaching the end of my shelf life at Fox.

'After all, you're twenty-six now.' He frowned.

I wasn't surprised. This was exactly what everyone, including my father, had warned me about. In fact, I was amazed that at twenty-six I was still around. According to the calculations of the studio hierarchy, twenty-four or -five was the usual cut-off time for nubile young actresses whose stock-in-trade was primarily their fresh youthful looks.

My immediate challenge was to lose the pounds I'd gained, for I, too, hated how I looked, but it wasn't a big problem – I just stopped eating at Dolores'.

I wanted to end my contract and go back to the theatre, but I thought Fox would never allow that. Movies were the only acceptable medium to them and anything else was demeaning.

However, I now began actively negotiating with Fox to end my contract. I wanted to take advantage of the new European ventures and the opportunities that were being offered to me there. Although Warren and I were by this time engaged, I realized he wasn't marriage material and so did he. We were right – Warren didn't marry until he was over fifty.

Much has been written about the Natalie Wood–Robert Wagner–Warren Beatty–Joan Collins interchangeable foursome; some of it is true, but much not, so I shall attempt to put the record a touch straighter.

Natalie Wood, who started her career as a child star in *Miracle on 34th Street*, had transcended the dangerous pitfalls of puberty, and had become a teenage favourite opposite James Dean in *Rebel Without a Cause* and one of the leading movie *ingénues* of the fifties. Dark and petite, she had a perfectly proportioned figure and a mischievous, gamine face. Her romances with Elvis Presley, Nicky Hilton and Robert Wagner provoked the kind of gossip that the columnists dream about.

Wagner and Wood were such a hot couple that they were forced to marry secretly in Scotsdale, Arizona, where the church doors were barred to ensure that a frenzy wouldn't break out among the fans or the *paparazzi*.

Natalie and I became friends shortly after I arrived in Hollywood. By a strange coincidence we often dated the same men – Nicky Hilton, Arthur Loew, Dennis Hopper, Bob Neal and others – and Natalie was gregarious, fun-loving and always ready for an adventure. We became even closer after she married my old partner from the *Lord Vanity* test, Robert Wagner.

Warren, the Wagners and I used to spend a great deal of time together, going to restaurants, playing poker and charades, night-club-bing, hitting the beach and generally having a compatible four-sided relationship. I've always found it quite rare, especially in Hollywood, for each individual in a 'couples' situation to like each other independently. Usually one of the women hates the other, or one man finds the other a crashing bore. However we all liked each other and got along like the proverbial house on fire.

A couple of years earlier I'd made *Stopover Tokyo* in Japan with RJ and the gossip mills of Hollywood had attempted to create a 'battle of the *femmes fatales*' between Natalie and myself because of RJ's and my 'affair', which was nothing but an enjoyable location flirt.

Natalie and I soon became confidantes. We shared a passion for shopping and could easily – and did – spend entire days in the depart-ment stores and fashionable boutiques of Rodeo Drive and Sunset Boulevard, and hours discussing the latest fashion trends. Natalie was a real girl's girl as well as being a popular guy's girl. She liked nothing better than a detailed discussion of diets, make-up and hairstyles, as well as serious gossip sessions. She was the perfect girlfriend.

I'd always been a profligate spender, although, at $2,500 a week, I was not earning nearly as much money as Mr and Mrs Wagner. Even when I was on suspension and not making any money at all, we didn't cut down on our sojourns at Saks.

By the time Warren was offered the male lead, opposite Natalie, in *Splendour in the Grass*, we had all grown close, and the four of us travelled together to the New York location where Warren and I had rented Joanne Woodward and Paul Newman's Fifth Avenue apartment.

RJ and I visited the *Splendour* location on the first day, to watch the genius director Elia Kazan work his magic. After two days I was bored with hanging around the set and threw myself into learning Italian at Berlitz, before leaving for Rome to make a Biblical sex-and-sandals stinker called *Esther and the King*. I had to do this picture because I simply couldn't afford not to. I'd turned down *Sons and Lovers* and spent the entire three-month period of that movie's shooting on suspension. What was galling was that *Sons and Lovers* was a wonderful film, and Mary Ure, who played the role I'd been offered, won the Oscar for best supporting actress. RJ went to the set of *Splendour* every day because, although Warren and I were officially engaged, and he'd given me a golden globule of a ring, studded with pearls and diamonds, to prove it, RJ was wary of Warren's sexual charisma.

I believe that Warren and Natalie developed a mutual crush while filming *Splendour*, and perhaps had a brief fling but, contrary to public speculation, their relationship wasn't serious until *after* he and I had broken off our engagement, and certainly long after the cameras stopped rolling on *Splendour*.

Things happen on location between actors and actresses which they would never dream of allowing if they were living in their own home base. Most actors are romantic, and far more good-looking and appealing than average. Couple this with being thrown into constant communication with each other on the set, and it's no wonder many succumb to away-from-home romance. Also, actors always see each other at their best, made-up and beautifully groomed for the cameras, so it's no wonder many fall for each other on location. But these flirtations or romances always have a dreamlike quality, as though it isn't really happening, and an intelligent actor usually knows subconsciously that when the director calls the final cut, he or she will return to their partner and loved ones and continue as before. Which is exactly what the Wagners and Warren and I did after shooting finished on *Splendour*.

Years later, Natalie confided that after she and Warren had lived together for eighteen months, their romance came to a ghastly end one night at Chasen's. Surrounded by such renowned figures as Alfred Hitchcock, the James Stewarts and the Gregory Pecks, Warren excused himself half-way through dinner to go to the men's room. He never returned. 'There was a rumour that he went off with the hat-check girl,' said Natalie, 'but, of course, he never admitted it. He just disappeared and I didn't hear from him until he turned up at my house a week later to pick up his stuff. But he was too late.' She laughed. 'I'd thrown *everything* into the incinerator.'

I'd often admired Natalie's signature thick gold bracelet, which she always wore on her left wrist. When I asked her why, she said, 'Because my wrist looks deformed.' She took off the bracelet to show me but I couldn't see any abnormality other than that the wristbone was minutely bigger than its twin. But Natalie was such a perfectionist that she believed this to be a major flaw.

I loved hearing her infectious laugh over the telephone. 'Hi – it's me, Nat, can you talk?' and our chats went on for hours, even across continents.

She had been so desperate to shed the moppet image that haunted her from *Miracle on 34th Street* that she admitted, 'I would have done *anything* to get the lead in *Rebel Without a Cause*.'

'Even sleep with the director?' I asked.

'Absolutely, and not just once.'

'Wasn't Nicholas Ray about thirty years older than you?'

'Yeah, but that was hardly a Hollywood secret.' She giggled. 'I tested twice but I still hadn't gotten the role. Then one night Dennis [Hopper] and I got into a car smash on Sunset and we were hauled off to the police station. We were so shook up and scared that I called Nick to come bail us out. When he saw how cut up, bruised, bandaged and way the worse for booze we looked, he said, "Right, honey. You've got the part. You look just like her."'

Natalie giggled again. 'You know, I guess there are *some* advantages to the casting-couch, but *looking* the part is still always the key.'

I thought the script for *Esther and the King* was one of the most appalling I'd ever read but I was now committed. Fox insisted that I leave for Rome immediately, so off I went back to my favourite city, to make what turned out to be my final film for Fox, and far and away the worst. The best thing about *Esther and the King* was that I became close enough to a young Italian actor, Gabriele Tinti, to become reasonably fluent in Italian.

The following year Warren and I went to Rome. He was starring as an Italian gigolo opposite Vivien Leigh, who played a middle-aged, lonely and abandoned American widow who goes to Rome to pick up the pieces of her life but, instead, is picked up by a handsome young stud. *The Roman Spring of Mrs Stone* was adapted from a Tennessee Williams story, and it was considered a brave move indeed for Vivien Leigh to play the role of the widow.

At forty-seven her great beauty seemed to have all but deserted her, and in many ways her character in the movie seemed to echo her own life. I was thrilled finally to meet this icon but when I did I was deeply disappointed. The powerful images of Scarlett O'Hara, Cleopatra, Lady Hamilton and Sabina were still etched in my mind and I was unprepared for this thin, quirky, papery-skinned lady, who chain-smoked and had ugly hands.

I met her before shooting started at a party at Peter Glenville's flat. Her greeting to me was perfunctory, but I'd become accustomed to the frequent coldness of older actresses towards pretty younger ones. Having shaken the hands of Marlene Dietrich, Bette Davis, Joan Fontaine, and the terrifying Joan Crawford, I was well aware of the jealousy that youth can often inspire in the middle-aged.

Vivien Leigh was wearing an elegant black dress from Balmain, which accentuated her tiny waist. Her hair was beautifully coiffed, although the style was rather old-fashioned and matronly, and she wore some pretty but discreet pearl and diamond jewellery. She held court in an armchair surrounded by admirers, in particular Jack Merivale, her current number-one beau. She and Laurence Olivier had recently divorced after some twenty years of marriage. Rumours abounded that Vivien always liked to have a romance or at least a flirtation with her current leading man so I clung to the arm of my fiancé perhaps rather more tightly than necessary.

The new London designs were all the rage for the young and I was wearing a rather avant-garde trouser suit. Vivien looked dismissively at me and my outfit. In a biography of her she is quoted as having said, 'Joan Collins was not to my liking at all.' But Warren was quite another kettle of cannelloni, and Vivien took to him with a vengeance. He looked dashing in his sharply tailored Italian suit, and the black-dyed hair and dark tan make-up suited him. He had quickly adopted the manners, mode and accent of a charming young Italian, and had told me he had to endear himself to Vivien. I didn't realize that he meant both on and off the screen.

I sat on the set in Rome one day, watching Warren play a scene in which he has to enter Mrs Stone's drawing room, push her roughly aside then admire himself in the mirror. Warren had been worried that this might make his character seem too unsympathetic, so he didn't shove Vivien roughly enough. After each take the director, Jose Quintero, yelled, 'Cut!' then insisted, 'Do it again, Warren, but do it rougher this time.'

By the time Warren had half-heartedly pushed her several times Vivien retired to her chair, lit another of her interminable cigarettes and remarked *sotto voce* to her hairdresser, 'If that fool doesn't get it right the next fucking time, I'm getting the hell out of here.'

Jose had a few tough words with Warren who, gritting his teeth, finally pushed Vivien against the wall so hard that she almost went through it.

I returned to London while the shooting continued in Rome. My mother was gravely ill and we were all desperately worried about her. She had been diagnosed with cancer, but Daddy was adamant that the nature of her illness be kept from all our friends and acquaintances.

Stories bounded back to me that Warren and Vivien Leigh were becoming more than friends, but I was far more concerned with Mummie

Left: Trying to look sophisticated at seventeen. My agent made me pose for a new set of pictures to try to land me some serious roles.

(JOAN COLLINS)

Below: Illustrating stories about 'girls gone wrong' in women's magazines gave my modelling career a small boost.

(LESTER ARWELL/EVERYWOMAN)

Right: Playing the vicious vamp Princess Nellifer opposite Jack Hawkins in *Land of the Pharaohs*, 1955.

(BRITISH FILM INSTITUTE)

Left: Fox's first studio glamour session in the dress I wore for my twenty-first birthday and the necklace my parents gave me.

(THE KOBAL COLLECTION)

Below: If looks could kill. Bette Davis as the frighteningly intransigent Queen Elizabeth does not take a shine to her lady-in-waiting Beth Throckmorton – on or off the set of *The Virgin Queen*, 1955.

(BRITISH FILM INSTITUTE)

Right: In *The Virgin Queen*, brilliant Charles Le Maire created the beautiful costumes which seemed more 1950s than Elizabethan.

(THE KOBAL COLLECTION)

Opposite: On the red velvet swing to stardom, 20th Century-Fox, 1955.

(BRITISH FILM INSTITUTE)

Above: Backstage
Broadway bitches. As
the predatory showgirl
Crystal Allen, I
challenge June Allyson
watched by Dolores
Gray in *The Opposite
Sex*, MGM 1956.
(BRITISH FILM INSTITUTE)

Right: Early shades of
Alexis as Crystal plots
and connives in the
bubbles in *The
Opposite Sex*.
(THE KOBAL COLLECTION)

Right: My first American comedic role in *Rally Round the Flag, Boys*. I play madcap Angela who has extraordinarily vivid dreams about her past life.

(20TH CENTURY-FOX CINEMASCOPE/NATIONAL SCREEN SERVICE LTD)

Left: Fox tested me three times for *Cleopatra* but the rest is history.

(JOAN COLLINS)

Above: Jayne Mansfield and I share a telephone but not a bra size in *The Wayward Bus* (known by the crew as 'The Wayward Busts').

(PAUL KEYLOCK)

Above: Having given up acting, I'm content to bring up my babies (but still manage to have my hair done at Vidal Sassoon), Hollywood 1966.

Left: Miniskirts were at their height on location in Malta for *Can Hieronymus Merkin Ever Forget Mercy Humppe and Find True Happiness?*, 1968.

Above: The Queen's Silver Jubilee in Beverly Hills – the Brits are coming and we celebrated with unbridled patriotism (Ronald Neame, Josie Pollock, Roderick Mann, Dot Spikings, Ian Le Fresnais, Christopher Lee, David Hemmings, Evie Bricusse, Samantha Eggar, Jackie Collins, Anthony Newley, Jacqueline Bisset, me, Rod Stewart, Dudley Moore, Sir Gordon White, Judy Bryer, David Niven Jnr, Leslie Bricusse (holding Shelby Newley), Sarah Douglas, Lynn Redgrave and daughter), 1977.

(EDDIE SANDERSON)

Left: Outside the 'honey wagons' with Michael Nader on location for *Dynasty*, 1984.

(JUDY BRYER)

Above: *Dynasty* became such a rage that Morgan Fairchild and I spoofed it for our own TV special *Blondes versus Brunettes*, 1984.

(PETER C. BORSARI)

than with any damn rumours, besides which, for both Warren and me, the romance gilt was fast wearing off the gingerbread.

Around Christmas the *Roman Spring* company came to England to start shooting at Shepperton.

It was at a party at costume designer Beatrice 'Bumble' Dawson's flat that I first met Binkie Beaumont, the famed producer, entrepreneur and intimate of many British theatrical legends, from Noël Coward to Olivier and Gielgud. As we queued around the buffet table he asked, 'Have you ever considered playing Amanda in *Private Lives*, my dear?'

'Have I ever?' I answered enthusiastically. 'I was *desperate* to play Amanda when I was at RADA, but there were too many girls in our class so I only got to play the French maid.'

'In a few years, when you look older and more sophisticated, I believe you would be a perfect Amanda. Come and see me then, my dear, and we will see what we can arrange,' twinkled the fabled Binkie, as he handed me his card. This was good news indeed. Amanda was a part I'd always wanted – I adored the wilful, witty, archetypal Coward heroine.

The general consensus of those in the know was that *The Roman Spring of Mrs Stone* was the classic case of A Star Rises and A Star Dies. Warren Beatty was destined for megastardom, while Vivien Leigh, whose looks and health were rapidly fading, was unmistakably on the slide. It was tragic to observe, and I sympathized with her, although she remained cold and cutting to me whenever she got the chance. Occasionally we'd play poker on set or sometimes at Bumble's apartment, for Vivien was, like me, fiercely competitive.

Although Warren was keen to get along with everyone, he put his foot in his mouth at the wrap party. It was held at the studios on the night-club set, where the final shooting had been, with an orchestra and fairly good food and drink. Everyone came in black tie or evening dress and had to stand up and say a few words. Finally Warren rose and mumbled in his usual self-deprecating way: 'I want everyone to know that this has been one of the great events of my life. I've *loved* working with Vivien and Jose, I've *loved* being in England, and even if this movie turns out to be a bomb, it will still have been one the greatest experiences of my life.'

There was a shocked silence at his gaffe, a few giggles then some embarrassed applause. Red-faced, Warren joined me at a corner table. 'I'll never make a speech again,' he muttered.

'I don't think you should,' I said. 'It's not *exactly* your forte, darling.'

A new *Road* movie was going to be made in London. The popular series from the thirties and forties had starred Bing Crosby, Bob Hope and Dorothy Lamour. Although they were now in their sixties, Bing and Bob didn't want the middle-aged Dorothy Lamour as their leading lady in *The Road to Hong Kong* and were searching for a young, pretty comedienne to play opposite them. Mel Frank, the producer, was considering several actresses for the role.

Natalie and I plotted how I could best go about getting it.

'Why don't you just call Mel Frank and say you want the part?' asked Natalie one afternoon in her dressing room, trying on a pair of tight capri pants she had just purchased at Saks.

'That sounds so pushy,' I said. 'Why don't I get my agents to do it?'

'Agents! Hah!' she scoffed. 'They're not worth the paper they're written on. You know Mel, don't you?'

'I've met him a couple of times.'

'Go on, call him now,' she insisted. 'It's morning in London, and he'll be there.'

Mel Frank actually answered the phone himself. I swallowed hard, pushed myself for the part, and a week later, to my *utter* surprise, I was offered the role.

A few days before I left for London, Warren and I amicably ended our two-year relationship, I having realized that he wasn't husband material, and as far as I was aware, Natalie and RJ were still happily married. But not for long.

Several weeks later, RJ came to London to make *The War Lover* with Steve McQueen. Broken-hearted about his recent separation from Natalie, he and I started dating. This caused furore in the press because Natalie and Warren were publicly dating too. Bizarre headlines proliferated, like 'Natalie and Joan's Love Swap', 'Joan and Natalie Always Go For the Same Fellas'. But RJ and I were, as the song goes, just very good friends. The Natalie–Warren romance caught fire, however, and they made headlines for several years and almost became a mini 'Liz 'n' Dick'.

While I was filming in London I met my future husband and the father of my two eldest children, Anthony Newley. After Tony and I married, Natalie and I didn't see each other for several years. I was in Europe most of the time, she in America, and correspondence was never a strong suit for either of us. Then, when she married Richard Gregson and had her first child, Natasha, I visited her in her charming house in Brentwood. She had changed from the fun-loving, party-going, frivolous girl into a mature, happily married mother, who adored her baby girl. By then I had my first baby, Tara, and we went through a period of exchanging happy snapshots through the mail.

But we did have the occasional falling out. One summer we were both staying in St Tropez at the Tahiti Plage Hotel with neither our children nor our current men. We spent our mornings on the beach, the afternoons in the boutiques and the evenings at restaurants and night-clubs hanging out with Jane Fonda, Roger Vadim, Johnny Hallyday, Charles Aznavour and other Tropeziens. One night we were invited to a new open-air night-club in town. Although we were girls who liked to have fun we were also girls who weren't supposed to court trouble, so we promised each other that, whatever happened, we would not succumb to the charms of the local Lotharios but just enjoy ourselves to the hilt. In the late sixties St Tropez in July was a magical, glorious place, a hedonist's paradise, and the night-club was a palace of delights. The music was by turns wild and mellow, and the atmosphere was charged with the kind of ravishing Riviera abandon that voluptuous days spent lolling on the beach can instil in one. For the first and last time, I was persuaded to snort a line of cocaine. Not knowing the effect, and willing to try practically anything once, I immediately took to the dance-floor and uninhibitedly, for what I thought was twenty minutes but which was actually two hours, I boogied and twisted away in my own little world. When I finally returned to our table Natalie had gone, leaving me to the tender mercies of four predatory Italians with flaming libidos and the fervent belief that I was on the menu. I made a fast escape and luckily found a taxi back to the hotel. Unable to sleep because of the drug I lay in the dark fuming about Natalie's disloyalty.

We were both leaving St Tropez the next day so I knocked on her door early in the morning and confronted her. '*Why* did you *leave* me? We were *supposed* to look out for each other.'

'Well, you seemed to be having such a good time dancing with all those guys that I didn't want to interrupt,' Natalie snapped sarcastically, in her best prima donna mode.

'But you broke our pact,' I said angrily.

'You were stoned,' she said simply.

'It's the first, only and *last* time,' I yelled. 'What kind of friend *are* you?'

She stalked off without a word. We boarded the plane to London in strained silence, and didn't speak to each other for six months. I remained in England, she returned to Los Angeles, and both of us were too stubborn to be the first to pick up the phone.

Fortunately we made it up, and stayed friends until Natalie's tragic death in November 1981, by which time she was happily remarried to RJ.

Natalie had always said she hated deep water, and wouldn't even swim in the deep end of her swimming pool. She drowned, inexplicably, during the night in the dark stormy sea off the coast of Catalina near her yacht, the *Splendor*, leaving a devoted husband and three young children. She was forty-three years old.

CHAPTER EIGHT

Settling down

As the sixties flowered I had begun to think seriously about what I wanted to do with the rest of my life. After almost nine years of being an actress I was disenchanted with the film world, and the thought of marriage and motherhood suddenly seemed very appealing indeed.

I was aware that I'd probably blown my movie career but I didn't really care. *The Road to Hong Kong* had done reasonably well but I was just 'the girl', the romantic lead, but at more than thirty years younger than my co-stars, Hope and Crosby, the relationships in the movie looked foolish. *Road* was an uninspired, black and white comedy in which I duetted with Bing – not what could be described as an auspicious singing début – and traded weak gags with Bob. The film was slightly enlivened by guest appearances from Frank Sinatra, Dean Martin, Sammy Davis and Peter Sellers.

Dean and Frank filmed for one day only, dressed as astronauts in silver foil costumes and helmets, arriving on the moon where Bob, Bing and I had been dispatched by wicked Robert Morley. Dean and Frank grab hold of me in turn, try to smooch and pull me violently from one to another while Bob and Bing look aggrieved. It was hard not to giggle because Dean and Frank were so full of pranks that they even succeeded in making the usually taciturn Crosby crack a reluctant smile. After shooting Frank took everyone to dinner at the White Elephant, the current favourite show business restaurant-club in Curzon Street, where Dean and Sammy kept us all in stitches until four in the morning.

I'd spent little time around the so-called Hollywood rat-pack. I'd dined with Frank and a group of his friends at Romanoff's-on-the-Rocks in Palm Springs, and been to parties at his house where I was amused to note that the only music played were Sinatra records. If you went to the Sinatra compound for dinner, you had to be prepared to stay awake and party all night. Early bedtime was not Frank's style.

I was living back at my parents' home at Harley House while making *The Road to Hong Kong*. Mummie was recovering from her operation, although we were all worried that she wasn't getting significantly better. But, as was the way in our family, nobody discussed it, and everyone pretended that everything was fine.

One morning Mummie came into my bedroom, a big smile on her face, the telephone in her hand. 'Guess who's on the telephone for you?' She sounded excited.

'I can't imagine, Mummie.' I was in my usual rush, trying to get ready for work.

'Frank Sinatra,' she hissed, in a pleased whisper. 'I wonder why he's calling you?'

I shrugged and plugged in the telephone and Mummie left the room, a small smile playing on her lips.

'Hello, this is Joan,' I said.

'Hi,' came the voice that had thrilled countless millions and still retained a pitch to melt icebergs. 'It's Francis. How're ya doing?'

'Oh, fine, thank you,' I chirped, in my English-schoolgirl voice. 'Just fine.'

'Good, good. Glad to hear it. Well, then – how'd ya like to have dinner with me Thursday night?'

'Oh, I think I'd like that very much,' I answered truthfully, wondering if I was being too hasty in my over-eager reply. I'd been dating Tony Newley but we were not yet at the serious stage.

'Okay, I'll send my plane for you.' Sinatra's voice now sounded briskly matter-of-fact.

'You'll send your *what*?' Mine rose several octaves.

'My plane.' There was a long pause. 'What's the matter?' he asked. 'Don't you like flying?'

'Oh, yes, I love flying,' I said. 'But – your plane? I don't understand. Where *are* you?'

'In Hamburg,' he answered brusquely.

'*Hamburg?* Oh, but I can't possibly go to *Hamburg*, I have an early call on Friday and I wouldn't get back in time for work.'

There was another ominous silence. Then Sinatra said, in a tone not to be argued with, 'I'll *change* your call.'

'Wh-what?' I stuttered.

'Mel Frank's a pal of mine. I'll tell him to change your call.'

'Oh, but – but – but –' I stammered, 'you – you can't do that. Mel will be angry with me and – I'm a *serious* actress. You can't just change my early call because of wanting to have din—'

There was a click and the line went dead. I stared at the receiver in astonishment. Had Frank Sinatra really hung up on me? I'd heard that he didn't like people to refuse him, and if 'people' happened to be a pretty girl he became even more offended. My stand-in or 'girl' told me she'd dropped *everything* at any hour of the day or night to meet Frank for fun and games. But, what the hell? Who wanted to go to Hamburg anyway?

Tony Newley was talented, successful and the hottest young man in town when I first saw him in *Stop the World I Want to Get Off*, which he'd written with Leslie Bricusse. The *enfant terrible* of the English theatre, Tony was the talk of London – and rightly so. He was the Renaissance man of entertainment – writing, singing, acting and directing, and doing it all brilliantly.

Born in Hackney, London, Tony had become a popular child star in the forties: he had been a memorable Artful Dodger in David Lean's *Oliver Twist* with Alec Guinness; the schoolboy opposite Roger Livesey in *Vice Versa*; and had had parts in several low-budget family films. Then in the fifties he became a pop star with hits like 'If I Say I Love You Do Ya Mind?' and 'De Dum De Dum De Dum', then wrote and starred in a cult TV show called *The Small World of Gurney Slade*. Now in his late twenties, sexy and good-looking, he lived with his mother Grace in a small flat in Kensington. He was – still is – very close to her. She had gone through a terrible time when she gave birth to Tony. In the thirties an illegitimate child was considered a terrible scandal, and poor Grace had suffered grievously for her 'sin'.

But this was now the swinging sixties and no one gave a fig for those old-hat rules any more. After several tumultuous months of on-and-off romance Tony and I decided to marry. He was still married to his first wife, although they were separated and, as a one-time matrimonial loser, I wasn't keen to make another mistake so we didn't immediately fix a date, although I was feeling distinctly broody.

One afternoon Tony and I were strolling around Harrods when a familiar voice hailed us. It was Sean Connery, who had just been signed to play James Bond in *Dr No*.

'Congratulations,' Tony said. 'You'll be great and I'm sure the film's going to be wonderful.'

'Oh, it'll be just another job.' Sean shrugged. 'Then I'll be waiting for the phone to ring again as usual.'

The three of us nodded knowingly – we all knew what it was like to wait agonizingly for the phone to ring, and the occasional euphoria when your agent announced that someone actually wanted to hire you. We hadn't an inkling that *Dr No* would be only the first of a series that was destined to become the most popular of all time, catapulting Sean to stratospheric stardom.

Tony and I married in 1963 in New York. His best man was his closest friend, actor Michael Lipton, and my matron-of-honour was my best friend Cappy Badrutt. Being with Cappy was like drinking champagne on an empty stomach. An international jet-setter, she was equally at home gabbling in English, Spanish or Arabic. A great beauty, she was like an older sister to me, and I subsequently based the style and sophistication of *Dynasty*'s Alexis on the delicious Cappy.

Tara Cynara Newley was born in October that year, and less than two years later our son, Alexander 'Sacha' Anthony Newley, appeared.

I embraced marriage and motherhood exuberantly. With several relationships behind me, I considered myself mature enough now to be a successful wife and mother; with two adorable children the delights of acting were dismissed. The new-found delights of nappy-changing, formula-making and pram-pushing became my passion, because Tara and Sacha were two of the most gorgeous babies in the world. I spent hours photographing their every move. Motherhood was an exciting but exhausting experience and I loved every minute of it. I wouldn't hire a nanny with Tara, preferring to look after her myself, carrying her around wherever I went.

I only made one film when she was a baby – *La Conguintura* in Italy with Vittorio Gassman – purely for the money and to keep my hand in.

My deep and abiding regret is that Mummie never saw my children. She had died peacefully in her sleep, eighteen months before Tara was born. Only in her mid-fifties, she was still beautiful, graceful and protective with that wonderful infectious sense of fun that endeared her to everyone.

Elsa Collins was an exceptional woman and they don't make them like her any more. Like many adult children I regret that I didn't really appreciate her enough until after her death. Hopefully, somehow, she realizes this.

Throughout the sixties Tony, Tara, Sacha and myself became true gypsies – Gulliver had nothing on our travels. Tony's career had taken off in a big way so we all played follow-my-leader. After his enormous success in England with *Stop the World* he subsequently became the toast of New York with it. Both our children were born there, which made them half-American, half-English, so we shuttled around with what appeared relative ease. I was often photographed arriving at or leaving Heathrow, dressed in the height of fashion, looking as if I hadn't a care in the world, one babe in arms and another clutching my hand.

Now that Mummie was gone, I finally felt that I was achieving what she had *really* wanted me to do. Although she'd been extremely proud of my career, she'd often told me that she wished I would marry and 'settle down'. Daddy adored his grandchildren and approved of my domestic situation, although he could never understand why we didn't put down roots in one place.

'Why are you always schlepping all over the world?' he would ask wearily. 'It exhausts me even *thinking* about your lives. In the last two years you must have been on a plane at least every three months.'

It was true. Tony and I and the children were constantly dashing about. A few months in New York, then a couple in London, and then several in Los Angeles where Tony's movie career was blossoming. Then on location to Devon while he made *Doctor Dolittle* with Rex Harrison and Samantha Eggar, off to London for interiors, then back to LA for him to make *Sweet November* with Sandy Dennis. It was such a dizzy whirl that I began to think it was even more exhausting than when *I* had been acting.

But the travelling finally began to frustrate me. I *needed* to settle down. I wanted to give my children a secure future where they could go to the same school, make friends and not feel that at any minute they were going to be moved again. In a strange way, Tara and Sacha were now living almost as Tony and I had during the war years, constant uprooting, different schools, homes and friends all the time. I knew it wasn't beneficial for them, although it did make them incredibly adaptable.

Reliable nannies were always a problem and any mother who finds a first-class one to look after her children is one lucky lady. I had a couple of trustworthy girls, but I also employed a few nightmares, so I felt more secure taking charge of my children alone. I was becoming used to people saying, 'Didn't you used to be Joan Collins?' as I wheeled a pram in either Central Park, Hyde Park, Regent's Park or down Beverly Glen wearing sensible shoes and a headscarf. I would smile sweetly and answer, 'Yes, I was, but not any more.'

When the children became old enough for proper school I put my foot down and insisted that we must settle down for their sake. Tony agreed and, now that his movie career was in top gear, we thought Hollywood was where we should pitch our tent. We bought a beautiful Beverly Hills colonial-style house on Summit Drive, and the children went to local schools. Tony's mother Grace and her husband Ron Gardner moved in and, along with with our Portuguese couple, Alice and Umberto Ferreira, we were a happy and thriving ménage.

What nobody had warned me was that 1151 Summit Drive was an unlucky house. It had been owned previously by Tony Curtis and Janet Leigh and several other couples who had separated and divorced while living there.

But these were halcyon days of laughter and fun.

We played, and played hard. Tony and I were involved with a primarily show business group in Los Angeles. Among them were Evie and Leslie Bricusse, David Hemmings, Samantha Eggar, Natalie Wood and Robert Wagner, Mart Crowley, Dyan Cannon; Asa Maynor and her husband Ed 'Kookie, lend me your comb' Burns, star of the hit series *77 Sunset Strip*; Barbra Streisand and her husband Elliott Gould; super-agents Sue Mengers and Stan Kamen; producers Freddie Fields, Arthur Jacobs and David Begelman; Mia Farrow, who was engaged to Frank Sinatra but we only saw her solo; Judy Balaban Kantor, now married to Tony Franciosa; Peter and Linda Bren, and Ronnie and Linda Buck. We met one or twice a week at each other's houses and we partied furiously. Disco and Latin-American dancing was the rage, along with the Madison and other group dances. Tony and I even bought a juke-box, which we installed in our huge front hall complete with all the latest hits.

Tara and Sacha used to love jumping around to 'Simon Smith and his Amazing Dancing Bear', as did the legendary Rudolf Nureyev and Margot Fonteyn for whom we gave a supper party after a performance of *Giselle*. Margot Fonteyn was elegant, charming and supremely ladylike while Nureyev, who had the cocky assurance of a man who had swum the Channel against a rip-tide, hovered in attendance. They were obviously extremely close to and fond of each other.

When supper was announced, it was every man for himself. I'd been warned that dancers needed to refuel after a performance so our buffet table groaned with a positive cornucopia of goodies. What I wasn't prepared for was that Nureyev, Fonteyn and a dozen of their dance troupe had the appetites of a battalion of navvies and the contents of the table disappeared in a flash, as though a swarm of locusts had flown in through my dining room windows. I stared in astonished admiration at a stick-like ballerina who was munching her way through a plate piled with enough food for ten strong men.

I dashed to the kitchen to beg the caterers to bring more food, anything they had, but they'd run out. Grace and I feverishly raided our larder and fridge and ended up putting out packets of the children's biscuits, potato crisps, odds and ends of soggy left-overs and piles of oranges. The troupe didn't care – they ate their way through every morsel of it, like a herd of goats, chattering and shrieking to each other animatedly. The Hollywoodians, who needed to watch their waistlines, looked on enviously. Is this what dancing does to you, I wondered. Soon the ballet company wandered into the hall where the juke-box was playing Sinatra's 'Come Fly With Me'. They all took eagerly to the floor, and Nureyev grabbed me and whirled me around like a teenager, jiving and bopping as expertly as if we were performing a choreographed and complicated *pas-de-deux*. We glided and pirouetted around the floor to approval from my other guests. Then, to my horror, I found myself huffing and puffing, trying to keep up with this Terpsichorean legend as he effortlessly threw me around in insouciant Fred Astaire-style.

'God I must be out of shape,' I mumbled to myself, trying to catch my breath and be more like Ginger. 'I'm only in my early thirties but I've got the stamina of a geriatric.' Nureyev had so much energy I couldn't believe that he'd just been on stage for two hours and we continued dancing till I dropped.

Tripping the light fantastic with Nureyev was as though I'd died and gone to a dancer's heaven, but I soon realized I'd better take dancing more seriously: it was obviously the key to enormous vitality.

In London I adored the Ad-Lib, Dolly's and Annabel's night-clubs and in New York Le Club, Arthur, and Ondine's, but in Hollywood there was only one place to dance the night away: the Daisy. This was the definitive sixties disco. Great music, great lighting and great-looking people. Disco fever had hit LA with a vengeance, and since most women now wore skirts so short that they often needed matching knickers, the guys thought it a sensational place to babe-watch. Most men were even more flamboyantly dressed than the girls, the current male look consisting of collar-grazing hair, masses of gold chains, a multi-coloured big-collared shirt open to the waist, wide leather belt and hipster bell-bottoms. They preened like peacocks and thought they looked fabulous and, despite some of the hideously excessive fashions, many did. Tony, not as crazy for dancing as I, liked to work at night, so I often went to the Daisy after dinner while he retired to his study to work on his blockbusting autobiographical musical movie, *Can Hieronymus Merkin Ever Forget Mercy Humppe and Find True Happiness?*.

Ronnie Buck, Tony's close friend, sought to cash in on the disco craze and suggested that a group of us open our own discothéque. 'I've found just the right place,' he enthused. 'It's an old factory on Robertson Drive – sensational place and *great* location.' Instead of the Daisy several nights a week I would be able to dance the night away at our own place *every* night. What bliss! With all that dancing I would never even need to think about diets or exercises. Just like Nureyev. I thought having our own personal disco was an absolutely fabulous idea, and eventually so did Tony, who'd said to Ronnie, 'You know those wind-up dolls? Well, I'm married to the original wind-up dancing dolly. You wind her up and she go-goes for twenty-four hours. I'll get involved so I know where to find Joanie at night.'

Plans went ahead to open the Factory, as we decided to call it, and we went into partnership with Sammy Davis Jnr, Peter Lawford, Peter Bren, director Dick Donner, Pierre Salinger – one of JFK's right-hand men, and, surprisingly enough, Paul Newman, who had not been known previously for his love of shuffling a nifty shoe.

The Factory itself had been built in 1929 and was actually a disused warehouse. It was strictly members only, and with its amazing thirty-foot-high stained-glass windows, rococo art-nouveau decorations, imposing oak furniture and extraordinary carved wooden bar complete with brass rail to rest the weary feet, it instantly became *the* place to go.

To get into the club, you entered an ancient creaking freight elevator which stopped at the first floor. The doors opened to reveal a twenties-style venue, with more Tiffany lamps suspended from the ceiling than in all the antique shops in Melrose Avenue, and an impressive glazed redwood dance-floor, which stretched a magnificent 7,500 square feet. It was the perfect place to dance the night away or chill out with friends. I was in my element, the Régine of West Hollywood, and as all the dancing had made my legs firmer, my skirts became micro-mini.

Ronnie and Tony had decided it was to be an exclusive club: 'The more exclusive and expensive the joint, the more people will want to join,' Ronnie had said sagely, and he was right. Three hundred and fifty dollars for annual membership was big money then, but it didn't deter the *crème de la crème* of Tinseltown. *Everyone* joined, and opening night was a veritable *Who's Who* of Hollywood, with Steve McQueen, Shirlee and Henry Fonda, Tony Curtis, the Billy Wilders, George Hamilton, Denise and Vincente Minnelli, Adam West, Sharon Tate, the Ray Starks, Laurence Harvey, Milton Berle, Tina Louise, Andy Williams, Judy and Tony Franciosa, Polly Bergen and Freddie Fields, Samantha Eggar, Jack Haley Jnr and, last but not least, Troy Donahue (Troy who?).

'We're a hit,' Paul announced gleefully. 'A mammoth hit. Let's have another beer.' The fact that Paul Newman was one of the owners and that he was often going to be there was catnip to the members. Paul was in charge of food. As the self-styled 'greatest barbecuer in the world', he informed Ronnie, 'You've got to buy just the right cut of cheap chuck to make the best burgers, and I'm the expert burger-maker.'

The press went mad trying to get into the Factory when they heard that Marlon Brando and Barbra Streisand were regulars – even Ingrid Bergman showed up one night. But Ronnie was adamant. No press and no punters. Every doctor, dentist, psychiatrist and shoe-salesman in LA attempted to join but were refused. It was total élitism, but it worked. We were a smash.

The Factory proved what I'd always suspected, that stars would rather be around other stars than anyone else. One enchanted night I caught Liza Minnelli staring at Barbra Streisand, Streisand staring at Loretta Young, and Young staring at Paul Newman. Stars, after all, are just people who can also be fans, just like 'civilians'.

There was tremendous anticipation when we heard that Robert Kennedy, brother of the assassinated and beloved President JFK, was going to attend a dinner at the Factory hosted by his brother-in-law Peter Lawford. I was particularly excited when Peter asked Tony and me to attend. I'd met Bobby Kennedy a few times before at friends' houses. The second time I was his dinner partner, at Andy and Claudine Williams', he had impressed me by remarking 'I loved the dress you wore last time we met.'

Incredulous, I said, 'Most men don't remember what one wore the previous *night*, and you remember what I wore over a year ago?'

'Yes. I love *point d'esprit* – especially black,' he said. 'It was a very pretty dress.'

I remarked what a fantastic memory he must have and he agreed modestly, adding that a politician needed a good memory. But his memory was uncanny. How many men even know what *point d'esprit* is?

Bobby Kennedy was immensely popular and many expected and wanted him to be the next President of the United States. Of medium height with thick sandy hair and ingenuous boyish blue eyes, he oozed bonhomie, charm, humour, intelligence and a ton of sex-appeal. He was stunningly attractive and utterly endearing. He had it all – including eleven children by his wife. But Ethel wasn't present on this glamorous night when Bobby, whose reputation for liking the ladies was well known, asked me to dance. In the eleven minutes (yes, I counted) that we were on the floor, I realized how potent were power, prestige and popularity in the United States, and how they could easily upset one's equilibrium. All I wanted was to dance with him.

Although the Factory was for members only, most of whom were celebrities or in show business, members were allowed to bring guests, and on this night many 'civilians' were present. Every five or six *seconds* some pushy jerk would tap Kennedy on the shoulder and gush how much they admired him and how they hoped he was going to be the next president. Each time Bobby would stop dancing, talk graciously to them, then turn back to me with a boyish smile and an apology. It was intensely frustrating – *I* wanted to talk to him too. I had worked with many of the world's top male stars – Gregory Peck, Richard Burton and Paul Newman – but none came close to having the amazingly charismatic aura that Bobby Kennedy exuded. There was no question that I was attracted to him and, I think, he to me. When we were walking back to the table, he implied that the dancing had been frustrating for both of us. 'Why don't you come to New York next weekend? I'll be there, we can catch up. I'd really like to see you again,' he said, with a heart-fluttering look from those guileless baby-blues.

I took a deep breath. I was a reasonably happily married mother of two. He was the Attorney-General of the United States, married with many children, possibly the future president, and one of the most important and famous men in America. This was opening up a enormous Pandora's box into which I wasn't prepared to peep. It was hugely tempting – but I shook my head and smiled. 'Thanks, Bobby, I'd love to, but I just can't. I hope you understand. But maybe I can take a rain-check?'

Always leave the door open – who'd told me that?

He squeezed my hand and gave me a long, penetrating look.

'You've got it,' he said sincerely. 'And I'll be waiting, I promise.'

Less than six months later I thought sadly about that rain-check.

I still keep on my bookshelf two black-and-white framed photographs, one of President John Kennedy inscribed, 'To Joan Collins, with my best wishes to her', which Peter Lawford gave me, and the other a memorial photograph of Bobby in a silver Tiffany frame, which was sent to me by Ethel Kennedy.

The sixties swung in Hollywood just as much as in London, but because the youth culture was a relatively new phenomenon in England it was more newsworthy there.

Certainly, at Summit Drive, things swung regularly in the Newley household. We partied with enthusiasm, our regular dinners usually ending with games or singing around the piano.

One especially memorable night in 1967, organized by Leslie Bricusse and Leonard Gershe, was attended by many of our regular friends plus Sammy Davis Jnr and Barbra Streisand. Ian Fraser played the piano, accompanying all the guests who were celebrating Tony's birthday and singing parodies of famous song lyrics. Sammy Cahn was famous for interposing his own lyrics to make witty ditties – a popular practice in Hollywood particularly on birthdays. After dinner, when we were all gathered around the piano in our huge yellow drawing room, Sammy said, 'We all know Tony's great ability as a song-writer, but tonight we're gonna sing a medley of songs Tony *didn't* write, but wishes he had.' He then launched into 'With a Little Bit of Luck' from *My Fair Lady*, singing 'with a little Ronnie Buck' instead.

I trilled, 'Daisy, Daisy, give us your members do, Aaron Spelling, Jack Haley Junior too', referring to our rival disco, to which we were still giving a run for their money.

Tony had just finished filming *Dr Dolittle* and there had been little love lost between him and the pompously irascible Rex Harrison. Rex was married to Rachel Roberts and she had never said no to a cocktail. Sammy crooned, to the tune of 'I Love Paris,'

'I love Rachel in the winter – when she's drinking;
I love Rachel in the summer – when she's stinking,
I love Rachel.
Why oh why do I love Rachel – because she isn't here.

Everyone screamed with laughter and had another drink or two.

Then to 'What Kind of Fool Am I?' Sammy sang to Tony:

What kind of fool are you,
You little Cockney Jew?

which brought the house down.

Judy Balaban Kantor Franciosa sang, 'Factory – Factory how I love ya –' to the tune of 'Mammy' and then came the *pièce de résistance*. Funny Girl herself, Barbra Streisand, sang, in that gorgeous magical voice, to the tune of 'People',

Newley – people who need Newley.
Are the luckiest people in the world.
Tony – lucky to have Joanie,
They're the luckiest people in the world.

Something in the way Tony looked at her while she was singing this made my feminine intuition kick in – 'He's fucked her – I'm sure he has!'

Tony and Sammy duetted 'After Today' and several more songs were sung, some of which were so politically incorrect that, dear reader, you cannot be party to them.

Tony had tears in his eyes as the song-fest finished and everyone was calling for him. 'This is one of the greatest nights I've ever dreamed about,' he said, then launched into 'What Kind of Fool Am I?' for which he would be forever famous.

Leslie whispered, 'It doesn't get any better than this, Jace.'

'How right you are,' I said, though still thinking of Streisand.

Tony was successful. We were young, with two beautiful children and loads of friends. It was truly the good life, and I counted my blessings fervently. But was it all too good to last?

While Tony was deeply involved in writing his new musical I started to find the days weighing heavily. My own reality had struck. Tara and Sacha were at school from eight until three in the afternoon and, after months of decorating the house, I now had nothing to do. I wasn't one of those women satisfied by the charity circuit, gossipy lunches, massages and endless shopping. Of course they were fine occasionally, but full-time they were about as appealing to me as spending a wet Wednesday in Wigan.

My agent Tom Korman called me several times. 'Look, Joanie, I've got lots of TV offers for you. You should be working. You can't just sit around in that house in Beverly Hills all day rearranging your knick-knacks.'

I knew he was right. I was becoming bored with domesticity and dancing like a dervish at night. I had too much energy – there were too many things I still wanted and needed to accomplish. I was only thirty-four. I had a lot of years left – I hoped. I'd toyed with various ideas. Decorating had been amusing for a while but it could never be my *raison d'être*. I'd always loved writing but I was still too involved with the children and didn't yet possess the necessary dedication. It was obvious what I wanted and needed to do. It was staring me in the face.

Tony and I discussed what would happen if I acted occasionally and we agreed that if I didn't go away on location, and if my work fitted in with the family's plans, I should take a stab at a career again.

'Go ahead, flower. It'll be good therapy for you. Get you out of the house.'

And get me away from the Factory and flirting and partying too, I thought. Suddenly the idea of getting back into my acting harness became extremely appealing.

I was well aware that my children would one day leave their nest. And what would I do then, I wondered. Start embroidering antimacassars or having affairs? No, my roots were calling and I needed to act.

Sometimes as Tony and I left for an evening's networking, my children would ask, 'Mummie, why are you going out again?'

And I would answer, 'Because Mummie wants to work, and I may meet a producer at the party who'll give me a job.' Being in the right place at the right time was the way it worked then, and it still does.

Within a few days Tom called. 'We've got a great part for you in an episode of *Star Trek*,' he crowed.

'*Star* what?' I asked. 'What's that?'

'Obviously you haven't been reading the trades.'

'No, I've been busy with Dr Spock and *Mother and Child Care*,' I answered flippantly. 'What's *Star Trek*?'

'Forget *Dr* Spock and start thinking *Mr* Spock,' quipped Tom. 'This series is developing a huge cult following. You *must* have seen it.' I suddenly remembered that once when Tara had been watching television I'd seen a funny-looking man with pointed ears. Other actors strutted around looking overly serious while stuffed into unflattering mustard coloured tops and too-tight trousers.

'Ah, yes, *Mr* Spock, the one with the ears,' I said.

'Right. I'll send the script over this afternoon,' said Tom. 'Read it – you'll like it.'

I thought the episode called *The City on the Edge of Forever* was quite good. I would play Edith Keeler, a saintly do-gooder who worked in a New York mission for down-and-outs in the Bowery district in the nineteen thirties. Edith was convinced that Hitler was a kind and caring sort of fellow, and because she was so appealing, intelligent and unafraid of speaking her mind, she was about to change the course of history. Somehow, single-handedly, she would persuade America, and hence the whole of Europe, to move on to Hitler's side and *he* would win the war.

There is poignancy in this story, though. Captain Kirk, played by the stalwart William Shatner, falls in love with Edith and she with him so they conduct a discreet romance. It is only when Mr Spock sees on his futuristic computerized TV what terrible damage Edith will create by changing the course of world history that he realizes she *must* be done away with. Accordingly, saintly Edith falls under an oncoming truck before things get out of control.

It seemed a slight premise but it hit the viewers' nerves. *The City on the Edge of Forever* became one of the most popular episodes ever made of *Star Trek* and is shown somewhere in the world every week.

The first day's shoot was in the mission, where Edith, sweetness emanating from every pore and complete with apron, ankle-length skirt, discreet make-up and neat hair-do, ladles soup into bowls for twenty grizzled tramps. Enter Cap'n Kirk and mysterious Spock, also dressed in shabby lumber jackets and trousers. Cap'n Kirk and Edith have eye-contact, and immediately fancy each other rotten.

Bill Shatner wasn't unattractive. Tallish, on the stocky side, he had a thatch of thick auburn hair, a mahogany tan and a cute sense of humour.

The following morning, as I lay back in the make-up chair while the hairdresser rollered my Vidal-Sassoon-cut hair, a gruff, sleepy voice from the other make-up chair said, 'Good morning, dear.' I glanced over to see a man I didn't recognize.

'Good morning,' I mumbled, closing my eyes.

'I thought our scene went quite well yesterday, didn't you?'

I looked back at the man and the penny dropped. It was Shatner himself, but he looked totally different from the tall, handsome man of yesterday. In frayed jeans and shirt, he was much shorter, whey-faced and a lot less hirsute, but his make-up was changing that, and his shoes, with three-inch lifts, would elevate him to the *de rigueur* six feet.

I smiled at Bill, he was rather a poppet, and he smiled back. But I didn't let my smile linger. I'd been warned that, like many leading men, he considered it his 'divine right' to make a pass at all his leading ladies, and he bedded as many as possible.

Although I didn't fancy him this only seemed to ignite his ardour for my screen character even more, and the passion between Edith and Captain Kirk positively sizzled.

I was amused to learn that the sexual tension on set during our love scenes was supposedly almost palpable. I even overheard some of the crew taking bets as to when and if I'd succumb to Shatner's macho charm – which I most definitely did *not*.

Star Trek was just another job, which I never realized would turn out to become such a memorable cult episode. Trekkies the world over still come up to me, saying, 'Weren't you Edith Keeler? Oh, you were terrific, but you shouldn't have died.'

Shortly after *Star Trek*, Tom called again with an offer for yet another cult series called *Batman*.

'It's in its third season and extremely popular,' said Tom. Obviously, only with morons, I mused, as I studied the script for an episode called *Ring Around the Riddler*, which was ludicrous. I would play a diva-type goddess called Lorelei Circe, a.k.a. the Siren, who uses her high-pitched voice to enslave people. Frank Gorshin played the Riddler and Peggy Ann Garner Betsy Boldface. She had been a popular child star at Twentieth-Century-Fox in the forties and starred in *A Tree Grows in Brooklyn, Jane Eyre* and many other hits. Like many ex-moppets, though, she hadn't had much career success since. We discussed the perils of our chosen profession while the hairdresser attempted to tame my enormous wig, which was probably one of the highest worn by any actress since Norma Shearer played Marie Antoinette. The two feet tall, white-gold acrylic edifice was a complicated concoction of curls, swirls and plaits and was so heavy that at the end of each day I had a severe migraine.

Adam West, who played Batman, was self-deprecatingly likeable, and desperate to break away from his type-casting. He was probably quite a good actor underneath his mask, cape and tight cod-piece, but who could tell?

During a discussion I had with him about the definition of a professional actor Adam suggested, ruefully, 'Someone who does his best when he doesn't feel like doing it, and for most of this season I haven't felt like doing it at all.'

'So what will you do when this finishes?' I asked.

'Oh, I guess I'll get another series. Although this show's a hit, how long can I go on playing a cartoon character? I have no privacy. I can't even walk in the street without people screaming and running after me for autographs.'

'Well, with this huge success as Batman you're bound to get a decent series playing a real person.'

'I hope so,' said Adam. 'But the rule of thumb is that after you finish a television series it takes at least two years to become employable again, and for the public to stop identifying you as the character you're known for.'

But sadly one of the most famous men on television didn't work for years. Becoming Batman virtually strangled Adam's career – but he didn't help himself much by making constant personal appearances as the Caped Crusader, complete with tights and pixie boots.

Although I had qualms about *Batman*, the children were so thrilled that I reluctantly agreed to a second episode called *The Wail of the Siren*. This time Mike Mazurki, a former wrestler who usually played hoods or Neanderthal types but was in reality articulate and well-read, played the lead. It's astonishing how many actors known for playing certain characters are so different in real life. Contrary to her sex-goddess image, Marilyn Monroe was shy, insecure, and naïve; Richard Burton, known for classical and romantic roles, was a down-to-earth Welsh boyo who liked nothing better than hanging out with his cronies, chasing girls, and drinking himself under the table; tough guy Humphrey Bogart was a quiet family man who loathed night-life and loved to stay home with family and friends.

At this point in my career I wasn't fully aware of how type-casting would come to haunt me. Television jobs kept rolling in and, since this was the only money I was earning, I was delighted to receive the going rate – which was $2,500 an episode.

Suddenly I was in demand on the TV circuit. David McCallum, one of my RADA contemporaries, who was making *The Man from U.N.C.L.E.,* offered me a guest role. Then in quick succession came *Policewoman* with the adorable Angie Dickinson, *Future Cop*, a stupid sci-fi stinker with Roddy McDowall, *The Bing Crosby Show* and *Run For Your Life*, a cops-and-robbers thriller with Ben Gazzara. Italian born Ben was a Method actor, which meant that to act rage he had to *be* in a rage.

This wasn't difficult for him, because he had, by his own admission, a short fuse. Many was the time the crew stood quivering on the set while Ben stalked to his dressing room, slammed the door and screamed obscenities to all and sundry in his mother tongue.

Ben was a compatriot of Tony Franciosa, now married to Judy Balaban Kantor. The Hollywood marriage merry-go-round isn't only confined to actors and actresses: it encompasses many other groups of people. Judy Balaban Kantor Franciosa was married three times and Cappy marched down the aisle four times.

So far I'd only wed twice – but storm clouds were gathering and I had a sneaky, sad suspicion that the Newley marriage was not going to stay the course. We were fast drifting apart.

With Tony's new-found cinematic success, Universal were funding him to write, direct and star in his own semi-autobiographical movie *Can Hieronymus Merkin Ever Forget Mercy Humppe and Find True Happiness?* It was to be shot in Malta, with pre-production in London, so was it just coincidence that the *Hieronymus* company offices were located in the Playboy club?

As the film was autobiographical I wanted to play the female lead, Polyester Poontang, a spoiled, wilful beauty who tames the chauvinistic polygamous Hieronymus. But Universal were lukewarm about me. I was no longer even tepid in Hollywood, and they wanted Samantha Eggar, Julie Christie or Vanessa Redgrave for the role. Even Natalie Wood, by now one of the top box-office stars in America, was approached to play Polyester but she wisely refused.

Universal developed budget problems and Polyester's part wasn't big, so after rejections from every currently popular actress, from Karen Black to Rita Tushingham, Universal reluctantly offered the part to me for the princely sum of $25,000 for three month's work. This decidedly was not a lot of money, but since I'd only made two movies in the past six years I accepted with alacrity.

Then, just before we left, another wrinkle occurred. George Jessel and Milton Berle had been cast respectively in the pivotal roles of the Grim Reaper and Good-Time Eddie Filth. Their combined salaries meant that Universal could no longer afford to pay me what they'd offered and I would have to play the role for $12,000, take it or leave it. I swallowed hard and took it. What else could I do? I had to be on the location anyway since Tony had cast Tara and Sacha as Hieronymus' children Thumbelina and Thaxted. Malta in the spring? Bound to be fun, I thought. Wrong.

Evie Bricusse, who is half Maltese, had often extolled the charms of this rocky, windy island, but during our time there, rocky and windy was the understatement of that year. Oh, the heat, the dust and the flies. A hurricane howled from the moment we arrived until the moment we left.

Much of the action of *Hieronymus* takes place on a glorious golden beach, and in many of the scenes with Tony we were emoting in a huge brass four-poster bed crunching sand between our teeth like granulated sugar.

Day after day we battled on, the wind whistling like an express train, the shifting sand getting into absolutely everything. The shooting conditions were truly appalling. It was a complete catastrophe for the cameras as the tiniest object on the lens will show up on-screen. The constant cry of 'hair in the gate – got to go again' was like a stuck record. The sand was embedded in our scalps, in our eyelashes, in our clothing. It was an itchy nightmare and there seemed no end in sight.

We were way behind schedule. In twelve weeks of shooting we'd only seen three days in which the sun shone without the damned wind, and everybody had a severe case of island fever.

Several weeks into shooting, exhausted by the elements, I trudged wearily back to the hotel, after another day of eating my hair while attempting to look beguiling on the beach. I fell on to the bed, turned on the radio, then sat up in shock. Robert Kennedy had been shot dead in Los Angeles.

I began to weep. I was far more upset by Bobby's death than I had been about his brother's assassination. While campaigning for the presidency he was assassinated in Los Angeles as he was walking through the kitchen of the Ambassador Hotel to escape the crowds. He was only thirty-eight and had had a brilliant future ahead of him. Judy Seal, Tony's secretary, who was becoming a good friend, was also distraught, so to comfort each other we went down to the Hilton bar to drown our sorrows in tequila sunrises. I was amazed that so many of our cast and crew were indifferent to the news of Bobby Kennedy's murder. The only thing that anyone seemed concerned about was the blasted movie – but, then, who could blame them? Everyone wanted out of this island.

Milton Berle was one of the bright sparks amid the gloom of exile in Malta. He had reigned supreme as America's most popular fifties television star. No Saturday night was complete without watching 'Uncle Miltie's' antics and he was the first TV superstar. As a comedian he was fearless, didn't mind making a fool of himself or embarrassing the audience. I'd adored his act which I'd seen several times in Las Vegas at the El Rancho Hotel. He only had to come onstage in drag, as one of his zany characters, put on his special 'feminine' face and audiences would be eating out of his hand. When I was a bachelor girl, Miltie and his wife Ruth would often come to my apartment to play charades, and they visited our grand Summit Drive house, too, where Tony and he formed a mutual admiration society.

One of Milton's earliest movies had been *Sun Valley Serenade*, with Betty Grable and John Payne, but he hadn't been in many films recently so he was anxious that the surreal, stylized *Hieronymus* would be a stretch for him, particularly the long speeches.

For my altercation scene with Good-Time Eddie Filth, Milton and I stood on a rock at the edge of the beach. I was dressed in a Victorian Alice-in-Wonderland full-length frock with a large white hat, starched pinafore and agonizing corset. Polyester loathed Eddie and in this scene was making no bones about it.

As usual it was like being in the eye of a tornado, and the whirling sand was building dunes in my false eyelashes and between my teeth. Milton and I were both wearing a ton of make-up, which the wind wiped off like Kleenex, and which the 'wrecking crew' had constantly to repair.

There was no problem with the first two long shots or my close-up, in which Milton was line perfect. Then came time for his close-up and he fell to bits. When Polyester said, 'Can't you see what you're doing to him?' Milton spat out his first line then dried. On the second line, he dried again, and when I said the third line he stopped.

'Sorry, folks, sorry.' He smiled endearingly. 'Wind's getting to me.'
Everyone sympathized. Three more takes later, when Milton had dried in
every one, he suddenly snapped, 'I can't play this scene properly because
Joan's looking at me so angrily.'

Wearing his sympathetic director's hat, Tony rushed up. 'Miltie, my
love, y'know she's *supposed* to look at you angrily. She hates you.'

'I know, I know, I know,' Milton said peevishly, 'but it's putting me
off. Tell her not to shout so much, and tell her to put her sunglasses on,
the sun's reflecting in her eyes.'

'Right, Joanie, put some shades on,' instructed Tony, who, doubling
as Hieronymus and our director, was wearing an archetypal Cecil B. De
Mille outfit – everything except the megaphone.

I was glad of the dark glasses as the sun was killing me. They were so
opaque that Milton now couldn't see my eyes, but he *still* dried. Take
after take, he dried and dried and dried. Expertly masking his frustration,
Tony put his arms around his friend and said, 'What's the problem,
Milton, old chap?'

'Joanie's mouth keep's moving,' he hissed. 'I can't remember my lines
with her mouth moving around like a snake.' They walked away a few
steps, whispering man-to-man. I sat in my director's chair and lit a cigarette, staring out into the stormy sea. I was boiling hot, covered in sand
and hardly able to breathe in my tight corset.

Then I heard Tony say, 'For God's sake, Milton, how can Joanie *possibly* talk without moving her lips?'

Milton whispered something back to him to which Tony listened
attentively, then ambled over looking sheepish. 'Sorry, flower, but would
you mind wiping off your lipstick? It's distracting Milton from his dialogue.'

'You've *got* to be kidding, Tony.'

'No, flower, no, I'm serious.' Apologetic, yet gently dictatorial, no
Henry Hathaway he. 'Your back's to camera so it doesn't matter.'

'No, no, of course. It doesn't matter.' The make-up girl handed me a
box of Kleenex and I wiped off the offending red splash. 'Ready when
you are, Mr De Mille.'

We started again. I was now wearing sunglasses, no lipstick, had a mouth full of sand and a corset that I was convinced was making permanent ridges in my waist. We were almost half-way through the scene when Milton went up again. Tony, patience personified, talked to him quietly. By this time my face, in front of the setting sun, was baking. The hat and sunglasses didn't protect it from the searing rays and I didn't relish third-degree burns. Weeks of shooting yet remained. I prayed that Tony wouldn't make us go again, but when he did Milton lost it once more.

Poor man, I empathized with him. Drying is one of an actor's worst nightmares – not to mention the sheer humiliation of it.

'Jeeze, Tone, I can *sense* Joan's looking angrily at me, and I can *still* see her lips moving,' said Milton waspishly. 'Can't you have her not look at me?'

'Well, it's a bit difficult, sweetheart, it won't match,' said Tony, patiently. 'If Joanie looks away from you we won't be able to edit properly.'

'Why don't you just do a close-up of Milton then I can stand behind camera, with my back to him?' I suggested, somewhat snappily through dry, cracked lips.

The assistant director whispered in Tony's ear while the crew fidgeted uncomfortably; they were fed up and far more sunburned than I. Tony nervously glanced at his watch and at the sun, which, inconsiderately, was setting.

Then Otto Heller, our genius septuagenarian director of photography, who had shot Hedy Lamarr's scandalous first film *Extase*, announced that we had less than twenty minutes of light left.

'OK, OK. All right, Otto, we'll do just a close-up of Milton. Now, Joanie, stand behind the camera. *Don't* look at Milton, keep your shades on, try not to move your lips and *don't* look angry.' Tony was in total De Mille mode now.

I obeyed, thrilled to be off-camera and not facing the sun, and we finally got the scene in the can. There were cheers from the crew and a few whistles, and Milton looked pleased with himself. Then came the dreaded words: 'Hair in the gate. Got to go again.'

The collective groan from the crew and actors was almost like a snarl, and I expected the hapless focus-puller to be lynched. We did it once more and finally I heard: 'Cut. Beautiful. Check the gate.'

'Gate's clear,' called the focus-puller thankfully and we cheered again.

Immediately Milton apologized profusely, and insisted on buying everyone a round of drinks at the hotel bar where he joked about his failure as an actor. But if he wasn't a great actor, Milton's prowess as a ladies' man in the forties and fifties was legendary: prolific rumours circulated that he was one of the best-endowed men in Hollywood.

Several years later Irving 'Swifty' Lazar, who was also supposed to be superior in that department, told me an apocryphal story. He and Milton were crossing a small bridge one night. They had both been drinking heavily and decided to relieve themselves into the river.

'Cold, this water, isn't it?' asked Swifty.

'Yeah – and deep,' answered Milton.

Because the Maltese location was so tough, Tony and I gave a party at the hotel every Saturday night. One night, standing in line at the buffet, I felt somebody hug me from behind. 'Why, Milton darling, I *knew* it was you,' I cooed.

'How did you know that, Joanie?' asked Milton.

'Why, no one else could possibly rival you down in *that* department.' I simpered, and he smirked back proudly. Milton loves this story and still tells it.

Polyester's big musical moment in *Hieronymus Merkin* was called 'Chalk and Cheese', a lavish production number in which the other performers are dressed as signs of the Zodiac.

In a burst of dramatic music, and to the crash of cymbals, the gorgeous Polyester appears as Gemini, clad in a clinging, off-the-shoulder white gown with a Grecian hair-do. (This costume was so similar to the one I had worn in *Batman* that in photographs they could have been interchangeable.) I was twirled around by the eleven other Zodiac signs, posing and posturing prettily until Libra, played by Hieronymus, a.k.a. Tony, appeared. We'd had many discussions as to what he should wear and I'd thought he was joking when he said he wanted to perform bare-assed. It wasn't a joke, though, and he appeared, stark naked except for a large key sticking out of his back. A diverse selection of blue camera tape and wads of Kleenex had been applied to his front and I was more than a little put off my stroke – in fact I could barely keep a straight face. When we sang our bitter-sweet little song about Libras and Geminis being totally incompatible, the camera kept discreetly above Tony's waist.

The number turned out well, but the lyrics of the song only seemed to underline the collision course that this particular Gemini and her Libra husband seemed to be on.

To break the Maltese monotony I went to Rome several times with Judy Seal. She was in a long-term relationship with Maximilian Bryer, who, like so many men, wasn't quite ready for commitment. And although Tony and I were married I didn't feel that we were truly committed to each other. With a heavy heart I'd realized, as the shooting of *Hieronymus* progressed, that our marriage was failing.

It's never been my style to stay on a sinking ship while it disappears beneath the waves. It's always better to jump off and grab the nearest life-boat – and I found mine in my trips to Rome, visiting Cappy in St Moritz, and telephoning my agent wondering about work. I'd now got the acting bit well and truly between my teeth again, and this filly was raring to go.

Tony's heart, however, was set on England again so, after the last insane seven years of flying back and forth across the Atlantic, buying and decorating houses and flats, then selling them sometimes before we'd even moved in, we decided to live in London. We kept the house on Summit Drive and settled into a large, rented flat in Park Street, Mayfair.

Judy married Max Bryer. He'd become so jealous because she was having such a whale of a time with me in Italy that he finally popped the question. At their wedding in 1970, Tara was a flower-girl and Sacha was a page-boy.

I thought *Hieronymus* was a thoroughly entertaining film, which, had it been made by a Fellini or an Antonioni would have been lavished with praise. It was avant-garde, witty and gorgeous to look at, but because it was so autobiographical the critics dipped their quills in venom and the film was universally panned. This always seemed to happen to Tony, who was never a critics' darling. Even with *Stop the World* and *Roar of the Greasepaint*, which were popular with the public, the critics savaged him. He was so talented but they *didn't* appreciate his huge healthy ego. Tony was desperately upset that his film had been so badly received and dived into his shell. I tried to comfort and support him but he was a loner, who preferred to lick his wounds privately, which only drove us even further apart.

I realized that, much as I adored my children, cared about Tony and wanted our marriage to work, there was no way that I could spend the rest of my life with him. As we sang in 'Chalk and Cheese', 'Libra and Gemini haven't a chance'. It was sad but true. We were such different people. I wished that Mummie had been alive so that I could talk to her about these problems. She would have been so disappointed at my second marital failure, for she had so much wanted me to be a contented and settled housewife as she had been. But it was not to be. The winds of change had turned in my direction, and were blowing me along with them.

Whatever will be will be

At the tail-end of the sixties, London was still swinging like crazy. All the usual haunts were jumping, and everybody seemed to be youthful, cheerful and in an optimistic mood. Mini-skirts soared to the limit, and crocheted knee-socks, white leather boots, striped PVC raincoats and psychedelic prints became the rage. Hair was back-combed high and reinforced with hairpieces, heavy make-up was worn, particularly around the eyes – false upper and lower eyelashes were the norm – and pale glossy lips completed a dazzling effect. In fashion-magazine photographs and personal snaps, everyone looked absolutely fabulous, *dahling*, and it wasn't because we were younger: clothes were *designed* to flatter women, and even though some abused the mini-skirt, most women looked great in it.

The greatest clothing emporium of that time was Biba, where you could buy flattering dresses, floaty chiffon shirts and wildly printed bell-bottoms for a paltry three or four pounds.

Alvaro's restaurant and Club del Aretusa were filled to bursting with 'the beautiful people', the trendy antique bric-à-brac shop Antiquarius was stacked with collectable art nouveau and deco *objets*, and the youth-oriented boutiques, like Granny Takes a Trip and Mary Quant, were thronged with gorgeous creatures dressed to the nines in multi-coloured chiffon, tie-dyed T-shirts, floating scarves, baubles, bangles and ethnic beads – and that was just the men! Unisex clothes were voguish and neither sex was embarrassed to embellish themselves – not only sartorially but with every artifice they could lay hands on from the hairdressers, chemists and make-up counters.

Suddenly my London agent had several offers for me, mostly for low-budget movies. I was happy, though, because an actor who loves working *needs* to act, just as a writer needs to write. Most actors feel like this because it's what we were born to do. Few have ever voluntarily given up this fascinating but infuriating profession – it usually gives *them* up.

By now television had stolen so many filmgoers from the cinema that movie producers had begun to fight back with a vengeance. They had realized that on the big screen they could show exotic foreign locations, which television couldn't, and speedily churned out a spate of glamorous films shot in gorgeous locations. One film that epitomized the late sixties and early seventies craze for location shoots was *If It's Tuesday This Must Be Belgium*. An ensemble movie, shot all over Europe, it aimed to show Americans all the Continental glamour spots, featuring one pretty girl in each city. In Berlin it was Catherine Spaak, in Rome Virna Lisi, in Paris Elsa Martinelli – and in London 'twas I.

The stars were Ian McShane and Suzanne Pleshette who, travelling London by bus, spot a 'dolly' striding along Kings Road *à la* Julie Christie in *Darling*. I wore the definitively sexy outfit of the day. A micro-short white crocheted mini-dress over a flesh-coloured slip, my long shaggy hair swinging in the breeze. It was only a day's work, and if you blink you miss me, but working in the King's Road, then at the pinnacle of its world-wide fame, was great fun.

After *Belgium*, in quick succession, I flew to Greece for *The Executioner* with George Peppard, New Mexico for *Three in the Cellar* with Larry Hagman, to Pinewood for *Quest for Love* and *Revenge*, to Trieste for *State of Siege*, back to England for *Fear in the Night* with Peter Cushing, Judy Geeson and Ralph Bates, *Tales from the Crypt* with Ralph Richardson, Richard Greene, Nigel Patrick and Peter Cushing again, *Dark Places* with Christopher Lee, Jane Birkin and Herbert Lom, *Tales that Witness Madness* with Michael Jayston and Jack Hawkins, *Alfie*

Darling with Alan Price, and *Subterfuge* with Gene Barry and Richard Todd. None of these films was particularly ground-breaking but I was doing what I loved best. Working.

I made twelve movies practically non-stop within three years, and by the end of it I was exhausted.

Now I'd decided I wanted to spend more time in London because of my budding relationship with Ronald Kass. Ron was now head of Apple Records and the music side of the Beatles company Apple Corps. He was tall, fair and attractive with burning ambition, charisma and enormous energy. I truly believed him when he said he wanted to take care of me and that he had the financial ability and drive to do so. He'd wanted to marry me almost from the moment we'd met, but in no way was I ready for yet *another* commitment. The headquarters of the Beatles' empire at Number 3 Savile Row was in the heart of the conservative part of the West End, adjacent to bespoke tailors and shoemakers to royalty and to the Establishment. The five-storey Georgian house, previously owned by impresario Jack Hylton and more recently known as the Albany Club, was an incongruous headquarters for the Fab Four who represented youth culture with a vengeance.

I visited Ron one day in his elegant new ground-floor office, with its finely carved panelling and ceilings, expensive paintings and extravagant all-white furniture. We had tea out of Limoges cups, accompanied by cucumber sandwiches, crackers and biscuits, and a two-pound tin of caviar from Fortnum and Mason.

'This is rather fine,' I remarked.

'Nothing's too good for Apple,' said Ron. 'The outgoings here are absolutely *astronomical*. Champagne, best wines, tons of *foie gras* and truffles are all ordered constantly, and as fast as anything comes in, out it goes again.'

'Why? Who eats it?'

'Secretaries, hangers-on, delivery boys, visitors – anyone who comes here doesn't leave empty-handed. I've told the administration but they simply don't seem to care that this place is leaking cash. If any goon off the streets comes in these doors carrying a joss-stick, smoking pot or wearing sandals, peace emblems or flowing robes, they're considered to give out what the boys call "Good Vibes". They'll usually get an audience with Derek or one of the guys right away,' said Ron. 'It's crazy, because if he's wearing a suit no one will give him the time of day. I don't know how much longer this place can keep going.'

'Can't you say anything?'

'I have, but I guess I'm just as guilty as the rest. Look . . .' He grinned and opened a cupboard to reveal jeroboams of Dom Perignon, boxes of Belgian truffles and every possible kind of liquor. 'Courtesy of Apple Corps – want to take some home?'

'No thanks.' I shook my head. 'I'm not into petty larceny.'

A cheery head popped around the door in a black-leather flat cap.

'Hi, folks. Time for tea?' He beamed. 'I smell cucumber sarnies.'

'Oh, hi, John. Have you met Joan?'

'*Miss Collins.*' John Lennon kissed my hand, eyes sparkling mischievously. 'What an honour.'

I shook hands with the most famous and most brilliant of the quartet. Tall and pale, he had a lugubrious face that looked either miserable or about to burst into giggles. He wore tight black pants, a flowing white shirt, and from around his neck a few peace symbols and ankhs caught the light.

'I used to *love* seeing your films when I was a little boy.'

'Thanks.' I laughed. 'You're only a few years younger than me – but I guess your mama let you see X-rated films.'

'Ooh, those pin-up pics of yours used to make me go all funny when I saw them in *Picturegoer. Very* nice.'

He plonked himself on to the sofa and spread half the jar of caviar on to a digestive biscuit. I poured him some tea. 'Three sugars, please.' He stuck out his long legs and put his feet on the glass coffee table. 'Aah, how I love a star-trek down Memory Lane,' he said. 'When I saw *Our Girl Friday* I was about thirteen, and I got that calendar of yours with the flowers all over your chest and stuck it above me bed.'

'That was some silly gear,' I said.

'Yeah, but it was horny for then. I like your gear now, girl, fairly fab.'

'I like yours, too. I covet that cap.'

'Well, you can't have it – *ooh*, you girls are all alike. I *won't* swap you.'

I was wearing a lilac shirt over trousers, tucked into knee-length brown suede boots and a brown velvet cap similar to Lennon's.

'Trendy chick, ain't she?' John observed to Ron. 'Gonna make it legal, then?'

John had a mind like a steel trap and switched subjects as easily as Jackie Stewart switched gears. I was glad he switched off this subject.

'Ooh, Ron, I see you've got a new picture.' He gestured towards a large painting of a watermelon.

'No, actually it's not new. I just moved it over from home.' Ron had a beautiful house in South Street, Mayfair.

'Nice.' John studied it. 'Could look good as a record sleeve. Why don't we call the company Watermelon instead of Apple?'

'Have to change the colour of the carpet,' I said.

'Right. Bad idea.' He polished off the caviar. 'What do you think of our first cover, then?' he asked. Ron handed me the sleeve which had nothing but a huge Granny Smith on the front.

'I think it's fabulous. It'll sell a million,' I said.

'*Is that all?*' He pantomimed shock. 'We'll all be in the workhouse if it only sells a million.' He checked his watch. 'OK, folks, time for the jam session. You coming to watch?'

We followed him as he dashed out, calling back, 'Thanks for the fish eggs, Ron. See you in five.'

I noticed that brand new apple-green carpet covered all the floors in the building, and pricy-looking pictures hung on the walls, nestling among dozens of gold records.

'The boys are doing a mini-concert on the roof for some documentary,' said Ron.

'Let's go,' I said. 'The last time I saw the Beatles in person at the Hammersmith Palais, I could hardly hear a note because of the screaming crowd.'

'Could be like that today,' said Ron.

On the tiny roof, a small stage had been erected where the four boys stood frowning and tuning their instruments. A camera crew was present and a photographer was snapping away. The smell of cannabis was strong in the air and the crowd, which consisted mainly of friends and hangers-on in jeans, flowing shirts and beads, was rowdy. I glimpsed John's girl-friend, Yoko Ono, skulking about.

The boys launched into 'Ob-la-di, Ob-la-da' to vigorous applause, and then a sweet new number 'Let It Be'.

There were so many people on the roof that I thought I might get pushed off, so I told Ron I had to meet the kids from school. As I left, John caught my eye, winked and raised his black-leather cap.

During *The Executioner* I was living in a rented house in Regent's Park with the children and a nanny. Charles Schneer, the film's producer, had invited me to a party to celebrate the beginning of shooting.

'I'll send George to pick you up,' he said.

'George who?' I asked.

'Peppard, of course, your leading man. He'll pick you up at eight. You'll love him.'

I was slightly apprehensive. I didn't like blind dates and I wasn't a fan of George Peppard, whose reputation as a boozer and womanizer had preceded him to London. But when he arrived promptly at eight, blond, tanned and casually well dressed, he seemed charming.

Peppard had become an instant success opposite Audrey Hepburn in *Breakfast at Tiffany's* in 1961, but his heavy drinking was beginning to take its toll on his once-dazzling all-American looks. In his late thirties, he prided himself on being a macho man and one of the boys.

There were plenty of interesting people at the party, mostly actors in the film, including distinguished Keith Michell, whose Hampstead house Tony and I had once rented, the drily acerbic Nigel Patrick, Judy Geeson and two great character actors, Charles Gray and George Baker. The director, Sam Wanamaker, was a charismatic American ex-actor, whose passion was to raise enough money to build a replica of Shakespeare's Globe Theatre in London.

That night I met the Columbia publicist who was to become a life-long friend, the diminutive, follically challenged yet perfectly groomed Jeffrey Lane. He and I sat in a corner giggling throughout most of the evening. I was unaware that I was offending Mr Peppard – until we both climbed into the chauffeur-driven limousine at midnight for him to escort me home. George had been at the cocktails all evening, was three sheets to the wind, and made no bones about his intentions towards me. 'How 'bout a buss?' he slurred, leaning in for the kill at my front door.

'A what?' I backed off, not about to swap spit with him.

'A buss.' He was barely coherent. 'C'mon, kid, let's go.'

'George, I'm married.' I clutched at that straw, although it was hardly a secret that I was now separated.

'Sho what? Come 'ere, babe.' He grabbed my shoulder, I lost my balance and we stumbled clumsily into the front hall.

'You'll wake the children,' I said weakly, loathing this situation, which so many women face regularly. Today it's called sexual harassment, in the seventies it was taken for granted that it was a guy's due.

'S'OK, s'OK, s'OK.' He gripped my shoulder again but I wriggled from his grasp.

'I'm afraid it's not OK.' I shoved him forcibly out of the front door, fully aware of the grinning chauffeur taking in this not-so-tender tableau. I felt like squawking, 'I'm a good girl I am,' *à la* Eliza Doolittle, but instead I said: 'I'm sorry, George, but it's just not on.'

Peppard stumbled down the steps, then his handsome face creased in a frown. He was drunk and angry and, for a second, I thought he might try to hit me. He stared at me, then hissed two words under his breath: 'Frigid bitch.' With that, he turned on his heel, staggered towards the car, and I slammed the front door, my face flaming in fury.

Ramifications of this incident haunted me for the rest of *The Executioner* for Peppard decided to send me to Coventry. We spent the entire film not speaking unless on camera, existing in a frosty vacuum.

But George wasn't as much of a macho man as he tried to be and I was amused one day to hear one of the make-up men ask the other, 'I hear Peppard is refusing to do the stunt that Wanamaker wants him to do – think he's too scared?'

'Yeah,' said his colleague, busily powdering my nose, 'most of his pluck is in his eyebrows.'

The most embarrassing incident for me during filming came when Sam insisted that, with the current more lenient censorship laws, our love scene had to be done in the nude. My squeaks of dismay left Sam and Charlie Schneer unmoved.

'That's what Columbia want and that's what Columbia are gonna get,' Sam said firmly. 'For Christ's sake, it's not the first time you've appeared nude on film, is it?'

'N-no,' I said hesitantly, 'but those two movies were for the Italian market only. I was guaranteed that they wouldn't be shown in the US or England.'

Sam stared at me crossly. 'I don't *get* it, honey. What the *heck* difference does it make if they see your tits in Italy or in the States?'

'A lot,' I said, then admitted, 'Well, I suppose it *is* a touch double-standard.'

'Sure is.' Sam lit a cigar and smiled. 'Don't worry honey, I'll protect you from the big bad wolf.'

That scene with Peppard was a horror. To have to make passionate love to a person who actively dislikes you (a feeling which by now was mutual) is an actress's nightmare. It wasn't so awful for George, who was wearing sturdy blue shorts. I, too, wore shorts, but above the waist there was nothing to protect my modesty except a tiny towel. It was a chilly day and every time Sam yelled, 'Action!' my dresser whipped away the towel leaving my frozen assets on display. Few women look their best lying flat on their back naked, particularly if their bosom is more than size 34 and I was convinced that mine looked like two fried eggs on a plate.

After our first fervent kiss Peppard, to his credit, forgot his *froideur* and plonked his body over mind. I thankfully gave in to his embrace.

Thence ensued a truce: George was now involved with Judy Geeson, and I'd finally come out into the open with Ron Kass.

The Executioner was another box-office bomb but I couldn't have cared less. I was happy in my personal life, working consistently, and thanks to my father's advice, I still believed that an actor is bloody lucky to be working at all. In my mid-thirties I wasn't going to sit around waiting for the hot script of the year to come along. That would go in any case to Julie Christie, Barbra Streisand or one of the younger girls.

'I've had my day as a movie star, so I'll work in whatever comes along,' I told Ron, which was fine by him as he seemed proud of my career. In fact, he seemed more in love with me than any previous man in my life. He also seemed settled, ambitious and hard-working, and although he was sometimes volatile and liable to fly off the handle, as I'd never yet met a flawless man – or woman – I was seriously considering his proposal of marriage.

In July 1969, while mulling over the possibility of becoming Mrs Ron Kass, I went to stay in Rome with two of my oldest friends, Gore Vidal and Howard Austen. They were always great company and lived in an enchanting roof-top apartment near the Piazza di Spagna with a killer view of the Eternal City and an enormous terrace with gorgeous blooms bursting out of terracotta pots. When I told them I was considering my third trip down the aisle, they weren't keen on the idea at all.

'You're absolutely *mad*, my dear,' drawled Gore, handing me another Negroni as we sat and watched the twinkling Roman lights. 'There's still *far* too much life in you to get tied down yet again. Why *must* you be so old-fashioned?'

'I like to make it legal, I guess.' I grinned.

Gore and Howard were voluptuaries who appreciated many of life's pleasures but often searched for more amusing or sensual experiences. Gore had made no secret of the fact that he thought my 'serial monogamy' was somewhat square, especially my insistence on fidelity to the current *amor*.

'You've got to live life, my dear. Live life! Live it to the hilt. Being with one person *all* the time is a drag, my dear, let's face it.'

When I'd told Gore a few years previously that I was considering *Star Trek*, he'd said, 'My dear, *never* miss a chance to go on TV or have sex.'

'In that order?' I asked.

'*Not* necessarily,' said Gore drily.

Howard laughed. He'd recently written a naughty cookbook, called *The Myra Breckenridge Cookbook* after one of Gore's more libertine literary heroines. For its cover he'd used an exceedingly salacious picture of me, taken on *Island in the Sun*, expertly devouring a banana. Ever since he and Gore had seen that photograph they'd been very fond of me.

Gore and Howard liked me because not only was I close to their friend Sue Mengers but also, as Howard said, 'Anyone who likes sex and food can't be all bad.'

Later that night, on their flickering TV screen, we watched as Neil Armstrong stepped out of Apollo 11 on to the surface of the moon. It was an eerily awesome sight, and even Gore, *blasé* as he was, was momentarily dumbstruck. He recovered quickly, poured himself another whisky and said, 'If you *must* marry again, my dear, why not try one of those astronauts? Neil Armstrong is quite cute. At least he'd be able to regale you with some amusing tales about life on the moon, instead of parroting on about the Beatles – oh dear me, *how* boring – and how boring most marriages are.'

I laughed then, but later that night thought about what he'd said. Was I *ready* for this lifelong commitment? I simply couldn't bear the idea of *another* divorce. And could I stay faithful to one man for the rest of my life? As Gore had pointed out, in these more or less permissive times, was that really so important?

Well, I thought it was, even though during my last marriage I hadn't always been the greatest proponent of fidelity. But hadn't that just been tit-for-tat? Whatever it was, I wasn't ready for marriage yet to Ron Kass, or anyone else, and I knew it.

Roger Moore was making a TV series with Tony Curtis called *The Persuaders*. They were playing two sides of the same coin: Roger, the urbane sophisticated Englishman, was Lord Brett Sinclair while Tony, the 'dese, dems and dose' Brooklyn tough guy, played Danny Wilde. One night during dinner at his Denham house, Roger asked if I would be interested in doing an episode.

'Everybody's going to be in it, Joanie,' he said, 'Sellers, Mike, even Albie. Forbesy's going to direct a couple so it's going to be a riot and we'll all have a lot of fun. And,' he twinkled, 'it's going to be shot in your favourite place. The South of France.'

'Great! When do you start shooting?' I said.

'We start pre-production over here next month, then we'll film in the South of France in June. There's only one *tiny* problem.' He paused.

'And what might that be?' Ever wary of the sting in the tail, I knew that the chances of getting Peter Sellers, Michael Caine and Albert Finney to star and Bryan Forbes to direct a mere TV show were slim to nil. But I was extremely fond of Roger and the Riviera. What could I lose?

'We're going to shoot all the location stuff with all the different actors in France first, and then all the interiors in England afterwards.'

He looked a touch uncomfortable.

'So what's wrong with that?' I asked.

'Weeeell,' he said, 'it means that between the time you finish in the South of France and the time you shoot in England there's probably about six or seven weeks when you won't be working.'

'Which means I can't accept another job if it's offered.'

'Well, *yees*,' said Roger. 'But the money's *fabulous*, darling.'

Since television guest-star money was seldom fabulous, I laughed when he told me the fee which was virtually scale.

'Rodge, do you mean to tell me you're getting Sellers and all your mates to guest for *that* salary?'

'Friendship is thicker than water,' came the reply.

Because we were close with the Moore family, because I adored the Côte d'Azur and because it wasn't too bad a part, I took Tara and Sacha with me. We settled in happily at the beautiful Hôtel Voile d'Or in St-Jean-Cap-Ferrat with the Moores, Tony Curtis, his new wife, and his daughter from a previous marriage.

Roger called Tony 'Sooty' because of his black hair, eyebrows – and for his often black temperament. I suppose Tony couldn't be described as a misogynist, but I was amazed by the vehemence with which I heard him dissecting Marilyn Monroe one day. 'Kissing Marilyn was like kissing Hitler,' he said disdainfully to the crew. He'd been quoted on this a million times but I couldn't believe he'd really felt that way about that sweet naïve star whom I'd so admired. I asked if it were true.

'Yup, Monroe was a real pain in the ass,' Tony said dismissively. 'And, what's worse, a no-talent pain in the ass.' Tony didn't approve of women who smoked or drank either, and since I indulged in both I wasn't at the top of his hit parade. But I didn't care. Anyone who didn't like Marilyn wasn't at the top of mine.

One boiling hot day in the hills far above Antibes, Robert Hutton and

I had to squat behind a small rock while being shot at by baddies. It was quite a tricky scene, because little holes had been drilled inside the rock for small explosives which were supposed to blow up close to our faces. Mindful of Gene Kelly's sage advice, 'Never do anything dangerous, kid, they pay stunt people to do that,' I asked director Val Guest if it were necessary to have my face just inches away from the rock.

'It's perfectly safe, dear, perfectly safe,' soothed Val. 'Nothing can go wrong. We have an excellent special-effects team.'

'Well, my face *is* my proverbial fortune.' I giggled inanely, glimpsing Tony glowering behind the camera. 'And, frankly, Val, I'm a bit worried about this stunt.' I felt in need of Roger's support but unfortunately he wasn't on call that day.

'Ah, Jesus Christ!' Tony stormed. 'Just do the fucking scene, will ya, for Christ's sake. What's all the fuss? Anybody would think you were a fucking princess or something. You're just an actress so get on with the fucking scene.'

I stared at him in his too-tight trousers, coldly remembering what Billy Wilder had said about him: 'All Tony Curtis is interested in are tight pants and wide billing.'

I ignored Tony and asked Val sweetly, 'Could you *please* just show me *exactly* what's going to happen? Why don't you set the explosion off without us in the shot? I'll watch and judge for myself if it's safe or not. After all, it *is* my face.'

'OK.' Val wasn't pleased but he told the special-effects man to set up the explosives and Bob Hutton and I stood behind camera watching.

'OK. Action,' yelled Val. The special-effects man pressed a lever and a huge sheet of flame shot out from the top of the rock, which then exploded into a thousand pieces.

'*Jesus!*' Special Effects looked crestfallen. 'Something went wrong, Val. I'm sorry. Probably a bit too much gunpowder in the load.'

'I don't think this stunt is *quite* ready for showtime yet – do you?' I asked Val, with an I-told-you-so expression.

Tony gave me a black snarl, stalked off, and Val started to restage everything.

I've often wondered what *would* have happened if our faces had been in the line of fire. Scarred for life, no doubt, and possibly blinded.

Many actors have been badly hurt and some have even died doing stunts in movies they shouldn't have done. Often they're made to feel 'chicken' if they don't perform, and for men particularly it can be tricky to get out of riding a recalcitrant horse or storming into a burning building. I have no such hang-ups. If it's at all dangerous, I will say, as Sam Goldwyn did, 'Include me out.'

The following day I was doing a scene with Tony, which consisted of him driving us in a jeep across a dried-up riverbed to a point in front of the camera. Every time we finished a take, Val called, 'Cut. OK. Let's go again, Tony.'

Tony would reverse, which he did so speedily and erratically that after the second take I started to feel sick. I climbed out to walk beside the jeep as he backed it along the bumpy riverbed to the starting point. Then I jumped in again and lit a cigarette. This absolutely infuriated him.

'Why do you have to smoke so much?' He fanned his hands in the air. 'It's disgusting.'

Everyone knew that Tony was more than partial to a joint, which was maybe why he had such incredible mood swings. He'd recently made headlines by being arrested at Heathrow airport for possessing a goodly stash of marijuana. His grandiose attitude towards my smoking a mere Marlboro annoyed me so I ignored him and continued to puff away.

When I jumped into the jeep after the fourth take, Tony screamed: 'You stupid *cunt*. What the *fuck* are you doing? Who the *fuck* do you think you are?' I stared at him, stunned. No actor had ever spoken to me so insultingly, certainly not in full view of the crew and with the sound department tuned in to every word.

'*What* did you call me?' I asked ominously. Tony repeated what he had said with a smirk, and the emphasis on the C word.

'I see.' I put my mouth close to the mike taped to the dashboard, said, 'Sound, did you hear that?' 'Yes,' an amused disembodied voice shouted from the base, 'and bloody rude it was too.' 'Right,' I said. I scrambled out of the jeep and stalked to my trailer calling: 'You'd better apologize to me, Mr Curtis, or I won't be coming back on the set.'

Frenzied Val Guest yelled to the grinning crew, 'OK, OK, OK, everyone, we've got that shot in the can, next set-up. Aw, shit, where the *hell*'s Roger?'

Half an hour later Roger arrived to find me pacing in my trailer.

'Roger, that *son*-of-a-bitch called me a cunt in front of the whole bloody crew. You've got to talk to him, and make him apologize.'

Roger laughed. 'There's only one cunt on this picture, Joanie, and that's Sooty himself.' He sat down next to me and put a comforting arm around my shoulders.

'I know *that*. But you can't let him get away with it, Rodge, you just can't.'

'Hollywood actors can be a real pain in the butt,' Roger said. 'I remember a few years ago working with . . .' He mentioned the name of a famous young actor. 'He was giving an excellent impression on the set of a pit-bull terrier having a bad day. The whole unit hated him so much that I took him aside and suggested he tried to behave a bit better and attempt to get along with everyone. "I'm not here to win a fuckin' popularity contest," he snarled. "I just want to be a damn good actor."

'"Well," I dead-panned, "since you've failed at that one, why not try for the popularity contest?"'

I laughed, and Roger said, 'OK, Joanie, now dry your eyes and let's get on with the show. I'll make the idiot apologize to you.'

Roger went to see 'Sooty', who suddenly became abject with remorse. 'Hey, man, look, I'm sorry, really sorry I called her a cunt. Tell the cunt to accept my apologies.'

Tony and I finished *Five Miles to Midnight* on frosty terms, but years later our altercation is now forgiven. Whenever we bump into each other these days we just laugh about it.

My new agent said enthusiastically what all new agents always say: 'We're going to get you some really good parts.'

All actors go through highs and lows, believing they're never going to work again – God knows, I'd been through enough to sink an aircraft carrier – but I was optimistic about this new agent.

Shortly thereafter, Michael Winner telephoned. 'Joan, dear, I've got this *fabulous* part in my new film, a remake of *The Big Sleep*. I think you'd be very good in it, dear. It's the role of Agnes, a sexy bookseller. It's got some nice scenes with Bob Mitchum. Lew Grade is producing and we'd like you to play it.'

'Great,' I said, 'it sounds fabulous. I think Mitchum's terrific.'

'So – who's your agent?' Michael asked. When I told him he gasped, 'I don't believe it.'

'Why?'

'I had lunch with him two days ago, and when I asked if he repre-sented any actresses who'd be right for Agnes he said no.' Michael started to laugh. 'I think you've probably made a mistake there, darling. You better change agents. Fast.'

I groaned. 'Oh, not again. I remember I used to have to answer the phone when Daddy was playing poker and tell certain clients he wasn't at home.'

'Most agents are useless,' Michael snorted, 'but a necessary evil, dear, because producers and film companies are even worse.'

I was glad I decided to make *The Big Sleep* because Robert Mitchum was one of the best screen actors I'd ever worked with. Some actors are unable to do violent or rough scenes without causing their adversary to end up either black and blue or in agony. Fighting with Mitchum was like playing with a kitten. He had to wrestle with me on the floor, fling me across the room on to a sofa, grab my hair, then throw me over his knee and spank me really hard while I wriggled around trying to dodge his slaps. It looked *totally* realistic on the screen, but Mitchum barely touched me and didn't leave the tiniest mark on my body.

I asked Bob his secret, and he replied, laconically, 'Honey, I'm an actor, and I know how to *play* rough. I've been doin' this stuff for about a hundred years so I'm not about to hurt an actress in a scene, 'specially not in *this* piece of crap.'

By 1972, newly married to Ron Kass, I was living happily in England full-time, with Tara and Sacha and a brand new adorable baby girl, Katyana Kennedy Kass. I considered myself extremely lucky because I was com-bining marriage, motherhood *and* a career, something that I'd always been told was an impossibility.

We'd bought a solid family house in Sheldon Avenue, Hampstead, Tara and Sacha were at day school, and Ron was running Warner Bros Music in London. As he had predicted three years previously, the financial situation at Apple had gone completely haywire and everyone had been given the sack.

Those were good years between '72 and '75, so I was utterly stunned when out of the blue Ron announced that we had to up sticks yet *again* and move to California. Much of this had to do with his tax problems, but there were looming difficulties with his current professional situation too. Things weren't going well for him at Warners.

I was appalled at having to move back to Los Angeles, and I did everything I could to persuade Ron we shouldn't go. I was particularly concerned about the children's schooling: Tara was almost thirteen, a difficult age for any girl, and Sacha at eleven was really enjoying his school. There had been dozens of articles about the drug problems in American schools, and the thought of leaving my children open to such temptation was an anathema. Ron, however, pooh-poohed my fears, the house was sold, and most of the furniture put in storage. I was particularly fond of my carved glass-topped dining-room table with matching chairs, which had been made from wood from William Randolph Hearst's San Simeon estate in California. Commissioned and designed by Tony Newley when we were married, it had a strong sentimental value. But 'Never miss anything that can't miss you' was a credo I'd made myself live by. Possessions weren't important, people were and I had to dump the table.

Roger and Luisa Moore came to the rescue. They'd always loved the table, around which we'd shared so many happy hours. Roger had just started playing James Bond and they had built a charming house in St-Paul-de-Vence on the Riviera. We sold the Moores the table and chairs, glad that they were going to a good home.

The one possession that I insisted on keeping was my gold Mercedes coupé. Although cars were never high on my list of priorities, this was the only one I'd ever really enjoyed driving.

With a heavy heart and a feeling of impending doom the Newley-Kass-Collins clan said 'Bye bye Britain' and moved lock, stock and Mercedes back to Los Angeles again.

CHAPTER TEN

Actress for hire

I f I'd thought that being an unemployed actress at twenty-five or thirty was depressing, being unemployed in my early forties was an eye-opener. Although I looked quite young, and in certain night clubs was still sometimes asked for my driver's licence, I was judged by Hollywood casting directors not by the age I *looked* but by the age I *was*. Consequently my American agent advised me to lop off a few years.

'*Everyone* does it,' Tom Korman assured me. 'It's no big deal.'

I remembered Johnny Cook telling me as a twenty-one-year-old Fox contractee to say I was eighteen. Obviously ageism raged in Tinseltown, no matter how you looked. If you were over twenty-five you were over the hill. As the producer Ray Stark once told me, as he lay in his bath trying to persuade me to climb in beside him, 'Twenty-five isn't young in this business any more, sweetie.'

My brief flurry of movie activity in England over the past few years was unimportant in Hollywood. I had been in foreign films, which meant nothing in the States. I might as well have not worked at all, as far as the casting people were concerned. It was hard to bite this bullet, but I did and told Tom, 'Since I'm obviously not going to get a movie job here, I'll settle for whatever's on offer.'

And what was on offer, of course, was television, tons of it. A guest star on television in the seventies made anything between one thousand and five thousand dollars an episode, depending on their considered worth. But the actor in question had a limited lifespan; if you appeared on more than three or four shows a year, casting directors considered you were overexposed so the roles dried up.

197

During this period I went through an incredible amount of rejection – hard, cruel rejection, much worse than I'd yet experienced. I'd actually been completely forgotten in the good old USA. Eventually, as a joke, I put a licence plate on my Mercedes that read 'JOAN WHO'. I'd never thought that Collins was a particularly difficult name to pronounce, but it certainly seemed that way to some.

A particularly horrendous experience took place one Saturday morning when Tom told me to go to a meeting with a television producer and director for a guest shot in some long-forgotten show. I arrived punctually at Nine Thousand Sunset Boulevard, dressed and coiffed as befitted the potential part. A receptionist of fearsome aspect asked, 'Your name, and what do you want?'

I told her my name, then said coolly, 'I'm here to see Mr Shields.'

'Are you *sure* you've got an appointment?' She sounded weary. 'What's your name again?'

I told her through gritted teeth.

'Cullings?'

'No.' I smiled like a barracuda, and spelled it out. 'C-O-L-L-I-N-S, Joan.'

'Oh, Colin,' she said. 'Yeah. Wait a minute, Jean, I'll see what's happening down there.'

I sat on a shabby leather couch, my stomach in knots, and picked up a well-thumbed copy of the *Hollywood Reporter*. What the hell was I doing here? I thought about where I would like to be, what I wanted. It certainly wasn't the bustle and competitiveness of Hollywood, I wanted the peace and tranquillity of a cottage in the English countryside, or perhaps a small but beautiful villa in the South of France. Who needed *this*?

Although Ron and I still owned a villa in Marbella, where we'd spent family holidays, we needed money to keep the place up, and to support the six children we had between us. The thought of escaping from Hollywood to live a more relaxed and real life seemed so appealing but it wasn't on the cards. Not this year. Ron had been released from Warner Bros records so I *had* to work and I couldn't afford to be fussy, because I was the family breadwinner now.

As I flicked through the magazine the door of the producer's office opened, one shaggy head appeared, and then a bald one. Their owners stared at me, shook them simultaneously and disappeared. The buzzer rang on the stone-faced receptionist's desk.

'Sure, sure. OK, I'll tell her.' She looked at me. Did I detect a delighted glint in those flinty eyes? 'I can't understand, Joanne, why your agent didn't tell you this, but the part was cast this morning.' She smiled, revealing badly capped greyish teeth.

'Oh, right,' I said. 'Thank you *so* much for all your patience.'

With as much dignity as I could muster I left and went to the nearest telephone kiosk outside the building to call Tom.

'How could you *do* this to me?' I yelled. 'How could you *possibly* send me up for a part that's already been cast? Do you realize how *humiliating* it is? What a laughing stock I am?'

Several passers-by on Sunset stared at this deranged virago, as Tom attempted to calm me down. 'I tried to call you before you left,' he said. 'They only informed me late last night that the part was cast. I didn't pick up my messages until late this morning.'

'Well, thanks a lot,' I said quietly, and hung up.

My Hollywood TV career seemed to be fading fast, and certainly no movie roles were going to come my way, that was for sure. As I drove down Sunset to our heavily mortgaged house, I vowed that I had to do something, *anything*, to get us out of this terrible financial bind. I was feeling really depressed and, for the first time in my life, terrified of the future.

The television gigs couldn't possibly cut it financially. They just about paid the grocery bills and the school fees. I racked my brains for ideas. Horror stories of once-famous actresses hitting Skid Row, working as waitresses or shop-assistants, or, worse, becoming down-and-outs relying on charity hand-outs swam into my mind. I tried hard to banish them, but I couldn't escape the nagging fear that, at over forty, I was over the hill.

My agent called with a small offer of salvation: to appear in *The Bing Crosby Show*, with my old partner from *The Road to Hong Kong*. Bing hadn't changed much: he was still recalcitrant and grumpy. The only thing that had changed was his silver toupée, which looked thicker and glossier than ever. Perhaps he fed it a diet of Pedigree Chum.

After that came *The Bob Hope Special*, which was good fun, and a few more odd jobs – nothing to write home about, but they covered the mortgage.

It was a frustrating period because in some quarters I was still considered a star of sorts, yet I wasn't being offered any rewarding work.

To make matters worse a few weeks after we moved into our imposing but, in reality, Mickey Mouse house on Chalette Drive, Tara came home excitedly from her Beverly Hills school, proudly displaying her latest homework. I was staggered. Her 'homework' consisted of listing all the different drugs that were available to buy in the stores for anyone to use. Although the idea was obviously to put kids off taking drugs, I saw it as giving them an excellent lesson in how to get hold of them, and how to derive the maximum high from them. I read in fascinated horror about how to sniff glue, how to get stoned on cleaning fluid, how to avoid the obvious people who sold marijuana on street corners, and all about the evils of cocaine and heroin.

I told Ron that we had to move immediately from this corrupt environment, back to the sanity of England: this was a terrible place to bring up children – not to mention terrible for my ego. He demurred. He wasn't ready yet, things were about to happen for him. What I didn't know was that my own husband was becoming hooked on the very drugs I so despised.

'How would you like to meet Mae West? She's giving a party.'

Ross Hunter was on the telephone. The ex-actor and prolific producer of the Rock Hudson/Doris Day films *Pillow Talk* and *Move Over Darling*, he had brought Lana Turner back from semi-retirement with box-office successes in *Madame X* and *Imitation of Life*. In his fifties, charismatic and knowledgeable about everything cinematic, Ross had discovered Rock Hudson, among others, and was an excellent commercial producer. Inspired by MGM's starry movies for Joan Crawford and Norma Shearer, he specialized in 'women's' films – love stories, lavish melodramas or fluffy comedies all made at Universal, and providing vehicles for older actresses whose careers were on the wane. Susan Hayward, Barbara Stanwyck and Jane Wyman had all benefited from his expertise in giving female audiences hope in his overripe sagas. Ross adored women and was particularly partial to fag hags – of which Mae West was the ultimate – and I was thrilled at the idea of meeting her in person.

'What's the event?' I asked.

'She's making a new movie. Something about a woman with a ton of lovers. It's called *Sextette*.' He snorted derisively. 'She's doing it with a bunch of young guys. Well, when I say young, at least three or four decades younger than she is. George Hamilton, Timothy Dalton, Tony Curtis.'

'Tony *Curtis*?' I giggled. '*He*'s going to play opposite Mae West? He could be her son.'

'Yeah, and Timothy Dalton and George Hamilton could be her *grandsons*. But that's Hollywood, kid. You wanna come?'

'You bet,' I said. 'Can't wait.'

Ross and I drove to the old section of Hollywood where Mae West lived in a crumbling baroque apartment house off Hollywood Boulevard. The building had been put up in the early twenties and evidently hadn't been redecorated since. The old doorman looked almost as unkempt as the crumbling edifice behind him. When we asked for Mae West's apartment he shrugged and pointed. 'Through there and up the stairs.'

We walked through a mosaic-paved courtyard with a small tinkling fountain in the middle, overlooked by apartments from which a few ancient faces peered down curiously. Strangely, they were all dressed in faded finery, heavily made-up and beautifully coiffed.

'This is where a lot of old actors live,' whispered Ross. 'It's the right place for Mae to be. She's Queen Bee around here.'

The sound of an out-of-tune piano echoed from a second-floor apartment.

'Why is she having this party?' I asked.

'It's a press conference. Mae likes the press, but she wants a few friends around too.'

'Who am I supposed to be? Friend or press?' I asked.

Ross grinned. 'You're with me so just keep your mouth shut and don't take your eyes off her. She's a legend, don't forget. There's no one else like her. There'll never be another Mae West.'

'How long have you known her?' I asked, as we climbed the shabby stairs.

'I met her with W. C. Fields when I was a kid in 'thirty-nine. They were shooting *My Little Chickadee* at Universal.' He shook his head and smiled. 'Boy, that was chaos. Both of them were so determined to be the biggest star of the picture that they each wrote their own scripts and it would have taken a scholarship in diplomacy to try and sort it all out. I haven't seen her now for about ten years.'

'Will she remember you?'

'Mae? Of course she will – but she'll probably pretend she doesn't. I mean, she's eighty-five for Chrissake. It's pretty difficult to remember how to stick on your false eyelashes at that age.'

An elderly dour-faced butler opened the door, checked Ross's credentials from a list, and motioned us into a long white hall. The walls were covered with black-and-white stills of the illustrious icon's early films, and posters of her most famous characterizations: *Diamond Lil, Klondike Annie* and *I'm No Angel*. Ross pulled me towards a large room from where I could hear the excited chatter of dozens of people.

It was a warm night but every window was tightly closed, and there was an atmosphere of heavy, cloying artificiality. The room smelled musty and of mothballs in spite of the perfumed and painted women packed into it. No photographers were present and when I asked Ross why, he said: 'She only wants pictures taken with *her* in them. There'll be one where *she* is, I guarantee.'

Ancient waiters staggered around with tarnished silver trays of shrivelled canapés – I almost expected OK Freddie to appear. The arms of the sofas and armchairs were covered in thick plastic antimacassars and the furniture, mostly fake Louis Quinze, looked distinctly shabby. On the walls hung several mediocre oil paintings of Mae West in her prime. When I pointed this out, Ross smirked. 'As far as Mae's concerned she's still *in* her prime. She started in movies in 'thirty-three when she was pushing forty. She *still* thinks she's forty and that time's stood still for her. Hence her choice of leading men.'

He motioned to a corner where Timothy Dalton, looking noticeably uncomfortable, was being interviewed by a dragon-lady gossip columnist.

'I *told* you. Young enough to be her *great*-grandson,' Ross whispered.

Then he grabbed my hand and we edged our way to the nether regions of the sitting room, where another corridor was barred by a hulking man. 'Hi, Paul,' said Ross breezily, 'how ya doing?'

'Hey, Ross,' the bruiser's face creased into a smile, 'I'm just fine.'

'Paul, this is Miss Collinwood,' Ross said introducing me with a fake name, 'honey, this is Paul Novak.'

'I'll go see if she's ready for you, Ross.' Paul lumbered down the passage.

'Who's he?' I whispered.

'Bodyguard, chauffeur, masseur, lover. You name it, he does it.'

'Lover?' My eyebrows raised.

'Lover,' said Ross firmly. 'Mae *loves* to love. Says it's the greatest for the skin.'

Paul Novak, who was probably in his late forties, returned smiling, which made his large flat face appear softer. He was enormous, over six foot two, with shoulders like two felled trees and biceps bulging out of his dinner jacket.

'She'll see you now,' he announced reverently, and ushered us into the inner sanctum.

A tiny woman reclined languidly on a soiled white *chaise-longue*. Her blonde shoulder-length wig was artfully arranged to cover what was obviously a pronounced dowager's hump. At her temples, the outline of the Sellotape which pulled them up was clearly visible. Her chin and cheeks were obviously also pulled, tied behind the wig by a rubber band – the famous 'Hollywood Lift'. Her face was a Kabuki mask of make-up: thick, white, almost lead-like base, gooey vermilion lips, accentuated by crude pink cheeks, and false eyelashes looking like two black crows that inadvertently crashed into a whitewashed wall. Her eyes weren't big, and the upper lids had drooped so heavily that it was impossible to see their colour.

After Paul had whispered in her ear Miss West greeted Ross with weary enthusiasm. 'How ya doin', deah?' she drawled in that unbelievably familiar voice, which was still going strong. She parted her lips and grinned at Ross. Her blatantly false teeth were far too big for her face and an unbecoming yellow, slightly smeared with lipstick.

'I'm fine, Mae darling, and you look beautiful as usual,' smarmed Ross. 'This is a friend of mine, J. C. Collinwood.'

The eyes flicked perfunctorily in my direction. I was about as interesting to her as steak tartare to a vegan but, nonetheless, she extended a tiny claw-like hand. Her extremely long false nails were painted a vibrant shade of pink, and her fingers were slightly curved as if she was permanently gripping something. Probably a part of Paul. Then her attention returned to Ross. A photographer snapped away at them as they talked, while I studied this Empress of Kitsch. Her off-white dress was in late thirties style, and it seemed too small for her. She wore a great deal of heavy paste jewellery which looked like it could have done with a damn good scrub. Although tiny in stature, she certainly wasn't in girth – probably about a size sixteen. Her vast cleavage was pale and powdered, but her face and bosom were both uncannily wrinkle-free. There was a mummified look about her, something not quite real, and I almost expected the scent of formaldehyde to waft over from her direction.

She was the central figure of a small tableau, surrounded by faded silken cushions, withered potted plants and a rickety occasional table holding silver curios and other dust-collectors.

She obviously adored Ross because they nattered away for ten minutes. Then, suddenly, she turned sharply to Paul. 'Where's Timothy?' she demanded. 'Bring him in heah.'

Her accent was a curious mixture of Brooklyn and received *grande dame*. Paul whispered to a minion, who hastened away and quickly returned with a rather sheepish Timothy Dalton, who looked even more embarrassed as a grinning Mae grabbed his arm with her claw and introduced him to Ross. Then, smiling like a Hallowe'en pumpkin, she announced proudly, 'This heah is mah new discovery, Timothy Dalton. He's as good an actor as Sir Larry Olivier, if not better, and after he plays opposite *me* in *Sextette* he'll be one of the biggest stars in the world.'

Timothy glanced at me with an abashed grin. It was hard to believe that this handsome actor in his early thirties would be playing opposite a woman in her mid-eighties. I wanted to ask why he was doing it, but I didn't get the chance until several years later when we made *Sins* together and Timothy told me, 'I needed the money, of course, and my agents – you know what they're like – convinced me it would be a good career move. Good career move! It practically finished me off,' he said ruefully. 'It took *years* for me to live it down.'

Mae continued to hold court with Ross and Timothy, batting her black crows at them flirtatiously, while a solicitous Paul hovered attentively. Occasionally she sipped from a glass of what appeared to be iced water but which could well have been vodka. I continued to nurse my warm plonk.

Later Ross assured me that Mae neither drank nor smoked, although she often held a cigarette, 'but just for effect,' he said. 'Mae's a purist, she believes in daily enemas, or high colonics, as she calls them, lots of sex and good clean living.'

Finally the legend indicated by a tiny yawn that our audience with her was at an end, and we said our goodbyes.

'She's quite extraordinary. She seems to have the confidence of a woman in her thirties,' I said as we walked through the party-goers on our way back down to the fountain in the courtyard.

'Yep,' said Ross, 'that's for sure. She *truly* believes that she's a great beauty and irresistible to all men. I guess that, in the final analysis, it's just mind over matter.'

'She believes, therefore she is?' I asked.

'Exactly. She liked you, though,' smiled Ross.

I looked at him in astonishment. 'How on earth can you say that? She only looked at me once and then for less than a second.'

'Yeah, I know,' he said, 'but if she hadn't liked you she'd have gotten rid of you immediately. She let you stare at her all night with your mouth hanging open. You think she didn't notice?'

'RJ's doing a series called *Switch*. He wants you in it. You don't mind wearing a bathing suit, do you?' said Tom.

'Of course not,' I answered with a touch more frost than was necessary. 'Why should I mind wearing a bathing suit?'

Robert Wagner was now a major television star, and although his series *Switch* was the usual cops-and-robbers stuff, he brought his own brand of charismatic appeal to it. He was also one of the show's producers.

RJ, as usual, was extremely charming, although we hadn't seen much of each other recently. He and Natalie Wood had remarried and were living in a big and beautiful house on Rodeo Drive where they had become the social doyens of the younger set. I was no longer a movie star, I was a television actress, and lucky to be getting roles at that. So, as the A, B and C social lists still dominated Hollywood, we didn't socialize as much with the Wagners as we once had. But my friendship with RJ, now going back over twenty years, was as strong as ever.

I was sitting with him in his trailer on the set one afternoon, when he asked me if I had what was euphemistically called in Hollywood 'fuck-you money'. I laughed hollowly. 'I barely have enough to buy the children new shoes.'

'JC, it's *real* important for an actor to try to put some money aside. We're *all* going to have our rainy days,' he said.

'Don't I know it!' I said. 'We do have a house in Marbella, but we're probably going to have to sell it.'

'Remember, you gotta get that fuck-you money, JC,' he admonished me. 'You don't want to end up like her, do you?'

He gestured out of the window to where Ida Lupino stood weaving drunkenly. She had been a big movie star and then an important director in the forties and fifties, but was now lucky to be offered cameo roles. In *Switch* she was playing my mother, but she could barely remember the few lines she had.

'No, RJ,' I shuddered. 'I definitely don't.'

'Then start thinking about your future, sweetheart,' he said. 'You should try to get a series yourself.'

'I'm trying, I'm trying,' I said, and I most certainly was.

'You make your own breaks in this world.' My father's words whirled around in my head and it was all true. No one gives you handouts. It's all up to the individual.

After *Switch*, my friend Angie Dickinson, who had also become a successful television star with *Police Woman*, asked me to do two episodes of her show and there was talk of me becoming a regular on it. But I knew that wasn't enough. I *had* to get some financial security for myself and the children, and there were only two ways that I could think of doing it: by appearing in something hugely profitable or by writing my memoirs. I decided to give the latter a crack but I never seemed to have enough time. There was such a lot going on in my household, with two growing children, a toddler and an out-of-work husband. But Irving 'Swifty' Lazar, the super-agent, kept encouraging me, and I finally started to write in earnest.

When my sister Jackie wrote her successful novel *The Stud* she said the part of Fontaine Khaled would be perfect for me if it were ever made into a movie. Rereading it, I realized that this raunchy, sexy tale with a disco background, about a sexually liberated older woman and a young hand-some night-club owner, contained some of the ingredients currently in vogue. *Saturday Night Fever* was big box-office and disco-dancing the new rage.

I asked Jackie to give me the rights to try to get financing and she agreed to write the screenplay. She wrote quite an erotic script, with many steamy scenes in lifts, jacuzzis and boudoirs, and thus armed, I set off to sweet-talk producers, believing that *The Stud* could resurrect my career.

I then spent the best part of two years encountering even more rejec-tion in my latest role as would-be producer. In attempting to get *The Stud* off the ground I pursued my movie-business contacts relentlessly, but the doors were closed in my face, however gently, by Lew Grade, Nat Cohen, Twentieth-Century Fox, Metro – you name it, they all said no. Nobody wanted *The Stud*, and nobody, it seemed, wanted me.

But I've never taken no for an answer, and when I asked Daddy's opinion, he told me to batten down the hatches and not give up.

We had recently moved from our house in Chalette Drive to a smaller, more economical one in Carolyn Way. Katy was living with us, but Tara and Sacha were staying temporarily with Tony, and Ron's children were with his ex-wife. But money was still in short supply. Ron's business ventures weren't happening, so I was forced to take practically any job that was going. Then I was offered *Empire of the Ants*, a low-budget Samuel Arkoff turkey, to be shot, aptly, in the swamps of Florida between Thanksgiving and Christmas.

I gritted my teeth and I made *Ants*. It certainly wasn't art – but in how many other jobs can you make $35,000 for six weeks' work? It was good money, which we badly needed.

At this point I can hear the reader ask, 'Why didn't they sell the house and live a more simple life?' Since I hadn't lived a simple life since I was a teenager, I wasn't about to start now. I'd always worked hard for a lifestyle I enjoyed and felt I deserved, and I wanted to keep that up. But I realized that I couldn't possibly keep on making films like *Empire of the Ants*. I had to get a grip on myself, and to point my considerable energy, drive and talents in a more lucrative direction.

Empire of the Ants, which also featured Robert Lansing, Albert Salmi and Jacqueline Scott, was not only a dreadful working experience but one in which I almost lost my life.

It was incredibly windy on location in the brackish swamps of the Florida Everglades and both putrid banks of the sluggish river where we shot were inhabited by river vermin, crocodiles, snakes and all manner of other nasties.

One particularly gusty morning I clambered into a Buick, driven by a large teamster, to go to the location base. The wind was howling like a demented soul and I thought grimly about the day ahead, trudging through the stinking swamps, soaking wet, clothes and boots covered in mud. I was starting to feel like one of those poor prisoners of war who staggered through the jungle, trying to construct the bridge over the River Kwai.

The gum-chewing teamster jumped out of the car and opened the back door for me. Since teamsters were not noted for their gallantry this was unusual but I thought, how nice. His gallantry, however, didn't extend to holding the door open while I stepped out on to the pavement. He opened it and left it. A blast of wind blew the door with all its force into my face and knocked me unconscious.

When I came to, I was lying on the floor of the hotel lobby surrounded by a dozen terrified faces peering down at me. There was an agonizing pain behind my left eye and, putting my hand up, I felt an enormous lump as big as an ostrich egg. When I realized I couldn't see out of that eye I became terrified.

'What's going on?' I asked weakly.

Jackie Scott comforted me. 'Don't worry, sweetie, please don't worry.' She was weeping – I could see that even out of my one good eye. 'You'll be all right.'

'I'll be all *right*?' I tried to sit up, aware that the curious circle now included onlookers from the hotel, savouring this break from an uneventful breakfast.

'But I can't *see*,' I yelled. 'What's wrong with me? Am I blind?' Suddenly I was Audrey Hepburn in *Wait Until Dark*.

'Ssh, honey. You're concussed,' Jackie said soothingly. 'You must relax, the doctor's coming.'

'You'll be OK.' Phil, the make-up man, gently laid a small bag of ice on my eye. 'Hey, c'mon, let's get her to a room, for Christ's sake. What is this – a friggin' floor-show?'

The tourists reluctantly drifted away while Phil took charge. Once in the hotel room, he made me lie on the bed, icebag pressed to my forehead, until the doctor arrived. Jackie held my hand and kept telling me that I was going to be all right. She was a good actress, but since she was weeping copious tears I knew she must be lying. Not only would I be blinded but I would be scarred for life. It was the end of my career – scarface parts only from now on.

The doctor arrived and examined my eye and the deep half-inch gash on the eyebrow.

'You're a lucky young lady not to have lost this eye,' he said gravely.

'Oh, gee, thanks,' I murmured.

'You won't need stitches because, although it's bleeding profusely, the wound isn't that deep.' He started to put a butterfly bandage on it. 'You probably won't look very good for a couple of weeks,' he said crisply. 'You must rest and you're not to work.'

'What about the shooting?' yelled the production manager, who had managed to ingratiate himself into the room. 'She's in every goddamned shot. She's *got* to work.' He obviously wasn't the slightest bit concerned about my injury, but only about how it might upset their wretched schedule.

'You're insured, aren't you?' The doctor stared at him coldly.

'Sure, sure, sure,' the production manager said hastily, 'course we're insured, but everybody wants to get home for Christmas, and if we've got to delay scenes, well, there's no way we'll make it.'

Christmas. That's right. *I* wanted to get home for Christmas too. It was already well into December and we had another two weeks' shooting to go before the longed-for end of this nightmare.

'Why don't we try shooting me just from the side for a few days? You won't see my left eye if you have the camera on me from the right. I'm sure I'll be fine to act tomorrow.'

Act. That was a joke. All my future scenes required me to do was to stumble about in a swamp then be annihilated by the noxious breath of a giant ant.

'Yeah. Great idea,' the production manager enthused. 'That'll be OK, won't it, Doc?'

'Well, she must certainly rest today.' The doctor looked dubious. 'See how she feels tomorrow.'

When I awoke the next morning, my eye was closed, the area around it black and blue. The egg had diminished slightly but the eye itself was swollen and remained tightly shut. The director, one Bert I. Gordon, strutted in to see me, tut-tutted and presented me with a bunch of red carnations – my least favourite flower.

'D'you feel OK to shoot today, sweetie?'

'Sure, I'm fine to shoot,' I said, desperate to get out of the Everglades, and away from the constant revolting stink from the sugar-cane factory, 'as long as you don't see this side of my face.'

'We'll work around it,' he said. 'Don't worry, we'll work around you, sweetie.'

And for two days they succeeded but on the third we all had to fall into the swamp while the prop men threw bagels at the crocodiles to keep them from nibbling at us. Although we'd been promised stunt-doubles, they, of course, hadn't arrived, giving lame excuses like 'bad flying weather'. The tempting carrot held out to all of us was 'Home for Christmas'. If we didn't do the 'falling in swamp scene' as scheduled, we wouldn't make it. What choice was there?

I've seldom been so petrified in my life as when our raft had to tip up into the jungle river and expel us four screeching actors into the filthy water. I was convinced that every river snake in the vicinity would wind itself around me – and maybe there were even bits of octopus egg floating around. Still barely able to see through my left eye, I scrabble-swam as rapidly as I could to the camera raft where the crew were. My screams of fear were real as I felt snake-like tentacles attach themselves to my legs, and when I finally scrambled on to the raft, they were bleeding from deep cuts. We were whisked immediately by jeep back to base where an anxious but efficient nurse insisted we shower, then put in eye-drops, nose-drops, throat-drops, and, for the ladies, douche thoroughly and immediately.

'You don't know what kind of disgusting germs are in that river,' she hissed. 'You can't *believe* the terrible diseases I've seen people contract who've swum in there.'

'Terrific,' I thought. 'Not only have I wrecked my face and my career by doing this piece of crap, but I've probably contracted some fatal disease into the bargain.'

The cuts on my legs became so infected that the nurse spent hours covering them in dressings. Between the bruised face, the half-blind eye and the infected legs I was an absolute wreck, and never have I been so relieved in my life as when shooting finally ended on Christmas Eve, and I caught the last plane home.

Much to my embarrassment, *Empire of the Ants* was screened at the Cannes Film Festival the following year, in 1977, and I attended a dinner given by Samuel Arkoff and various dignitaries from American International Pictures. I sat next to George Walker, the ex-boxer, who had recently started to distribute small-budget films. When I gave him my spiel about *The Stud* he was immediately enthusiastic. He loved the idea and within months we were in production and shooting in London.

The search for an actor to play the title role suddenly became another media event as close to the search for Scarlett O'Hara as we could make it. Any male celebrity between the ages of twenty and forty was suggested by an eager press, avid for some newsworthy trivia. Many names were put forward, among them Adam Faith, Terence Stamp, George Best and even Tom Jones, who actually appeared the most anxious to play it. I thought he wouldn't be bad at all, but director Quentin Masters wanted someone younger and he wanted someone new. We tested several handsome young actors, and finally chose the darkly brooding, saturnine, but undeniably sexy Oliver Tobias.

In the past few years Britain had been producing only rather downbeat films, almost as though the English were frightened by their sexuality. It was acceptable to titter and leer at the antics of Sid James and Barbara Windsor in the *Carry On* films but Britain wasn't any good at portraying the down-to-earth eroticism of foreign films such as *Belle de Jour* and *Last Tango in Paris*. I'm not suggesting that *The Stud* was in any way a work of art comparable with *Belle de Jour*, but it had a raw, pulsating sexual energy right for the times, a good story and perfect casting.

During *The Stud*, Ron and I entertained regularly at South Street, and often gave buffets for twenty or thirty. Sometimes I would cook something simple, like pasta and salad, for, contrary to most people's ideas, not only *can* I cook but when I apply myself I'm really not too bad.

At that time our core Saturday-night group consisted of *The Stud* team, and sometimes Alana and Rod Stewart, Tricia and Robin Guild, my brother Bill and his wife Hazel, Cappy Badrutt, Peter Sellers, Doug Hayward, Luisa and Roger Moore, Leslie and Evie Bricusse, Jan and Johnny Gold, Bianca Jagger and whoever else was currently in town.

One night a girlfriend of mine arrived with an extremely good-looking young man in tow. 'He's an American actor,' she whispered to me. 'Isn't he cute?' He certainly was. Thirtyish and tall, with an open-faced boyish charm and quizzical eyes, he sat quietly in a corner not really joining in and seeming somewhat shy.

Wearing my good-hostess hat, I went over to chat to him. 'Are you working here?' I asked.

'Yes,' he replied.

'What are you doing?' I asked.

'I'm making the sequel at Shepperton—'

'Sequel to what?'

He didn't answer and looked at me with a pained expression. 'What's it called?' I asked helpfully.

'Er . . .' He seemed puzzled, shifting uneasily on the sofa. 'Er – *The Empire Strikes Back*,' he replied.

'Oh, that does sound interesting. Is it about the British Empire?' I asked blithely.

He looked at me blankly, probably thinking, Who *is* this stupid woman? 'I – er – don't *think* so.' He said slowly. 'It's – er – well – it's the – er – sequel, y'know?'

Since I didn't know what on earth he was on about, I changed the subject and asked him his name. 'Harrison Ford,' he answered. Did I detect another pained expression crossing his handsome face? Neither his name nor the title of the movie meant a thing to me. I had been fully preoccupied with finishing off my autobiography, being a full-time mother and working on *The Stud* and I had been oblivious to the movie scene for a while. It was only when I passed the Odeon a few days later and saw '*Star Wars* – starring Harrison Ford' that I realized what an idiot I'd made of myself.

One would have thought that I'd entertained an entire fleet by the attitude the irate watchdogs of English morality took towards me in *The Stud*. They stood on their soapboxes and castigated me with a hypocritical vengeance. Although I had shown far less flesh than Glenda Jackson had in *Women in Love* or Jane Fonda in *Barbarella*, I bore the brunt of sizzling fury from the prudish, as though a woman over forty semi-nude on the screen was something truly shocking. Never mind. As Grandma once told me, 'You can please some of the people *all* of the time, and all of the people *some* of the time, but you can't please *all* of the people *all* of the time.' She was right and, in any case, I didn't think I'd committed a crime by revealing, on screen, for about forty seconds my not-to-be-sneezed-at bosom. Some of the stinging things that were written about me were searingly hurtful, but I shrugged them off as best I could.

To show how successful *The Stud* and its follow-up, *The Bitch*, became, in 1979, in a poll of Englishmen between the ages of twenty-five and thirty-five I was voted the sexiest woman in the world, ahead of Brigitte Bardot, Jane Fonda and Raquel Welch. I received an enormous amount of flattering praise on one hand and vicious criticism on the other. 'Over forty, takes clothes off. Shows breasts.' Shock, horror and disgust. But there was a lot of positive interest too. I was approached to write a beauty book in which I would share my health and beauty tips with other women. My first autobiography *Past Imperfect* had been published and went straight on to the bestseller list and I realized how much I truly enjoyed writing.

For *The Bitch* credits I was shot straight on, with no make-up and hair wrapped in a towel. As the credits run, I transform my scrubbed face into a glamorous one which I don't think had been done before and was highly effective. Some people even criticized me for *that*, resenting these two 'exploitation' films and me for being in them. Brent Walker merchandised our movies as if they were a brand of shampoo or tomato soup, and we weren't shy about going along with it. *The Stud* became enormously successful and was one of the highest grossing British films in years. The ads for the video-cassette shrieked, rather embarrassingly, 'Give your boyfriend Joan Collins for Christmas!' and I couldn't pass a building site without whistles and ribald remarks.

I thought Oliver Tobias was excellent in a fairly demanding part. It can't have been easy to play a man whom every woman has to fancy. Although some of his notices for the film were derogatory, on the whole most critics agreed that he had the right degree of sullen masculine appeal. I was surprised that he didn't become a star after this movie: there are few English actors with his brand of sultry dark looks, talent and sexual charisma – rather like James Mason in his prime.

I think Oliver's problem was that he was so embarrassed at having played the Stud role that he spent the next several years denigrating it, and turned down any similar roles. That was his mistake, for I've realized that the public *want* their actors to play the parts that they expect them to play. Judging from box-office takings, they don't want to see Sylvester Stallone or Arnold Schwarzenegger playing comedy, they want to see them being tough macho-men. Oliver Tobias became a torrid sex-symbol

Above: Bob Hope, Bing Crosby to my right, Frank Sinatra and Dean Martin to my left. How lucky can a girl get? *The Road to Hong Kong*, London 1962.

(UNITED ARTISTS)

Left: Bill and I with Mummie and Daddy at a charity ball at The Dorchester, London 1961.

(JOAN COLLINS)

Above: Evie Bricusse, me, Liza Minelli, Tony and Grace Newley after Liza's Broadway opening of *Flora the Red Menace*, New York 1964.

(JOAN COLLINS)

Right: At our fabulous disco 'The Factory' in de rigeur Sixties mini-mesh and with our resident group, Hollywood 1968.
(JOAN COLLINS)

Below: You'd look sulky too if you had to wear this hairpiece. As the Siren in *Batman*.
(A.B.C.)

Above: Happy families in Malta. My birthday party on the beach with Tony, Tara and Sacha, 1968.
(THE PRESS ASSOCIATION)

Opposite: As the randy Hieronymus Merkin in the eponymous film, my real life husband Anthony Newley croons a tune on the Maltese beach where the wind never stopped blowing, 1968.

(THE PRESS ASSOCIATION)

Right: Checking out
Captain Kirk's hairline
in *Star Trek*.
(N.B.C.)

Below: With Natalie
Wood and Sacha in St
Tropez waiting for our
ship to come in, and not
very happy about it,
1968.

(THE KOBAL COLLECTION)

Below: With Tara and
Sacha at London
Airport off once again to
Los Angeles to continue
our gypsy life, 1968.

(THE KOBAL COLLECTION)

With Tara, waiting for
her to appear in a
charity dancing
exhibition, 1968.
(HULTON-DEUTSCH COLLECTION LTD)

Above: Yes, we *do* have bananas – and were all in the height of 70s chic. This was the outfit John Lennon liked me in. Mike Winters, Des O'Connor, Sacha Distel, Bernie Winters and Lionel Blair.

Above: As the Sixties peaked so did my eyelashes.

(JOAN COLLINS)

Right: Although we disliked each other, George Peppard and I manage to make our smooch look authentic on *The Executioner*, 1970.

(COLUMBIA)

Above: So many mouths to feed, Marbella 1972.
(EDDIE SANDERSON)

Left: With my two least favourite things, guns and horses, for *The Bawdy Adventures of Tom Jones* as the bloodthirsty highwaywoman Black Bess, 1974.
(UNIVERSAL)

Above: Orson Welles always had everyone on their toes in *The Man Who Came to Dinner* for Hallmark TV. Don Knotts peers behind the door wondering if he'd incurred the great man's wrath, 1976.

(PETER DICKENSON)

Left: How do they do that? Stabbed to death by a plastic knife in *I Don't Want to be Born* (UK)/*The Devil within Her* (US), 1975.

(BRITISH FILM INSTITUTE)

Above: Robert Mitchum trying to pull my wig off in *The Big Sleep*, London 1977.

(THE KOBAL COLLECTION)

in *The Stud*, and if he'd played a few more roles like that he might well have become a hot property.

I discovered that my tag of 'sultry, nymphomaniacal bitch' was one that the public loved and actually believed in! No matter that I was a mother of three and stepmother to another three, that I was married, albeit to my third husband, and that I didn't live the sybaritic, hedonistic, man-eating life of Fontaine Khaled. They *wanted* to believe that I was exactly like her, and however much I denied it, the bitch label stuck with me for a long time.

Of course, in many ways, that epithet was my good-luck charm, for in 1981 when Aaron Spelling started to think about casting an archetypal bitch goddess in his slipping soap opera *Dynasty*, luckily one of the first actresses he thought of was me.

When the contracts for both *The Stud* and *The Bitch* had been drawn up, the video industry was in its infancy and nobody could have foreseen what a money mountain video would become. However, Brent Walker denied that either *The Stud* or the two videos made money, and refused point-blank to let us have any of our share of the box-office from the two movies. There was nothing for it but to undertake a lengthy and costly lawsuit to try to recover some of the money we were due. Seven years later, after thousands spent on lawyers and endless time and effort, we won.

Evie Bricusse and I were lunching together one day at Ma Maison, then Hollywood's trendiest restaurant. The alfresco atmosphere and décor lent it the air of a St Tropez bistro – with plants and flowers everywhere, shady palm trees and a cool lattice roof to keep the Californian sun off the tanned and relaxed patrons.

I was now famous again in England, mostly because of *The Stud*, and was shooting *Zero to Sixty* in LA, although I hadn't worked in the States for some time. I was acutely aware that I was no longer a well known face here.

David Niven Jnr, almost as celebrated as his father had been for his charm and wit, dropped by our table on his way to his Friday gin-rummy game, upstairs from the restaurant.

'I'd like you to meet Madame Claude,' he said, an amused glint in his blue eyes, and Evie and I shook hands with a short, unexceptional-looking middle-aged woman. 'Why don't you join them for coffee?' said Niven to Madame Claude. 'I'm late for my game.'

Off he dashed, the woman sat down and we chatted until it suddenly began to dawn on me who she was. Madame Claude had been the most famous madame in France. Throughout the past couple of decades, she had procured some of the most beautiful girls in the world for her clients, some of whom were the richest and most prestigious men in the world. Kings, princes, emperors, heads of state and movie stars were known to call Madame Claude when they wanted female companionship, and she would supply girls of such a high calibre of beauty, charm and intelligence that often these alliances would lead to the altar. Indeed, several leading socialites I know in Paris and New York were once reputed to have been on Madame's books.

We discussed French furniture, and she asked us if we would like to visit her apartment to see her own collection.

'It's nearby, only two blocks away, in West Hollywood,' she said.

'Why not?' I nudged Evie. 'It'll be fun.'

Madame Claude gave us a short tour of her apartment, which was nothing exceptional. She had some interesting red chalk drawings and etchings, and a few pieces of what looked to me like genuine eighteenth-century furniture. But she seemed more interested in Evie and me than in showing off her goods and chattels. As we stood in the sunlight admiring a bronze sculpture, she asked pleasantly, 'Have you girls ever thought of making a little money on the side?'

I thought I knew what she was getting at but Evie didn't. I prodded her, then answered innocently, 'I don't understand what you mean, Madame.'

Madame Claude smiled like a cat. 'I have quite a few clients who don't always like their women – how shall we say? – to be in the first flush of youth. Some men prefer their female companions a little more – what is the word? – seasoned.' Evie looked stunned. The penny had dropped.

'I think you two girls could do well, very well indeed. Your husbands don't have to know, and I believe you could make enough money to buy yourselves a few little extra baubles.' Madame Claude was as smooth as a silk shirt, and not unobservant. Evie and I were adorned in Buccelatti and Bulgari baubles so it was obvious we both liked a jewel or two.

'Do you mean like Catherine Deneuve in *Belle de Jour*?' I asked.

She smiled craftily. '*Exactement*. There is a great deal of pleasure to be had from these erotic encounters, *n'est-ce pas*? And no one will ever know, of course.'

'Let's sleep on it, shall we, Evie?' I said.

Evie nodded, speechless, and after accepting Madame Claude's card and promising to call her, we stumbled out on to the street, giggling and shrieking like hysterical schoolgirls.

'She obviously didn't have a *clue* who you are,' laughed Evie.

'Ahh, but maybe she did,' I said. 'Maybe she was just testing.'

Niven Jnr called the next morning for a full report on our adventure.

'You never know, Niv,' I told him, 'next time you order up one of Madame Claude's girls for an afternoon's delight you might *well* be getting more than you bargained for, darling.'

CHAPTER ELEVEN

The lull before the storm

Although *The Stud* and *The Bitch* had done well, money still wasn't rolling in, so I continued writing and started a novel. I'd now been writing for what seemed ages. There was a trunkful of half-written essays, stories, compositions, bits of novels, bits of my life.

We were living a strange nomad-like existence, flitting between L.A. and London with monotonous regularity. We had bought another house, Bowmont Drive in Beverly Hills, with a huge mortgage, but Ron still had his London house so we lived in both places, depending on the children's schooling and my work schedule. Ron was still not working much, if at all.

Meanwhile, I teamed up with Sir John Gielgud for one of Roald Dahl's more macabre stories, in Anglia Television's series *Tales of the Unexpected*. I was delighted to be working with one of England's finest classical actors. I hadn't seen Sir John since I'd visited him backstage as a RADA student, which I certainly didn't expect him to remember, but he'd hardly changed physically at all. I was the *grande dame* of the Manor, the headstrong bitchy wife of a newspaper tycoon, and he was playing my snooty butler, who looked down his aristocratic nose at Milady's naughty antics with nubile toy-boys.

I adore John Gielgud. He has a prodigious memory and could report in exact detail a costume that Edith Evans wore in a play they had done together in 1930, or what Nöel Coward had said to Vivien Leigh at some wartime party. He loved gossip and was deliciously self-deprecating. One day we were discussing critics and he said crossly, 'Do you know what that blasted Kenneth Tynan said about me?' Seeing the nods of encouragement, he continued, 'He said I was the greatest actor in England – from the neck up!'

'How rude,' I said.

'Ah well,' he sighed, 'clothes make the man, and what God hasn't given us we can but disguise.'

Sir John, indeed, was always impeccably dressed, even though we were shooting in the unlikely venue of Great Yarmouth, staying at a seafront hotel.

Every morning, throwing on jeans, shirt and headscarf, I'd totter down to the car where Sir John awaited, dapper in tweeds, a tie, a waistcoat and elegantly smoking a cigarette, his mind already as sharp as a whip.

In the half-hour drive from our hotel to the stately-home location, Greystowe Manor in the middle of Norfolk, Sir John would regale me with stories. One day I looked out of the window and remarked inanely: 'It's beautiful countryside here, isn't it?'

Sir John glanced at the landscape and, with a disdainful sweep of his cigarette, drawled, 'Very flat, Norfolk.'

He is, however, notorious for dropping bricks and one of my favourites has him holding court at some Hollywood party, with several attractive women sitting at his feet. They were discussing British actors, past and present, when he announced, 'I've always been fond of Richard Burton, but he's *always* marrying such awful women.' Then, looking down, he saw the large violet eyes of Elizabeth Taylor staring crossly up at him. 'Not you, Elizabeth, of course,' he added hastily.

However, he was courtesy incarnate when he spoke of me in an interview with *The Times*: 'People seemed to expect some kind of cataclysmic happening when Joan and I were working together, but Joan is a very professional actress and we got along extremely well together. In fact, she was quite perfect in the part.'

Neck with Gielgud was so well received that Anglia asked me to do another of Roald Dahl's bizarre tales. *Georgy-Porgy* was about a young vicar played by John Alderton, driven mad when he was a boy by the unnatural attentions of his mother. I played his evil, controlling mother (an eight-year-old played John's character as a boy) and also the woman who tempts him when he's a vicar, finally driving him out of his mind.

In a scene when the vicar starts to lose his mind and hallucinates, he looks into the pews and sees instead of thirty soberly dressed matrons the same women all naked. Anglia placed an ad in the local paper for ladies willing to fill these minor roles, thinking they would get few candidates. Wrong. Dozens of eager females in all shapes and sizes arrived to audition. They came from Norwich, and even as far afield as Cambridge, Kings Lynn and Peterborough – a couple even arrived from Nottingham. The producers couldn't believe that so many women would be so eager to strip for a TV film, but they didn't bat an eyelid when they were asked to peel off. The assistant director was spoiled for choice and we ended up with overflowing pews full of naked women, including my body-double, as by this time I'd had enough of on-screen stripping.

Waiting to shoot, excitement was at fever pitch as the ladies temporarily covered their modesty with large cotton bibs, thoughtfully provided by the wardrobe department. Suddenly, the white-faced production manager ran to director Christopher Miles with a missive from the Bishop of Norwich, no less. 'I don't bloody *believe* it,' yelled Chris. 'It's ridiculous.' Then he called over John Alderton, myself and the crew to tell us the gist of the letter, which was that the Bishop felt that the scene could not be shot in church, because the naked women would desecrate it. Reconsecration would be necessary afterwards!

Panic ensued. We were all set up to shoot the nude scene, and the Bishop's ultimatum had seriously upset Anglia's limited budget. The producer rang the Bishop's office, but the Bishop remained adamant. No naked naughtiness was going to take place in *his* church.

The ladies put their kit back on with sighs of disappointment and returned themselves to their homes and their conservative county look. The location manager then went on a frantic recce for a suitable location to shoot this pivotal scene. Luckily he found an old crypt and two days later most of our matrons returned, still eager to strip.

But when the story hit the press, a furore erupted. Terrified not to offend the sensor, *Georgy-Porgy*'s editor had to cut the scene to the bone. 'No tits. We mustn't see the *tits*,' cried the frantic producer. But only if you freeze-frame can you see that *all* the women are wearing flesh-coloured body stockings.

My image as a sort of basqued sex-queen who swanned about perma-nently in black-lace stockings, suspenders and a come-hither expression, had in many ways contributed to my success and popularity, but in other ways it certainly had not. I discovered that the body of my work, over forty movies and dozens of TV shows, had been forgotten, and that most people only thought of me as I was in *The Stud* and *The Bitch*.

The Stud changed my life for ever. It also changed my children's lives. Billboards and ads appeared everywhere picturing me in revealing clothes and my children were teased at school about their outrageous mother. Fourteen-year-old Tara was still living with Tony and his wife in Los Angeles so she was not affected, but Sacha, at an English boarding school, and Katy, at her London day school, certainly were.

The seriousness of this was brought home to me when the head-mistress of Connaught House School called to say that Katy was being relentlessly bullied because of my unsavoury image. She asked if there was something I could do to correct the children's impressions of me. One of the things Katy's classmates had said to her was 'Your mummy can't be a good mummy, because it says in the Underground that she's a bitch.'

'I think it would be helpful for Katy if you could give a little talk to the children,' said the headmistress. 'Would you?'

'Absolutely,' I agreed, and one morning, conservatively dressed in tweed, I stood in the assembly room before a group of excited pre-teens and seven-year-olds, and tried to tell them what it was *really* like to be an actress. My lecture was illustrated by clips from other films and TV shows, like *The Virgin Queen, Sea Wife* and *Star Trek*. Naturally I didn't talk about *The Stud*, other than to make the point that if you play a mur-derer on screen, it doesn't mean that you really are one, just as if you play a good person, you're not necessarily one of those either.

'An actress tries to portray as accurately as possible all the differences and characteristics of another person – even if that person is someone she doesn't like and wouldn't want to behave like.' Afterwards the children all clustered around me eagerly asking for autographs, and from then on their attitude to Katy changed completely.

With Sacha there was a different problem, which I wasn't even aware of until he told me about it several years later. Whenever I visited on parents' days, apparently I was stalked by five or six boys wherever I went. They constantly snapped secret pictures which they then had enlarged and teased him with mercilessly. As I had just been voted the sexiest woman in England, it must have been a huge embarrassment for my twelve-year-old son. Sorry, Sacha!

In 1978 I made two amusing tongue-in-cheek commercials for Cinzano with the incredibly skilled Leonard Rossiter. These were so successful that we made two or three each year until 1984. Leonard was such a brilliant comedian that when rehearsing with him my main problem was to stop shrieking with laughter. His comedy timing was superb, wacky, iconoclastic, and slightly different on every take – the true sign of a marvellous actor.

I played a glamorous *femme du monde* to Leonard's buffoon and the ads were so popular that when ITV went on strike viewers wrote in complaining not about the lack of programmes but about not being able to see Leonard and Joan.

Then I was offered a dream deal with British Airways. 'You've been asked to make a commercial for BA,' my agent said. 'No salary but as your fee you'll get free travel on British Airways as many times a year as you like for three years.'

'I'll take it,' I said, accepting with alacrity. I don't think BA realized that I was going to trip blithely back and forth between America and London at least twelve times a year, not to mention a score of other Continental trips. That was my favourite commercial and I've remained faithful to British Airways ever since, even though now, of course, I pay full fare!

In 1980 I played the eponymous heroine in *The Last of Mrs Cheyney*. We opened in May at the elegant theatre-in-the-round Chichester Festival Theatre. It was the first time I'd trodden the boards since *Claudia*, at the Q Theatre.

My salary was a staggering £170 a week, which barely paid my hotel bill. But who cared about money? This was to be Art, and the main thing was to get bums on seats, which we did. *Mrs Cheyney* was a sell-out before it had even opened.

I played a beautiful jewel thief masquerading as a society woman, who insinuates herself into a country-house set to con them. Simon Williams – urbane, affable, charming and funny – was my leading man. I'd always thought that he would become a second David Niven but, alas, it didn't happen. The adorable Elspeth March played the dowager, and on many matinée afternoons, Katy would visit backstage with Lucy Fleming's daughter, Flora, and the girls would play with Tucker, Elspeth's little dog. Lucy was the daughter of Celia Johnson, my probation officer in *I Believe In You*, and had her mother's fine-boned looks and charm. She was then living with Simon.

The run was not only enormously enjoyable but so successful that our producer, Duncan Weldon, wanted us to play the Cambridge Theatre, London, later that year. But before that happened, the worst event of my life occurred.

Even now it is hard for me to write about the dreadful accident that Katy had that August, while staying with a girlfriend at Ascot. She was knocked down by a car and sustained a serious trauma to the brain. One of the worst parts was that I was in Paris with Ron and Tara, meeting with the artist, Erté, who would design my costumes for the West End run, and I wasn't told about the accident until two o'clock in the morning. Unable to get out of Paris, because there were no flights, I called my father in hysterics. He suggested that his friend Roger Whittaker, the folk singer, would perhaps fly to Paris in his private plane to pick us up. Daddy rang him and, bless him for ever, Roger picked us up and flew us at dawn in his little plane over the Channel to the Central Middlesex Hospital, in Acton, where Katy hovered between life and death for days.

The next two months were so harrowing for both Ron and me that it's difficult, even now, to relive them. Needless to say, we sat constantly at the bedside of our darling, beautiful eight-year-old daughter, willing her back to health by the grace of God, good luck, miracles, the power of prayer and positive thinking and the brilliant neurosurgeon, Mr Robin Illingworth. We lived in a caravan in the hospital car park, so that we could be with Katy night and day.

I didn't want to continue working on *Mrs Cheyney*, but Mr Illingworth insisted that once Katy was on the road to recovery there was no reason for me not to. Soon my darling girl was back home, in her own little room in South Street, and making enormous progress every day. Ten weeks after her accident *Mrs Cheyney* rehearsals began.

By the time the first night dawned, in January 1981, Katy had started to walk and talk again. The best present I could have received was the first-night note she sent me:

> Dearest Mummie
> I love you very much.
> Good luck.
> Love Katy
> XXX

The writing was a little shaky, but it was a gift from God, as was she.

The Last of Mrs Cheyney was not quite as successful as it had been in Chichester. Sadly London audiences were not as enthusiastic about this frothy 1920s comedy, but we struggled on regardless although the West End was, like everything else at that time, suffering a severe recession.

One night an ashen-faced Simon came into my dressing room before the show, and sank into an armchair unable to speak. 'What on earth's wrong?' I asked. I poured him a small brandy, even though one of the theatre's cardinal rules is no drinking before the show, but Simon seemed so shattered that it was obvious he needed something.

'What is it? Please tell me.'

The stage manager rapped on the door, announcing the quarter, and Simon rolled his bloodshot eyes and sighed heavily. 'Can I use your telephone?' he whispered. 'I've got to call Lucy.'

'Of course. But what's happened?'

'We've lost Flora.' His voice was barely audible, his face a heart-breaking mask of pain.

I couldn't believe it. Flora was the same age as Katy, and she and her brother Miles had visited the hospital many times during Katy's convalescence.

'It's not *possible*. What do you mean, you've lost her?'

'She was staying with her father in a houseboat on the Thames,' Simon said haltingly, knocking back the cognac. 'When they stepped into the dinghy to go ashore for some supplies, it overturned. Flora hasn't been found.' He couldn't go on. His voice tailed off and he looked at me, his eyes filled with horror and dread.

'Oh, my God, Simon, you can't possibly perform tonight. We'll get the understudy to go on.'

'No, no, I must, I will, I will, don't worry, I have to. I'll go mad if I don't.'

We told the stage manager that performance tonight might not be up to scratch, and both of us staggered through the play with aching hearts. I couldn't bear to look at Simon as I felt I might cry, and played most scenes with him looking upstage.

In the interval Simon came into my dressing room again to make a phone call. When he turned round his face was even whiter than before. 'They've found Flora's body,' he said shakily. 'I've got to go to the morgue after the show and identify her.'

Simon's bravery was astonishing. That he was able to go on stage and perform after hearing such ghastly news showed the iron discipline and will-power which is the strength and backbone of so many actors.

The next night, after he had identified Flora's little body, during our most tender love scenes we locked eyes and both started to weep. As I looked at Simon and saw the tears sparkling in his eyes, my own eyes started to fill as I thought about those two precious little girls, Katy and Flora, backstage at Chichester a few short months ago playing with Elspeth's dog, laughing and giggling like all eight-year-olds. Now one was dead, and the other learning to walk and talk all over again.

I knew that Katy was going to recover, and I was determined to do everything in my power to see that she did, so to this end I did very little except be with her. Most of 1981 passed in a blur, but the main thing was that she was getting better all the time.

When *Mrs Cheyney* was playing we had bought a charming little cottage in Holmbury St Mary, near Dorking, with which we had fallen in love. With our six children it was a great place to spend the weekends, and tremendously beneficial for Katy to run around in the lovely garden.

That summer saw the wedding of Lady Diana Spencer and Prince Charles. Katy cut out photographs from newspapers and magazines to make a Royal Wedding scrapbook. I loved helping her with this as I'd made one myself for Princess Elizabeth and Prince Philip's 1947 wedding.

My old friend Duncan Weldon, who lived near our cottage, called to ask my opinion of a script he'd sent me, called *Murder in Mind*. I told him I thought it was pretty bloody awful but offers were thin on the ground, which was more than I could say for the bills which kept dropping on the doormat. Duncan finally persuaded me to try it out at the Yvonne Arnaud Theatre in Guildford. Nothing else was on the horizon so I studied this dire drama, wondering, yet again, if my career was kaput. I was still being offered movie roles but they were all clones of Fontaine, awful films made on the cheap and on location. I didn't want to leave Katy so I had finally accepted, with the possibility of bringing it later into the West End. *Murder in Mind* was about Mary, a middle-class county woman terrorized by three psychopathic criminals, who break into her house. It was an extremely physical role: Mary hides in cupboards, is chased around the set, jumps athletically in and out of a trunk stage centre, then holds the marauders at bay with a long shotgun. Guns have never been my scene and I actually loathe them. Just pointing the thing at another actor gave me palpitations, and squeezing the trigger, even though I knew it was filled with blanks, terrified me. Nevertheless needs must, and with half-hearted enthusiasm rehearsals began.

During the dress rehearsal the night before we opened, I ran off-stage into the pitch darkness, and instead of there being just one step down, for no explicable reason there were now three. I took the brunt of the fall on my elbow, and was immediately rushed in agony to the local hospital. There they calmly informed me that I had broken my elbow.

'I can work with a broken elbow,' I insisted.

'No, you can't,' said the doctor brusquely. 'We have to give you painkillers. Your understudy must take over.'

'We haven't got an understudy,' Duncan yelled. 'This is a low-budget production. You've *got* to let her go on, Doctor, you *must*.'

'*Go on?* With her arm in plaster from wrist to shoulder and full of drugs? Impossible,' scoffed the doctor.

'I'll look like a complete idiot,' I said. 'And how can I possibly climb in and out of the trunk and the cupboard with my arm like this, let alone hold that bloody shotgun?'

'You'll manage, darling,' Duncan said soothingly. 'You're very inventive and you're a trouper. You've *got* to do this, darling. *Please*, you must – as a favour for me. Without an understudy we'll have to close the show. It'll cost me a fortune.'

'Oh, Lord,' I said. 'OK.'

So, as a favour to Duncan Weldon, I performed on opening night, in agony, arm in plaster and a sling.

The curtain rose to reveal Mary on the telephone, explaining that she'd had a skiing accident, hence the broken arm. When later I confronted the three marauders with the shotgun it was balanced so precariously it pointed at the ceiling. The whole thing was ludicrous and I'm amazed the audience didn't all scream with laughter. To their credit, they didn't even titter, not even when I tripped, fell on my bum and several blanks exploded into the air causing the three hoods and half the punters in the audience to jump out of their skins.

At the drinks party afterwards – warm white wine and dead bits on toast – Duncan thanked me profusely for saving the show, congratulating me on a gutsy performance.

'You owe me one, Duncan,' I smiled.

'Oh, I know I do, Joan dear,' he agreed. 'I most certainly do.' Unfortunately Duncan didn't live up to his word.

Shortly after the run finished, Tom Korman called. 'Aaron wants you for *Fantasy Island*.'

'Oh, Tom,' I sighed. 'You know that's schlock. I *told* you I don't want to do any more episodic TV.'

'Not even if you get to play Cleopatra?'

I could hear him twinkling down the long-distance fibre optics. Cleopatra! Now *that* was a different matter. I'd always wanted to play the Egyptian Temptress, and having been pipped at the post by Elizabeth Taylor for the 1960s movie, I decided that, yes, it might be fun to play her on TV. I asked Robin Illingworth if Katy was fit to travel, he said she was, so Katy and I trundled off to Los Angeles. Wardrobe rooted out an ancient costume that had been worn by one of Elizabeth's handmaidens, and I tottered through a naïve drama about a woman who believes she's the reincarnation of the Queen of the Nile.

Little did I know that this would prove to be the most fortuitous television work I'd ever done.

CHAPTER TWELVE

Infamy, infamy, they've all got it in for me

'**A**aron wants you for *Dynasty*.'

It was July 1981, and Ron and I, with all the children, were on holiday at a friend's villa in Marbella.

'Aaron *loved* you in *Fantasy Island*. And now he wants you to do *Dynasty* for him,' said Tom Korman.

'What's *Dynasty*?' I asked.

'It's a television series, along the lines of *Dallas*.'

Ah, *Dallas*, now *that* was a fabulous show. When Katy had been in hospital, I'd watched it faithfully every week – it starred my old friend Larry Hagman – and I'd thought several times that this was just the kind of television I'd like to do. I could have played one of JR's mistresses or his adversary.

'Aaron and his co-producer Doug Cramer want you to play a sort of female JR. She's a real juicy bitch.'

'Aah, a change of pace at last. What's the script like?'

'Well, it's been on air for ten or eleven weeks, it's not doing badly but it's way down in the ratings. With this new character they think they can heat it up. They've gotta bring some spice into the female department, and they want you, Joanie – they love you.'

'What's this juicy bitch called?'

'Alexis,' he said. 'They're modelling her on Lucretia Borgia, Mata Hari – you name the wickedest women you can think of and that's what she'll be.'

'Alexis? Mmm, I like that name.'

'I'll send you a video of some of the shows,' said Tom, and hung up.

I viewed the *Dynasty* tape but thought it a pale imitation of *Dallas*. The latter was a lusty, action-packed, sexy romp with sizzling dialogue, great characters and a delicious love-him/loathe-him villain in Larry Hagman. The *Dynasty* cast were competent but, with the exception of Pamela Sue Martin who played the feisty daughter, there wasn't much bite to the characters. When I expressed my doubts to Tom he said, 'Look, they're making *your* character the one with the bite. Alexis is going to be so racy and wicked and volatile that the show will ignite when she's on the screen. God knows they need it, and they need you. Aaron's *desperate* for you.'

I had a lot of faith in Aaron Spelling's canny acumen. Every TV show he produced turned to gold – *Charlie's Angels, Fantasy Island* and *Love Boat*. It looked as though *Dynasty* could be in with a chance.

'I've got one small problem,' I said slowly.

'What's that?'

'I'm signed to star in this ghastly play in October. We start touring the provinces prior to a possible West End opening, which isn't even definite. What can I do about that?'

'We'll just have to get you out of it,' insisted Tom. 'No problem.'

'I hope you're right, darling,' I answered sweetly, 'because having just signed the contracts with Duncan Weldon, I have a nasty feeling he's *not* going to be too thrilled about letting me go.'

And was I right. Duncan was not thrilled. *Au contraire.* No *way* was he going to let me out of my *Murder in Mind* contract to do *Dynasty*. This was July and rehearsals for the play weren't starting until September, so there was more than enough time to find another actress for this trashy thriller. Appealing to Duncan's better nature did no good whatsoever.

He and his wife had been neighbours in Holmbury St Mary, and close enough friends to share our anguish over Katy's accident. 'It would be great for Katy to be in California,' I ventured.

'I'm not a charitable institution,' snapped Duncan.

'But, Duncan, remember you said that you owed me one after I played Guildford with that broken arm because you couldn't afford an understudy? Doesn't that give you *any* twinge of conscience?'

'As far as *I*'m concerned it would be OK, but my partners at Triumph Productions are adamant. I've just received a telegram from the manager of the Theatre Royal, Birmingham. I quote: "We will not accept Joan Collins' non-appearance in *Murder in Mind* unless we have her death certificate in our hands."'

'Charming,' I said. 'How utterly, *utterly* charming.'

'You can't do *Dynasty*,' he said, and I slammed down the phone on him.

I was now more determined than ever to play in *Dynasty*. Having read the first script I saw Alexis's enormous potential, and for Katy to be in sunny California this winter was infinitely preferable to being dragged around the English provinces in the freezing cold.

My father agreed. 'Go,' he insisted. 'You've got to do it. It's a great opportunity and you should know by now that they *don't* grow on trees. How many times have I got to tell you how tough and hard the business is? You know it too. If you can make an impact in an American TV series you must go for it, darling.'

So I called Duncan again. 'I'm leaving for America to do the series. I just have to.'

'Please, Joan, you can't. There will be other *Dynasty*s,' Duncan pleaded. 'There will be *many* other parts as good as this Alexis woman. Please, I beg of you, please do *Murder in Mind* for us. Otherwise –' he dropped his voice threateningly '– we're going to have to sue you.'

'Thank you, Duncan, for your friendship and loyalty, it's meant *so much* to me, but let me tell *you* something. Roles like Alexis do *not* come along in an actress's life as easily as you seem to think. So don't be so bloody hypocritical. I haven't had a decent part for ages, and you know perfectly well that *Murder in Mind* is a ghastly play and Mary's such a standard role she could be played by a million actresses. You could get Judy Geeson, Nyree Dawn Porter, Juliet Mills, Samantha Eggar – all of them are just as big if not *bigger* stars than I am. It doesn't *need* a particular kind of actress to play Mary and you bloody know it.'

'No,' he boomed, 'the theatres want *you*, and we're going to hold you to your contract. Can you afford to go to litigation?'

'Look, Duncan, what if I *guarantee* that I'll do a play for you every eighteen months in my hiatus for *exactly* the same salary as *Murder in Mind*? A thousand a week. Isn't that a good deal for you? If I do *Dynasty*, I have this gut feeling it might just be very successful.'

'I've got to think of what happens *now*. I've got to think of those provincial theatres empty because Joan Collins isn't appearing. You can't disappoint your public. They'll think you even more of a bitch than you are,' he snapped.

'Well, then, I won't be disappointing them, will I?' I said, hanging up.

These negotiations had gone on for so long that Aaron Spelling was getting understandably restless. He wanted an answer. Yes or no. Lawyers had now become involved as Triumph Productions had contacted both the actors' unions, Equity in England and the Screen Actors' Guild in America, to prevent me working on *Dynasty*. Ron and I decided it would be best if I didn't return to London, but went straight to Los Angeles from Marbella. I called Daddy for advice and, for the first time I could remember, he used a four-letter word. 'Go to Hollywood, darling. Take Katy and the family. Do that *Dynasty* show. You can fight 'em out there. Fuck 'em all,' he said vehemently.

So I went, and on a cloudless California day, twenty-five years after I'd first driven on to the Twentieth Century-Fox lot as a raw young contract girl, I returned there with the Bitch-of-the-Year part in my pocket.

The more *Dynasty* scripts I read, the more I realized Alexis Carrington's potential. Conniving, brilliant and beautiful, Alexis was bent on revenge. She was the epitome of a woman scorned, and if she had to use her undoubted charm and sexuality to achieve her goals she wouldn't hesitate. She was a fearless, independent, brilliant dynamo, totally in control of her life. Because of her breathtaking jewels, exquisitely elegant clothes and undoubted glamour, the jet-setting socialite Alexis never went anywhere without becoming the centre of attention. But she was also a power-player with important contacts in government, international politics and big business. A talented painter, she also spoke fluent French, Spanish and Italian and could converse on any subject with absolutely anyone. Her romantic conquests included men of every nationality, and she had charmed and captivated diplomats, dilettantes, kings, princes and billionaires. Alexis Carrington was the personification of Kipling's observation that the female of the species is deadlier than the male.

Since all these qualities weren't apparent in the early scripts from Esther and Richard Shapiro, Eileen and Robert Pollock and Ed de Blasio, I created Alexis's rich tapestry of a back-story, which they approved.

In the first season *Dynasty* took off like a rocket and as the plots involving Alexis became increasingly pivotal, everyone's popularity soared.

Let me give you a brief background history of Alexis Morell Carrington. The British-born daughter of a diplomatic attaché, she married the ambitious oil wild-catter Blake Carrington at seventeen, gave birth to a son Adam the following year, to a daughter Fallon the next, and two years later to Steven. Blake was so busy making money he had no time for his wife but when he found her in bed with their estate manager, Roger Grimes, he beat Grimes senseless, then blackmailed him into saying the most dastardly things about Alexis in court. The most galling of these was that Alexis was an unfit mother. Because of Grimes's perjury Alexis was banished, not only from Denver but from ever seeing her children again.

Still in her twenties, with half a million dollars a year alimony from Blake, Alexis began her frenetic jet-set life, establishing residences in Acapulco and Paris. The anguish she suffered over losing her children was only assuaged by her constant love-affairs and endless travelling.

Her dramatic return to Denver, as a surprise witness in Blake's manslaughter trial over the death of his son's homosexual lover, stunned the entire Carrington clan. Blake, on discovering Steven embracing his boyfriend Ted Dinard, had knocked Dinard to the ground and he had died. Alexis with sugar-coated venom told the court about Blake's violent past, and how he had abused her.

But after sixteen years of not seeing Blake, Alexis suddenly decides that he is the only man strong enough to stand up to her, and also that he's the only man she's ever really loved. With nothing to lose, she decides to stick around and attempts to steal him away from his wife, the saintly Krystle. Alexis moves into a studio in the grounds of the Carrington mansion, to which she still holds the deeds, all hell breaks loose and the floodgates open to major conflict.

But Alexis doesn't have the financial clout to fight for what she wants. She needs serious money, Blake Carrington-type money, and she soon gets it after marrying Blake's much richer arch business rival, Cecil Colby. When Cecil dies while making love to her, Alexis becomes one of the richest women in the world and from then on it's a fight to the finish, no holds barred.

Alexis's first entrance created such a furore that the studio was immediately flooded with fan-mail for me. Dressed in a white fitted suit with black lapels, a huge veiled white hat and sunglasses, I appeared on the witness stand to testify in court against my brutal ex-husband Blake. The English tabloids, realizing that something big was going on, head-lined 'Joan Set to Take Over from JR'. This seemed to be the popular opinion, but I always believed that JR was infinitely more evil and manip-ulative than Alexis.

'Alexis is *not* a murderer,' I patiently explained to the journalists who asked me what it was like playing the wickedest woman on television. 'Blake is a murderer, JR is a murderer, but Alexis would *never* kill anyone, she's as pure as driven slush.'

Alexis was a wonderfully meaty role, but even so I was astonished at the speed with which the American public took to her. Just one of the many lines that endeared Alexis to them comes when she sees her daugh-ter, Fallon, after being estranged for fifteen years. Fallon zaps her with a zinger and Alexis comes back with, 'I see that your father had your teeth fixed, but not your mouth.'

People were fascinated by Alexis, and her *alter ego* Joan Collins, and the American public, having forgotten Joan Collins, became confused between myself and Alexis. Because *Dynasty*'s schedule left little time for shopping, I often borrowed from Alexis's flamboyant wardrobe for social events so she and I often looked indistinguishable.

It was around this time that Judy Bryer came in as my personal assistant and companion during *Dynasty*. She was invaluable to me and we became extremely close.

Dynasty was a hugely expensive show to produce. In the first season a fifty-minute episode cost $1 million. But after the second year when all the actors had received salary increases the cost escalated to north of $1.5 million. The wardrobe alone cost $25,000 a week, but as the ratings soared the producers felt that their investment was paying off and no expense was spared. On set our food came from the best grocery shops, the caviar Alexis consumed with such relish was Beluga and the hot-house flower arrangements came from the finest florists in Beverly Hills. Only the champagne was fake – watered-down diet ginger-ale.

Before I joined *Dynasty*, Linda Evans, Pamela Sue Martin and Pamela Bellwood wore simple all-American type clothes, pants, skirts, shirts and sweaters – not a designer frock anywhere. But as the seasons rolled by, and Diahann Carroll came aboard as glamorous Dominique, followed by Heather Locklear as vixenish baby vamp Sammy Jo, all the girls insisted on being more extravagantly dressed. Since Alexis was supposed to be the most glamorous, this meant that Nolan Miller had to design still more excessively ostentatious and dazzling clothes for me.

Nolan's influence was instrumental in making *Dynasty* so successful. A talented costume designer in his late forties, who had been in films and TV for years, he was very good looking, six feet five with thick wavy auburn hair and amused blue eyes. Although he was shy he had a wicked sense of humour and sometimes gave screamingly funny imitations of his more *outré* clients. Nolan is one of the few designers who *really* wants to make his women look their absolute best. Not for him the grungy rags that some other designers push us to wear. No, sir, Nolan wanted his actresses to look fabulous, so we did. I adored him and we became close allies, conferring daily about Alexis's clothes or, in come cases, her lack of them, for Aaron loved to place me between the satin sheets with nothing on except an actor.

Among the other actresses Nolan dressed, on and off screen, were Barbara Stanwyck, Elizabeth Taylor, Sophia Loren, Eva Gabor and Carole Channing.

Linda Evans and I loved big shoulder pads, because it made our waists look smaller, our hips slimmer and they were more flattering than an Italian waiter. In the second season, at the height of shoulder-pad passion, I bought a stunning suit from Pierre Cardin in Paris. This creation had such vast shoulders, in the shape of angel's wings, that when I turned my head sideways, they touched my nose. When I wore it for a *Dynasty* telephone scene the cameraman could barely find my face. I received a stern edict from Doug Cramer: '*Never* wear that ridiculous suit again. The public want to see your face not your shoulder pads.'

Soon, though, shoulder pads had reached such epic proportions that in some evening dresses with huge puffs and ruffed shoulders I had to turn sideways to walk into a room, as women had done in the eighteenth century.

Planning what Alexis would wear to plot and scheme and seduce was enormous fun. I spent hours with Nolan in the wardrobe department designing outfits with an eye on what Alexis was up to. The duller the scene, the more outrageous her clothes, and vice versa.

Krystle, played by Linda Evans, swiftly becomes Alexis's arch enemy. The two women loathe each other, each standing for everything the other despises. In the first season Linda and I had two of our famous fights. The first, the feather-and-cushion fight in Alexis's studio, was memorable because while we were hitting each other furiously with cushions and screaming insults the feathers flew up our noses and we couldn't stop sneezing and giggling like hyenas. But when we had to fall into the lily-pond to fight like demented goldfish, it wasn't quite so much fun. At the beginning of the fight Linda was meant to haul herself off and pull back her arm as if to sock me in the jaw, but before her fist connected with my face director Irving Moore would yell, 'FREEZE,' which she was supposed to do. Then Irving would call, 'CUT,' and our doubles would take our places, mine to receive the brunt of the thump. But on the first take Linda let rip on me. 'FREEZE!' yelled Irving but Linda ignored him. Ever a jock, her fist connected hard with my chin and I shrieked. 'Freeze my *ass*!' I yelled. I fell back into the pond, half laughing, half wondering if my jaw was broken.

Luckily I'd moved my head just quickly enough for the punch to glance off my chin but that woman had a right hook like Mike Tyson. She was suitably repentant. 'Gee, I'm so *sorry*.'

'You just don't know your own strength, dear.' I smiled up at the Amazon, spitting out a water-lily stem, which had tasted surprisingly appetising.

Krystle was always the aggressor in our fights. Linda was taller and bigger than me, fond of weight-lifting and active sports, and she and I had different attitudes towards our battles. I didn't enjoy them, would often say, 'Alexis uses her *tongue* not her fists to win battles,' and refused to do anything even faintly risky. But Linda loved our skirmishes, and even fought her own double so that she could do some of the rough stuff herself.

After the débâcle in the lily-pond I encouraged my double, Sandy, to do as much as possible. Since she was paid every time she performed a stunt, she seemed delighted.

There was also the famous mud-slide down a hill, which ended in a long struggle in a filthy puddle. Nolan said that for this scene the front office had decreed that Linda and I must wear mini-skirts.

'No doubt they want us to flash as much leg as possible,' I said. But edicts from on high had to be obeyed, so in unsuitable stilettos and thigh-high skirts we prepared to do battle. We tussled in a desultory way, careful not to mess up each other's *maquillage* and hair, then lost our balance. Krystle and Alexis tumbled into the mire. Down they went, rolling over and over, skirts over heads, legs revealed almost to the crotch. Luckily, Sandy's and my legs are similar.

Once in the puddle, covered in mud and screaming at each other, our make-up people came into their own. They appeared to get enormous enjoyment from smothering Linda and me from top to toe in thick gooey mud, which was actually fuller's earth and water, but tasted like horse dung. We had to scrub ourselves for hours to get it off – and Sandy did *not* do this bit.

Contrary to popular belief, the Californian climate isn't always warm and temperate and this scene was shot on a freezing January day, so cold that the sound man complained he could hear our teeth chattering.

Sound was always giving us problems on location. Whenever we did any scene in which a normal boom mike couldn't be used, we had to be wired. As our costumes were usually as tight as the skin on a grape, this was often an intricate operation. It wasn't difficult to attach the tiny receiver mike to a bra – the sound man could always manage that – but the cigarette-pack-sized transmitter gave us huge problems. Our waists were already squeezed in too tightly for it to go there and the hips weren't possible either because we had to look snake-hipped and slinky and the bulge would show on camera. Eventually soundman Dan solved the problem: he invented a microphonic device which we had to wear inside our upper thighs. The pack was attached to our legs by a massive wrap-around bandage contraption fastened with Velcro. It was highly uncomfortable as the lump would rub against the other thigh as we walked. Pamela Sue and I always groaned when Dan arrived with his appendages, announcing, 'It's bondage-time, girls.'

Why did *Dynasty* become so unbelievably successful? Maybe it was simply the right show with the right cast at the right time. Maybe America and the world were starved of romance and glamour, which had been in short supply both on television and in the movies. The Carrington clan represented the ultimate American fantasy family, larger than life and colossally rich beyond the dreams of avarice.

The Denver-based Carringtons' principal business was oil, but they also owned mega-corporations, a football team, hundreds of horses, several private jets, helicopters, limos, priceless classic cars, an enormous opulent 'mansion' and several holiday homes. The men enjoyed being men, and the women mostly enjoyed being girls. But these ladies weren't for buying. No man could use them, for none of the *Dynasty* women were doormats or victims. They all represented a breed of powerful women with goals, thriving businesses and exciting romantic lives.

For many years in the cinema, if a woman wasn't prepared to give her career up for a man, she was considered inadequate: an uppity, unfeminine ball-breaker who would come to a bad end, or would finally see the error of her ways, quit being an interior decorator/actress/business-woman and fall willingly into the arms of Cary Grant, Rock Hudson or some other hunk.

All the *Dynasty* characters represent ideals to which many people aspired. Blake is older but still attractive, a take-charge, no-nonsense conservative who has made his own fortune. His is the definitive American success story. *You really can do it.* A poor guy working in an oil-rig *can* end up running a vast empire. Blake behaves as many of the male audience would like to, if they were strong and articulate enough.

Krystle epitomizes the good woman that some women still aspire to be – and some men want their women to be like – yet she has almost complete disregard for Blake's wealth, and with all her sweetness can often be pig-headed. The Carrington children are fascinating prototypes. Steven is honest and brave and makes no secret of his homosexuality although still constantly searching for his sexual identity. He has tremendous problems with his father, who doesn't approve of his lifestyle although his mother, Alexis, does. In the early eighties it was a radical departure for *anybody* on television or the movies to talk openly about homosexuality, and our audiences were soon swollen by thousands of gay men who identified with Steven. Fallon is beautiful and witty but discontented: everything she touches falls apart, and she always picks the wrong man. Pamela Sue Martin had the exact combination of sassy wilfulness and bristling sexuality for Fallon but, alas, she grew tired of the role and left after only two seasons.

Then came Alexis who does what every woman secretly wants to do: she says 'Fuck you' to the world and to anybody who stands in her way. However, she says it most of the time with charm. She digs her stilettos into the ground and believes in herself and in her power. If she wants something she'll damn well go out and get it, and nothing and *no* one can get in her way. Devious, manipulative, outrageous, acquisitive, completely self-possessed but with a dazzling sense of humour, Alexis, with her one-line put-downs and sensational clothes, became the woman that everybody loved to hate, but many women wished they could be.

Then there were the business rivals, the arch-enemies, the husbands, the glamorous wives, the lost children, the poor forgotten relations who came in and just as quickly went out again. *Dynasty*'s popularity grew and grew throughout the seasons and we became as intrigued by what we were going to do next as our audience.

But with all the on-set fighting, most *Dynasty* actors were immensely supportive of each other. It was sometimes difficult for us to learn dialogue because it was so often similar to something we'd said the previous week, so we were always running lines with each other. We often 'corpsed' because sometimes the dialogue seemed so exaggerated and absurd, and often just a twinkle of amusement in an actor's eye was enough to cause someone else in the scene to collapse in hysterics. When you corpse you simply *cannot* stop laughing – even if someone told you your grandmother had died. It's like some ghastly attack of hiccups. Sometimes, out of boredom, someone would try to start one of us off. One of my biggest and most disconcerting 'corpsing' days was when I tried to say this immortal line to Michael Nader, who played Dex, one of Alexis's innumerable husbands: 'I'll get those ships if I have to steer them back myself. I'll get them if I have to steer them back over every wimpy little wart-hog who ever crossed my path. And *no one*'s going to stand in my way. *No one*, do you hear?'

I started out word-perfect but by the time I came to the word wimpy I'd started to smile, and by wart-hog I couldn't speak. To my supreme embarrassment we needed sixteen takes, at the end of which I was pouring with sweat and hoped never to see a wart-hog again.

Things were always falling off and breaking in *Dynasty*. Door handles would fly off, earrings would plummet to the ground, stiletto heels would get stuck in the carpet causing the unfortunate actress to fall flat on her face, and celery sticks lodged between many a front tooth.

Once I had to say *this* deathless line, with the utmost disdain, 'It's too bad, Krystle dear, that, despite your Carrington millions, you never seem to have developed a sense of *style* about how to use it socially.' I bit into a spring onion, then started to choke until tears ran down my face and they had to call the unit nurse.

Another *faux pas* occurred when I complained in an aggrieved manner, 'Look here, Dex, I'm a *very* busy man.'

One April Fool's Day Michael and I were rehearsing a passionate love scene. Dex comes close to Alexis wearing a gorgeous silk dressing-gown, and suggests, smoothly and sexily, 'Alexis, aren't you going to open your surprise present?'

'Of course,' says Alexis. I slid his dressing-gown off his shoulders, equally smoothly and sexily, gazing seductively into his eyes until his naked chest was revealed – wearing a white Wonderbra.

'Surprise!' yelled the crew. 'April Fool.'

Very droll, I'm sure.

We actresses encouraged each other in our diets, watching to make sure no one scoffed too much from the tempting Craft Service trolley, sometimes even yanking a doughnut or candy bar away from someone. This trolley was loaded with temptation: from dawn till dusk it groaned with cereals, cookies, crisps, nuts, pretzels, doughnuts, five different kinds of bread (with toasters beside it), bagels, cream cheese, smoked salmon – and that was just breakfast. It must have cost the producers a fortune. The crew made regular trips to Craft Services and I didn't blame them. They worked every day, and longer hours than the actors. Sometimes we had several consecutive days off, but never the crew, so during the shooting season most of them put on about two stone.

But, our divine clothes wouldn't fit us if we gained any excess baggage. The correct weight for the camera is roughly five to ten pounds *under* one's normal weight, and this meant *constant* dieting. When I see *Dynasty* reruns now I'm amazed at how thin I am and how all of us looked so good – at least, most of the time. Believe me it's tough to look good at seven o'clock in the morning, and self-discipline isn't always easy to muster. Most people's faces aren't at their best until at least three or four hours after they've woken up, but we had to be picture-perfect and ready to shoot at 7.30 a.m. Often I'd find myself at a restaurant looking at my watch in a panic at eleven o'clock in the evening and bleating, Cinderella-like, 'Oh, God, I've got to get home. I'm up at five.'

Linda and I met recently at a Valentino fashion show and I noticed that she, like me, had gained several pounds, which I suppose is only natural really.

As my career soared into a stratosphere that I'd never imagined, so my wretched marriage eroded. It was terribly hard to keep up the façade of being happy with Ron, who was now into serious substance abuse. However hard his family and friends tried to help him, it was useless. Until he wanted to help himself nothing could be done. To add insult to injury the sympathetic friend in whom I used to confide my bewilderment at Ron's drug problem was actually his supplier.

Ron had been the organizer of our financial life so when newspapers started printing headlines like 'Joan Owes the Milkman Twenty-three Pounds for Pintas, Potatoes and Eggs' and 'The Gardener Has Got to Keep Digging at Alexis for the Hundred Quid He's Due', I realized that Ron had been ignoring all the bills.

Writs poured in; our Cadillac was repossessed; the bailiffs attempted to remove the furniture from South Street and even the television while Sacha was actually watching it with some schoolfriends.

But all of this paled into insignificance beside the huge strides my darling Katy was slowly but surely making in her recovery. That was the *only* thing that mattered.

My position as Television's Favourite Bad Girl, gave reporters the excuse to gleefully examine every aspect of my life to try to dig up dirt. Dirt sold tabloids, and dirt about one of the wickedest women on TV made those papers fly out of the supermarket. A series of bizarre, scurrilous and untruthful stories suddenly hit the presses, and I was referred to by such juicy epithets as Superbitch, Queen Bitch, Queen of the Bitches, Soap Bitch and Vicious Vixen. To counter that, I was receiving almost ten thousand letters a week from fans who loved to hate me.

Then for the cherry on the icecream sundae, Triumph Productions, led by my ex-friend Duncan Weldon, actually sued me for £35,000 for breach of contract, which I had to fight in the High Court.

I knew it was terribly important for Katy to feel that she had a united mother and father. Only eighteen months had passed since her accident and she was the centre of my life. But when I finally realized the crashing state of disrepair into which my finances had fallen, and acknowledged the despair I felt about my marriage, I knew I *must* make the heart-break-ing decision to end it.

Fuelled by the report that I had spent an entire transatlantic flight in floods of tears, rumours of Ron's and my split were rampant. In January 1983 we finally went public and I filed for legal separation. First, how-ever, we resorted to the usual desperate measures to try to save it: thera-pists, psychiatrists and marriage counsellors. I even spent a whole weekend in a 'finding yourself' seminar, which is completely out of char-acter for me. But I came sorrowfully to the conclusion that unless both parties are *equally* dedicated to changing and working together, one can-not save a ruined marriage. Ron was unable to give up drugs, and sadly we parted.

After the separation I flew to London for a long weekend to visit Tara and Sacha. There, I went through South Street, with my brother Bill, packing as we now *had* to sell the house. In Ron's desk Bill dis-covered hundreds of unopened letters addressed to Ron and to me from the merchant bank Hill Samuel. Bill, who was in the property business and infinitely more knowledgeable than I about all things financial, went even paler than usual. He spent several hours reading them, then announced: 'It looks like you owe this bank hundreds of thousands of pounds.'

'That's impossible.' My voice sounded hollow. 'How could I possibly owe them money when I don't even know anything about this account?'

'I don't know,' said Bill, 'but while you're in California I'll try and find out.'

A few months later, Bill had unravelled this saga of woe. In 1980 Hill Samuel had granted Ron a loan. With compound interest this bank, who had accepted my *forged* signature on the loan mandate, then somehow allowed the debt to reach the ridiculous, staggering sum of £228,000. The interest was ticking up at the rate of £87 a *day*. I'd known *nothing* about either the loan or the debt, but unfortunately ignorance is no protection in the eyes of the law, and *everything* had to be sold to pay off this vast amount: the weekend refuge cottage at Holmbury St Mary, the villa in Marbella where we'd spent so many happy holidays with the children, and Ron's town house in South Street. I was cleaned out of absolutely everything except the heavily mortgaged Bowmont Drive house. In mid-1983 I faced the future with nothing in either my pocket or my bank account – and with only my fame and my ability with which to survive.

CHAPTER THIRTEEN

Dynasty daze

'**S**ex and venom, that's what we hired you for,' snapped one of the second banana producers. I'd been called into his office to be carpeted for some minor infraction. Frequently the *Dynasty* cast were treated like naughty schoolchildren, and it was galling to us to be had up before the 'headmaster'.

When my contract negotiations with the network broke down in the second year, because my agent was requesting parity with the other two leads, the producers stamped their well-shod feet. But I had to take a stand; John Forsythe was making $20,000 an episode, Linda Evans $17,000, while I was on $15,000. After some extremely unpleasant negotiations, in which I was made to feel like a grasping virago, ABC gave in and I received a comparable raise.

I knew that if I'd been a male actor in the same position having helped to pull *Dynasty* up from low down in the ratings to be the number-one show, the network would have been falling over themselves to give me parity, without my having to beg. But no, that is *not* the way it goes in this male-oriented world of ours, and as a woman, I had to fight for my rights, and when I fought I was called a bitch. And so it went on, the endless vicious circle.

About this time I went to court again, to prevent the newspapers from constantly referring to me in real life as 'The Bitch'. I was becoming sick to death of being constantly described with this horrible epithet, but the main reason why I *had* to do something fairly drastic was that Katy, who was recovering, doing well and back at school, was once again being teased about her mother's screen activities. The *Concise Oxford*

Dictionary gives the definition of a bitch as 'female dog' or 'a lewd, malicious or treacherous woman'. My lawsuit claimed that 'the constant use of this epithet is extremely insulting and offensive to our client, and her family, and has caused her much distress. We write in the hope that our client's wishes are accepted and the practice of reference to Miss Collins as The Bitch ceases.'

To their credit, most of the up-market newspapers stopped giving me that label, although they continued to confuse me with my on-screen image.

I'm always surprised that so many people believe the Carringtons and the Colbys are super-rich denizens from another planet.

'*Nobody* lives like that,' journalists often scoffed.

'Oh, really?' I answered. 'You won't *believe* how many people I know who make the Carrington clan look like paupers.'

Dynasty was like a hand-mirror that reflected a tiny fraction of the luxury, opulence and wealth of some of the richest people in the world, and gave the public the tiniest taste of how they lived.

But for me, the money that I was making on *Dynasty* finally meant freedom. The freedom to be able to have my children visit me whenever and wherever I wanted. The freedom not to think twice about travelling first class, to whatever the destination. The relief of knowing that maybe now I could stop worrying about ending up in the Motion Picture Relief Fund Home. The freedom to turn down work if it wasn't suitable, and the freedom to think about buying that little villa on the Riviera.

Unfortunately most actors are rarely free of the nagging feeling that they'll never work again. Since it's a horrifying fact that over 90 per cent of our profession is unemployed at any one time, it seems an understandable paranoia. Although I was riding high, at the pinnacle of my success, I knew full well that it was *impossible* for it to last. I was only too aware of the fickle nature of the public, particularly Americans who, unlike the British, French or Italians, always want someone new and have a great capacity to quickly forget their stars.

One of the many things I cherish about England is that people remember me not just from *Dynasty* but from the movies I'd made as a girl. I am, perhaps, to many people in Britain, 'good old Joanie', somebody they've grown up with, seen all their lives, and read about with their breakfasts for years.

By 1983, watching the Carrington saga had become a weekly ritual for over a hundred and fifty million people worldwide. More than seventy countries had bought the series, and viewers not only watched it in their homes, but in bars, pubs and restaurants. *Dynasty* nights were the rage particularly in gay bars, and every Wednesday at nine o'clock many a restaurant-owner would curse us as they would do such lousy business. It was the number-one show in America, the UK and in dozens of countries throughout the world. In Norway theatre managers protested to the Government that *Dynasty* should not be aired on Saturday night as it was ruining their business. People rearranged their work schedules, their sports nights, their card games, their dates, to spend an evening with Blake, Krystle and Alexis. In Germany where it was called *Der Denver Clan*, I was known as *Der Denver Biest*, and in Italy it was so popular that they had to air it twice a week. In some Middle East and Arab countries *Dynasty* was banned because it was considered too immoral and licentious and, in other places, too politically incorrect. Sales of unauthorized video-cassettes were phenomenal in those countries. If I had been given a dollar for every black-market *Dynasty* video sold I'd be as rich as some people think I am.

The *Dynasty* set ranked number three of the places in Los Angeles visiting dignitaries most wanted to go; Disney was first, then Universal City, then us. Within two years our visitors had included the entire Grimaldi family of Monaco, several members of the Jackson family (Michael himself was a huge fan of the show), and dozens of minor royals, politicians and tycoons from all over the world.

Doug Cramer loved entertaining these visiting dignitaries on set: they were just as star-struck as ordinary people and so enthusiastic about watching they would often get in our eyeline.

By 1983 *Dynasty* had usurped the position of *Dallas* in the ratings.

Despite being so busy with *Dynasty* I was still ready to accept new challenges, so when director Jim Fawley offered me the dual role of the glamorous wicked stepmother and the hideous wicked witch in Hansel and Gretel, for *Faerie Tale Theatre*, I quickly accepted.

Hansel was Ricky Schroeder, the Macauley Culkin of his day. I gave a reasonable performance, in which I was totally unrecognizable, warts and all, with false rubber hooked nose and chin, rotten yellow fangs, thick bushy hanging eyebrows and a raggedy grey wig. And guess what the newspapers called me? Yes, Superwitch – however for this performance I won best actress from the National Cable TV Association.

A flurry of television work came in my direction in the way of specials, variety shows and one-hour semi-documentaries.

One ghastly embarrassment was *Battle of the Network Stars*, a yearly event in which performers from the three major networks' current shows compete against each other in such sporting events as javelin-throwing, swimming, long-distance running and relay-racing.

In my late forties I found myself competing against nubile twenty- and thirty-somethings, such as Heather Locklear, Heather Thomas and Morgan Fairchild, for the dubious honour of winning for my network. My sports prowess had never been something I'd bragged about. Even on the netball court at Francis Holland my face turned scarlet after twenty minutes – and any kind of sport bored me to tears. I'd been reluctant to participate but John James and Linda Evans had egged me on. So I reluctantly donned baggy T-shirt with ABC logo (my least-favourite garment), baseball cap with logo (my second least-favourite garment) and a pair of skimpy shorts.

One day before practice – or rehearsals, as we thesps referred to those exhausting, sweat-inducing endurance tests – I saw Heather Thomas donning flesh-coloured tights under shorts.

'What on earth are you putting those on for?' I asked.

'Honey, I'm twenty-four years old and if you think I'm gonna go on TV in front of zillions of people and let them see these white flabby thighs and cellulite waving about – forget it.'

This girl obviously knew her onions. In the clinging tights her legs looked, if not exactly Cyd Charisse then certainly not Phyllis Diller either.

'Judy darling,' I called, 'pop down to Saks and buy half a dozen pairs of flesh-coloured tights, a.s.a.p.'

'Make sure they're Calvin Klein 'Buff' opaque panty-hose – plain knit, seamless and with no gusset,' instructed Heather crisply. When I saw the special, and realized how much better the legs of the girls wearing tights looked compared to those without, I realized there is always something new to learn in Tinseltown.

As for my career in active sports, it died then and there – as I almost did during the relay race, in striving to keep up with all those super-fit jocks.

'Never again,' I told Judy breathlessly, clutching my heart as I came in last in the relay race having dropped the baton *twice*. 'From now on my idea of sports will be reading *Variety* while stretched out on a lilo in my pool.'

In *Blondes versus Brunettes* with Morgan Fairchild, then the wicked lady of *Flamingo Road*, we spoofed *Dynasty,* she as Alexis, I as a frenetic Krystle. This was far more my cup of tea. Morgan's a great girl, and a great giggler, and our resulting effort did well in the ratings and was said to be one of the better specials that season.

My picture had now been on the cover of practically every magazine, and my personal life was constantly dissected, discussed and exaggerated worldwide. Because I was now husbandless, every man I even looked at was supposedly a contender in the marriage stakes.

One of my escorts to screenings and dinners was my hairdresser, Dino Gigante, a charming gay friend who was always great company. Much lewd fun was made at the expense of his name, but I couldn't believe it when people started taking this 'romance' seriously. Neither could Dino, who could hardly have been described as in the closet. I adored him and was devastated in 1984 when he was one of the first of my friends to succumb to the dreaded AIDS.

I'd never made a secret of having a predilection for younger men. In this day and age where practically anything goes in relationships, I fail to see why anyone should be a conformist. But in one way I am. I believe that for one's own happiness and peace of mind, it's preferable to have a partner.

After my separation from Ron, several girlfriends had become concerned about my casual and seemingly pointless dating. One in particular, a popular Dallas socialite, asked me to stay with her for the weekend to 'find a husband'. Even though I told her I wasn't interested in another husband, she was insistent. 'Ah'll give you a paarty and introduce you to ahll the most eligible and faabulous men in Texas,' she drawled. 'At least you'll find wern to have *furn* with.'

'Wonderful,' I said, and the following weekend went to stay with her in Dallas. The party my friend gave was filled with what I considered to be boring, middle-aged codgers. There was nobody in whom I was even remotely interested, although many of the men present were reputed to be billionaires. However, later on several of us went to a disco where I struck up an interesting rapport with a handsome young man.

At breakfast the following morning my Dallas friend asked curiously, 'So, you disappeared last night. Did y'all meet anyone interesting?'

'Y-e-e-e-s,' I said tentatively.

'So, c'mon, who was he?' she asked excitedly.

There was a pause and I looked her steadily in the eye. 'Your son,' I said.

'Mah *son*—' She swallowed hard then smiled with good grace – she was only a couple of years older than me. 'Gee, that's *great*. Y'know, he really *is* a nice boy,' she managed weakly.

Then in quick succession I was linked (erroneously) with a New York businessman, who later became engaged to Elizabeth Taylor, Clint Eastwood, Dudley Moore – that was a quaint one, almost as quaint as Prince Albert of Monaco.

Morgan Mason, the twenty-nine-year-old son of James, was sophisticated, intelligent and extremely witty. So, much to the shock of the more prudish members of Hollywood society, we started going out. He was a PR on Ronald Reagan's team and used to bring me some of the President's favourite jelly-beans in a glass jar with the presidential stamp on it. The *paparazzi* quite liked our pairing, and one night, leaving a screening, Morgan and I were walking rapidly towards his car with the anxious snappers as usual walking backwards when one tripped, which caused three others to topple over his inert body like ninepins and caused Morgan and I to dissolve into helpless mirth.

In *Dynasty*'s hiatus I played Kay Dillon, another sophisticated, scheming woman who ran a model agency in Aaron Spelling's movie of the week, *The Making of a Male Model*. My co-star was a new young actor called John-Eric Hexum. He played a beautiful but unsophisticated cowboy plucked from the wilds of Nevada whom Kay tames and trains to become America's number-one pin-up boy. The script was amusing enough and John-Eric was adorable, so we started dating, which caused another furore because he was in his twenties to my forties. But to me this was water off a duck's back. I wasn't attracted to older men and when I observed people in their forties and fifties, most of the women looked in *far* better shape than the men. I was at a stage in my life when I no longer cared what people thought. So many lies had been written about me, what did it matter? I liked John-Eric and Morgan, they liked me – so out we went.

Then, in the summer of 1983 at a party near Windsor, I met Peter Holm, a handsome Swedish ex-pop-star who seemed to be the answer to this matron's prayer.

Maybe because of my desultory dating I was ripe for a takeover, and so our doomed relationship began.

Michael Nader came into my life at the same time as Peter, when he joined the cast of *Dynasty*. We hit it off immediately: he was sexy, fun and a terrific kisser. Dex immediately makes a play for Alexis; she initially turns him down, foolish girl, then eventually marries him, making him her third husband. Alexis and Dex were both totally passionate and totally amoral and Dex more than balanced Alexis's sexual excesses. After one of their many break-ups, Dex sneers, 'Alexis, you are a slut, with the morals of a bitch on perpetual heat.'

'Look who's talking,' Alexis mocks. 'We're *meant* for each other, darling.'

Although Alexis stays more or less happily married to Dex, that doesn't stop her trying to entrap Blake in Rome. She flaunts herself before him in a revealing purple bathing suit insisting he run tanning lotion on her back, while purring like an alley-cat. Blake almost succumbs to her charms in this scene, but subsequently the writers decided that Blake would *never* be unfaithful to Krystle, and John Forsythe fervently agreed.

A couple of seasons later Blake loses his memory so, encouraged by this, Alexis whisks him off to the Mexican hacienda where they had spent their romantic honeymoon.

I think one of the ingredients that made *Dynasty* a huge hit was that it was such a sexual merry-go-round. Everyone was leaping into bed with everybody else and the ratings soared. Eventually the producers decided that they *wanted* Blake to have a romantic liaison with Alexis, thinking that these two together would raise the ratings to even greater heights, but Forsythe refused point-blank. When the lead actor on a hot show puts his foot down, the producers are powerless, and Forsythe was adamant: 'Blake is a one-woman man, he would never be seduced by a tramp like Alexis.' So out went *that* plot. I thought John was being ridiculous. This wasn't real life, this was fantasy, but he cherished his good-guy image and couldn't bear the viewers to think ill of him. Alexis later played the field for several seasons after catching Dex in bed with Amanda no less, one of her long-lost daughters.

Heather Locklear joined that year as Krystle's niece, the wilful nymphet Sammy Joe. Some of the producers thought, unjustly, that she wasn't much of an actress, and there were rumours that she would be axed by the end of the season. I thought she had talent, lots of cute charisma, and the camera loved her.

The producers liked to see Alexis eating. In fact there was rarely a scene in which I wasn't either stuffing my face with caviar, celery, sausages or a dead bit on a stick, always sipping champagne or smoking black cigarillos. The producers believed the only actors in *Dynasty* who could eat and talk at the same time were Heather and me, so she, too, often tagged her scenes with a bite of hot-dog and a saucy smirk.

She is now one of TV's biggest stars, maybe because during her *Dynasty* years she never stopped studying her craft. She admitted she learned a few things about playing the devious manipulating Amanda on *Melrose Place* by watching me play the devious manipulating Alexis. If that's true, then she's a great student. When she married Tommy Lee, a tall, strange-looking rocker from the group Motley Crue, everyone avoided him whenever he visited the set. He looked like a walking cadaver, his body covered in tattoos, and had a weird aura around him. 'He's a womanizer, a drug addict and an alcoholic,' one of the more informed crew members whispered. 'They say he's great in bed and she's wild for him.'

'He's a debauched son-of-a-bitch,' said the make-up man. 'The sooner that kid dumps him the better for her.'

Eventually Heather did, and several years later Lee married Pamela Anderson. As the French say, *on va voir*.

Hugh Heffner's offer proved impossible to resist. At an age when many women were thinking about future grandchildren and putting their feet up, I was taking off some of my clothes for the famed photographer George Hurrell, posing for the cover of *Playboy* and a series of exotic, semi-nude shots inside. I was fed up with the prevailing attitude that women over forty were unattractive non-persons on the slag-heap of life.

The Christmas 1983 edition of *Playboy* became a collector's item and one of the biggest-selling issues ever. I thought the pictures were excellent, and I was pleased with the whole thing. Unfortunately, John Forsythe was somewhat less than enthusiastic. He complained bitterly to Aaron that I was 'a disgrace to our fine show'. But that soon passed, cordial relations resumed once more, and I became a sort of heroine for the over-forties.

Soap operas get away with murder. They can even replace one actor who plays a character with another. For example, Al Corley played Steven Carrington in the first season but by the second year he was bored with the part, and antagonized ABC by appearing on talk-shows saying, in essence, '*Dynasty*'s just a load of crap and only fools watch it.'

Inevitably Steven was conveniently blown up on an Indonesian oil-rig, but several episodes later, he is seen recovering in hospital, heavily bandaged. A few weeks later when the bandages are removed, lo and behold, Steven was no longer Al Corley but Jack Coleman.

When Pamela Sue Martin left, Emma Samms was substituted as Fallon. This time audiences were given *no* explanation as to why Fallon had not only a completely different face but also a completely British accent. However, they accepted it, as they accepted everything in *Dynasty*: we could do no wrong in the first seasons, and by 1984 we were still the number one television show in America.

Nolan had a penchant for dressing Alexis in red, so when I was flung into jail with a bunch of hookers Alexis had on three-quarters of a million dollars' worth of jewels, a scarlet *décolleté* gown and a tear-stained face. Standing behind bars screaming, 'I'm innocent, *innocent*, do you hear?' while twenty-five female vagrants jeered and hassled her – it was an incongruous sight.

Alexis was proving such a successful character that the producers decided to bring in another bitch to keep her in line: Stephanie Beacham. Stephanie and I had much in common. Both British, we'd started in the theatre, then gone into movies, and we were both known for playing assertive, tough, competitive women.

Stephanie was cast as Sable Colby, Alexis's cousin, her most deadly rival. Alexis's fortunes were failing, and Sable was supposed to be richer than the cousin she hated with a virulent passion.

In Sable's first episode she announces grandly to Blake: 'I'm going to obliterate Alexis,' and from then on she does her damnedest to do just that.

By 1984, although I was making $50,000 per *Dynasty* episode, I still supplemented it with other projects. I'd been working for most of my life, but still had little to show for it in property terms and I wanted my own house.

Long before our divorce Ron and I had bought a medium-sized house on Bowmont Drive, on the wrong side of Beverly Hills, and I was still paying off the mortgage as fast as I could. It wasn't a grand house by Hollywood standards, but it was conveniently easy to run, and spacious enough for the occasional Saturday *soirée*.

I was amused by the way the media promulgated the theory that I was rich beyond the dreams of Croesus. There seems to be some bizarre notion that when you *earn* thousands of dollars a week you get to keep it all. Would that it were true. If you manage to hang on to 20 per cent, you're lucky. Between the high American taxes, both state and federal, the 10 per cent agent's commission, the business managers and press agents, who become a necessity, housekeepers, mortgages, maintenance and, of course, the children, the money just vanishes.

One *Dynasty* actor complained during the third season: 'I've got to tell Aaron I need a raise. I can't *possibly* exist on twenty thousand dollars a week.'

I laughed in his face. 'Do you really think Aaron's going to sympathize with that? Most people don't get to live on twenty thousand dollars a *year*.'

'You don't know what it's like,' the actor whined.

'Oh, but I do know *exactly* what it's like,' I said. 'Every actor knows what it's like, and we *all* have this horror that we're going to end up, *if* we're lucky, in the old actors' home when we're seventy or eighty with nothing but a book of yellowing press cuttings and our shabby little anecdotes to keep us company.' He looked shocked as I continued. 'Well, darling, I *won't* let that happen to me. I intend to make enough money to buy a villa in the South of France, with olive trees and mimosa, a fabulous view of the Mediterranean, and enough money to keep it all going. And *that*'s what *I'm* working towards.'

In *Dynasty*'s 1984 hiatus I played opposite that handsome hunk David Hasselhoff in a comedy spoof about Hollywood called *The Cartier Affair*. I was Cartier Rand, a glamorously flamboyant but ingenuous TV star who comes out with such camp lines as: 'An *Emmy*? You think I want a stupid *Emmy*? Do you really think I *need* a silly little gold-plated statuette to vindicate my career?'

'Yeah,' says David ironically, 'I do.'

The cherry on my cake that year proved actually to be an Emmy nomination for best actress in *Dynasty*, and although I didn't win, I was flattered to be in the running.

I was being showered with accolades and awards: I'd won the Golden Globe award for best actress as well as having been nominated for three consecutive years, *and* also received 'People's Choice Favorite TV actress' plus many others, some important, some not. The media were pulling out all the stops on me now, the labels ever more extreme. 'The Greatest Glamor Queen of Them All', 'The Great Survivor', 'The Queen of Hollywood', 'Queen of TV', 'America's Favorite Wicked Lady', 'The Most Beautiful Woman on TV'. The headier the headlines, the more everyone thought it *would* go to my head, but I took none of it seriously, neither the bad nor the good. When I was asked by some journalist, 'How will you feel if your career slows down?' I answered, 'It isn't a question of *if*, it's a question of *when*. Careers don't last for ever, certainly not in *this* business. If you try to make it last for ever, you will only end up bitter, jealous and cynical.'

For this tiny moment in time I was flavour-of-the-month, I knew it – and I knew full well that it couldn't last.

In 1984, at a BAFTA première in Beverly Hills, the guest of honour was Princess Anne, and I stood next to a newly slim and blonde Elizabeth Taylor. Recently emerged from the Betty Ford clinic, she was no longer the fat lady whom Joan Rivers had mocked so often on her talk show. She looked stunning with short blonde hair and trim figure. On my other side stood Stewart Granger, a friend of Maxwell Reed and one of the English movie idols of the forties. He was extremely rude, and quick to tell the newspapers the following day how vulgar and untalented he considered me. Gee, thanks, Stewart. I've always disliked actors who gratuitously slag off other actors. It's bad enough that we get it from the media, without receiving it from someone in our own profession.

One accolade that delighted me was Madame Tussaud's decision to make a wax-work figure of me – or was it Alexis they *really* wanted? Whichever it was, she looked fantastic, and I had great fun choosing her dress and jewellery, and instructing them on her make-up. That same year I was given my own 'star' on Hollywood Boulevard, an honour curiously enough not bestowed on everyone. I thought it fascinating to be embedded for ever in cement on the sidewalk for Hollywood tourists to drip ice-cream over my name.

Fan mail was still pouring in for me by the sackload, letters in which women wanted advice on how to control their lives like Alexis, how to deal with their cheating, brutal husbands, how to be more attractive –

some of them were heart-breaking. I believe Alexis and some of the other *Dynasty* actresses were more popular than the *Dallas* actresses because when things went wrong in their characters' lives, rather than becoming whisky-soaked wrecks or behaving like Goldilocks, Alexis and Co would swivel round on their slingbacks to face their opponents, give their men hell, and be seen to get away with it. Fabulous!

With our runaway success, Aaron and the Shapiros decided that if one *Dynasty* was so successful, two would be a triumph, and in 1985 they created a spin-off called *The Colbys*, peopled by relations, descendants, friends and enemies of Cecil Colby, Alexis's second husband.

As one of the series' protagonists they picked John James, *Dynasty*'s Jeff Colby. The other stars were Jason Colby, to be played by none other than Ben Hur himself, Charlton Heston, and Billy Wilder's favourite actress, the legendary Barbara Stanwyck.

The producers were so excited about *The Colbys*, that to raise its ratings, they insisted that every *Dynasty* actor must guest on it. But I saw no reason why I should commit to this blatant crossover which I thought would harm *Dynasty*. I'd heard murmurs about a possible spin-off of my own, to be called *Alexis*, but I was considered too valuable to the original to be let go so I didn't push it – in retrospect, perhaps, a mistake.

That season, *Dynasty* and *Colbys* audiences became utterly confused. The shows' time-slots were constantly mixed around so that if the viewer switched on to see *Dynasty* at eight o'clock on a Wednesday night, he'd see *The Colbys* instead.

Charlton Heston was playing the Blake Carrington-type role, Katharine Ross the good girl *à la* Krystle, and Stephanie Beacham crossed over as the Alexis-type vixen.

'If the mountain won't go to Muhammad, Muhammad will have to come to the mountain,' Esther Shapiro joked to me one day. '*Guess* who's going to guest with you on *Dynasty* next episode?'

'President Reagan,' I quipped.

'Charlton Heston!' Esther seemed puffed with pride and I could understand why. Charlton Heston was an enormously respected movie star, not to mention also the President of the Screen Actors' Guild, and although his movie career hadn't been flourishing recently, he still commanded enormous respect and admiration in the industry.

I'd never seen *Dynasty*'s crew in such a state of excitement than they were in on the day of our scene. Even Aaron made one of his rare on-set appearances to shake the great man's hand. It was as though God himself was gracing us with His presence, one of the many commanding roles that Chuck (as he *didn't* like to be called) had played.

We said cordial 'Good mornings' in the make-up room. Gerald Solomon was doing my hair and Jack was pancaking 'God'.

The patriarch of the Colbys was about sixty-two and looking good. Tall and muscular, with strong facial features and an authoritarian, dignified image, he gave new meaning to the word imposing.

When he left I commented on his impressive head of thick grey hair. Gerald soon set me right. 'It's a toupee,' he hissed. 'He wears it all the time, but it moves around on his head.'

'How do you know?' I whispered. One can never be sure who's listening in a movie studio – spies are everywhere.

'Because he comes into make-up in the morning with it already stuck on. Jack has to put the panstick on *around* the tuft that falls over his forehead, and he's *forbidden* to touch it.'

'I knew another actor like that,' I said, remembering a famous horror-movie star. 'He wore a "toup" and I had to play a scene with him in which he'd been so frightened he'd gone completely bald.'

'So, obviously he didn't wear his piece, then?' said Gerald.

'Certainly not.' I laughed. 'He came into make-up with his piece *on*, and the hapless hairdresser had to put on the bald cap *over* it!'

'Now *that*'s a challenge,' said Gerald laconically. 'Why didn't she complain?'

'Because the actor absolutely *refused* to admit that he wore one. *Swore* it was all his own hair.'

'Like our own dear Chuck,' said Gerald.

Heston had brought along his gigantic leather-backed director's chair, with his name embossed on the front, and 'from the crew of *Ben Hur*' inscribed on the back. It was so heavy it took five prop men to move it.

Mr Heston was exceedingly dignified and seemed to take himself very seriously indeed. Sometimes I liked to clown around on set, but I realized I must behave sedately while working with this icon, so not a single quip passed my lips. Charlton Heston was a consummate professional who never needed more than one take. Our scene, a classic 'Alexis-pitting-wits-against-man', was in the can in under two hours.

Afterwards Heston stood, shook hands with me, the director and the lighting cameramen in a dignified fashion, and said what a pleasure it had been working with all of us. Then off he strode back to *The Colbys*, leading with his famous profile, an authentic old-fashioned gentleman film-star.

CHAPTER FOURTEEN

Life's a bitch

By the mid-eighties the three major television networks had lost so much of their dominance to the cable companies that they were becoming almost manic in their pursuit of ratings. Money was suddenly no object at ABC, and 'raising the ratings' was their call to arms.

Bringing other stars into *Dynasty* was an expensive ploy but one that the network believed would boost them to the top. We in the cast were somewhat dubious – after all, *Dynasty* was still performing brilliantly, continuously in the top five, before the likes of Rock Hudson, George Hamilton, Charlton Heston, Ali McGraw and Helmut Berger were brought in to help out. But ABC and Messrs Spelling and Cramer didn't agree with us; stars and yet more stars was their new credo, and on to our sets they trooped, at enormous salaries and with preposterous story-lines seemingly cobbled together at a moment's notice.

Rock Hudson was the first superstar to grace us with his presence. He had been the all-American hero of the fifties, a tall, clean-cut, handsome matinée idol who always tried to seduce the professionally virginal Doris Day in frothy comedies. Rock's popularity had been centred mainly on his dazzling beef-cake looks. Universal had signed Roy Fitzgerald after his demobilization from the Navy after the Second World War, changing his perfectly reasonable name to the ludicrously fake Rock Hudson – and unaware that he was a promiscuous closet queen. Over the years, his wild homosexual parties became the stuff of legend in Hollywood for the battalions of gorgeous young studs he'd always invite. I went to one of his famous costume parties in the late fifties. Wearing a beaded flapper frock, it was there that I first met the devastatingly gorgeous young Elvis Presley dressed in glitter and white as a rhinestone cowboy. But Elvis, a well-brought-up boy, seemed almost as stunned as I was by the excesses at Rock's party.

In 1985, though, Rock's stunning looks had long since gone. I sat beside him in the make-up room on his first day of *Dynasty*, watching out of the corner of my eye as he stared gloomily into the mirror at his rav-aged features. Jack Freeman, the make-up man, was attempting to Polyfill that once beautiful face for a love scene with Linda. I thought that he had his work cut out as Rock looked terrible: pushing sixty, gaunt, hollow-eyed and much too thin. He looked exhausted, like a man who'd been on a severe bender for a month.

He chain-smoked during his make-over, and we chatted politely about our own forthcoming scene. The entire time he sat there, he scratched himself continuously and rubbed his back up and down against the leather chair. This was unusual, to say the least, and I wondered what the problem could be. After he had left, Gerald Solomon, my hairdresser, whispered, 'I've heard he's got AIDS.'

'I'm not quite sure what that is,' I said.

'Neither am I, but I hear it's deadly,' responded Gerald.

In the early eighties few people knew anything about AIDS, how it was contracted or how contagious it was. The first time I'd even heard of it had been in August 1982. I'd been on the cover of *US* magazine, and next to puffs for other features was a sinister headline: 'Mysterious Cancer That's Killing Gay Men'. It hadn't even been given a name then, but now, less than two years later, it had become an issue about which many people were becoming hysterically paranoid.

'Don't touch *any* of those brushes,' Gerald warned, as he and Jack disinfected their professional equipment more thoroughly than usual.

'But how can one catch it?' I asked.

Gerald, who was openly gay, shrugged. 'No one really knows – but they say you *may* be able to get it by touching someone who has it, or drinking from the same glass, or even using cutlery an infected person has used.'

Linda came in and we both listened solemnly to Gerald's theories.

A highly infectious disease for which there was no known cure was pretty scary. Linda was uncharacteristically silent as she prepared for her love scene with Rock, which was to be shot after my next sequence.

After I wrapped, I went over to Rock and Linda's set where the tension was palpable. They rehearsed the scene up to the embrace, when the director then called, 'Cut.' But when they finally kissed, Rock pulled out every stop. He embraced Linda fiercely, kissing her with aggressive passion. As the saintly Krystle, who has never been unfaithful to Blake, Linda was supposed to struggle to escape from him, but Rock was almost savage in his love-making. As Gerald and I watched from a corner of the set, I was astonished at Linda's courage.

'She could catch it!' I hissed.

Gerald nodded and said, 'I only hope he doesn't bite her.'

As soon as the director called, 'Cut. OK, kids, that's a print,' Linda dashed to the bathroom where she spent fifteen minutes brushing her teeth, gargling with antiseptic and scrubbing her face.

'You're a braver man than I, Gunga Din,' I remarked to her in make-up the next day.

'What could I do?' she said simply. 'I didn't want to hurt his feelings.'

I admired Linda's altruism but not her carelessness. As it turned out I wasn't the only actress concerned about catching AIDS from a kissing scene. When the news that Rock had the disease and his indifference towards possibly infecting Linda hit the media, frenzy erupted. Dozens of actresses rang their agents refusing even to *touch* actors whom they suspected might be gay.

It was an uncomfortable and uneasy situation for everyone, particularly for actors, who are usually known for their tolerance and liberalism.

The issue was fuelled by ignorance, for in those early days *no one* knew much about AIDS, least of all the doctors. People even began to believe that AIDS and herpes were synonymous.

Within a month our union, the Screen Actors' Guild, had received so many petitions from actresses and their agents that a new clause had to be inserted into all contracts: no producer or director could force any actor or actress to do love scenes if they didn't want to. 'Kissing doubles' were suddenly all the rage, and many actresses looked upon actors whose sexuality was the tiniest bit dubious with considerable suspicion.

Media stories of Rock's secret homosexuality opened a Pandora's box in Hollywood. Suddenly every actor who had never been married or wasn't screwing three girls at once was suspected of being gay. Paranoia and fear became endemic as Hollywood hostesses started to use only plastic cups and cutlery at their parties, and ordered industrial-strength dish-washers to clean everyone's potentially deadly germs off their finest Limoges. This was the time when people thought you might catch AIDS from shaking hands, so much air-kissing ensued, which still exists today. We have AIDS paranoia to thank for the dreadful *mwah-mwah*. It was only when Elizabeth Taylor became the spokesperson for AMFAR (The American Foundation for Aids Research) and the public was told that AIDS could only be transmitted by shared needles or unprotected sex that calm was eventually restored.

On the *Dynasty* set, we watched Rock's disintegration with deep sorrow. Each week he seemed weaker, more vulnerable, his face horribly drawn, but he still wouldn't admit he had the disease; he carried on smoking forty cigarettes a day and slugging back neat vodka like a sailor on leave.

Two weeks later I had to shoot another scene with him. By now he was so frail that he had to sit down between each shot, and so emaciated that his clothes hung on him as if he were no more than a wire coathanger – but like the consummate professional he was, he played the scene without a hitch. A few weeks later he went for more treatment to the American Hospital in Paris but returned to the US because there was no cure.

Rock Hudson died in October 1985 in his Hollywood house, The Castle. This tragic trailblazer had become more famous for being a homosexual killed by AIDS than he'd ever been as one of the most popular pin-up boys in movies.

Elizabeth Taylor said at his funeral, 'Please God he has not died in vain.'

Several weeks later Tom telephoned to inform me that I had to do an episode of *The Love Boat*, called *The Captain's Crush*.

'*Love Boat*?' I squawked. 'Oh, Tom, that's such a trashy show. Please don't make me do it. *Dynasty*'s a top series, and guesting on *Love Boat* seems so demeaning.'

'I'm afraid you've got to,' he said bluntly. 'It's in your *Dynasty* contract.'

I studied the fine print and saw that he was absolutely right. Spelling and Cramer were no fools: every star of their other shows was obliged to guest on *Love Boat*, which was shooting on the same Warner Hollywood lot as *Dynasty*.

Although tremendously popular, *Love Boat* wasn't of the calibre of *Dynasty*. It was lightweight fluff for the tabloid/talk-show housewives.

My first day on set, almost the entire stage was taken up by an amazing facsimile of an enormous cruise liner. It had a swimming pool, filled with properly chlorinated water. There was a bar with actual drinks, albeit the whisky was diluted with Coca-Cola and the wine was apple juice, there was even an area where 'passengers' could play deck quoits and deck tennis.

The captain of the Love Boat, and my leading man, was Gavin McLeod, an avuncular, cropped-hair actor in his fifties, easy-going, popular with the crew and glad to be working in such a successful series. He looked dashing in his sparkling white uniform, lavishly trimmed with gold braid and medals. Supposedly he had a twinkle in his eye for my character, a glamorous movie star, suitably overdressed in Nolan Miller's most flamboyant creations.

After our first flirtation scene, I went back to *Dynasty*, and when I returned a few days later to shoot the love scene with Gavin, Gerald whispered as he was tweaking at my hair, 'Have you *seen* what's on Gavin's upper lip?'

'No,' I murmured. 'What is it?'

'Herpes,' he said intensely. 'And that's *seriously* contagious.'

'Oh, my God. *Herpes*.' My mind reeled. 'Herpes and AIDS are almost the same, aren't they?'

Gerald gave a who-knows? shrug and then I was called to the set.

I spotted the enormous sore in the centre of Gavin's lower lip immediately we started rehearsing. To my dismay it was exactly where I was supposed to kiss him. My heart sank and after we blocked the scene, *sans* kiss, I told the director, Jerry, that I thought the scene would play better if Gavin bent me backwards over the rail of the boat far enough so that the camera couldn't actually see us kiss.

'Why do you want to do that?' Jerry said suspiciously. 'Love scenes are what make our series sizzle. This is the Love Boat, dear, didn't you know?'

I trawled my mind for inspiration. The charming Mr McLeod was smiling at me, his sore – which I had now convinced myself would kill me on contact – glistened in the arc-lights. I glanced over to where Gerald stood, brows raised questioningly, wondering how I was going to get out of *this* one.

'Of course, it's *fine* by me to do the kissing scene any way you want, Jerry. But the problem is that I wear so much lipstick that not only will it get all over *my* face, but all over Gavin's too.' My smile was full of altruistic concern. 'He's wearing such a wonderfully spotless white uniform, it would be a pity to ruin it with *Framboise Fuchsia*.'

The wardrobe girl's ears pricked up. 'Gee, that could be a *real* problem,' she wailed. 'Gavin's only got one other dress uniform and that's at the cleaners.'

There was a pause while Jerry looked at my make-up man Bob Sidell. 'Is this lipstick thing true?' he barked.

'Absolutely,' said Bob seriously. 'We always have problems with Joanie and her lipstick, don't we, hon?'

I nodded vigorously and Jerry looked nonplussed. Then, in a confidential whisper, he said to me, 'Give us a break, dear. Why don't you take off the lipstick for this scene?'

I drew myself up and stared haughtily at him, with the Edith Evans dragon-lady look for which I was so famed in the tabloids. 'Take off my *lipstick*? I'm playing a flamboyant movie star. You couldn't *possibly* expect her to wear *this* outfit,' I gestured dramatically to my emerald heavily ruffled dress, 'without lipstick. Sorry Jerry, but that's carrying Method acting *too* far.'

Jerry looked so crestfallen that I said, 'Look, I'm *happy* to do the scene, darling. I'm just telling you it will take at *least* half an hour to redo my make-up after the kiss unless we fake it.'

'Half an hour?'

I nodded vehemently. 'Well maybe I *could* do it in twenty-five minutes.'

Seconds ticked away. Jerry looked at his watch, and Gerald and Bob stood on the sidelines unable to meet my eye. Then Jerry consulted with the assistant director who shook his head and said, 'There's no time to redo her make-up, boss. We're behind schedule as it is.'

'OK, OK, OK,' said Jerry. 'You win. We'll do the scene your way, Joan.'

So the handsome captain swept the beautiful movie star into his arms on the moonlit deck and murmured sweet nothings in her ear. Then he bent her backwards over the rail and we stared into each other's eyes.

'Was it because of this?' whispered Gavin, with an understanding smile. 'It's only a cold sore, you know.'

'Oh dear, I'm sorry, Gavin, but you know all these rumours are going around about herpes, and I'm afraid I have a touch of hypochondria.'

'I don't blame you,' said Gavin conspiratorially. 'I told Jerry this morning that we shouldn't do the kiss, but he insisted. You know, the ratings.'

'Oh, yes, I know,' I said.

Even though the audience didn't actually see the captain's lips meet the diva's, this episode of *Love Boat* still pulled in a huge number of viewers.

For plot purposes and studio economies, in the 1985 season Alexis's offices and apartment were moved into the hotel owned by cousin Sable. It seemed ludicrous to me that Alexis would deign to live in a residence owned by her deadliest enemy, but I had no say in it. Aaron had bought an enormously expensive hotel set, which he had to use, so suddenly all the main action centred around it. That, I believe, is when *Dynasty* started to lose its sparkle.

I was sorry to move as I had loved my sets. They were totally Alexis, modern, stylish and glamorous. My desk epitomized her, sleek, sharp and streamlined, with a thick glass top supported by four giant elephant tusks. Make of that what you will.

Another star brought into *Dynasty* to add more heat was the German actor Helmut Berger. I'd known him for many years: he was beautiful, mad as a hatter and enormous fun. He'd had a varied career since being discovered in 1969 by Luchino Visconti who had cast him in *The Damned*, when he'd become a cult icon because of his wickedly dazzling looks. Helmut made no secret of his penchant for night-clubs and carousing, and back in the seventies we'd done our fair share together in Paris and Rome. Always surrounded by a laughing group, Helmut was great company and I was delighted that he was going to be in *Dynasty* playing Peter de Villes, Fallon's latest boyfriend.

'Hello, darling,' a vaguely familiar voice rasped one morning. It was 6 a.m., and, clutching a styrofoam cup of coffee, I was *en route* to my dressing room to begin the tweaking process. A skinny, pale, tired-looking creature stood in the doorway of his tiny trailer.

'Hi.' I wasn't inclined to chat to someone I didn't know and before my morning caffeine fix I'm less than scintillating. I continued walking.

'It's Helmut!' He bounded down the steps to give me a European bear hug. 'Don't you recognize me, darling?'

We *aah*ed and *mwah-mwah*ed, both secretly analysing each other's washed-out morning faces.

'God, what a *night*.' He ran a hand through his luxuriant long blond hair. '*I'm exhausted.*'

'Surely you didn't go out last night, when you had to get up so early this morning?' I asked.

'*Daarling, of course.* Oh, you Americans, you all take acting so seriously,' he scoffed.

'*Daarling*,' I reprimanded him, 'may I remind you that I'm *not* American. Listen, you'd better take this stuff seriously. The dialogue might look easy to learn but it's a bitch.'

'Don't worry, *daarling*. I've never had any problems with *my* dialogue.' He hugged me again, and off we went to make ourselves beautiful.

Within a week, word came back from the set that Helmut was having enormous problems with his lines. So much so that a new character, an American lawyer, was quickly written in to be his representative. Much of Helmut's dialogue was given to the lawyer, and as the episodes for which he was contracted rolled by, he had less and less to say in them. One day he confronted me. He looked fabulous, and the excesses to which he openly admitted were well camouflaged by a deep tan make-up.

'Why are they *doing* this to me, *daarling*?' he asked despairingly. 'Tell me the truth – please.'

It wasn't my business to tell him the truth, so I asked in a schoolmistressy tone, 'Were you out on the tiles again last night, darling?'

He smiled endearingly, the consummate little-boy-lost.

'Of course, *daarling*. Camilla had a wonderful party. Why didn't you come?'

'You know why, darling. Work comes first. You *must* realize that we can only party in this town on Friday and Saturday nights.'

'Boring,' Helmut trilled, '*very* boring. You're missing out on things, Joanie. You've got to live your life to the hilt, *daarling*.'

'Well, getting plastered at parties with a bunch of people I don't know and partaking of weird substances does not a picture-perfect actor or actress make,' I said primly.

He shrugged. 'You need to have some fun, *daarling*.'

'I have my fun when I go to London and party at Annabel's or Tramp. Helmut, LA's a working town, and if you're going to be in front of that camera you've *got* to get six or seven hours' sleep.'

'*Daarling*,' he winked, 'you're really becoming *so* square. Is this the girl who used to dance the night away with me at Régine's?'

'Sure is,' I grinned, 'but now I'm saving all my energy for the set – and you should too.'

'Boring, *daarling* – too, *too* boring.' He jumped into his red convertible. 'There's more to life than acting.'

Sadly, the powers-that-be at *Dynasty* were not satisfied with Helmut's performance, and shortly thereafter he was dropped. There's a moral there somewhere.

*

Ali McGraw did somewhat better than Helmut. I'd known her since the seventies when she was honeymooning with Bob Evans in Acapulco. She was a fabulous girl – warm, witty and down-to-earth, but overly modest about her own talent. She had started as a model and then become the box-office golden girl after *Love Story* and in *Goodbye Columbus*. Catapulted to superstardom she'd become America's favourite actress, but gave up movies when she met and married Steve McQueen. Since their divorce she had seldom worked. As I keep saying, our business is unbelievably precarious, and Ali was a prime example of the fickleness of both the public and the producers.

Since *Dynasty* was such a big deal, Ali was understandably nervous on her first day. Our great mutual friend, Sue Mengers, had told me to 'be nice to Ali', so I took her to lunch and told her about some of the pitfalls. 'It's like a factory here,' I explained, 'and we're the product. We've got to get ten minutes of film in the can each day and if we *don't* manage it by six or seven o'clock, we'll go on shooting until we do. It's essential to know your lines backwards, forwards and inside out because we shoot so fast that if you blow them you'll soon find yourself up to your neck in shit.'

'Doesn't sound like the movies,' Ali said warily.

'It's *not* like the movies at all.' I laughed. 'In the movies you can take all the time in the world to work on your scene. Here you've got to get it right, preferably in the first take. If you dry, they'll cut away from you to another actor. If you dry too many times . . .' I thought of poor Helmut '. . . they'll axe you. They're *not* a charitable institution.'

'Thanks for warning me,' said Ali. 'I'll try to be a good little team-player.'

Ali had been brought in as a potential love-interest for Blake. Ever since Krystle had had a fling with Rock Hudson's character, ABC wanted to show the other side of the coin. Alexis was certainly busy in the romance department, as were Adam, Fallon and Steven. In fact, everyone was at it like rabbits – everyone, that is, except stalwart Blake and saintly Krystle. ABC wanted to change that and thought Ali was the perfect foil for John Forsythe's austere, distinguished character. She was beautiful, elegant and classy, just the kind of woman Blake could fall for. But no. It was not to be.

When John Forsythe saw the script in which he begins a romantic flirtation with Ali, he threw a wobbly and demanded script changes. He still believed that Blake would never, *ever* look at another woman, so Ali's scenes were soon sliced to ribbons and the romance was nipped in the bud. Ali was kept around for decoration, or maybe because of her contract, until the infamous finale of the 1985 season.

In this scene Catherine Oxenberg, who played Amanda (the long-lost daughter of Blake and Alexis), is marrying the handsome Prince of Moldavia played by Michael Praed. During the lavish wedding, in which all the *Dynasty* cast are present, a group of terrorists bursts in through the windows, machine-gunning the entire congregation. The final shot is of everyone lying on top of each other, completely motionless, playing dead. Now *all* our futures hung in the balance: none of us knew whether we would be coming back for the next season because none of us knew whether we had survived or been killed in the massacre. I was off to France to make *Sins*, a mini-series for CBS, but still in the middle of renegotiating my *Dynasty* contract, I didn't have a clue as to Alexis's fate.

The end-of-season *Dynasty* party was held at the Beverly Wilshire Hotel. Everyone – cast, crew and their spouses or 'significant others' – gathered to eat, drink and gossip, and then to watch the *Dynasty* gag reel, a compilation from the editors of all the amusing things that had happened during the season. It was usually hysterical: actors dropped props, fluffed, swore and generally made fools of themselves, crew members dressed as Carrington caricatures sang ribald songs.

At the end of the evening, Aaron Spelling went to the dais to bring on John Forsythe, who then introduced all the other actors. One by one we all went up to take a bow. Then John said, 'And now a lovely lady who, unfortunately, will not be back with us next season – Miss Ali McGraw.'

There was an audible gasp from the audience as an ashen-faced Ali walked slowly up to the dais. Everyone stood up to applaud her but Ali looked shattered. Her huge brown eyes were wide as a child's and she seemed on the point of tears. I couldn't believe the insensitivity of the person who had instructed John to relay the news of her dismissal in such a callous manner. All the cast whispered uncomfortably to each other as we stood about on stage, some probably thinking, 'There but for the grace of God go I.'

It was a most unfortunate evening. So I was thrilled I was leaving the next day for Paris and *Sins*.

CHAPTER FIFTEEN

For my sins

When my relationship with Peter Holm began, he had seemed to me like a take-charge kind of guy. He'd helped to organize my financial affairs, tried to take some of the pressure off, and to look after all the thousand and one problems that needed almost constant attention. When one spent twelve hours a day working flat out, this seemed like an enormous relief. In effect Holm became my manager – which, in retrospect, was one of the most foolish moves I'd ever made in my whole life.

In 1985 I decided it was time to work for myself. In every hiatus I'd worked for either Aaron or another producer, so Peter and I had begun to look for a suitable project. I wanted to produce as well as to act this time, and with the help of Jon Feldheimer and Justin Pierce at New World production company, we found a book by Judith Gould called *Sins*, which we started to prepare as a mini-series for CBS.

I felt that at last I was taking control of my career and being executive producer and star of *Sins* was one of the most exciting and rewarding, if gruelling, experiences of my professional life.

The production was to be supervised by line producer Steve Krantz, husband of the hugely successful novelist Judith Krantz, myself, and a CBS line producer, Anna Hall. But the aspect of producing that interested me most was casting. I'd always thought that I could be an astute casting director ever since I'd spotted the possibilities in a sexy dark-haired young man who used to whistle at me outside Metro's mail room. As Carolyn Jones and I had tottered past on our way to *The Opposite Sex* set I said, 'He's so good-looking, he should be an actor.'

'I've heard he's trying,' Carolyn whispered.

The young man later asked me for a date but, nose in the air, I turned him down. A few years later, in some Roger Corman horror film, I recognized his devilishly handsome face. His name was Jack Nicholson.

Sitting next to him at a dinner recently, I asked, 'Do you remember me from Metro during your days in the mail room?'

He shot me his famous quizzical grin. 'Course I do.' He twinkled. 'I fancied you, Yvette Mimieux and Liz Taylor – I was a brash kid and I asked you all for dates, but all of you turned me down.'

'More fool us,' I laughed.

Casting *Sins* was a joy. So many talented international actors were available, and since we had a sizzling, first-rate script, agents swamped us with calls about their clients. I had definite ideas about whom I wanted for several key roles. My character, Hélène Junot, who runs a fashion magazine, has a second-in-command called Luba. I thought Marisa Berenson would be perfect to play her: several years before she had been in Kubrick's *Barry Lyndon*, but hadn't worked recently in America. We had difficulty in persuading CBS to cast her as the networks always had their own favourites and they wanted someone whom American audiences would recognize. But I was insistent.

'Marisa knows the world of fashion. She's Schiaparelli's granddaughter, for heaven's sake. She dresses naturally in a chic, high-style way, which is *exactly* how Luba would. You'll *never* get that look from a Hollywood actress. Most of them have no interest in fashion at all.'

Marisa got the part.

For ZZ, Hélène's arch-enemy, I insisted on the acerbic, independent model/actress Lauren Hutton, and for Hélène's love interest I wanted Timothy Dalton. Unfortunately the network didn't think he was sexy enough, which we all thought was ridiculous. 'Timothy has *tons* of sex-appeal and is very good-looking,' I pleaded. 'Even Mae West thought so.'

But CBS knew best, and this time they were adamant, so James Farantino played Hélène's lover, and Timothy Dalton was cast as her brother. Several years later Timothy took over from Roger Moore as James Bond, which proves that networks aren't always infallible.

Our final cast was superb. Marisa Berenson, Gene Kelly, Lauren Hutton, Jean-Pierre Aumont, Giancarlo Giannini, Capucine, Arielle Dombasle, Joseph Bologna, Catherine Mary Stewart, William Allan Young, plus some stalwart English supporting actors, like Paul Freeman, Neil Dixon, Peter McEnery and Judy Bowker.

Hélène Junot's other arch-enemy, the hateful Nazi Herr von Eiderfeld, was the most difficult part to cast. He must be Hélène's nemesis throughout, and her life-long vendetta with him is driven by the horror of having seen her mother beaten to death by him. We interviewed several actors in London and the man who impressed me, rather menacing-looking, shaven-headed and intense, was Steven Berkoff. He was a cult figure in England, and several of the English cast seemed quite intimidated by him. Several years later when I worked with Steven in *Decadence* I discovered several reasons why. But on *Sins* I was the boss, and we had an excellent rapport.

Steve Krantz wanted Gene Kelly to play Hélène Junot's older husband, a concert pianist with whom she falls madly in love. Although I'd bumped into Gene at various Hollywood gatherings over the years, I hadn't been close to him since my early days in LA. Although most famous for his brilliant musicals, he was also a distinguished dramatic actor and had given impressive performances in *Inherit the Wind, Marjorie Morningstar* and many others. CBS were hot for the idea but left it up to us, the producers, to deliver. Gene was a tremendous Francophile, which we hoped might entice him to take part, and by sheer coincidence he was in Paris at the time. Steve called him at the Crillon, he seemed eager for a meeting. We were off.

At seventy-three Gene looked terrific, like a man fifteen years younger, and still had the energy and *joie de vivre* with which he had so enchanted audiences in *Singin' in the Rain* and *On the Town*. After we'd reminisced about old times and old friends, he told me he was impressed that I was producing. 'Good for you, kid. That's showing 'em that a gal can do it too.' Gene was of my father's generation, always slightly amazed that 'the little woman' could manage to cut it in a man's world.

We left him the script after he gave us his sincere assurances that he would read it immediately. Within a week, he'd agreed to play this relatively minor role and everyone was thrilled.

In Paris with Katy, Judy, her daughter Victoria, and a nanny, Peter (my Swedish partner) and I checked into the Ritz Hotel, giving new meaning to the word excess. This entourage took over almost an entire floor and we called it Camp Ritz.

One entire room housed the exercise machine with which I attempted to keep myself in shape for my demanding part. Hélène Junot had to age from eleven to fifty and although, of course, I could play the latter years, there was no question of attempting to play Hélène under thirty. Catherine Mary Stewart did an excellent job until I took over.

Assorted guests often dropped in from all over the world for flying visits and I fell in love with the City of Light once more. Unlike London and LA, Paris had barely changed since the fifties. When not working, I explored and revelled in it with a vengeance. I felt a tremendous affinity with France, and Peter and I discussed buying a small house on the Riviera.

Our Parisian location was made even more memorable by the annoying fact that I had to watch my friends devour wonderful food in this gourmet heaven, while I picked at celery and grilled sole in an attempt to stay svelte. Every pound I put on added a year to my face, so I couldn't gain more than a couple. It was a crashing bore, but worth it in the end.

Valentino designed Hélène's divinely elegant modern wardrobe, but my 'boom-booms', as he euphemistically called them, presented a problem. During one fitting he sighed, 'To look *really* chic in clothes, my dear, a woman must be more flat-chested than rounded.' Unfortunately I tended towards the latter and, however thin I became, bore little resemblance to his stick-elegant models.

'Never mind, I know how we will solve this little problem.' His teeth flashed in his perfectly tanned face, and at the next fitting one of his dressers produced, with a flourish, what could only be described as a rubber liberty bodice. With this uncomfortable and hideous contraption strapped over my chest, it immediately looked several inches flatter. Valentino seemed delighted, and indisputably my clothes hung better. Proudly I went on set to display my new shape to Steve Krantz.

'That dress looked much better at the first fitting. What have you done to it?' asked Steve.

'Don't you think I look chic, and, er – *thinner?*'

'Yeah, yeah, you look thinner, you look good, but I liked it better when you had more . . .' He waved his hands vaguely as men do when describing a curvy woman. By this time the lighting cameraman and operator had both offered their opinions, which concurred with Steve's. 'In France, we *like* our women to 'ave some shape,' said the cameraman.

'I'll see what I can do.' I dashed to my dressing room, removed the painful contrivance, put on a 'minimizing' bra, and went back to see Steve and the boys again.

'Much, *much* better.' Steve smiled approvingly. 'Now you look womanly, like Hélène should look. We don't want any more of that flat-chested stuff, not after *Playboy*, dear.'

Even though I was one of the executive producers, I still had to fight hard for control on *Sins*. The networks didn't like the inmates running the asylum. 'Never the twain shall meet' was the way networks and studios preferred it with performers, and historically there had always been friction between those in front of the camera and those behind it.

Although he hadn't appeared in a film for some time, Gene Kelly was still a major star, so when he was due to arrive at the beautiful villa in the South of France where we were to shoot Stanislaw and Hélène's honeymoon sequences, the crew were excited. I've always found it fascinating to gauge the unit's opinion of actors. Some current superstars whom the public worship leave the crew cold; others, like Gene, Charlton Heston and Gregory Peck, inspired the utmost respect and admiration.

Although more than twenty years older than me, Gene looked frisky, with a roguish twinkle. He'd always had an eye for the ladies and in our first love scene, which director Douglas Hickox staged on the lawn, Gene was in fine fettle. Flashing his winning lop-sided smile he took me in his arms and whispered this tender dialogue, 'Hélène, oh, my dear Hélène, I love you so.'

'And I love you too,' I cooed back. At which point we were tentatively to kiss. Well, it started out tentatively but then Gene, encouraged, perhaps, because I'd flattered him excessively at the Crillon by telling him how I had adored him since I was a little girl, decided to take it further. To my absolute astonishment he bestowed upon me a classic French kiss and thrust his tongue deep into my mouth.

'Cut,' called Doug. 'What's all *that* about, Gene? This is supposed to be a tender kiss.'

'I couldn't resist this little gal,' said Gene, in his throaty high voice that always sounded like a chuckle. 'I've wanted to do that to Joanie since she first came to Hollywood, but she was always too busy with someone else!'

Gene had a slight complex about his hair. When he was young it had been thick and black but in his forties it had started to recede and now he always wore a silver-grey toupee both on and off screen. I too prefer wearing wigs when filming because the arduous daily process of washing, setting, combing out and being tweaked is time-consuming and unnecessary. On the windy afternoon when we were to shoot another love scene on a *bâteau mouche*, chugging down the Seine, we were both beautifully bewigged.

Then from nowhere a hurricane suddenly blew up and swept through Paris: gale-force winds whipped the river into Atlantic-sized waves. We were freezing and our respective wigs were in grave danger of flying off. I stuck dozens of hair-pins through mine, attaching it firmly to my own hair, but this was difficult for Gene as he didn't have too many strands of his own to work with. Wardrobe presented him with a black French beret, which he jammed jauntily on top of his toupee, and I was given a white one. In our twin berets we looked like two Gallic onion-sellers. But even with them well squashed down, the wind was so ferocious we were in danger of losing our headgear altogether. Gene was totally good-natured, cracking gags throughout, and when a particularly vicious gust almost removed the hat and raised the front of his hair he joked, 'This ain't *nothin'* compared to the four-day downpour I went through for *Singin' in the Rain*. Don't worry, kids, this is a piece of cake.'

Gene was a delight, an absolute professional, and I was devastated in early 1996 to hear of his death. To me he epitomized the Golden Age of Hollywood: the glamour, the dedication and the larger-than-life quality that all true old-time movie-stars possessed.

There is no one standing in the wings to take Gene Kelly's place, nor will there ever be. Each time we lose a Greer Garson, a Bette Davis or a Cary Grant, the sad fact is that they were unique, which one cannot say about most of today's stars. Those wonderfully exciting, glossy Technicolor musicals, with their simplistic plots and enthusiastically extravagant numbers, have also gone for ever. Thank God for videos, so that we can see again the greats of that Golden Age at the mere flick of a switch.

Peter and I eventually bought a tiny *maison de pecheur* in Port Grimaud on the Riviera and a boat, a large Riva, we called *Sins*. Each day we watched rushes of *Sins*, and began to think we had a real little jewel on our hands. So did CBS. By the time shooting finished the rival network, NBC, had decided they needed damage control for the Sunday night *Sins* was to air.

NBC had just put the finishing touches to *Peter the Great*, their block-busting mini-series, which cost three times as much as *Sins* to make, and starred such icons as Laurence Olivier, Vanessa Redgrave, Omar Sharif and Peter O'Toole. To prevent CBS from winning 'sweeps' night (when the channels compete for the highest ratings and the future highest advertising rates) the following February, NBC decided to schedule *Peter* in the *exact* time-slot opposite *Sins*. Not only that, but just to ensure that *Sins* would sink, they moved *The Bill Cosby Show*, the most successful sit-com on air which commanded sixty-eight million viewers, into their first half-hour slot opposite us.

'We're doomed,' I said gloomily to Steve, as we sat together digesting this latest piece of news. 'We'll *never* beat that line-up. It's *impossible*.'

Steve, a producer for many years, was more sanguine. 'I think we've got a chance,' he said. '*Peter the Great* is a big, heavy historical epic that Mr and Mrs Average might think is too cultural for their taste. You're still so popular as Alexis, and we're frothy and light with a great plot and cast, and a story that all women are going to want to watch. Yes, we've got more than a chance,' said Steve optimistically. 'And I believe we may even win the night, because *Sins* is wonderful fun. It's dramatic, campy and kitsch with enough glamorous clothes and glitzy events to keep every

Left: With Sean
Connery, Jackie, and
Michael Caine after
lunch at the Caines',
Beverly Hills 1985.

(JOAN COLLINS)

Above: I'd always
adored Gene Kelly and
was thrilled to work
with him in *Sins*, Paris
1985.

(SIPA PRESS/VLADIMIR SICHOV)

Right: With Roger
Moore and Stephanie
Powers the evening
before 'Night of 100
Stars', Regines Club,
New York 1985.

(JOAN COLLINS)

Above: Elizabeth Taylor and I compare cleavages watched by George Hamilton, London 1987.
(JOAN COLLINS)

Right: I'd played Queen Elizabeth in a costume-party episode of *Dynasty*. *Life* magazine made the photo appear like an old master painting.
(BRITISH FILM INSTITUTE)

Left: As Marilyn, with a facsimile of the famous evening gown she wore when she sang 'Diamonds Are A Girl's Best Friend'. I thought the effect was quite remarkable.
(BRITISH FILM INSTITUTE)

Above: With Donald and
Ivana Trump at the
Trump Tower. Launching
'Spectacular', my
short-lived signature
scent, which was a
spectacular failure,
1990.

Left: Tony Newley and
I emulate Noël and
Gertie in 'Red Peppers'
in *Tonight at 8.30* for
the BBC, 1991.

Above: After dinner at Irving Lazar's famous Oscar party. Miss Ciccone is cool with Alek Keshishian and Robin, whilst I chill out with Alan Nevins, 1992.

(PETER C. BORSARI)

Left: Katy and me in 1993 at a party to celebrate my editing of *Marie Claire* magazine.

(ALAN DAVIDSON)

Opposite: Fans caused such a furore when *Dynasty* went off the air that *Dynasty: The Reunion* was made in 1991 – but Alexis didn't change her style.

(EDDIE SANDERSON)

Above: The high life meets the low life. Roseanne plays my unlikely cousin in *Roseanne*, Hollywood 1993.

(EDDIE SANDERSON)

Left: Sharon Stone tells it like it is at Valentino's party, Ledoyen Restaurant, Paris 1994.

(GIANCARLO GIAMMETTI)

Opposite: Sacha had just finished his portrait of Billy Wilder and we celebrate at the Wilder's apartment, Los Angeles 1995.

(JOHN COLAO)

Above: Signor Pavarotti insists that we both go temporarily off our diets, Barbados 1994.

(CHRISTOPHER BIGGINS)

Right: Me with my financial advisor in the South of France 1993. (He's better than most I've had!).

(ROBIN HURLSTONE)

Right: My darling Robin at Destino, 1995.

(JOAN COLLINS)

Overleaf: Emerging triumphantly from court, having won the case Random House brought against me, New York, February 1996.

(MALCOLM CLARKE)

Dynasty fan happy. So don't worry, dear.' But I did. I had a lot riding on this.

We all crossed our fingers. In February, after both shows had aired, when the overnight Neilson ratings came in, *Sins* took second place to *Peter the Great*. Gloom pervaded, but by the end of that day, when the complete ratings had been compiled from all over America, *Sins* had won by a significant margin. We'd taken the night in spades. *The Bill Cosby Show* and *Peter* had been pipped at the post, and elation ran high.

The newspapers went wild with hyperbole. *USA Today* said: 'Joan the Great Takes the Lead.' The *LA Times* said: '*Sins* Wins, Overtakes *Peter*' and the *Hollywood Reporter* stated succinctly: 'CBS's *Sins* Stops *Peter the Great*.'

Now the toughest question was, what should I do for an encore?

Shortly after *Sins* wrapped Peter and I married but it didn't take long for the problems to start.

Barbara Walters was, and remains, the most important and influential of all the television interviewers. Attractive and extremely powerful, she had the pick of any star in Hollywood for her in-depth interviews, which were usually shown after the Oscar broadcast or at other prestigious time-slots during the year. When *Sins* publicity people informed me that Barbara wanted to interview me, it was a coup.

The crew arrived at my Bowmont Drive house and proceeded to set up in the living room. The house was a mess, bursting with lights, cables, technicians, TV monitors and the usual associated hustle and bustle of a television crew. I was upstairs in my dressing room, getting ready, when Peter burst in, red-faced and furious. 'I hope you're getting paid for this,' he yelled.

'Getting *what*?' I looked at him scornfully. 'You must be *joking*. People should pay Barbara Walters to appear on her show.'

He took a rather menacing step towards me. 'If you don't tell her that you want to be paid, I'm throwing all those people out.'

'Peter you really *must* be joking. For God's sake, don't be so stupid. I'm *not* going to tell Barbara Walters that. It would be an *incredible* insult to her and an enormous scandal for me.'

A hearty crockery-throwing row then ensued, as the stubborn Swede refused to take no for an answer and barred the doorway. When I finally told him that it wasn't Barbara Walters who was going to leave the house but him, he stalked out muttering angry Swedish curses. I went downstairs on trembling legs to do Barbara's sympathetic interview, and several times became over-emotional as I talked about my 'new happy marriage'.

There was no question that serious cracks were developing between Peter and me, and we'd only been married a month.

CBS was so gratified with *Sins'* brilliant ratings that they immediately started to search for another project for my next *Dynasty* hiatus. New World found another book, called *Monte Carlo*, by Steven Shepherd, which, although not as strong storywise as *Sins*, was still the kind of frothy drama the network believed that the public liked to see me in.

Monte Carlo is set in 1940, while France is occupied by the Nazis and the inhabitants of Monaco continue their glamorous, hedonistic pre-war existence. George Hamilton was cast as my leading man. I'd always thought that his wit and Cary Grant-type charm should have made him a major star, but he seemed happy enough in his life as an urbane man about town, never terribly concerned whether he worked or not. I'd met him when I first arrived in Hollywood at a party at Cappy's house. He had immediately asked if I wanted a ride in his new car. 'It's a classic Rolls,' he announced proudly. 'One of only fifty made. Goes like a dream.' He was probably about nineteen, but possessed the impeccable manners and bearing of someone much older, a gentleman to the manor born. Tall, tanned and now in his fabulous forties, George was the perfect romantic lead, and I cherished his support and friendship during shooting, because at this time *everything* began to hit the fan with my six-month-old marriage.

Monte Carlo was again shot in the South of France, and I played Katrina Petrovna, a glamorous half-Russian night-club *chanteuse* who moonlights as a spy. Naturally, I again wore the most sensationally flamboyant costumes, but I also had to sing. Although I'd duetted with Bing Crosby in *Hong Kong*, and with Tony in *Hieronymus*, I'd never thought that Barbra Streisand had anything to worry about. 'The Last Time I Saw Paris', the song Katrina warbles in a night-club, entrancing her audience, needs tremendous range from the vocalist but I decided to give it my best shot, and hired a top local voice coach. However, I'd reckoned without the interference of Peter Holm who, flushed with his success as one of *Sins'* executive producers, decided to put in his two cents with a vengeance.

As a Swedish pop star some twenty years previously, he'd tasted some of the fleeting fame that seems to be the lot of that profession. 'You don't need singing lessons. You haf a nice voice,' he insisted, putting his large foot firmly down, shod as it was in grey mock-croc.

'But not nice enough, Peter.' I sighed. 'Look I *desperately* need some voice coaching to create a believable singing performance. Katrina is supposed to be a singing sensation. I'm *not*!'

After another interminable and predictably boring argument, I went to a studio in Nice to work on the song with my coach, our music supervisor and a pianist. But someone snitched to the Swede, for on the second day he came storming into the rehearsal room, screaming at everyone in sight. The gist of his tirade was that my voice was 'sweet' and 'natural' and rehearsals 'would ruin it'. This was so patently ridiculous that a blazing row erupted in front of everyone, which made me so emotional and so inhibited my singing that I stopped rehearsing. I made a rough playback with my voice *au naturel* and, needless to say, it was pretty dire.

Everyone involved in *Sins* and *Monte Carlo* was scared of Peter. His anger was venomous, and when he gave full vent to his fury he could be terrifying.

This was just one of the many senseless fights that had occurred since our marriage and which had opened my eyes. The marriage was a fiasco, I was seriously worried and had to admit that I'd made the greatest, most stupid mistake of my life.

It must seem pretty pathetic that a successful woman, more or less in the prime of her life, should allow herself to be mentally abused and pushed around by a bullying Jekyll and Hyde ex-rocker who'd become a petty tyrant. The trouble was that I remained too stubborn to admit my marital blunder, just as I'd been too pig-headed to listen to all my close friends and family who, without exception, had *begged* me not to marry Holm. I also knew that if I left him, he would make our divorce horrendous.

By this time Peter had also succeeded in alienating many of those closest to me, including my agents at the powerful William Morris agency. I thanked my lucky stars for George Hamilton, who became my rock, confidant and adviser during *Monte Carlo*. 'Bit by bit he's tangled you in his web,' George said sagely one night, as we sat with Sacha at the Voile d'Or restaurant. 'You've *got* to get out of this marriage for your own salvation. *Why* does Peter throw such terrible tantrums and always insist on everything being done how *he* wants it? Why does he sulk for days if he doesn't get his own way?'

'He's like a wilful four-year-old, and he's a desperate sociopath as well,' said Sacha.

'But he did organize my finances and get rid of a lot of parasites in my life.'

'Yeah, he did that to suck you in,' said George. 'Now it's time to get rid of *him*.'

'You're both right,' I said.

'For God's sake, Alexis wouldn't put up with it for a second. She'd eighty-six the evil son of a bitch,' said George.

'If *only* I could be more like her.' I sighed. 'Half the people in the world think I'm just like her and *admire* me for her strength and assertiveness but I'm *not*.'

'Get a life,' said George insistently. 'You must leave Holm. Otherwise he'll destroy your career and you along with it.'

Sacha nodded vigorously. 'Ditch the creep, Mummy. When you finally do, we'll *all* be thrilled.'

During shooting, I realized that *Monte Carlo* didn't have anywhere near the opulence and plot twists of *Sins*. It was much too kitsch, and some of the performances – including mine – were distinctly hammy at times, although we had a good cast that included Malcolm McDowell, Peter Vaughan, Lisa Eichorn and, again, the witty Lauren Hutton.

During Katrina Petrovna's first entrance, I had to sweep into the dining room at the Hôtel de Paris on the arm of a three-star Italian general. My full regalia consisted of a strapless evening dress, high-piled hair, which gave me a slight resemblance to Lily Tomlin, the ubiquitous ostrich feather stole and the *de rigueur faux* diamonds. The assembled diners hush with admiration when they see the famous *chanteuse*. Then Lauren, also exquisitely dressed and sitting with George, whose tan was so dark he looked as if he'd been turned on a rôtisserie, was supposed to utter admiringly, 'Ahh. So *that's* Katrina Petrovna. I've heard that her voice has even fascinated Hitler.'

I'd informed Lauren that my voice would probably have made Hitler capitulate to the French Resistance, so we'd tried to think of an alternative line but couldn't come up with one.

'I'll surprise you,' Lauren said.

On take one, stalking by her table, nose in air, general on arm, I heard Lauren say, 'Ahh, so *that*'s Katrina Petrovna. I didn't realize she was so short!'

I bit my lip hard to stop myself laughing until Tony Page yelled, 'Cut. You can't say that,' whereupon everyone collapsed in hysterics. On the next take Lauren said, 'I thought she'd be taller.'

Later I said to her sweetly, 'Darling Lauren, if you bit your tongue you'd probably die of food poisoning.' She thought that was pretty droll too.

The portents for both my new marriage and my new mini-series weren't good. When Peter and I did speak we usually argued; he was the most combative person I'd ever met and he was successfully killing any shred of affection I'd once harboured for him.

CBS were in too much of a hurry to air *Monte Carlo* for the all-important 1986 November sweeps, which appalled me because it was barely nine months since *Sins* had gone out. I believed the viewing public was being overdosed with Joan Collins, so I called Kim Le Masters, then head of CBS mini-series, to beg him to show *Monte Carlo* the following year.

'Certainly *not*. Our network isn't going to be told what to do by some *actress*. It's none of your business, honey. We're airing in November and that's final.'

'But Tony Page has said that everything's too much of a rush. The lab are working day and night to get it finished, but the film's not even scored properly yet. Both editors say they *can't* do *Monte Carlo* justice in such a hurry. Can't you bring it out later, *please* – maybe for the February sweeps?'

'I don't believe I'm hearing you say this,' snapped Kim. 'This is CBS's business, not yours, honey, so mind it.' And he hung up.

But I sincerely believed that this *was* my business. I was the star and one of the executive producers. *I* was the person on whom the brunt of the criticism would rain if it failed. But I knew I was powerless against CBS scheduling. You can't fight City Hall. Few actors win battles against networks or big studios – unless they're mega-superstars and I was not one of those.

So I gritted my teeth and, on the November night that *Monte Carlo* aired, threw a party for thirty friends at Bowmont Drive. By this time Peter and I were barely speaking, and George was dating Elizabeth Taylor, newly divorced from husband number seven. George asked if he could invite her but I was a touch reluctant – everyone knew Elizabeth's penchant for unpunctuality.

'George, you *know* Elizabeth is *always* late. *Monte Carlo* airs at nine, we're serving drinks at seven thirty, dinner *promptly* at eight, and I want everybody to be seated well before the show.'

'I *assure* you Elizabeth will be there in plenty of time.' George smiled suavely. 'I'll *make* her be punctual.'

I remembered a dinner the previous week at which everyone had waited for hours in a Greek restaurant for Elizabeth. George had called her several times and she had kept assuring him she was on her way. At eleven o'clock when she still hadn't arrived, and as I had to rise and shine for *Dynasty*, I had swept out. But George was insistent: 'She'll be there, I promise you. She's dying to see *Monte Carlo*.'

'She couldn't tape it?' I asked pragmatically.

I'd known and liked Elizabeth for years. Shortly after I'd arrived in Los Angeles we'd double-dated at the old La Rue restaurant, and had chattered away girlishly: she is, like Natalie Wood had been, a girl's girl. Many people would disagree and say that she is more of a man's woman.

Whatever, there is no bitchiness, envy or venom in Elizabeth as there is in so many Hollywood women. If she likes you, she genuinely likes you, and is your friend for life. Throughout the years our paths had continued to cross. I'd dated her first ex-husband, the dissolute Nick Hilton, then she had dated my ex-boyfriend Arthur Loew Jnr. I had been the 'utility infielder' ready to take over from her in *Cleopatra* when she was at death's door with pneumonia. I'd also been at a dreadful dinner party, with a group of horrified acquaintances, in the Roman villa she had shared with husband Eddie Fisher when she had insulted and berated him while everyone there knew about Liz 'n' Dick. Everyone, of course, except Eddie.

We had several friends in common and before her fiftieth birthday party which she threw in her Bel Air house, I'd asked them, '*What* do you buy for the woman who has everything?' Elizabeth made it no secret that she adores being given presents and I'd compromised on that good old stand-by, a Victorian silver photograph frame. She adores giving too, and is extremely generous to her friends. When I married Peter Holm a large box beautifully wrapped in lilac paper arrived from the most exclusive bed-linen shop in Beverly Hills. Inside was a gorgeous peach cashmere blanket with our initials embroidered on it. Unbelievably luxurious, it was one of the most expensive gifts we received. Written on a card in violet ink was a message of love and congratulations. Elizabeth likes seeing her friends get married almost as much as she likes doing it herself.

All the usual suspects were present at the *Monte Carlo* party. The pasta was delicious and at five to nine everybody started congregating in front of the TV sets. Although Bowmont wasn't big, the living room was large enough to accommodate several televisions which were hired and placed, *à la* Swifty Lazar, in various parts of the room so that everyone could have a good view.

At three minutes to nine, the doorbell rang. George raised his eyebrows. 'I guess that's her.' He grinned.

'I guess it is,' I said. 'Well I suppose she *is* on time – for Elizabeth.'

In came the fabled star, wearing tight black silk trousers, a matching beaded sweater and a gorgeous art-deco diamond, ruby and emerald bracelet, reputedly a gift from an Egyptian potentate. She was abjectly apologetic and insisted she wasn't going to eat. 'I'll just have a cigarette,' she said, trembling slightly as she lit it. We stood in the entrance hall and she looked nervously into the living room where everyone was pretending not to notice her. Hollywood people are just as starstruck as ordinary mortals and Elizabeth is the last of the glamorous superstars.

That night she was wearing very long acrylic nails, and as the match flared so did one of these.

'Oh my God! My nail's on fire!' Elizabeth shrieked.

George gallantly threw his drink over her hand and Elizabeth stared at the dripping mess with dismay. In the other room I could hear the music credits beginning to roll, but many of my guests were too busy craning their necks at Elizabeth to look at the screen.

'Do you have an emery board?' she whispered sweetly, pulling herself together.

'Of course. Come up to my dressing room.'

It was a shocking mess of discarded clothes, jumbled cosmetics and open jars and bottles and looked as if it had just been subjected to a terrorist attack, but amazingly, Elizabeth seemed impressed.

'This is *so* tidy,' she remarked. 'You must be very neat.'

'It's a pigsty,' I said.

'You should see mine.' She smiled.

I handed her some manicure equipment and asked if she needed anything else.

'No, I'll be just fine,' she said. 'And I'll be right down, I promise.'

I dashed back downstairs to watch *Monte Carlo* and a few minutes later, realized that, rather than watch George and me emote, many of the guests kept glancing around, waiting for Elizabeth to re-emerge. Eventually she appeared and sat down demurely on a sofa, nail neatly manicured, every hair in place and looking terrific. I noticed that some of those present seemed totally in awe of her.

But then Elizabeth is true Hollywood royalty, and has evoked admiration and respect for decades. She has one of the heartiest down-to-earth laughs I've ever heard, and in the few amusing moments of *Monte Carlo*, she was one of the first to giggle.

Unfortunately I was right about *Monte Carlo*. It was not nearly as good as *Sins* had been, nor as successful in the ratings.

I was sad that my mini- series hadn't worked, but even sadder my fourth marriage didn't seem to be working either.

CHAPTER SIXTEEN

When she was bad . . .

A long with Elizabeth Taylor, Cher, Catherine Deneuve, Victoria Principal, Linda Evans, Mikhail Baryshnikov, Omar Sharif, Sophia Loren and Uncle Tom Cobley and all, I launched my own signature scent, 'Spectacular'. Although I'd done some promotion for Revlon's 'Scoundrel' fragrance several years previously, if 'Spectacular' was successful, it could lead to cosmetics, skin care and bath products. I already had a successful line of spectacles with Marine Optical, and a less successful line of hats, costume jewellery and lingerie, so I was prepared to pull out all the stops for my scent. The boss of Parlux Fragrances, Gerard Simone, was an Italian-American fond of his food and especially of his wine. He decided that it was unnecessary for me to do such a crass thing as a TV commercial to make the public aware of 'Spectacular', and that we would get far more coverage and public visibility if I made store appearances all over the United States. 'We'll get you into every major store. It'll be great,' he enthused. Since America has thousands of towns and cities and probably tens of thousands of department stores this seemed an awesome if not impossible task, but Gerard was not to be daunted. 'We'll take you by private plane,' he bragged. 'All over the States. You'll be a riot.'

And there almost *was* a riot when my publicist Jeffrey Lane, Judy Bryer and I first saw the private plane. About the size of a Mini-Cooper, the fuselage all but touched the ground. Could it be true that we were really supposed to take America by storm in this fabulous executive flying machine? It would be like trying to empty a swimming pool with an egg-cup.

The plane trips were a nightmare – it began to seem as though the pilot deliberately flew through every patch of turbulence he could find. We only survived nervous breakdowns by drinking as much champagne as we could lay our hands on, and stuffing ourselves with stale sandwiches. Little did I realize that this marketing ploy was all the Parlux Company could afford, and that there *was* no money for print ads or commercials. Or for fresh sandwiches.

For a week we criss-crossed the fifty states while I enthusiastically barnstormed 'Spectacular', preaching to the hopeful, horizontally challenged housewives of Seattle, Phoenix, North Carolina, Dallas and Tucson that if they wore my scent a little of the *Dynasty* aura would become theirs. *Dynasty* was still such a craze that it seemed that half the women in the world wanted to look like Alexis or Krystle, while the other half loathed their guts.

Many people still clamoured to be on *Dynasty*, even for a walk-on, and one day Gary Pudney, head of ABC talent co-ordination, received a call from Donald Trump. Then one of the twenty richest people in the US, Trump was on a winning streak and always got what he asked for. The following day when he walked into Gary's New York office he made no bones about what he wanted.

'I'd like to have a part on *Dynasty*,' he announced. 'I just love that show.'

Gary was nonplussed. 'This is very flattering, Donald, but unfortunately all the roles are cast. Maybe next year when we film the Carousel Ball again, we can find a cameo part for you, like we did for Gerald Ford and Henry Kissinger.'

'But you don't *understand*,' said Donald. 'I *am Dynasty*, and I would be *great* as one of Alexis's lovers.' He stared at Gary with the arrogant self-confidence that had helped make him one of America's most successful and famous men. Gary made some excuses, then assured Donald he would do what he could to find a suitable role for him.

Donald Trump was an authentic American success story, although it had been his father, Fred, who had started the family real-estate business after the war and had made it flourish.

Knowing that Donald was such a huge *Dynasty* fan, Gerard Simone suggested to him that he might like to have my 'Spectacular' perfume launch in his brand-new glittering building on Fifth Avenue, the Trump Tower. Donald agreed with alacrity, and I was amazed but delighted. Since 'Parlux' weren't doing anything much to launch it, it would receive a much-needed boost if Donald Trump threw open the doors of his 'spectacular' glass palace, apparently the most exciting and expensive new building in New York.

The Trump Tower is like a vast monument to capitalism. On launch night I arrived with my mini-entourage and walked through the sliding glass doors into an enormous atrium made of vomit-coloured marble blocks. Four escalators wove their way up to the several floors of lavishly expensive shops, and waterfalls cascaded down to where pseudo-alfresco dining areas had been created for shoppers to sit and sip, while mind-numbing Muzak soothed their ravaged wallets.

We took the elevator to the penthouse suite and were ushered into The Donald's (as wife Ivana called him) inner sanctum. He bounded over to greet us. About six foot tall, he had a good-looking face on the verge of running to fat. His fine gingery hair was so long that it curled over his fashionably high collar, and he had thick bushy auburn eyebrows, rather like Michael Heseltine's, smallish aquamarine eyes and a tiny mouth, which appeared to be permanently pouting.

Ivana, a vision in Ungaro pink, lemon-yellow hair tumbling over her shoulders, and a ton of jewellery, was charming and slightly more laid-back than I'd expected. We drank champagne and chatted, Gerard overly impressed to be shooting the breeze with this illustrious captain of industry. Donald had several of his plaqued magazine covers hanging on the walls, and photographs were scatted about of himself and Ivana with movie stars and heads of state.

The champagne had fortified me so I felt no pain as Donald took my arm and, with a 'This is it, kid', escorted me by escalator down to the main floor. On the other escalators dozens of violinists rode up and down enthusiastically playing Hungarian rhapsodies. We descended to their accompaniment, along with that of the tinkling waterfalls and the heady sound of applause and cheers to the main lobby where dozens of flash-bulbs and TV news cameras lay in wait. Donald was thrilled. 'Just *look* at this turn-out,' he boasted. 'Fan*tas*tic.'

The ground floor of the Trump Tower was an absolute mêlée. It seemed that half of New York had been invited, and Donald and I were immediately separated by the sheer force of the crowd. I talked to as many media people and reporters as possible, and met Donald's brother Robert, and Robert's beautiful wife, Blaine. Ivana stuck to me like glue, and was incredibly supportive because when a reporter asked her, 'Mrs Trump, what scent do you wear?' she answered sweetly, 'Why, I always wear "Spectacular", of course.' This was said with such sincerity that I was not only surprised but truly flattered. No wonder she became so successful as a saleswoman for her own lines of jewellery and clothes.

Later I asked Donald why he had thrown this bash for me, someone he hardly knew. 'It's the next best thing to being in *Dynasty*!' he replied.

'Well, if it were *my* decision, I'd have you playing opposite me next week.' I smiled. 'I guess you really must love show business?'

'Show business is my *life*,' he said seriously, gesturing to his glitzy palace. 'This is *all* show business. That's why I've got Atlantic City too, and that's why I have my toys.'

I knew what toys he meant: the executive Trump jet, the Trump heli-copter and the Trump yacht, all of which were bigger and better than *any-thing* that Blake Carrington owned. Ivana and Donald were the eighties' golden couple, the dream ticket. It was no wonder that he'd been nick-named the Midas of Manhattan.

To launch a new product to the consumer, a heavy publicity cam-paign *must* be mobilized to push it. People will only buy what they know about and unfortunately this didn't happen with 'Spectacular'. A few ads appeared but too few to make it a success and within eighteen months 'Spectacular' had died an ignominious death – as did the heavily hyped fragrances of Cher, Baryshnikov, Omar Sharif and many others. Only Elizabeth Taylor has stayed the course to rule the roost with her signature scents, backed up as they are with multi-million-dollar advertising campaigns.

In October 1985 I was asked to introduce several songs at the Royal Variety Performance. This is a prestigious British show business event, a tradition for the past forty years, and is always attended by two or three members of the Royal Family. I was somewhat nervous because the titles of the five songs and the song-writers' names that I had to memorize, were rather complicated. Each song had at least two or three lyricists and composers, there were no cue cards and we'd had scant rehearsal. It didn't matter how many times I mumbled to myself, ' "Three Coins in the Fountain", lyrics by Sammy Cahn and Jimmy van Heusen, music by blah blah blah', I was convinced I would dry – particularly galling in front of Her Majesty and Prince Philip.

I gibbered nervously to Jeffrey Lane as we drove to the Drury Lane Theatre, trying to assuage my idiotic first-night nerves. Five other actresses shared my dressing room, including the rather abrasive and out-spoken Lauren Bacall, whom I'd known since my early Hollywood days.

I changed into a wildly over-the-top Bob Mackie creation, freely copied from one worn by Marlene Dietrich. The skintight, flesh-coloured chiffon gown was appliquéd with sparkling rhinestones in strategic places and, although it was incredibly flamboyant, it was also strangely simple. I turned this way and that in front of the three-way mirror until a voice called, 'Five minutes, Miss Collins' and Jeffrey came in. He handed me my wrap, an enormous chiffon shawl edged with a forest of peach ostrich feathers, which I threw round my shoulders. Betty Bacall, in a simple black silk pant-suit, looked at me disapprovingly. 'Eighty-six the feathers, JC.'

'Why? It's what *makes* the outfit,' I said.

Bacall tut-tutted again. 'Too much. Get rid of 'em.'

'I *know* it's theatrical but it's a Royal evening, it's *supposed* to be.'

'Well, I think it's totally over the top,' said Betty brusquely.

'*That's* what I'd wear to a bistro for dinner.' I indicated her simple suit, not intending bitchiness, but the other actresses smiled at each other knowingly.

'If I were you, dear, I' just wouldn't wear those feathers, they're much too much,' Bacall insisted.

'Well, darling, you're *not* me,' I said brightly, 'and the feathers stay in the picture.'

As Jeffrey and I departed, trailing moulting ostrich feathers, I heard someone say, 'Done up like a dog's dinner, dear. Wonder where she left the kitchen sink?'

We stood in the wings as I scanned the palm of my hand where I'd written the composers' names in Biro. Suddenly I was worried about my feathers and said to Jeffrey, 'You don't think they're over the top?'

'Are you kidding? Never. Not for you.'

Just at that moment the MC announced my name, and Jeffrey pushed me on stage, feathers and all, where I managed not to forget a word – or a name.

When the performance ended all the participants, including Lauren Bacall, Rula Lenska, Gloria Hunniford, Celeste Holm, and Paul Nicholas, stood in a line-up on stage to meet and be photographed with the Queen, who was looking particularly lovely that night in full combat gear – tiara, diamond earrings, necklace and nice frilly frock.

The next morning Jeffrey looked pleased as we skimmed through the newspapers. 'Every photograph in *every* paper is of the Queen talking to you. So much for eighty-sixing those damn feathers. A bid of advice, Joan. Don't *ever* take another actress's sartorial advice.'

Joan Rivers, the blonde, acid-tongued chat-show hostess, has long been a friend and I always enjoyed doing her shows in which we had plenty of rowdy badinage. Doing her *Tonight* Show, with Boy George in 1986, it was hard to judge which of us was the most camp, as we were all trying to outdo each other in the frock department. Boy George won, his kitsch outfit far surpassing my strapless white dress and Joan's chic red gown, and he certainly outdid us in the make-up stakes too.

On one of Joan's shows she became particularly intrusive about my private life. 'Come on, now, Joanie, tell us, *please* tell us *which* husband was the best lover,' she asked inquisitively.

'Oh I can't answer that,' I said.

'Yes, you can,' she said eagerly.

I smiled like the Cheshire cat, then answered sweetly. '*Yours*, darling.'

Joan, seldom at a loss for words, was speechless for a moment, then she laughed, albeit a touch timorously, and said, '*Touché*.'

In the commercial break she asked, 'Is it *true*? Did you *really* sleep with Edgar?'

'Of *course* not,' I said. 'Are you mad?'

Apropos of my recent fourth marriage to Peter Holm, and perhaps for revenge, Joan then asked, 'Is it true that the towels in your house are marked "His", "Hers" and "Next"?'

I replied, 'Darling, I don't bother to have anything embroidered on them. Nobody's ever lasted that long.'

This made everybody laugh because I was simply applying the public's image of Alexis to my own persona; I knew it was what they expected.

'Always give 'em what they want,' as Daddy said.

Now well into his eighties, he'd been happily married for some twenty years to Irene Korff, and their daughter Natasha, my half-sister, was between Sacha and Katy in age. One night Daddy admitted how proud he was of my success. 'Good thing I didn't become your secretary, wasn't it?' I said.

A staunch royalist, Daddy was thrilled when in 1987 I was to be presented to Queen Elizabeth the Queen Mother and to the Princess of Wales at a Royal Film Performance of *84 Charing Cross Road*. He was far more impressed about the Queen Mother than about the Princess.

'She's just a lightweight,' he said dismissively. 'Now the old Queen – *there's* a great woman for you.'

Nolan ran up a gorgeous pink satin, slightly over-the-top gown, and I flew to London for a long weekend. In the receiving line I exchanged pleasantries with my old adversary George Peppard, who seemed to have mellowed since those tense days on *The Executioner*.

I watched the Queen Mother walk graciously down the line of stars, chatting bewitchingly, then she stood before me, resplendent in a lace dress and a beautiful diamond tiara, necklace, brooch, bracelet and earrings. This great lady, whom I'd met several times before, was old-world charm personified. She oozed gentle humour and that overworked word 'niceness'. She also possesses a strange sensuality, which is probably why she has remained the most popular of all the Royals.

'What are you doing over here, my dear?' she enquired, in her high sweet voice.

'They've given me a few days' break from *Dynasty*, ma'am. I'll be going back to it next week.'

'Oh, isn't that nice?' She smiled and nodded while the press corps strained to hear our words.

'Do you ever watch it, ma'am?' I asked boldly.

'Oh, *yes*.' She beamed. 'I love it. We always watch it. *All* of us.'

'I'm sure you must all hate me,' I said ruefully.

'Oh, no, my dear. We all *love* you and think you're marvellous. Keep up the good work.' She flashed her enchanting smile and was on to Mr Peppard.

'Queen Mum meets Queen Bitch,' I thought. 'That'll be a tabloid headline tomorrow.' And it was.

I was flattered by the Queen Mother's compliment because recently I'd become used to receiving insults. As television's most hated woman I was fair game for the comedians, the wise guys and the snippy late-night talk-show hosts.

I received the ultimate insult when I was guest of honour on Dean Martin's *Celebrity Roast*. This was a televised tribute to performers from all walks of show business, in which other performers, usually comedians, sat on a dais dressed to kill, hurling hideous barbs at the roastee. It took place in the wonderfully garish Ziegfeld Room at the MGM Grand Hotel in Las Vegas. Among the guests were the female impersonator Charles Pierce, dressed, coiffed and made up to look like Alexis, Angie Dickinson Milton Berle, Red Buttons, John Forsythe, Don Rickles, Anne Baxter and, last but never least, Aaron Spelling. He seldom ventured out of his house or office, and here he was in Vegas – quite an honour.

Comedienne Phyllis Diller, who admitted to having had more facelifts than anyone in the world, but who looked like a donkey in drag, threw the first barb. 'By the time Joan was thirteen she had sown enough wild oats to make a grain deal with Russia.' I thought this was about as funny as a funeral, but the camera was focussed on me so that the world could judge if I was being 'a good sport'. I couldn't allow my fixed smile to crack.

So, this was the way it was going to go, was it? The joke was that I was a loose woman with the morals of an alley-cat, man crazy and married many times. America was still extremely moralistic, so I gritted my teeth and prepared myself. The insults didn't disappoint – but the flaccid jokes were so bad that the whole thing was cringe-makingly embarrassing.

I realized that most of the stars were here not for me but for the exposure they'd receive when the show was aired. I barely knew Anne Baxter or Bea Arthur although, of course, Angie and Milton were friends.

Dean said in his sleepy half-corked manner, 'Joan's cut down on her smoking. She only has a cigarette after making love – she's down to two packs a day.'

I grimaced wryly. Ironically I wasn't even dating anyone.

On and on it limped.

Angie: 'Joan darling, you've done more than *anyone* else on TV to bring moral decay to the masses.'

Was that why I was riding so high, I wondered.

Milton: 'Joan's show has everything. Incest, adultery, wife-swapping, lesbianism – and that's just in Joanie's dressing room.'

I forced a chuckle. The more the cheap shots were aimed, the cooler I was determined to remain.

When the final guest had had their say, I girded my loins for war then stood up. 'When they asked me here tonight I expected to see some of my own countrymen – Sir Laurence Olivier, Sir John Gielgud, Maggie Smith – and what do I get? You lot!'

I went on in this vein and the audience seemed amused, but then TV audiences are trained to do what they're told. They would laugh at a beheading if the stage manager held up a card with LAUGH written on it.

'Never again,' I said to Judy afterwards. 'It was quite fun, but I prefer my roasts strictly out of the oven.'

Around this time some English newspapers decided to call me the third most famous Englishwoman in the world. 'But even Joan would admit that Princess Diana and the Queen are more famous than she,' gurgled the *Daily Mirror*. Such utter nonsense. What about Mrs Thatcher, the Queen Mother, Princess Anne? I thought it was ridiculous, over-effusive stuff, which I took with the usual bucketful of salt.

When I made a visit to London to turn on the 1985 Christmas lights at Liberty's, Regent Street was packed and traffic practically at a standstill. 'They told me you have more people here than Princess Diana had last year,' said Auntie Pauline, one of the guests invited to sip champagne at the festivities. Daddy was also there, with Bill, Irene and Natasha, and they all looked happy for me.

My heart tried to punch its way through my ribs as I stepped out on to Liberty's balcony and looked down the length of Regent Street. Thousands of people were standing below, and everyone seemed to be screaming my name. I remember thinking for a few seconds that this is what it must have been like every day for someone like Evita Perón or Hitler or Mussolini. A scary thought. However, what was most gratifying was that they were all calling for Joan and not for Alexis.

CHAPTER SEVENTEEN

Fourth time unlucky

I spent most of 1986 in a lather about whether or not to divorce Peter. His tyranny, dual personality and definite sociopathic tendencies were making me feel as though I was playing the Ingrid Bergman character in *Gaslight*.

In retrospect I cannot believe my naïve stupidity over this marriage. That Peter had alienated so many of my friends and business acquaintances and that my children detested him – Katy had begged me not to marry him – should have given me more than a clue that something was wrong.

Admittedly, the early months of our relationship had been reasonably happy, and I had been smitten enough to keep the rose-tinted spectacles clamped on firmly. I was also working between ten and twelve hours a day, so I had little time to think.

They say that love is blind, in which case I was more than ready for my guide dog and white stick. Peter had wept buckets during our marriage ceremony at the tacky little White Chapel in Las Vegas; whether they were tears of joy or merely of relief that he had finally succeeded in talking me into it, I had no way of knowing.

I suppose I should have smelled a very large rodent when our wedding photographs appeared in a supermarket tabloid. They had been taken during the ceremony by Peter's best friend, Hassa Olafson. I was furious: all his photographs were supposed to be for our own private album, and not for sale to some third party for his financial benefit. Peter pretended shock, horror and outrage. But as the two Swedes were joined at the hip, always closeted away together in Peter's office jabbering away in their mother tongue, I became suspicious. Hassa finally admitted that he *had* sold the pictures and when I accused him of being a disloyal parasite, Peter sided with him, saying 'He needs the money because he has two young daughters to support.'

Why his parental responsibilities were anything to do with me is anyone's guess.

During our honeymoon, in Palm Beach and London, Peter had refused point blank to pose for photographers at the airport. He suddenly presented a side of himself that I'd never seen before, behaving so appallingly that we had even more rows.

It wasn't long before his ex-girlfriends started coming out of the woodwork, selling their stories to the tabloids. One stated in the *Sun* that 'Peter was mean-spirited, selfish and totally obsessed with money and sex.' I certainly agreed with the latter observation and I was beginning to see the light about the former two. Yet underneath Peter's rudeness and pig-headedness – which are hardly the basis for a good marriage – he could also be caring and considerate. He showed his worst side to my staff, however, becoming so rude and overbearing that one by one they all left. As anybody who's been involved with a bully will know, they usually win in the end by continually wearing people down.

Peter had taken over as my financial jack-of-all-trades, and I was giving him 20 per cent of my income, a staggering amount of money. He assured me, though, that this arrangement was saving me vast sums and showed me columns of figures on his computers. But by August 1986 I discovered that while he had made almost half a million dollars, I had paid for the running of the house, entertainment, my clothes, my travel – everything.

'Your power has gone to Peter's head,' Judy remarked sadly.

During one of our many fights, I took all the cheques and unpaid bills from his office and gave them to our accountant, Larry Turner. A friend of Larry's told me that Peter had said to Larry, 'If Joan doesn't give everything back to me I'm filing for divorce. I'll get every penny I can from her. I'll get more than anybody's ever got. I'll sue the ass off her, then I'll go to the *National Enquirer* and sell them stories they'll pay a fortune for.' What a charmer.

My contract had recently been renegotiated again, to an astronomical

$100,000 an episode, but instead of doing twenty-eight episodes a year I would now only make ten. This allowed me to escape from Peter to England and see my children as well as Daddy and Auntie Pauline – who were both now, alas, getting old, but still very sprightly. Also, Ron Kass died that year. He had been very ill with cancer and Katy was deeply distressed. She was living with my secretary Cindy Franke in a rented flat and going to school in London, but after her father's death she needed me more than ever.

Because it was imperative that I keep my head above water, and behave normally on the *Dynasty* set, I tried to brush my marital problems aside.

One night I went to dinner at Dyan Cannon's house, and confided in her. She is a gutsy, down-to-earth girl with an infectious laugh but also a deeply spiritual side. 'Shine a flashlight right into the dark corners of your relationship and see what you find there,' she told me. 'That's where the truth lies.'

I thought this sound advice so although not usually an analytical person, I did exactly that and told Peter that I was seriously considering divorcing him. 'You'll be a laughing stock, not only in Hollywood but everywhere. Divorcing after less than a year, and your *fourth* marriage at that. What kind of person will they think you are?' he mocked.

'Just like Alexis, I suppose,' I snapped, but I still couldn't make up my mind.

One day, out of the blue, I started getting heart palpitations. The relentless arguing every night and having to be at the studio each morning at five a.m. were getting to me. No one but my closest friends knew how much stress I was experiencing. But Dyan had said I must listen to my innermost feelings, and my irregularly beating heart was definitely trying to tell me something.

My doctor said that he would like to monitor my heart for twenty-four hours and attached me to an electrocardiograph, with a complicated arrangement of rubber plugs and wires, and told me to go about my life as normally as possible.

When the Swede saw the machine that night he demanded, 'What's that?'

'It's something the doctor said I must wear for twenty-four hours,' I explained calmly.

'Crap,' he said. 'Absolute crap. You don't need that, *sveethaart*. You don't need that *stupid* thing, you're perfectly healthy. Take it off.'

After an argument, in which my heart kept doing flip-flops, he wrested the machine off me and threw it into a corner. 'That's what I think of that crap, *sveethaart*. Stop being such a drama queen.'

Anyone who's experienced the painful break-up of any relationship, marital or not – and who hasn't? – knows that agonizing decisions *must* be made. My closest friends and family all stood by me as I vacillated, but in the end I knew I had to bite the bullet.

I was in London at a party at Annabel's when I suddenly felt this incredible lightness: even though I was still married, I felt free, and suddenly it hit me with absolute certainty that what I had to do must be done immediately. But I knew it was going to be far from easy.

Peter and I had been getting ready to move into our new house and together had taken some bits and pieces from Bowmont to Cabrillo Drive. However, I had also smuggled across much more, which Peter didn't know about, helped by Cindy Franke and my housekeeper Yvonne McClure. Hidden in cupboards at Cabrillo were suitcases of clothes, books, photograph albums, pictures and mementoes. I removed as much as I could for I had a feeling that shortly all hell was going to break loose.

Peter had taken to hiding himself away each day, in his office at Cabrillo, which was in the process of complete renovation (costing *me* an arm and a leg, of course). His office door had three locks on the outside and several dead bolts inside. In padlocked metal filing cabinets were stored all of my financial papers, everything from contracts, tax returns, accounts, bank statements, papers, investment portfolios, receipts, cheques and even the children's birth certificates. I finally realized that Peter's repeated threats to ruin me financially if we ever parted were in no way idle. Also, he had an industrial-size paper shredder, which I believed he wouldn't hesitate to use to destroy the indispensable red-tape of my life.

One Friday night, after another particularly horrible row, I stormed out of Bowmont. I stayed the night with Judy and Max and on Saturday morning contacted Marvin Mitchelson, the premier divorce lawyer in LA. He was known for his favouritism towards women clients, among them Bianca Jagger and Lesley Ann Down, and he had handled the palimony case against Lee Marvin. After he had heard all of the gory details, he agreed to take me on, and we thrashed out a plan that was more devious, cunning and manipulative than anything Alexis Carrington Colby might have come up with.

Early on Monday morning, Marvin obtained an order from a Santa Monica court for the return of all my papers in Peter's office and the right for me to live at Cabrillo. At the same time he filed my petition for divorce. The timing of the next part was critical. News of divorces being filed, and injunctions on property belonging to celebrities, usually hit the media within minutes so we had to be exceptionally clever.

I was shooting that day, and immediately Marvin called to tell me that the injunctions had been filed, I telephoned Peter. In a little-girl voice, which would have done justice to Alice in Wonderland, I asked him to come and lunch with me at the studio, so we could talk things over.

As we hadn't spoken for three days he immediately accepted, sounding pleased. 'I'll be there in forty-five minutes, *sveethaat*,' he said.

Judy, Jeffrey and I sat in my dressing room, trembling with anticipation and smoking like fiends forty-five minutes later, peering out of the window, we watched Peter drive on to the Warner Hollywood lot in his flashy black Morgan. As he jumped out of the car, my process-server, ironically called Doug Collins, handed him an envelope saying, 'Peter Holm, these are your divorce papers.'

Peter looked so stunned that for an instant I thought he was going to hit Doug, but Doug was bigger than him, and a real tough guy, so he must have thought better of it. We watched, fascinated, as Peter's blanched face changed to a bright vermilion. Obviously the penny had dropped that things were happening up at the Cabrillo house, probably at this very moment.

Then he turned and stared venomously up at my dressing-room window, no doubt seeing three faces peering down at him. For a few seconds it looked as if he might try to storm our sanctuary. Jeffrey became paranoid and started yelling, 'He's got a gun, he's got a gun!' and Judy began hyperventilating. They almost fell over each other as they scrambled to hide in my wardrobe. Like Lot's wife, I couldn't have moved if I'd wanted to – frozen with fear, I think they call it.

'Fuck you,' Peter screamed at Doug, slammed his car into reverse and drove off at such speed that he almost knocked over an astonished John James.

Outside Cabrillo, Peter found himself confronted by three burly LAPD officers and a notice on the door forbidding him entry. He cursed and threatened the police until they hustled him away, saying that he would be slung in jail if he couldn't control himself. They told him that he wasn't allowed to set foot in Cabrillo, but that he could return to my house in Bowmont Drive.

The moment Peter had left for the studio, Cindy had driven over to Bowmont in her car, a removal van following her. She had about two and a half hours to grab as much of my stuff as possible and we kept in close touch with her by mobile phone. When we heard from the police that Peter had left Cabrillo and was on his way to Bowmont, we called her at once.

'Get the hell out, Cinders,' I yelled. 'God knows what he'll do if he finds you there. Leave *now*.'

Cindy was in the garage stuffing her car with more of my possessions. She jumped into it, then remembered that she'd given the remote control that opened the front gates to the removal men – who had already left. Cindy was trapped. We exchanged more frantic calls.

'You've got to get out of there. Scramble over the fence – anything – but for God's sake *go*.' I begged.

'Oh, my God,' Cindy squeaked. 'It's him.'

Paralysed with terror, she watched a black car draw up across the street.

But it was only my next-door-neighbour Jon Voight, of *Midnight Cowboy* fame. He turned into his drive and pressed his clicker to open his own garage. Miraculously the frequency of his remote and that of Bowmont's front gates were the same, so with a screech of tyres Cindy reversed and was up the hill to safety within seconds of the Swede arriving in an apoplectic rage.

Our separation made global headlines and I was instantly hounded by *paparazzi*. Helicopters buzzed Cabrillo and we had to post full-time guards at the front gate. I was convinced the Swede would try to get to me, but I was determined that from now on the only showdown we would have would be in a courtroom.

Peter remained in Bowmont, with his red-wigged factotum, James. I had now realised that Peter was a total misogynist with no respect whatsoever for women. Michael Caine's nickname for him had been 'The Swedish Comedian', because socially he made no effort at all. Dear Daddy, never to be outdone while a media frenzy was going on, was quoted as saying, 'Thank God she's got rid of that Swedish geezer, I always hated him.' Aaron allowed me to take extra trips to London to visit Katy, Tara and Sacha, who were all thrilled that I had finally dumped the dreaded Swede.

All my friends and children were so delighted that I had finally filed for divorce that I decided to have a huge celebration. Elton John, Sue Mengers and Jean-Claude Tramont, Swifty and Mary Lazar, Barbara and Marvin Davis, Jackie and her husband Oscar, Michelle Lee, Dani Jannsen, Tina Sinatra, Alana Stewart, George Hamilton, John James, Alan Carr, Jolene and George Schlatter, Wendy and Leonard Goldberg, Joe Bologna and Renee Taylor, Jackie Bisset and Alexander Godunov, Dyan Cannon, Candy and Aaron, Camilla Sparv, Nolan Miller, Steve and Judith Krantz, Willie Brown and dozens of others toasted my new-found freedom.

David Niven Jnr brought me a stack of different T-shirts on which he had had slogans printed: *'You Can't Go Holm Again', 'No Place Like Holm', 'Holm is Not Where the Heart Is', 'Go Straight Holm', 'I don't want to go Holm with you'*. There was a special one for me: *'Holmless'*.

After all my shilly-shallying I thought that finally this unfortunate chapter of my life had closed. However, I had reckoned without the divorce.

Peter became a complete jerk: he refused to leave Bowmont Drive, and gave press interviews while lounging on a lilo in the swimming pool in minuscule leopardskin trunks spouting stuff like, 'Joan is consumed by Alexis, that's why she's doing this. She really loves me and I love her and we'll get back together, I know it.'

Fat chance. He then decided to picket me with placards which read 'JOAN, YOU HAVE *OUR* $2.5 MILLION, 13,000 SQ. FT. HOME WHICH WE BOUGHT FOR *CASH* DURING OUR MARRIAGE. I AM NOW HOMELESS. HELP!' He even persuaded James to hold a placard reading 'JOAN, YOU NOW EARN OVER $100,000 A WEEK, BECAUSE PETER NEGOTIATED, SUPPORTED AND ASSISTED YOU FOR 2½ YEARS. PLEASE GIVE HIM A DECENT HOME.'

To say that I was delighted when the judge ruled both in my favour, and of the pre-nuptial agreement would be putting it mildly. Peter had the right to only a nominal amount, and I left the courtroom no longer heavy-hearted, but free at last and looking forward to the rest of my life.

After divorcing the Swede, I wanted to be rid of *everything* connected with him, so the *maison de pecheur* in Port Grimaud was put on the market. The boat, called *Sins*, was nothing but a liability, constantly *en panne*. According to the boatman it worked perfectly whenever he tested it during the winter but, come early June when we needed it, *Sins* would invariably break down. It spent more time in the boatyard than in the Mediterranean.

That was when I fully understood the truth of the saying: 'There are only two great events in a boat-owner's life: the day he buys his boat, and the day he sells it.'

Otherwise life went on. Back on the *Dynasty* set, no actor's personal problems were ever allowed to interfere with their character's even more pressing difficulties but even *Dynasty* wasn't quite as rosy as it had been. The former golden girl of TV, with her glossy, slightly exaggerated storylines and glamorous, flamboyant characters, was having troubles of her own. After yet another reshuffle of ABC executives, the new administration were *not* fans of our series, and decided that they no longer wanted it on their network. New shows – brighter, fresher, more modern than ours – were popular. Series like *Murphy Brown, Roseanne* and *The Golden Girls* were getting the ratings and ABC believed viewers were tired of the glitzy unreality of *Dynasty*. The only night-time soap opera doing fairly well was *Knotts Landing*, which was a more 'real life' show.

One of the ABC brass said to us: 'Those women look like real women in that show, and not painted-up Barbie dolls like you gals.'

Then, for the 1986–87 season, ABC made a foolhardy move – or perhaps it was deliberate. They changed *Dynasty*'s regular time-slot from Wednesday at nine p.m. to Thursday at eight. The cast thought this suicidal. Fans who had been riveted to *Dynasty* for years expected it to air at its usual time. Since ABC had not even taken ads to announce the time switch, we immediately lost a vast number of viewers, and *Dynasty* began to slip inexorably down the ratings, losing viewers at an ever-increasing rate.

There was no longer enough money in the show's budget to bring in high-powered movie stars like Rock Hudson and Charlton Heston, and ABC complained bitterly about the *Dynasty* cast's huge star salaries. It was true, we were all making a *ton* of money. I was now in only one out of every three episodes and ABC began getting letters of complaint: 'Where is Alexis? We miss her' and 'These new episodes stink'. But the TV viewing public is fickle and their interest in *Dynasty* was on the wane.

Then, to add to our problems, the writers who had been with the show since its inception left, and David Paulson, a new line producer/writer, was hired. ABC wanted *Dynasty* modernized and made more like *Roseanne* and *Murphy Brown*. But Aaron and Doug didn't agree: they wanted *Dynasty* as glittering and glamorous as always and there was much behind-the-scenes squabbling among *les grands fromages*.

The old-time movie moguls usually kept their jobs for twenty-five or thirty years. Now, with giant corporations gobbling up the studios and production companies at an alarming rate, the average tenure for a network boss was twenty-five to thirty *months*! The new breed of ABC studio heads were all in their early thirties. They thought that *Dynasty* was out of date and wanted to kill it off. When *Dynasty* had still not died by the 1987/88 season, one executive was heard to remark, 'This show is like the Wicked Witch of the West. It just won't die. I guess we'll have to put a stake through its heart.'

The cast anxiously discussed each script's ever weaker plots, and wondered *why* ABC wanted to destroy a golden goose that was still playing successfully in over eighty-six countries. What inverted snobbery made them despise a show that featured wealth, opulence and beauty? Why did they want to bring everything and everyone down to the level of Roseanne and her slovenly clothes and chaotic house?

Granted that *was* real life to many Americans but, in my opinion, real life isn't what TV and movie viewers want to see all the time. They like to be swept away by fantasy and escapism. But, sadly, by the end of the eighties, everything began to change and the word glamour became a synonym for something negative.

In the 1986/87 season I left town at every opportunity – for London, Acapulco, Hawaii, Palm Springs, San Francisco or New York. I was disenchanted with LA, its smog, floods, mud slides, brush fires, terrifying riots and, most of all, the earthquakes.

I'd also had an unnerving experience shortly after my divorce from the Swede. The two highly paid guards at my front gate had been given instructions to check all guests and not to let in anyone unless they'd been specifically instructed to do so. It was a Sunday, my housekeeper's day off and I hadn't been expecting visitors. For the first time since the divorce frenzy, the *paparazzi* seemed to have disappeared in search of fresh prey. Along with them had gone the ubiquitous helicopter, which had buzzed my house several times a day with a black-bearded *paparazzo* hanging out of it from a strap attached to his waist. I was relaxed, and looking forward to a lunch party.

I had just stepped out of the shower, wrapped myself in towels and had strolled into my bedroom.

As I stood at the window admiring the view and thinking that life was going to be great from now on, two teenagers marched into my bedroom, arms outstretched.

Fear curdled my stomach. 'What are you doing here?' I gasped. Newspaper headlines flooded into my mind: 'Star Stabbed in Luxury Boudoir', 'Four-time Divorcee Brutally Slain by Teenage Gang', 'Dynasty Diva Dies'. Where were the forty-dollar-an-hour guards, for God's sake? I took a deep breath. I had to take control and I mustn't let them see my terror. I moved towards the uninvited guests in my most menacing Alexis manner. But it isn't easy to be menacing when your costume consists of two towels.

'What do you want?' I demanded.

The teenagers didn't answer, just smiled, and walked boldly towards me.

This is it, I thought, as their hands reached into their pockets. Now a knife or a gun will come out. Blade or bullet, which would it be? For some unknown reason, I didn't feel frightened any more. I'd survived worse things than this. I'd been through Katy's accident, trapped in fires, had some close calls in aeroplanes and cars, and these two kids were *not* going to finish *me* off. They were going to get a piece of my mind.

'How *dare* you come into my house!' I stormed, as one of the towels slipped a few inches. My voice was strident with fury but they didn't flinch. They just stood there gaping. 'Get the *hell* out of here *now*!'

'Ooh, Alexis, we love you!' said the girl, who had brought out of her pocket nothing more lethal than an autograph book. 'You're our favourite star.'

'We just wanted to see you in real life,' said the boy, in hurt tones. He was at least six foot three and loomed over me intimidatingly.

I had two strangers in my bedroom – I was alone, wet, and clad in only a towel—

'They're only a pair of autograph hunters,' said one inner voice.

'No, they're not! They're muggers and murderers,' said the other.

I started to push the kids forcibly out of my enormous bedroom and into the even more enormous living room.

'Get out of my house! How *dare* you come into my bedroom? Why did the guards let you in?'

'We told them we was your nephew and niece,' said the girl. My mind boggled. Then fury took over. I must have terrified them because they took to their heels and fled. I felt almost sorry for them. Then, looking down, I discovered that the towel had slipped to my waist, and realised that the kids had been confronted by a topless, screaming virago.

My heart was pounding so hard that I felt my blood vessels would start bursting like fireworks. I threw on a terrycloth robe and stormed out to where the two gum-chewing guards were leaning nonchalantly across the gateposts, staring down the hill at the retreating backs of the intruders.

'What the *hell* is going on around here?' I roared. 'Are you *mad*? How *dare* you let those people in?'

'Oh, gee. I'm sorry, Miss Collins,' said Brad, whose IQ was evidently about the same as his hat size. 'They told us they were relations of yours.'

I stared coldly at him, then said, 'Are you colour blind as well as half-witted?' I stormed back into the bedroom to call Judy and tell her to fire the guards.

'I'm safer just having the alarm on,' I reasoned. 'At least if somebody tries to get in the house it will go off, I'll be warned and the police will arrive in less than three minutes.' Ah, the perils of global fame – I was fed up with this goldfish-bowl existence.

At Christmas in 1986 I escaped to a rented chalet in Lake Mammoth, California, near the Bryers, with all my children, Jeffrey Lane, and Tony's mother Grace. I've always loved family Christmases and each year I buy an enormous tree and bring out all of its decorations, some of which I've had for over forty years and others that I had made instead of knitting baby clothes when I was pregnant with Tara and Sacha. Each year after the celebrations they are carefully packed away for next time, but I didn't have room to take them to Mammoth, and although we had a beautiful big tree it wasn't the same without all our old favourites hanging on it.

Since I don't ski, I stayed in the chalet while everyone else went off to the slopes, and started working on my first novel, *Prime Time*.

Dynasty was obviously winding down so now I was going to write. I love writing and knew that I didn't want to commit myself to another long-running TV series. I needed peace of mind and I needed it badly. Fame is such a two-edged sword, and I craved anonymity. I thought *Dynasty* would probably get the chop in a year or two; then I could move back to England, where my three children were living, and get back to the theatre. I kept thinking about Binkie Beaumont's words to me. Now *Private Lives* was becoming almost an obsession and I was determined to play Amanda. But before then I had to finish my novel.

Most people in public life receive a considerable number of requests either to represent charities or to give to them. There are thousands of different ones and each seems to be for such a worthy cause, but you would have to have unlimited funds to support them all. Consequently my main thrust is to support only charities that help children, particularly babies, although I'm active with several cancer foundations too.

I was already on the committees for the Philadelphia Institute of Human Potential and the National Society for the Prevention of Cruelty to Children, as I was well aware of how desperately brain-damaged people needed rehabilitation care. After they had been sent home from hospital, it was often up to an untrained parent or guardian to look after them so I became involved in a new charity to rehabilitate brain-damaged children.

I helped to form the Kerland Foundation, who were pioneering revolutionary and controversial techniques to help handicapped children overcome their disabilities by encouraging them to challenge themselves physically – clambering through wooden frames, hanging upside down from equipment on the ceiling and stimulating every part of their bodies and putting their unused brain cells to work again. I became active with other charities, among them the International Foundation for Learning Disabilities School, an offshoot of the Philadelphia Institute. When the Duke and Duchess of York came to LA they visited the school, and were impressed by the innovative techniques they saw being used.

In 1987 the Detroit Children's Hospital named a wing after me, which I opened, and also a new cardiovascular unit for children. That same year I was honoured by Variety Clubs International for my 'artistic and humanitarian achievements' – whatever they may be. America adores 'honouring' celebrities and any excuse for a party often blossoms into a TV special, which in this case it did yet again. It was a star-studded evening at NBC studios and Clint Eastwood, who had been the previous year's recipient of the award, was Master of Ceremonies.

When I walked into the ballroom, the *Dynasty* theme playing at full blast, friends, celebrities, family and co-workers gave me a standing ovation and I was hard pushed not to burst into tears. I walked to the centre table, greeted along the way by Charles Bronson, Jill Ireland, Angie Dickinson, Tony Bennet, Michelle Lee, Michael York, almost the entire

Dynasty cast and Paul Henreid. He was the actor most famous for lighting those two cigarettes at the same time for himself and Bette Davis at the end of *Now Voyager*, and for leaving with Ingrid Bergman at the end of *Casablanca*. He bent over to kiss my hand with old-world gallantry and whispered, 'You are so wonderful.'

'So are you,' I said, wondering if he'd light my cigarette later.

At the main table Clint introduced me to his girlfriend Sondra Locke and I greeted James Stewart, who was also a previous recipient. There was no time to chat because the cabaret started immediately, but I leaned across to James Stewart and whispered, 'Do you remember that film we made in London, *The Big Sleep*?'

'We never made a movie together, m'dear. I certainly don't recall it,' he answered, in that familiar drawl.

Was I putting my foot in it, or was he having memory problems?

'Well, we didn't actually have any scenes *together*,' I said. 'But we did have lunch at the studio.'

'You're right,' he said, and smiled triumphantly. 'But you *still* weren't in that movie, m'dear.'

I shrugged. After all, he *was* a legend.

Robin Leach, of *Lifestyles of the Rich and the Famous*, was hosting. I've never heard a voice like Robin's: a nasal blend of Cockney and Brooklyn, he sounds like a mixture of Bruce Forsyth on speed or Jerry Lewis on Prozac.

He introduced impersonator Rich Little, who sang 'You're Just Too Marvellous For Words' to me, in the voices of James Stewart, Jack Nicholson, James Mason, John Wayne and Ronald Reagan. The line that got the biggest laugh was, 'You're just too marvellous for words, like glorious, glamorous, and that old standby, alimony!'

I still never understand why it's funny when a woman is legally obliged to pay money to a man, but sarcastic references to divorce no longer hurt.

Then Robin in his inimitable 'champagne wishes and caviar dreams style' introduced Michelle Lee, of *Knotts Landing*, and Michael Feinstein, a brilliant Cole Porter-style pianist, who performed a medley of all my favourite songs. Starting with 'You're the Tops' they segued into 'Lady Is a Tramp', 'You Are My Lucky Star', 'You Do Something To Me', 'I've Got You Under My Skin', 'I'm Glad There Is You', 'Thou Swell', 'You Are Too Beautiful', 'Why Can't You Behave', then a version of 'My Way', in which they sang 'She always did it her way'. They ended with 'You're Sensational' and this line: 'Alexis acts like a four-star rat/But underneath you're a pussycat.'

This attracted a roar of applause and I was sincerely moved, but the whole thing was straying into the territory of toe-curling embarrassment: these 'toast-roasts' are an American phenomenon and I consider I'm far more English than American, in spite of all the years I've lived in California. But then Bea Arthur and James Stewart sang to me, and I almost burst into tears again. I wished that Mummie was here – she had adored Jimmy Stewart. After many more tributes Tony Bennet sang the grand finale. It was quite an evening, particularly when Clint read a telegram from President and Mrs Reagan: 'We are so happy to join this tribute to someone who cares so much about children and who has also brought glamour back to Hollywood.'

In Hollywood there is at least one celebrity roast every month, and I've been to many, notably for Gene Kelly and for Aaron Spelling. Hollywood loves a star, and how they love their own. They also revel in grand charity events. At a gala dinner in Palm Beach for Prince Charles and Princess Diana, the press gave free rein to their imagination. Prince Charles had been married to the ravishing Princess Diana for two years and at the time I had just married Peter Holm.

During the ball, given by the elderly philanthropist Armand Hammer, an equerry came to my table to 'request the pleasure of my company' on the dance floor with his Royal Highness.' I was conscious of the massed rows of media sitting in the bleachers at the end of the room, watching everything for a possible titbit of gossip. I was wearing a low-cut taffeta gown with perhaps rather too much cleavage, but I couldn't refuse HRH, so I nodded graciously.

I'd met the Prince of Wales several times before, and that night, as always, he was exceptionally charming. He has the most mellifluous, beautiful voice and while we were dancing I told him that, with his voice, he could have been an actor, which seemed to amuse him. He is a great fan of the performing arts, so we exchanged views of current theatrical happenings.

I saw Peter dancing with Princess Diana. How on earth had he managed *that*? Prince Charles is an exceptional dancer, as well as an entertaining conversationalist with a great sense of humour, and I enjoyed our twirl around the floor. So apparently did the watching press corps, for the following day there was much innuendo about our 'close dancing', and a cartoon by Griffin appeared in the *Daily Mirror* showing the Prince leering at me, and Peter doing the same to the Princess.

It was all just good clean fun, and I thought nothing more of this innocent little episode until several years later when a biography of Prince Charles was published. I was amused to read that in his diary he had written of the incident as follows:

> I asked Joan Collins to dance; she was very amusing and with an unbelievable cleavage, all raised up and presented as if on a tray, so eye-wander was a problem.

I suppose you *could* call that a favourable review.

CHAPTER EIGHTEEN

A bumpy ride

A new man had come into my life in the miniature form of Irving 'Swifty' Lazar, a true legend in his own remarkable lifetime. I had known him since my early days in Hollywood when I had been taken to his flat for drinks with Gene Kelly and a group of friends. Gene had whispered to me, 'C'mon you've got to see Swifty's closet.' He sneaked me into a vast dressing room in which was arranged the most well-organized and fastidiously tidy collection of tiny men's clothes I'd ever seen.

Irving was a 'snappy dresser'. His perfectly tailored suits, mainly cut in London to fit his five foot one inch frame, were arranged in serried ranks in order of colour and texture, starting with white and cream for Palm Beach and the Riviera, grading through the acceptable spectrum of colours for the well-dressed *homme du monde*, beige, grey, fawn, navy and black. Beneath all these sartorial masterpieces, stood the biggest collection of men's shoes I'd ever seen – all tiny, and all hand-made by the likes of Lobb and Maxwell.

Swifty had encouraged me to write my first autobiography, *Past Imperfect*, in 1978. When I signed the contract for it, with Simon and Schuster, they had insisted on inserting a clause to the effect that if I ever wrote a novel they were to be given first refusal. In 1985 Simon and Schuster read *Prime Time*, liked it, and immediately contracted me for two more novels.

Swifty gave me a lot of advice, among which was 'Listen, kiddo, Hollywood's like any other industry town, everybody knows everybody else's résumé, and everybody knows what everyone is earning and *exactly* where they are on the totem pole with their careers.'

I often think about that statement because it's totally accurate. The entertainment industry *does* thrive on itself. People eat, drink, breathe and sleep movies, movies, movies, and they're interested in little else. Many people are so uninformed about what's happening in the rest of the world that it's quite bewildering.

'If you want to survive in Hollywood climb up that totem pole,' Swifty said. 'That has to be the main thrust of your life, so get out your pen and start writing. I'm getting you a great deal so you can give up all this acting crap.'

Swifty knew absolutely everyone and an invitation to one of his famous parties was the hottest ticket in town. He knew the international society set, the *crème de la crème* of show business, and all the high-powered political and social movers and shakers of the world: Gianni Agnelli, Irving Berlin, Lauren Bacall, Humphrey Bogart, Truman Capote, Dietrich, Gable, Garbo, Hemingway, Cole Porter, Noël Coward, Tennessee Williams, Somerset Maugham, Moss Hart – the list of his friends and acquaintances included some of the most exceptional figures of the mid- to late-twentieth century.

Irving was bombastic and something of a bully, and insisted on having his own way. His wife Mary, twenty-five years his junior, was an ethereal, witty beauty who kept him in line, which was far from an easy task. She made an enormous contribution to Irving's life, both personally and professionally. Her inner kindness and serenity were immensely appealing, and their house became one of the most glittering salons in California.

The first Lazar dinner party I attended was up at their house in Truesdale. Amid the Van Dongens and Matisses, and the elegant French furniture from Mallett's of London, I found myself seated between Cary Grant and Freddy de Cordova. Freddy, the man whose wit is as dry as the finest martini, was the producer of Johnny Carson's show *Tonight* and wanted me on it as a guest. 'Listen, Joanie, we don't want you to pull that serious-actress stuff on us like you did last time. We want you to lighten up, giggle, flirt with Johnny, dear.'

Since this was the seventies, when feminism and political correctness had reared their heads, I disagreed, and asked him why it should be okay for a man to talk to Johnny on serious subjects but not a woman.

'Viewers *hate* feminists.' Freddy laughed. 'Why do you think Dolly Parton's one of our favourite guests?'

To my left sat Cary Grant, who looked every bit as heart-stoppingly handsome as he did on screen, and recently separated from Dyan Cannon. British-born Grant, tall, tanned and still devastating in his early seventies, had been for decades a great Hollywood leading man. He was suave, gorgeous, and great fun as a dinner partner. He asked me if I'd seen Marlon, as the last time we'd met had been at a Broadway opening when Grant's fascination with Brando had rivalled that of the rest of the audience.

Looking at him, I wondered if the rumours about Cary were true, namely that he was bisexual and also terminally stingy with money. The former seemed hard to believe. Sophia Loren had reputedly almost left her husband for him and Dyan Cannon had been deliriously happy during their marriage, and they'd produced a pretty daughter from an obviously successful union. But what about the latter? As if reading my mind, Grant, who had finished every scrap of the delicious food on his plate, turned to me and said, in that uniquely urbane voice, 'Aren't you going to finish your dinner? Waste not, want not.'

'I'm on a diet,' I shrugged. 'You know how it is.'

'Luckily I don't. That's one problem I've never had.' He stretched over to remove the untouched chicken leg from my plate and I noticed that the button on his cuff didn't seem to match those on his shirt. I leaned forward to check. Yes, it was true. They were *definitely* odd buttons, and on closer inspection his shirt collar seemed a touch frayed, too.

When I told Dyan on the telephone the next day that I'd sat next to her ex-husband, she said bitterly: 'That son-of-a-bitch. You have no *idea* what a tight-wad he was with his money. I used to buy baby food for Jennifer in bulk because it was cheaper and he *still* used to complain to me about the price – his own daughter, can you imagine?'

'His shirt looked like it had seen better days,' I said.

'No wonder. He used to hang on to his shirts till they were falling to pieces. Then when I'd finally persuade him to throw them out, d'you know what he used to do?' asked Dyan. I thought I might be able to guess the answer but feigned ignorance. 'Cut off all the buttons so that the housekeeper could save them for his *other* shirts!'

She laughed. Then I told her another story I'd heard about Grant's fabled parsimony. 'Roddy Mann told me that when he'd been a house-guest of Cary's, he'd noticed that all the towels in his bathroom were shabby and worn.'

'Typical,' said Dyan.

'So for Christmas he'd sent Cary a stack of beautiful new Porthault towels. When Roddy went back to stay with Cary the following year, he noticed that the same old threadbare towels were still hanging in the bathroom.

'Why haven't you used the new ones I sent you?' asked Roddy.

'Oh, there's plenty of life left in the old ones yet,' answered Cary airily.

'Yeah, that sounds like him,' said Dyan. 'Mean as a two-dollar hustler. But he *certainly* wasn't gay. At least not with me, honey.' And she burst into her infectious and explosive laugh.

Perhaps it was the secret of Swifty's success, but his one admitted failing was that he never read his clients' manuscripts. He was, however, a champion vendor of these properties, and it was only when a suspicious client delivered his work with $100 bills stuck between the pages that this eventually came to light. The manuscripts were returned with the cash still inside them.

Another time, Alan J. Lerner, also believing that Swifty never read anything, taped together several pages of *An American in Paris*. Swifty sent back the unread manuscript with a note, 'Alan, this is a *rare* work of art.' Alan was incensed and fumed to a friend, 'Swifty has the nerve of a one-armed paper hanger.' But, whatever he did, Swifty was never ignored. He was loved or loathed in Hollywood yet was one of the pillars of the community. When it came to representing his clients he had true killer instincts. He was the first master agent, the all-time super-negotiator, who knew *exactly* which buttons to press and how to manipulate a buyer like a true virtuoso. He demanded such huge fees for his clients that when the buyer came back offering 50 per cent, his ploy would be, 'I

can't *possibly* go back to my client with that. It's too insulting to them.'
Nine times out of ten this trick worked, and he'd end up with exactly
what he'd asked for.

He was nicknamed 'Swifty' by Lauren Bacall. During lunch one day
her husband, Humphrey Bogart, had asked, 'How many deals do you
think you can make for me, Irving, and in what period of time?'

Swifty thought about the many current movies being cast, and
replied, 'I bet I can make you three deals in one day, Bogey.'

'No way,' scoffed Bogart.

'Give me twenty-four hours,' said Swifty. 'By this time tomorrow,
Bogey, you'll have three movie deals. Guaranteed.'

Swifty legged it round to three different studios and, sure enough,
secured Bogart three separate deals in the said twenty-four hours – and
for more money than the actor had ever received before. When he told
Bogart he'd lost his bet and was now booked solid for the next two years,
Bacall promptly christened him Swifty.

Sue Mengers was another super-agent. She was *the* power-house film
agent of the seventies and eighties and her client list read like a *Who's
Who* of movies with Jack Nicholson, Barbra Streisand, Michael Caine,
Ali McGraw, Ryan O'Neal to name but a few. She also counted among
her closest friends movie moguls Barry Diller, Ray Stark, Robert Evans
and David Geffen. Her hysterical wit and down-to-earth honesty have
been entrancing me since we met in the sixties when she was a secretary
at William Morris. Blonde, pretty and *slightly* on the chubby side, she has
a bubbly personality and became the prototype for many archetypal
agents in current movies. Her story-telling talents could have easily
landed her a job as a stand-up comedian in a night-club, and her imitations of famous folk, particularly Joan Crawford whom she once represented, are all hilarious.

In 1968, Hollywood had been stunned by the most horrific murder
the town had ever experienced. Sharon Tate, the beautiful pregnant wife
of Polish director Roman Polanski, hairdresser Jay Sebring and several
other friends were brutally killed in Sharon's house by the now notorious
Charles Manson gang. At six o'clock the following night my telephone

rang and a frightened, squeaky voice bleated, 'Joanie, it's Sue. What are you doing tonight?'

'I'm staying in babysitting as Nanny's off.'

'Have you got anybody else in the house?' she asked plaintively.

'Just the housekeeper. Tony's in London,' I replied. 'Why?'

'I'm scared.' Sue sounded as if she was eight years old. 'Can I come stay with you?'

'Of course you can. Everyone's scared, but I've got pretty good security here.' I found it rather endearing that this all-conquering super-agent was behaving like a frightened schoolgirl. She came over for the night, and we watched the reports about the murders on television.

A week later, on a glorious California day, we attended Sharon Tate's funeral together. Black-clad, the celebrity mourners, many of whom were weeping uncontrollably, looked strangely out of place under the azure sky. I wept too. A few years earlier Tony and I had attended the couple's wedding reception at the Playboy club in London. Sharon had looked ravishing, her long blonde hair, laced with 'baby's breath', like a cloud around her exquisite face. The pixieish Roman, in his Beatles jacket, had looked like the cat who'd found the dairy.

After the funeral everyone adjourned to producer Robert Evans's house for drinks and a buffet lunch. Most of the guests wore the blank expression you see on people's faces in elevators, and Roman wandered around like a zombie. For once no one was discussing business.

'This is a truly exceptional phenomenon at a Hollywood function,' Sue said, *sotto voce*. 'There sure are some people here *I*'d like to talk shop with.' She looked up as Bob Evans, whom I'd known since he was a contract actor at Fox, came over and asked us, 'Right – are you ready for the second feature?'

'What *are* you talking about?' I asked.

'Well, Jay's funeral, of course.' He laughed, but his eyes were empty and sad.

I couldn't face the 'second feature' and neither could Sue so we went back home, got drunk on Pouilly Fumé and reminisced.

When Sue married the French writer-director Jean-Claude Tramont, in the early seventies, they'd bought an old Hollywood star's baroque mansion where they proceeded to entertain lavishly at least twice a month. A positive *Who's Who* of Hollywood would come to wine, dine and network. Sue's parties were almost like an audition because they always featured some of the most important producers and directors. Deals were often made over the buffet table or after dinner in front of a roaring fire, but unfortunately many would be cancelled in the cold light of the following day.

One particular 1977 party boasted a more star-studded cast than usual: Elizabeth Taylor, Natalie Wood, Ali McGraw, Jackie Bisset, Ryan O'Neal, Farrah Fawcett and Dudley Moore. Wall-to-wall stars glittered and, out of the corner of my eye, I even spotted Woody Allen. I'd adored all his work for years, especially *Annie Hall* which had just been released and contains one of the funniest lines about California I've ever heard: 'The only cultural advantage about living in LA is being able to turn right on a red light.' I've thought Woody Allen a comic genius ever since *What's New Pussycat* and I'd recently read an article about him in *Esquire* in which he had talked openly about his phobias, which included desperate shyness. I noticed he was about to leave and dashed over to him. Here I must mention that I was wearing a low-cut beaded dress with a good deal of jewellery and a good deal of hair.

'Excuse me, Mr Allen,' I said eagerly, 'my name is Joan Collins and I just wanted to tell you that I'm a huge admirer of yours.'

'Why, thank you.' He blinked owlishly and backed away, unable to meet my gaze. His shoulders were hunched in a tweed jacket and he looked like a cornered mouse.

I crashed on regardless. 'I feel we have something in common, Mr Allen, because after reading that article in which you said you were shy, I empathized completely because I'm shy too!'

I gave him a beguiling yet tentative smile.

Woody glanced at me, blinked several times, then peered at my cleavage. 'You could've fooled me,' he stammered, looking me up and down and wriggling sideways out of the door like a bewildered crab.

At another of Sue's parties, Kirk Douglas was deep in conversation with Billy Wilder. Billy's a master humorist who gives the best hatchet job in town, a true iconoclast, and from barbed wit no one is safe. During dinner I was seated next to Billy, who said drily, 'Kirk told me a few years ago that he'd just finished a movie about Vincent Van Gogh, and how did I think it would do? So I told him, "Kirk, *everybody* who owns a Van Gogh will go and see the movie, so what are you so worried about?"'

America was coming to the end of the flamboyant Reagan era, and the message was clear: 'George Bush is America's future.' The *Dynasty* producers valiantly attempted to cut down on the old-fashioned opulence by trying to dress some of the younger cast members like Emma Samms, Heather Locklear and Tracey Scoggins in more casual clothes. Stephanie Beacham and myself, however, were still relentlessly done up to the nines.

It seemed as though 1987 was going to be a good year. Peter was history – at least until the divorce. I was only contracted for ten episodes of *Dynasty* so I could spend time playing, which I needed to do. Because I'd been working non-stop I hadn't really 'played' much for years. So for a while I became an habituée of the saloons and night-clubs of Europe.

I rented a flat off Berkeley Square with Katy and Cindy, where friends used to congregate so often both before and after our Annabel's 'fix', that it was nicknamed the 'Annabel's Annexe'.

I flew back and forth across the Atlantic so often that when I woke up I sometimes wouldn't know which side of the ocean I was on. Was I in Los Angeles or in London? I seemed to spend an equal amount of time in both places.

Dynasty was sinking fast in America but was still enormously popular in Europe, and I was unable to walk down any street in Italy, France, England or even on some tiny Greek island without hearing shrieks of recognition.

However, at the same time as I was enjoying my four-hour lunches in London and sojourns in Paris, Rome and Marrakesh, my lawyers were preparing for what Peter Holm had vowed was going to be the most bitter divorce of the decade. I was nervous and started drinking more than usual to try to forget the viciousness that lay in wait for me in a Los Angeles courtroom.

Just before I was due there for yet another hearing, concerning one of the endless threatening problems Peter was creating – he was now claiming maintenance of no less than $80,000 a month – an unfortunate incident occurred. I was making over a dozen London to Los Angeles round-trips a year and the British Airways staff knew that I always arrived *exactly* forty-five minutes beforehand, with or without baggage, that I always went first class and that I always paid for my own ticket – no more freebies, unfortunately. Arriving at the airport, upset over the fax I'd just received containing the Swede's $80,000 demand I was told that, because I was late, my seat had been given to producer David Puttnam. This meant I must now travel club class. I had night shooting that evening in LA, so I became understandably angry. To his credit, David Puttnam argued with BA and told them they were being most unfair, but he *didn't* offer to swap seats. I remonstrated with the person in charge, telling her that I'd arrived forty-five minutes before the flight time for the past three years, and that there had *never* been any problems before.

Toffee nose in the air, the woman sniffed. 'There's absolutely nothing I can do. You were late so you'll just have to go club because first is full.'

My frazzled nerves and the woman's arrogant couldn't-care-less attitude got the better of me and I have to confess that I did call her a 'fucking old cow'. Then I told the group of airport *paparazzi*, who'd all been photographing me regularly on this trip for years, what had happened and that they could print what I'd said. Which they did, their editors, however, omitting any reference to my seat having been given away, so that the front pages next day declared: 'Joan Collins Does an Alexis at Heathrow', 'Joan Collins Loses Her Class' and 'Fly-Nasty'!

Club class is not bad if one can totter off to bed on arrival, but I had to go straight from the airport to the set. On this nightshoot my face, never picture-perfect after a twelve-hour flight, blew up like a balloon. A local *paparazzo* sneaked a picture of me and sold it to an English tabloid, which was delighted to show its readers how fat the bitch was who had insulted the Heathrow airport staff. It appeared that my name was mud at BA. So I was delighted to receive, the following day, three dozen plump roses from Lord King, the Chairman, accompanied by a letter of apology for the manner in which I'd been treated.

I was having a fitting with Nolan in my dressing room early one morning when the telephone rang and my stepmother Irene informed me that Daddy was ill.

'Nothing's really *wrong* with him, though,' she said. 'He's perfectly all right in every respect except that he seems to have lost the will to live. Remember how he used to adore playing cards, football matches, walking the dog, even just watching television?'

'Yes, and he enjoyed writing his book too,' I said. A couple of years previously Daddy had penned his show business memoirs.

'Well, it's all changed. He's lost interest in everything, even eating and drinking.' Irene sounded distressed, although trying hard to put on a brave front.

'I can't believe it. Daddy isn't really *that* old. Look, I promise you I'll get to London as soon as I can.'

I hung up and thought about what I'd just said. That Daddy wasn't really that old. But he *was* old. Eighty-five was a little younger than Irving Lazar and a year or so older than Billy Wilder but both of those venerable gentlemen seemed to be still in their prime, full of curiosity and energy. Why wasn't Daddy?

I wangled some time off from *Dynasty*, flew to London and went straight to their house in Regent's Park. Daddy, who had barely eaten for two weeks, was sitting in bed staring blankly at cartoons on the television set. It broke my heart to see my truculent, dogmatic father in this torpor. Irene, Natasha and Bill were dancing constant attendance, all behaving as though everything was normal. But it wasn't normal for an old man to refuse anything other than a teaspoon of liquid and one tiny bit of food a day – far from it.

'The doctors have said that if we can't persuade him to eat he'll die soon,' said Natasha. I felt so sorry for her. She was only in her early twenties and I remembered how shattered I'd been to lose my mother at that age.

'I think he *wants* to die,' said Bill sadly. 'After all, he's had a great life and it's his choice to end it.'

'I guess you're right,' I said.

I tried to get Daddy to eat some smoked salmon, which he'd always loved. I told him I'd brought it from Los Angeles but after only one bite he couldn't face any more. However, he seemed extremely pleased to see me and listened avidly as I told him anecdotes and gossip about *Dynasty* life. 'I still prefer *Coronation Street*.' He looked at me defiantly then chuckled.

'I know you do, Daddy. *Dynasty*'s far too glamorous for you,' I teased him.

The next day he went into hospital and I had to leave for LA. He returned home a few days later, but the following week Joe Collins died peacefully in his sleep.

I was surprised that Daddy, who was only half Jewish and had not been remotely religious, had requested a traditional Jewish funeral at Golders Green cemetery. It was a low-key affair, with only immediate family and close friends present, including Kathy and Lew Grade, Roger Moore, some artists whom Daddy had represented and all my children. I flew in from LA the night before and was escorted to the synagogue by Bill and Sacha. I found myself weeping uncontrollably. Silly as it may sound, I was an orphan now. It had been the most shattering blow to lose Mummie in 1962, and now I was the eldest of the diminishing Collins clan, although I didn't think I was matriarch material quite yet.

Auntie Pauline looked terribly frail and seemed to have had what the French call a *coup de vieux*. She had worshipped my father and she, too, died, the following year, probably from a broken heart.

With the death of my father in 1988 I grew closer to Swifty. Although he was a close adviser I now thought of him as something of a father figure. He had loathed Peter Holm, which is why, he informed me, I hadn't been invited to many of his parties during my relationship with 'that dreadful Swede'.

Michael Nader and I had been insisting that Dex and Alexis should reunite because everyone thought we were a terrific couple. The producers finally relented and gave us a few episodes in which our love scenes sizzled, and fan-mail started to pour in for us again.

Our romance is rekindled when Sean Rowen, Alexis's fourth husband, attempts to kill her in a bubble bath. Dex comes in, saves Alexis, kills Sean, and we're off.

The writers had watched the débâcle of my own divorce and used aspects of my unfortunate marriage in Alexis's equally unfortunate marriage to Sean.

'Sean almost ruined me. I handed him everything, *everything* I worked for all my life, on a plate,' Alexis says bitterly. Then shortly before she and Dex make love Alexis says to him, 'You're the only man who's man enough to give me my space and I'm never going to let you go,' and Dex, who's lolling around in bubbles for a change, pulls Alexis into the bath.

But, alas, Alexis and Dex aren't together for long. Another row ensues, and Alexis's hated and most deadly enemy, cousin Sable, grabs him and, catching him at a weak moment, beds him.

James Healy, a mediocre actor who played Alexis's husband Sean, was a strange young man who didn't endear himself to the cast by bragging constantly that 'Laurence Olivier was a great mate of mine.' Since everyone knew that Lord Olivier's 'mates' were the likes of Ralph Richardson and John Gielgud, we found this hard to believe. But everyone tried to get on with him, even though he had an ego the size of a small country.

Alexis and Sean's wedding ceremony was performed in a Mexican hacienda, decked out with native artefacts on the walls and hanging from the ceilings. It was built on Stage 7 but looked entirely authentic even down to the copper pots and pans suspended above our heads, and the bougainvillaea crawling up the walls.

On 18 October I stood with James in front of the preacher, wearing a low-cut red lace dress with red orchids in my hair. ('I don't think this marriage is long for the world,' I'd said, sagely, to Nolan, so we decided rather cynically that, since this was to be Alexis's fourth wedding, red was the appropriate colour.)

When director Irving Moore yelled, 'Action!' the pastor said, 'Alexis, do you take this man to be your lawful hus—' and was interrupted by a tremendous roar like an express train. All the copper pots above us shook as did the walls of the adobe hut. Never one to yell 'Cut' in the middle of a take, I tried to ignore what was going on – until I heard terrified yells from the stage hands.

'Earthquake! Earthquake! Jesus Christ, it's the Big One!' someone screamed. *'Get the hell outta here!'*

The rumbling became louder, pots and pans rained down on us and the whole set started to vibrate, literally swaying from side to side. Everyone ran for their lives, and James Healy, pushing me out of his way, ran faster than anyone. I was out of there so quickly I left my red sling-backs on the set.

Outside Stage 7 pandemonium reigned. All the actors and crews from other shows had also rushed outside, to what they thought would be safety. How wrong we all were. The ground was *writhing*, asphalt and paving stones undulating like snakes under a blanket. The noise was deafening. There was nowhere to escape to and it was impossible to keep one's balance on the shuddering ground.

A six-foot-five electrician called Big John put his arms around me comfortingly. I clung to him and quivered, 'Oh, Big John, I'm so scared.'

I could feel his huge body trembling as he said, 'Honey, I'm scared, too, *real* scared.'

I put my hands to my ears to try and block out the horrendous noise. People were running around screaming in complete panic. The sound stages looked close to collapse. Was this at last 'the big one' that Los Angelenos had been threatened with for so long? As we stood there the tremors gradually subsided, and Bobby Dee, our assistant director, told everyone to go grab some coffee and they would try to find out what was going on.

I disentangled myself from Big John's bear-like embrace with a promise to return for the after shocks, and dashed off with Judy and a few of the others to the make-up room for a smoke.

James Healy sat stiffly in one chair looking even paler than usual and I sat in the other. We lit up and soon everyone started to laugh hysterically as people do after a severe shock. Judy went for coffee and we were chatting excitably, when suddenly that dreadful, ominous train-rushing-through-a-tunnel noise began again. The room started to teeter.

'Oh, my God, it's going to kill us all!' screeched James, in a high-pitched, panicky voice, and rushed out, yelling, 'Get the hell out before this building collapses.'

'Such gallantry,' I murmured to myself, but I didn't need to be told twice and leapt down the back stairs. Judy followed, balancing several styrofoam cups of coffee.

'Forget the damn coffee!' I gasped. 'We need brandy.'

'Where are you going?' yelled Judy.

'To the parking lot.' I broke into a run across the quivering tarmac. 'That's got to be the safest place because there aren't any buildings nearby.'

I sat with my 'wrecking crew', laughing fearfully in the middle of the empty car-park. The sweet prop-man brought my director's chair and a bottle of brandy. I was convinced the earth was going to split asunder in front of us, and we would all be sucked into its gaping jaws.

That warm October morning, the parking lot at Warner Hollywood studio was a vast empty space. The photographer Eddie Sanderson had arrived to shoot Alexis's latest nuptials, and we listened to his car radio. 'Still more after-shocks expected,' said the announcer, stoically. 'Probably almost as strong as the first quake.'

'That's it,' I said to Judy, through clenched teeth. 'I've got to get out of LA. I can't stand this.'

The earth continued to shake intermittently, but each time the tremors lessened, and two hours later I returned to Stage 7 to finish getting married.

Television newsreaders attempted to soothe worried Angelenos: 'This was only a 7.5 on the Richter scale. It's *definitely* not the Big One.'

Well, I *wasn't* reassured. Everyone knew LA was due for a massive, destructive quake before the century ended and the radio reports were horrifying: buildings had collapsed, people had died and dozens of others had been imprisoned for hours in elevators. Since my idea of hell has always been to find myself trapped in an elevator during an earthquake, I made a decision. I was going to sell Cabrillo and move back to Europe as soon as I possibly could.

CHAPTER NINETEEN

Things are looking up

I t was 31 December 1987, and I was staying with Carole and Anthony Bamford and Robin Hurlstone, in the Bamfords' magnificent house in Barbados. In the Parish of St James, Heron Bay is undeniably the most sensational residence on this gorgeous island. To say it is the most beautiful beach-house in the world would not do it justice. I had shot here for *Island in the Sun*, but Carole had transformed the house into a paradise which bore little resemblance to the movie set I remembered, when it had been used for 'Government House'.

Robin Hurlstone was one of their closest friends. He was tall, blond, green-eyed and extremely handsome, with a wicked sense of humour, great taste and perfect manners. An art dealer by profession, he was the most observant person I'd ever met, as well as being one of the most attractive. However he was much younger than me, which rather bothered me, but didn't seem to bother him at all.

On that magic night, we all went to Pamela Harriman's New Year's Eve party. Pam, dazzling in red, asked me to do the traditional countdown to 1988 on the balcony overlooking her terrace. I looked over at Robin as I did this, and felt distinctly that another chapter of my life was about to unfold.

Indeed, I was proved right, for since that holiday I have shared my life with Robin, and have never been happier with anyone.

I flew back to *Dynasty* in January, secure in the knowledge that things were definitely looking up.

It amazes me to think that there has probably been more written about my banishment from the Royal Enclosure at Ascot than about any other aspect of my career, other than *Dynasty*. The actual facts of this episode are simple: I had applied for my Royal Enclosure badge in February 1987, but the application, for which I'd been sponsored by several big-wigs, was apparently mislaid by someone at the other end, so no badge was sent. I wasn't at all concerned. Ascot is fun enough without the Royal Enclosure and I had a jolly lunch in John Chalk's tent with many friends, among whom were Malcolm Fraser, a handsome property developer, who was also a close confidant. He was with his girlfriend Fiona, who was wearing a Royal Enclosure badge that read Mrs Malcolm Fraser – which she wasn't. After a liquid lunch Malcolm and John bet me that I couldn't manage to get into the Royal Enclosure unrecognized. I wagered that in my huge hat, sunglasses, and elaborate frock, strangely not looking dis-similar to many other women there, I would *not* be recognized.

'I'll bet you five hundred pounds,' said Chalkie, waving some readies in the air. 'You're far too famous, Joanie.'

'You're on,' I said. 'Can I borrow your badge, Fiona?'

I pinned it to my lapel and Malcolm and I strolled in the sunshine to one of the gates leading into the Royal Enclosure. There I was heavily scrutinized by several stewards.

'Are you *sure* you're Mrs Malcolm Fraser?' asked one suspiciously.

'Oh, yes.' I linked my arm through Malcolm's. 'Yes, we're newly-weds,' I said, voice pushed into upper Sloane-Ranger register, and smiled.

The official looked even more suspicious. 'Would you please take off your sunglasses, madam,' she commanded.

'Oh dear, it's so bright,' I twittered.

'Take them off,' she repeated, rather too aggressively, I thought.

I obliged, then stared boldly into her face. The game was up.

'You're Joan Collins, aren't you?' she asked, but so accusingly that I felt I was being interrogated by Torquemada himself.

'Yes, I am, and I suppose I've lost my bet.'

'You know this is a *very* silly thing to do,' she finger-wagged, in a schoolmistressy voice.

'I know,' I said brightly. 'I'm terribly sorry. It was just a bet, and a stupid one at that. Come on, Malcolm, let's go.'

'*Don't* do it again,' called the voice from behind us, as we walked back to John's tent. I scribbled my cheque to him, saying, 'I guess I'm more famous than I thought. I honestly thought that, with every woman dressed up to the ninety-nines, I was camouflaged well enough to get away with it.'

The next day, every tabloid front page declared in hyperbolic headlines: 'Joan Is Given Ascot Elbow', 'Joan Booted Out of Ascot,' 'The Queen Bars Joan, the Royal Loser.' I thought it was all rather a giggle and didn't take it seriously. After all, Fiona had worn Malcolm's wife's badge, so what was the big deal? But suddenly the newspapers started to write about me as though I was some pushy *nouveau-riche* hustler, and the story was embroidered and exaggerated *ad nauseam*.

The following year, invited to Robert and Susan Sangster's box for lunch, I was again without a badge for the Royal Enclosure and had absolutely no intention of going near it. I arrived in pouring rain with Dieter Apt, who was trying to make sense of Robert's directions. Of course, we took a wrong turning and, in the drizzling rain, cowering under an umbrella, with eight *paparazzi* following us, where should we end up? You've guessed it. Right outside the Royal Enclosure again. I couldn't *believe* my ill-luck. We made no attempt to enter, just said, 'Sorry, we've made a mistake, we've come the wrong way.'

But, the following morning the newspapers had another field day at my expense.

'She does this every year, she's a *very* silly woman.' Laura Thompson-Royds, assistant to the Queen's representative at Ascot, and obviously a very important person indeed, reportedly snapped, 'She never *stops* trying to gatecrash the Enclosure.'

It really wasn't important to me to be seen prancing about in the Royal Enclosure – and I forgot about the incident, although it was and still is constantly written about.

In 1995, when I was finally sent the damn badge, I entered the hallowed grounds of the Royal Enclosure, but stayed for only ten minutes. No big deal, I can assure you.

My attraction for the French Riviera kept growing. I'd enjoyed it as a teenager when I'd stayed with Lalla and Pauline in Cannes. Over the years several of my friends had bought homes there and when I returned to the Côte d'Azur in the eighties I knew that this was where I wanted to spend most of my time.

Robin shared my love of the South of France. He had spent a great deal of his childhood there and spoke excellent French, at which I was, and still am, a miserable failure. Throughout the summer of 1988 we looked at several houses, but we had exacting requirements and nothing seemed quite right.

Over Easter 1989, Robin was staying with his friend Hugo Guinness in Gassin, a charming little village fifteen minutes from St Tropez. He called me in Los Angeles, full of enthusiasm, to say that he and Hugo's father, James, had found the perfect house. I had three more weeks before *Dynasty* rolled up its tent, but Robin told me that I should come to see this exceptional place the moment we wrapped.

I was now appearing in only half the episodes of *Dynasty* and was disappointed that, even in those, I had only a few scenes. David Paulson, our new boss, was desperately trying to fulfil his brief to bring the show into the same milieu as *Roseanne* and *Golden Girls*, so to this end less of Alexis – but they were sardines on toast and *Dynasty* was caviar. We were losing our style, our mettle and our remaining viewers.

We knew *Dynasty*'s death was imminent but we had not been told when it would take place. The final script was unbelievably ridiculous. The last scene of the last episode shows Alexis, Sable, Dex and Adam having a blazing row on the first-floor balcony of Sable's hotel. As Alexis walks in, Sable sneers, 'Ahh, here comes Mummy dearest making one of her grand entrances as usual.'

Since I was wearing quite a simple black pant-suit while Stephanie had on a tight cyclamen satin mini-suit encrusted with sequins, her hair backcombed high, huge shoulder pads, deep cleavage and dozens of diamonds, this line didn't actually make sense.

Then Sable brags that she's pregnant by Dex.

'How sweet.' Alexis calmly lights a cigarillo. 'Sable's having a change-of-life baby.'

This infuriates Sable and the row builds as Alexis sneers, 'Naturally she'd go to the *only* man in Denver who found her attractive.'

'I gave her a shoulder to cry on,' says Dex furiously.

'That's not all you gave her, dear,' says Alexis.

'What else can you expect from a stud horse?' Adam screams at Dex.

A frantic fight then ensues, which ends with Dex and Alexis falling off the banisters and plummeting through the air, watched by a horrified Adam and Sable.

Then Blake is shot by a crazed gunman, Krystle goes stark staring bonkers in a Swiss sanitorium, and Blake's daughters Fallon and Kristina are trapped by a homicidal maniac in an underground tunnel.

None of us could get over how bad the final script was or that the network were so cynically ending the show with the fate of almost every major character left hanging. We all felt that our loyal audience had the right to a reasonable resolution – or, *even*, a happy ending.

I confronted David Paulson and asked why.

He shrugged. 'What can I do? ABC insist on pulling the plug on us. They hate our show so we've got to do what the bastards want.'

'Talk about throwing the baby out with the bathwater,' I said bitterly. 'Well, at least we'll get tons of residuals [income from foreign showings and repeats].'

Wrong!

My last day on the *Dynasty* set was highly emotional, and when shooting finished I stood at the top of the Carrington mansion's stairway blowing kisses to the crew below, many of whom were in tears. We'd been 'family' for almost nine years and I knew them so well. I was particularly sad to say goodbye to our brilliant director of photography, Michel Hugo. I'd ordered champagne for them all and a cake, which said: '*Dynasty* 1981–89. It's been the best. I love you all. Joan.'

In March 1989 *Dynasty* came to its disappointing end. I felt a mixture of relief and sadness. As Judy and I packed up my minuscule dressing room, where I'd practically lived for years, we both shed more tears.

My life, however, was branching out in different directions. I definitely felt a pull towards the stage: I wanted to feel the rush of an audience's presence, to be able to experiment every night, to work on different ways of creating laughs, to polish and hone my performance instead of walking through it, as I felt I'd been doing lately in *Dynasty*.

I'd recently lunched with Michael Codron, the distinguished English producer, and my agent, Peter Charlesworth, when we had discussed fulfilling my long-standing ambition to play Amanda in *Private Lives*. The deal was being hammered out now: a short tour of the provinces, and then London. Added to that, Robin was becoming more and more excited about the South of France house, which I couldn't wait to see.

Judy and I drove off the lot in her station wagon, piled with all the accumulated detritus of years, and I waved goodbye to the guards. Then I gave Warner Hollywood Studios one last, lingering look. An unremarkable collection of shoddy tract houses, where writers, editors and producers slaved, rickety wooden buildings that held the art and wardrobe departments and editing rooms, and the hideous white concrete bunkers, which were the sound stages. It all looked like nothing. Certainly not the fantasy factory that had created *Dynasty*'s magical saga of passion, hatred and greed. I hate goodbyes and endings, but I couldn't stop the tears rolling down my cheeks.

CHAPTER TWENTY

Private lives, public life

The first time I saw my potential new home in the village of La Croix-Valmer in Provence, I was taken aback. The villa was high on a hill, surrounded on all sides by rolling hills covered in umbrella pines and oak trees.

Right on the St Tropez peninsula, and designed by Roger Herrera, one of the finest local architects, the half-finished house was set in six acres of land. The view out to the sea and the Iles d'Hyères in the far distance was staggeringly beautiful and romantic. It was totally peaceful and completely protected and remote. There were few houses within sight of the villa and the smells of jasmine and mimosa were overwhelming.

As I stood with Robin, looking out at the beauty and tranquillity of the Provençal surroundings, I realized that he was right: this *was* the place that I had been dreaming about for decades. This would be our bolt-hole and we both knew we would love it for ever. We christened it Destino – *la forza del destino*, something I've always believed in.

To me, France is a magical country and I love it. From Paris – the most enchanting city in the world – to Provence, every part of it is special.

According to an ancient Provençal legend, when God had created the earth, the sky, the plains, the rivers, springs, seas, mountains and light, he leaned back with a contented smile. Then he discovered he still had a bit of everything left over and created Provence, a paradise he intended for himself.

With plenty of nagging, encouragement and endless telephone calls, we persuaded our laconic French builders to install the kitchen and finish the pool by the end of June and, on 14 July 1989, the two hundredth anniversary of the storming of the Bastille, we moved in. Judy came over to help, and for two months we camped out like happy gypsies. I'd put Cabrillo Drive on the market expecting, rather optimistically, an immediate sale. But real-estate prices had plummeted in LA and any chance of an offer even close to the asking price looked remote. There was also still the problem of selling my tiny *maison de pecheur* in Port Grimaud. I was shocked to discover that recession had also hit the South of France, so there were no buyers there either.

That first summer in Destino was wonderful, as indeed have been all subsequent summers. We lazed, gardened, ate delicious food, swam, made future plans, and had dozens of friends to stay. I was thrilled that I didn't have to act for a while, although I did spend several hours each day writing. To rid oneself of a lifetime of self discipline is no easy task – and I'd never been just a lady of leisure, not even for a few weeks.

In October 1989 Robin and I were invited down to lunch at Houghton Hall in Norfolk. One of the most beautiful stately homes in England, it had been built in the 1720s by Sir Robert Walpole, the first Prime Minister. I had been looking forward to meeting Sybil, the Dowager Marchioness of Cholmondeley, the remarkable owner of this Palladian palace. Now aged ninety-four, she had been a great beauty and famous society hostess since the First World War, and had married the Earl of Rocksavage in August 1913. 'Rock', as he was affectionately known, was considered the most beautiful man of his generation.

Robin and I arrived, with Sybil's grandson Charles, at the gates of the estate at midday. As we motored up the drive, I looked out at the large herd of white deer who peered back at us inquisitively, and spotted several magnificent peacocks strutting about on the manicured lawns.

'Her ladyship is waiting for you in the coffee room,' announced the butler.

My first sight of Lady Cholmondeley was an image I shall remember for the rest of my life. In the middle of a long sofa, with a grizzled miniature red dachshund in her lap, sat this remarkable old lady – directly beneath a full-length portrait of herself by John Singer Sargent as a ravishing beauty in her mid-twenties.

She got up, with the aid of two walking sticks, and greeted us warmly. While we talked, I found my eyes wandering about the room, marvelling at the dozen or so other Sargents, some of which hung on the walls while others rested on easels.

Lunch was announced, and we followed Lady Cholmondeley into the dining room, where we ate off a stunning eighteenth-century Sèvres dinner service. This tickled Charles, who later told me with a twinkle that not even when his grandmother's royal neighbours from Sandringham (the next-door estate to Houghton) came to lunch or to dine was this particular service used.

We chatted away effortlessly about a whole range of subjects, but I kept trying to bring the conversation back to her. She startled me when she said, 'Well, you see, I was brought up in the Playboy Club,' with an amused gleam in her eyes. It turned out that her family's vast London house had stood on precisely the same spot in Park Lane, until it had been demolished in the late 1950s to make way for the monstrosity which contained the club. She talked of H. G. Wells, Noël Coward, the painter Sir William Orpen and the great pianist Vladimir Horowitz, who used to come often to her houses to play.

She spoke most precisely, each word chosen with care and in what I can only describe as 1920s English. For example, things were 'lorst and gorne for ever', she could either be 'crorse' or 'vexed' about something and Pall Mall was pronounced 'Pell Mell'.

After lunch Lady Cholmondeley insisted on giving us her own tour of the house. The state rooms at Houghton are all on the first floor, filled with suite after suite of William Kent furniture, all designed for the house in the 1720s. She showed us everything, even taking me (without the men) into her bedroom, to see some of her extraordinary clothes, period couture by Fortuny, Charles Worth and Chanel. We were pursued everywhere we went by the incontinent dachshund, who left small but telling reminders of her latest visit to some of the grandest rooms, much to the amusement of her mistress.

Of the pictures, I can recall several vividly, but perhaps especially 'The White Duck', the mid-eighteenth-century masterpiece by Jean-Baptiste Oudry. Painted only in shades of white, it must be the greatest still life of the 18th century. Lady Cholmondeley told me that it had belonged to her brother, Sir Philip Sassoon, the famous aesthete, patron and collector, who had died in 1939. Tragically, 'The White Duck' was stolen from the house after Sybil's death.

She also showed us a second, still more ravishing, portrait of herself by Sargent, this one having been given to her by the artist himself as a wedding present.

We then had tea in the 'yellow drawing room' – yellow to distinguish it from drawing rooms of other colours. Here there was another Sargent, this time of Lady Cholmondeley's mother, Lady Sassoon, and the magnificent portrait by Hans Holbein of 'The Lady with Squirrel', which is now at the National Gallery, in London.

At six o'clock, it was time to leave. I said, 'I can't thank you enough, Lady Cholmondeley, for such a marvellous and memorable day.' She put her hand on my arm, and said, with touching simplicity, 'My name is Sybil.'

I asked her if she might come and see me in *Private Lives* the following autumn, as I knew she'd been such a great friend of Coward's. She replied in that precise way of hers: 'My dear, I'm not accepting *any* social engagements after January.' This seemed such an odd thing to say, as she seemed so full of energy and spirit. But did she have some sixth sense?'

As we drove away I looked at the now tiny figure, still waving, dwarfed by the vast palace behind her to which she'd given so much of her life and love.

Sibyl Cholmondeley died peacefully on Boxing Day, some two months later.

The following summer I threw myself into preparations for *Private Lives*.

Edward Duke, one of Robin's and my dearest friends, who was to play Victor, Amanda's second husband, came to spend two weeks with us in France. He was a highly accomplished comedy actor; tall, dark, attractive, acerbic and full of humour. He had recently starred in his own one-man show, *Jeeves Takes Charge*, playing not only Jeeves and Wooster but also a host of other eccentrics, including Bertie's fearsome aunts.

Every afternoon he and I settled down under an umbrella by the pool to learn our lines, both determined to be word-perfect before rehearsals began in September. Within ten minutes, though, he'd have me in stitches: his impressions of John Gielgud, Ralph Richardson and Laurence Olivier were absolute classics.

Keith Baxter was cast as my leading man Elyot; Sybil the *ingénue* was played by Sara Crowe, known for television commercials as the cream-cheese girl, who turned out to be excellent; and Tim Luscombe directed, who didn't. During rehearsals I was fascinated by a huge rent in his jeans, right under his balls. Every time he squatted down, in his eager-under-graduate way, I expected one or other of them to pop out. When I mentioned this to him, he laughed gaily and said, 'It's the style, darling.' Oh really?

When he was young Keith Baxter had been very good-looking. Now in his fifties, he hailed from the Alan Bates/Albert Finney/Peter O'Toole era but, unlike them, he'd never achieved major stardom. Respected in the theatre, he had a reasonably good marquee name, and Michael Codron was enthusiastic about our pairing.

Rehearsals went quite well, although I thought Elyot should have made more physical contact with Amanda. Since Coward's play is based on a strong physical attraction between the couple as well as their mental and emotional bond, this should be conveyed to the audience. But Keith never seemed keen to touch and caress me, although he liked putting his hands on my rear, particularly in Act II when I wore yellow silk pyjamas with nothing underneath.

'Why are you always grabbing my bottom?' I asked him one night. 'Can't you stroke my shoulders, my arms, or my neck?'

'But, darling,' Keith lilted, in his faint Welsh accent, 'I *love* your bottom. It's just like a boy's.'

I was ecstatic to be back on the stage again. After two weeks at the Theatre Royal, Bath, *Private Lives* opened in London at the Aldwych

Theatre in October 1990 and a fortnight later, it had recouped its investment.

The second act of *Private Lives* is gruelling: Elyot and Amanda are
alone on stage for thirty-two minutes, bantering, bickering, making love
and making up. It is a *tour de force* for the actors, who need sparkle and
plenty of energy. However, to my dismay Keith lacked the spontaneity
which we needed for this scene to truly sizzle.

One of the great joys of theatre is that one can change one's
performance constantly – improving, improvising, polishing, eradicating
business that doesn't work and replacing old stuff with new. One *never*
changes dialogue, of course, but one certainly changes one's 'line read-
ings'. I was always trying to improve my Amanda, both during rehearsals
and performances, thus hopefully getting in return a freshly revitalized
rendition from my stage partner. Most actors find this stimulating
because they can explore different depths in *their* own performance and
keep it lively and interesting not only for the audience but also for the
other actors. Saying the same lines in *exactly* the same way eight times a
week, day after day, month after month, becomes mind-numbingly boring and stultifying, and horror of horrors, the more you know the lines
the stronger the chances of drying – which often happens in dreams,
known in the profession as actor's nightmare. Unfortunately, after we had
opened in London and Keith had read the mainly favourable reviews, he
was either unable or unwilling to change his performance and said everything with *exactly* the same inflexion every *single* night.

In vain, during the difficult second act, would I give different inter-
pretations of different sections of dialogue. Keith would *always* answer
any line in *exactly* the same tone as he had done from the start. It didn't
matter whether I uttered it sweetly, bitterly or sarcastically, I always got
the same look, mannerisms, movement and intonation in return. It
started to drive me mad, and poor Robin had to bear the brunt of my frus-
trations every night.

'He's got all the flexibility of a telegraph pole, darling. What am I
going to do?' I wailed to him and Edward.

'And all the animation of the leg of a billiard table, my dear!' Edward
shot back. 'His only flair is in his nostrils. That old Welsh pit-pony's set

his performance in concrete. Just get on and do it. Take no notice of Blodwyn. Think of England. Think of your salary, darling.'

It's extraordinary how often critics can disagree so vehemently about performances and naturally my Amanda caused controversy. One critic accused me of hamming, mugging and tearing up the scenery, another said I gave an exceedingly bland, tame performance. Hard to believe they saw the same show on the same night.

But there was no doubt that *Private Lives* had instantly become a major smash hit. We were a sell-out.

'I've never *seen* so many flowers, dear,' said my darling dresser Charlie Routledge on opening night. 'Place looks like bleedin' Covent Garden. I'll 'ave me work cut out 'ere I can see.' He scrupulously watered and tended them every day, so that three weeks after opening my dressing room still looked like a Mafia funeral.

During our run celebrities by the score came backstage afterwards, even ex-President Ronald Reagan and his wife Nancy, who had been told by Jerry Zipkin, the doyen of New York social 'moths', that it was a 'must see!'.

But the biggest celebrity was the Princess of Wales who attended a charity gala performance for the Royal Marsden Hospital. Nervous that she was out front, everyone was terrified we'd blow our lines. In my opening scene with Edward, I was suddenly, and inexplicably, panic-stricken. I'd been having the actor's nightmare more regularly lately, waking up shaking and sweating with fear. As I stepped downstage, looking beyond the audience to say, 'Look at the lights of that yacht reflected in the water. I wonder whose it is?' which I'd said hundreds of times, I dried. I gave Edward a terror-stricken look and he came in helpfully with his next line. I was so seriously rattled, though, that I could think of nothing except that I couldn't remember any lines, which is absolutely *fatal* for an actor: if you *think* you're going to dry, chances are that you will. Oh horror of horrors.

Drops of sweat ran down my back. Only actors can understand the sheer terror of those few dry-mouthed moments that feel like a century has passed. In that heavy silence, the audience usually realizes instantly what's happening, and even those who are dozing become wide awake, eager for whatever will happen next. What came next from me was absolutely *nothing*. My mouth gaped like a fish until Edward said, apropos of nothing except that it was in the script, 'I hate sunburned women.'

What the *hell* did he mean? That line was meaningless to me. I turned upstage, my pleading eyes on the prompter. Whispered gibberish spouted from his mouth. I took a step towards the table stage left, and picked up my drink, playing for time. What must Princess Diana think at being subjected to this disaster? That made me even more flustered.

Edward, now also a nervous wreck, tossed another *non sequitur*, which threw me even more. I glared at the prompter signalling for help with my upstage hand.

'Ahoo-na-elian Sanboo,' I heard him hiss.

It was no good. I was done for, tongue-tied and finished in show business. Oh, the humiliation and the giggles at Kensington Palace later, no doubt.

I collapsed into a chair and asked Edward for a cigarette, which was not in the script. His eyes opened wide in shock, for although we smoked in the scene, Props only put the required number of fags in his case, and we'd already smoked those.

'I – er – I think I've run out, Amanda,' Edward stammered.

'Oh, I'll go and ask the maid for some,' I trilled, and rushed offstage to the prompt corner where in a millisecond I scanned the proffered page. Suddenly the whole scene rushed back into my head and I bounced back on stage where Edward was insouciantly sipping from an empty champagne glass, trying not to look like a total twat. The lines rolled back into my brain and we were off again, thank God.

Edward and I were covered in sweat at the end of that scene but at least he understood. 'Darling, it happens to *all* of us,' he said as we hugged. 'It's worse than a nervous breakdown, it's as though one's been struck as dumb as poor Philomena.'

We finished the rest of the play without incident, and when Princess Diana came backstage to meet the cast she was her usual charming and effervescent self.

When I was presented to her, I said, 'I'm so embarrassed, ma'am, about fluffing my lines and drying tonight.'

'I didn't notice you drying.' She smiled.

'Well, I'm glad, but I did, horribly, so we're all going to Joe Allen's later to get roaring drunk.'

'What fun,' she said.

'Would you care to join us?' I asked boldly.

The Princess gave a wistful smile. 'I'm afraid not. But thank you. Maybe some other time.'

The finale of Act II was a volatile knock-down drag-out fight between Elyot and Amanda. I was more than twenty years older than Amanda should be, not keen to be thrown over the sofa and tumbled on to the floor every night and, of course, there would be no convenient stunt-doubles to help out. But the play's the thing, and the fight was an integral and necessary part of it. Every night at the end of Act II the stage was littered with debris and broken glass, which made it difficult to manoeuvre in my bare feet.

All went well for the first two months until one matinée when I stubbed my toe against the sofa while running away from Elyot. I thought it was just another minor battle wound, but by the next morning it had swollen to the size of a small banana. The doctor told me it was broken, and that I couldn't wear a shoe until it had healed.

'But I'm in a play.'

'That's a problem, I'm afraid,' the doctor said. 'Can't you get out of it for a few weeks until it's healed? Put your understudy on.'

I sighed. Here we go again. Doctors never understand our business. The show *has* to go on. *Private Lives* was doing capacity business, some of which was because I was in the cast. If my understudy went on, many people would want their money back. I'd also heard stories of actors getting hate mail when they didn't appear. I told the doctor I was going on, hell or high water, and consulted with Charlie, my dresser, as to how to disguise the disfigurement.

In his eighties, Charlie was one of the great backstage legends of the British theatre. The title role in *The Dresser* had been based on him and he had dressed, among many others, Diana Rigg, Peter O'Toole and Tom Courtney. Impeccably turned out himself, and never seen twice in the same sports coat or sweater, he was always ready with a smile, a quip, a cup of tea and an answer to most backstage problems.

Amanda's first two outfits were a floating peignoir, and a long evening dress so it was relatively easy to disguise my deformity: Charlie bought some black ballet slippers and cut a discreet hole in the side of one so that my toe could flap through unconfined. We hoped that the audience wouldn't notice it. There was no problem in the second act as, wearing lounging pyjamas, I could play the scene barefoot. But the third act posed a dilemma. Amanda's costume here is a chic black and white suit in which the only possible footwear is high-heeled court shoes. The ever-resourceful Charlie found the solution. He bought two pairs of cheap black shoes, one in my normal size and one four sizes bigger. Then, with considerable patience and a sharp razor blade, he cut a hole in the large right shoe for my wounded toe to peek out. Then, because it couldn't stand imprisonment in tight stockings, he cut a tiny hole in the end and painstakingly painted my toe black! God knows what the first few rows of the audience must have thought – it must have looked ghastly.

The first few days in this footwear were agonizing, but the third act is blessedly short, and when I wasn't onstage I sat in the wings, foot propped up, while Charlie brought me sustenance.

A week later Robin and I were meeting Valentino and Giancarlo Giammetti at Harry's Bar for dinner after the show. Valentino is the most immaculate, fastidious person, and I knew this droll shoe arrangement wouldn't be appropriate for tonight. I settled on a pair of black trousers, wore a flat black shoe on my left foot and two black silk socks on the right.

'No one will be able to tell, dear,' Charlie assured me as I left the theatre. 'I promise you.'

Robin and I walked into the restaurant to be greeted by the ever-elegant Valentino, who kissed me on both cheeks and said, without even glancing down, 'My dear, you look wonderful, but what happened to your foot?'

Because of *Private Lives*' success, Michael Codron had extended the run several times, but it finally ended in March 1991, by which time ABC had capitulated to public opinion. Infuriated by the unfulfilling *Dynasty* cliffhanger fans had bombarded them with angry mail and thousands of viewers had threatened to boycott all ABC shows. To appease them *The Dynasty Reunion* would be shot that summer. First, though, I was due for another fling with Noël Coward.

In *Tonight at 8.30*, which I also co-produced, I played eight different roles in eight BBC half-hour shows. These ranged from a grumpy, fat seventy-year-old spinster, to a dizzy blonde socialite, a scrawny shrew and a blowsy red-haired barmaid, my bottom heavily padded. It was enormously challenging, *huge* fun and our cast was tremendous. Again, I'd been heavily influential in the casting.

Simon Williams, from *Mrs Cheyney*, was debonair in white tie and tails in *Shadow Play*, while I sang to him in a shrill falsetto and a platinum wig. John Nettles from *Bergerac* was a bearded and commanding naval captain in *Hands Across the Sea*. Tony Newley was brilliant in *Red Peppers* and as the meek put-upon clerk who turns on his nagging wife in *Fumed Oak*, and Edward Duke played several small but telling roles. The distinguished Shakespearian actor Dennis Quilley was the domineering patriarch in the saga *A Family Album* and Miriam Margolyes, Bernard Cribbins, Tony Slattery, Jane Asher, John Alderton, Bonnie Langford, Siân Phillips and John Standing rounded out an exceptional group of actors.

Tonight at 8.30 had been created by Noël Coward for Gertrude Lawrence and himself, and I'd always wanted to do it, mostly because it contained *Red Peppers*. For the hilarious backstage sketch of a bawdy, bickering second-rate variety act, Tony and I had to learn two complicated dance routines so the early tap training came in useful. We clowned in carrot-topped wigs and white satin sailor suits as we sang 'Has Anybody Seen My Ship?' and attempted to be Jack Buchanan – suave in white tie, top hat and tails, wielding canes while doing a soft-shoe shuffle dance called 'Men About Town'. For our screaming fight scenes in the dressing room we drew heavily upon our own marital experiences – no Method acting needed here – but those were far behind us.

With the passing years, and our affection for Tara and Sacha, Tony and I had become friends, and in some way we were almost family. The bad times of our marriage were behind us. Life is far too short to bear grudges or continue feuds so we buried the hatchet and got on with it. I'd always appreciated Tony's tremendous talent and I was glad that he'd given up crooning to the punters in Vegas saloons and had moved back to London.

In June 1991 ABC made *The Dynasty Reunion*. To say that it was a massive disappointment would be like saying Hitler was a naughty boy. It was appalling, cobbled together without rhyme or reason to placate viewers.

Al Corley, the original Steven, came back to play the gay son again, but we had to manage without Gordon Thompson, who played the other Carrington son, Adam. His agent hadn't been informed of the shooting dates so Gordon couldn't get away from his daily soap opera. With remarkable alacrity, and immense stupidity, the English actor Robin Sachs was rushed in to play Adam. He looked and sounded *nothing* like Gordon, which must have also been confusing for the audience.

All the main players had miraculously recovered from whatever had befallen them in the final episode: Fallon and Kristina had escaped from the maniac in the tunnel; Blake's supposedly fatal gunshot wound was passed off in a one-liner as, 'It was only a flesh-wound – nothing serious.' And of Alexis, last seen plummeting over a balcony, a minor character explains: 'Can you *believe* it? She twisted her body in mid-air and fell on top of Dex, poor thing.'

This, of course, was the reason in the script that Dex couldn't be at the reunion but the real one was that Michael Nader had gone on to the daytime soap *All My Children*.

Krystle miraculously had come out of her coma and is seen, shabby and confused, tottering to an auction of the Carrington loot. There she spots Alexis, who sneers, in classic Alexis fashion, 'What's the matter, dear? Was the Alpine air too heady, or did you wander away from the sanatorium and get lost?'

This time the producers had been determined to hire a forceful, dynamic actor to play opposite me. They had not been happy with James Healy (less so a year later when he was sentenced for assaulting his sister's estranged husband with a piece of glass). They finally decided on Jeroen Krabbe, arguably Holland's finest actor. He had recently specialized in villains in American action films, and was about to play the baddie opposite Harrison Ford in *The Fugitive*.

Tall, good-looking and burly, with cropped light brown hair and piercing blue eyes, I was delighted that our love scenes sizzled and our fights crackled. But Jeroen wasn't an actor to pull his punches as I discovered at the finale. Having turned out to be far more villainous than Alexis, he drags her by the scruff of her neck to a shed, ties her up, gags her, then starts to poison her with carbon monoxide fumes from a lawnmower! No Robert Mitchum he. Rough he most certainly was, and my screams and shrieks of agony were for real.

'I guess you apply "The Method" in Holland too,' I said as he gallantly kissed my bruised hands at the end of every brutal take.

'Yes,' he murmured. 'Just wait for our love scenes.'

Although my two novels for Simon and Schuster had been bestsellers, both in the UK and the US, there were problems with another author at the publishing house, so Swifty decided he'd better move me out of there.

Accordingly he signed me to a two-book deal with the giant conglomerate publishers Random House for a staggering $4 million.

I was delightfully stunned when Swifty told me, in his usual jocular fashion, 'Listen, kiddo, they want you in the worst way. Now all you gotta do is write the books.'

This was right up my alley, I was sated with television: all the years of *Dynasty* had left me with no desire to be on a long-running series again, and I was objective enough to understand that movie roles weren't going to fall into my lap.

Which left the theatre, and although I'd adored doing *Private Lives* in England, I felt a certain trepidation about the forthcoming four-month tour of America followed by two months on Broadway. The theatre is a bloody, grinding slog, and you need immense reserves of energy and concentration to make lines you have spouted hundreds of times sound spontaneous. Long runs can drive you crazy.

I was anxious to get my novel published by 1992, and even more anxious to make it better than its predecessors so I was going to dedicate considerable effort and time to this project. I felt that my career in the future would depend more on writing and less on acting. I spent most of the summer of 1991 in the South of France, writing my novel for Random House, then again started rehearsals for *Private Lives*, produced by Charles Duggan and directed by Arvin Brown. Edward Duke remained as Victor but Elyot would be played by Simon Jones, best known for playing Sebastian Flyte's brother in *Brideshead Revisited*, with Sibyl to be played by Jill Tasker.

Simon and I worked well together, and during rehearsals I felt that he was a lucky improvement on Keith.

Never one to travel light, on this American tour I excelled myself in the excess baggage department. As we were going from one extreme of temperature to the other, I'd packed for every contingency from anoraks to bikinis. Between us, Judy, Robin and I had twenty-eight pieces of luggage, about which I was constantly teased because most of it was mine.

Chen Sam, my publicist, was a wizard at packing and unpacking. She was taking a short sabbatical from Elizabeth Taylor, who was in the process of becoming Mrs Larry Fortensky, and as she had worked for and travelled with Elizabeth for several years I understood why she was so dextrous with the tissue paper.

In October, we arrived in Denver for opening night. Downtown Denver was like Switzerland, almost surgically clean, and it seemed somehow appropriate that we were to begin our tour in the city where Alexis had reigned supreme.

The Center Theater was so enormous, with over two thousand seats, that the actors had to be hooked up to microphones. Simon Jones had decided to wear a hairpiece – which made him look, as he said with a wink, 'more sexually confident' – underneath which his microphone was wedged. However, sometimes the sweat on the poor man's brow caused the sound to short out. Sometimes he would inexplicably get loud messages from police cars, which was so disconcerting that I corpsed helplessly.

'How come *you* never sweat?' Simon asked accusingly.

'Do you think I could have got through all those years on *Dynasty* if

I'd sweated,' I answered. 'I'd have been fired. It's mind over matter – and a *great* deal of powder.'

Robin thought Edward's performance was excellent, but confided: 'When Victor says to Amanda: "I *can't* believe it's true – you and I here alone together – married!" he always manages to look as though the income tax inspector is waiting for him in the wings.'

On the first night, I was predictably nervous. Edward burst into my dressing room, ebullient as ever. '*Darling*, the audience is Denver's finest! It's a surging *sea* of cosmetic surgery out there. I've never *seen* quite so much glitter. They look as if they've all put on their best bib and tucker for the mighty Alexis.'

'Well, let's hope they laugh,' I said. 'And at least get some of the subtleties.'

During the first interval Simon said, 'My God, did you see all those women with their binoculars out? It's as if they were at a race meeting. What the hell are they doing?'

'They're looking at Joan, darling! Looking for scars behind the ears.' Edward beamed.

'Oh, great,' I said. 'Maybe they'll spot our microphones instead.'

But the audience must have liked the play because we received a rapturous ovation at curtain call, and a man who looked exactly like Elizabeth Taylor's new husband presented me with an enormous bouquet of red roses. Later, at the party, the Mayor of Denver gave me a plaque declaring that the following day was to be 'Joan Collins Day in Denver'.

'Does that mean she gets to shop free?' Edward asked innocently.

The critics were kind, although one huge woman, of at least sixteen stone, criticized the size of my stomach rather than my performance. Charles had persistently told our temperamental costume designer William Ivey-Long, that my white evening dress was too tight, but he had never fixed it. He appeared to be too busy worrying about his first night seating arrangements. Twelfth row, centre stalls wouldn't apparently do for him, so on the first night he'd stormed out before curtain up, shredding his programme and throwing the bits into the shocked face of an usherette. We were all upset at his breach of theatrical etiquette. A touring theatre company is like a family; we *always* stick together. We might bitch among ourselves but we *never* do it publicly.

The news that I'd broken every Denver auditorium box-office record, including those set by Lauren Bacall and Katherine Hepburn, was most encouraging and we toasted our continuing success. But opening night in Dallas was a disaster: there was hardly a titter from the vast auditorium and we sank into gloom during our run there.

It is extraordinary how audiences change from one night to the next: lines that have them rolling in the aisles in one city are greeted by stony silence in another. In the theatre you can never take *anything* for granted, which is one reason why it's so endlessly intriguing.

But Dallas had its bright spot. One morning the telephone rang and the honeyed voice of a friend of a friend of Robin's asked, 'Would you and Miss Collins care to come to tea with me tomorrow?'

'It's Greer Garson,' he whispered, having had to sit down.

Mrs Miniver, Goodbye, Mr Chips, Random Harvest . . . images of Greer Garson in her prime flooded into my head. I wished that Mummie was still alive so that I could have told her about meeting one of her favourites in person. Greer Garson had been the number-one female star in America during the early- to mid-forties. Between 1939 and 1945, she had been nominated for the best actress Academy Award an unbelievable six times, for her performances in *Goodbye, Mr Chips, Blossoms in the Dust, Madame Curie, Mrs Parkington, The Valley of Decision* and, of course, *Mrs Miniver*.

On Friday afternoon, Robin picked me up after rehearsals, and off we went to the address we'd been given on Turtle Creek Boulevard. This turned out to be a huge and exclusive apartment block, so exclusive in fact that some of the richest citizens of Dallas lived within its impressive walls. Robin told the apartment block's security guard that we had come to see Mrs Fogelson, and we were told to go up in the elevator to the penthouse. We emerged into a tiny corridor, tentatively pressed the apartment's door bell and were let in by a tall black maid in a white starched uniform, who ushered us inside. The white rooms were enormous with high ceilings and huge African masks and sculptures adorning the walls. In a glass case stood an Oscar. We looked at the attached plaque, which read: 'Best actress 1942 Greer Garson – Mrs Miniver'.

After a few minutes, Greer came in, followed by her nurse. She must have been in her mid- to late-eighties yet walked well, head up, filled with both energy and enthusiasm. She wore black trousers, a white Mexican-style shirt and her eyes were bright and alert. She wore bright lipstick, mascara and a touch of powder. Her hair was a mixture of white and pale auburn. When she spoke, her magical voice could, even then, have calmed a tempest.

She kissed me and took both of Robin's hands. We sat at a large round table, where tiny cucumber sandwiches and sponge cake had been made in our honour, and talked as if we were all old friends. Greer was full of humour and boundless Anglo-Irish charm.

She told us how much she'd adored Ronald Colman: 'So kind and gentle and shy. Such a gentleman.' It turned out that *Random Harvest* was her own favourite film, as well as Robin's. 'Robert Donat was a joy – adorable – such a marvellous timbre in his voice. Clark Gable was a poppet, too, although you know that halitosis business was sadly true. And Walter Pidgeon – divine. Yes, I've been very lucky with my leading men.'

'Of course, when I married my first husband – he played my son in *Mrs Miniver* – well, my dear, such a *scandale*. He was a few years younger than me but, then, he always did have a terrific tendency to minimize his age. We were married on a Friday and he left for the Pacific on the Sunday. He was in the Navy, you know. We wrote to each other a good deal, but I suppose that wasn't really enough . . .' Her voice trailed off with a delicious hint of amusement.

Robin asked her where the art-deco black and white snakeskin table, which stood in front of the fireplace, had come from.

'From a python,' came the answer, in a tone of voice which can only be described as sounding like a giggle.

I complimented her stunning pear-shaped diamond ring. 'Oh, thank you so much, my dear, it's worn in your honour. I'm afraid it's a bit dirty. It's my engagement ring from Buddy [Fogelson] – circa 1949.' It was truly magnificent, large but not that ghastly vulgar size so prized by *nouveau-riche* ladies the world over.

She went on to tell us of how two or three years ago, when she had been in a Dallas hospital suffering from heart trouble, the nurse came into her room to turn on the television to cheer her up. As the evening news came on, she saw some footage of a terrible fire in an apartment block.

'"Oh dear!" I said to myself, "I do hope no one's been hurt." Then the wind blew, and the smoke drifted a little, and I recognized with horror my own apartment block in Los Angeles. At that moment my lawyer came bounding into the room, out of breath, sweating, and said to me, "Do you want the good news or the bad news?" I said, "Please give me some good news," and he said, "You're in a hospital bed in Dallas." "Humph, and so what's the bad?" "Your apartment in the Wilshire Building no longer exists."'

Greer told this story without a hint of bitterness or self-pity, although, she told us, 'I lost *everything*. All my letters, diaries, photograph albums, pictures, furniture, even my Oscar melted. The one you see over there is a replacement that the Academy were kind enough to give me. Everything went except one little Georgian silver teaspoon. Well, possessions are only possessions. Lucky, I suppose, it wasn't me melting.'

We sat with her for another hour and then it was time to go. She took my arm to walk me to the front door, kissed Robin and asked us both to sign her visitors' book. I wrote, 'Tea and cucumber sandwiches with Mrs Miniver. What heaven.' Robin wrote something about her still looking like a bright new penny, a line that Ronald Colman says to her in *Random Harvest*.

Then she kissed us both again, and said, 'You are both absolute heaven. So beautiful. Be happy, my darlings. Enjoy life – love it and live it to the full. Goodbye, my darlings, I've so enjoyed seeing you both. You've made me so happy. Goodbye.'

The front door closed and Robin and I were left with tears in our eyes, as the ping of the arriving elevator broke the spell. As we descended, we clutched each other, both with the imprint of her lipstick on our cheeks.

'She was so like Mummie,' I whispered.

After Dallas came Houston, where Robin and I stayed at Sandra and Ricky di Portanova's house. They gave us an opening-night party at which Sandra, resplendent in black and gold Oscar de la Renta, looked like some beautiful ambassadorial envoy from Ruritania, and Simon and I, who had been rehearsing a camp tango for New York, performed it to wild applause.

The Music Hall Theatre was an enormous opulent barn with three thousand seats – eminently suitable for *Phantom of the Opera* perhaps, but for an intimate little comedy it was disastrous. We must have been on a roll, though, for we received another first-night standing ovation and social Houston loved us, pulling out all the stops to entertain us, with a party or a luncheon practically every day.

My darling friend Lynn Wyatt gave us a fabulous party. (Lynn in her charming Texan accent always called me 'mah sistah'.) Jose Quintero, the director of *The Roman Spring of Mrs Stone*, sweetly told me that he had always believed that I would have a flourishing career. 'Even when I just sat around on the set watching?' I asked. 'I thought my career was over then.'

'Yes, dear Joan. Even then.'

Our next stop, Sacramento, California, was a city about as glamorous as a whist drive in Tulse Hill. (Thank you, Noël.) To publicize the play, I had to do non-stop interviews and I was amazed that my vocal chords hadn't packed up from talking so much. 'Selling yourself to death,' Robin called it, and he was right.

Although the Sacramento reviews were wonderful, ticket sales weren't. When a review says, 'Don't miss this at *any* cost!' you expect that at least a certain number of die-hard theatre-goers will turn up but, in short, they didn't.

In San Francisco, which I happen to think is the most beautiful city in the States, I turned on the Christmas tree lights in Union Square. But I was sad to see such a huge number of beggars, some wearing signs saying, 'Homeless, hungry and HIV positive'. We went around town with pockets full of dollar bills and handed them out on almost every street corner.

The first night in San Francisco was to be a black-tie AIDS benefit without the critics in attendance. Robin's evening trousers had fallen into the bath, so he had to wear a pair of black jeans, which he wasn't thrilled about. He needn't have worried, though. The mostly male audience turned up in full black-leather gear, many sporting spiked dog-collars!

This was by far the best audience we'd ever had. Shrieks and laughs on practically every line and thunderous applause. We were all flushed with success and perhaps overplayed just a touch.

Robin sat beside Graham Payn, the executor and beneficiary of Noël's estate, who was wildly pleased. '*So* much better than London, my dear, and I thought it was terrific there.'

Just before the curtain went up on the official San Francisco opening night when the critics were supposed to be out front, Charles Duggan appeared, pale and stricken, to tell us, 'The critics were in last night when all the leather queens were here. I've heard we're going to get stinking reviews, because the gay audience loved the show so much it irritated the critics.'

This seemed totally illogical but, sure enough, the reviews were dreadful, and completely disheartened us all. Yet San Francisco audiences came anyway and adored the show every night.

The following week we arrived in Los Angeles. I did the *Tonight* show and several interviews and was again filled with optimism about *Private Lives*. We would be there for two weeks, Robin and Katy and I staying at Cabrillo which still hadn't been sold – although the public had trooped through it in large numbers, most of them, no doubt, to see how Alexis lived.

Then, fast-forward in a whirl of numbness, we played Miami, Washington, Seattle, Pittsburg, and finally New York. We opened on Broadway at the Broadhurst Theatre in March 1992 and ran for an exciting and stimulating two months, even though, back in Miami, I'd been persuaded to give an interview to the aptly named Alex Witchell, wife of Frank Rich, then known as 'the butcher of Broadway'. Rich was feared and loathed, because his usually scathing reviews appeared in the tremendously influential *New York Times*. I didn't wish to talk to this woman, but our press agent repeatedly told me it was *essential* for our New York success. 'If Alex does a good piece and likes you, so will Frank.'

Because I was fed up with interviewers, particularly the females, always criticizing me for being too groomed and for wearing too much make-up, I wore a plain white T-shirt, jeans and no make-up whatsoever. Witchell seemed friendly, describing me in her piece as 'looking like Joan

Crawford's younger and prettier sister'. Apparently she hadn't noticed that I hadn't worn even a smudge of mascara.

But, as I had predicted, although *Mrs* Rich had written quite a fair piece on me in the *New York Times*, there was no guarantee that Mr Rich would like *Private Lives* and he was typically scornful. Many of the other reviews were good (*Variety* described me as 'dead perfect as Amanda', and the *Post*, the *News*, the radio and TV reports were mainly excellent), it mattered not. Frank Rich was King of the Critics and ultimately he was the only reviewer to whom theatre-goers would listen.

I was astonished that the Broadway theatre could allow itself to be decimated and dictated to by just *one* critic. Why hadn't the powerful producers and backers banded together years ago and stopped paying for these expensive ads in the *New York Times* until Frank Rich was fired or, at least, told to tone down his vicious attacks? *How* can a business, in which even finding the funds to put on a show is such a desperate struggle, allow itself to be destroyed by the whims of *one critic*?

After six months in America with *Private Lives*, I made another vow. No more touring. Exhaustion had set in with a vengeance and all I wanted to do now was collapse at Destino, stare at the view and write my little heart out.

CHAPTER TWENTY-ONE

Million dollar icons

Swifty and Mary Lazar's legendary Oscar parties were always spectacularly star-studded and their 1992 bash at Spago on Sunset Boulevard proved no exception. I was asked and, as the Lazars were particularly fond of Robin, so was he. Nearly every major movie and television star, mogul, producer, writer and director poured into the restaurant at the ridiculously early hour of five p.m. Jet-setting socialites had flown in from all over the world and the assembled throng glittered, gossiped and gaped at each other in palpable anticipation of what the night might bring. The Oscars are the *raison d'être* of Hollywood – apart from profit, of course. Many people profess to scorn them, but to win this naked little golden man is the apotheosis of movie-making.

Spago was the most 'in' restaurant of the moment. Wolfgang Puck, the owner, was famed for making the best pizzas in the world, which were passed round to the guests as soon as they arrived. With exotic toppings of smoked salmon, Beluga caviar and truffles, his reputation proved well deserved and dozens of diets simultaneously bit the dust. Waiters circulated with glasses of chilled Krug which everyone sipped while waiting for the broadcast to begin.

Competition for invitations to this swankiest of all Tinseltown *soirées* was so fierce that Swifty and Mary spent months fending off calls from eager moguls and stars, who would do *anything* to be invited. But Swifty was always adamant about whom he would and would not ask, and no matter how much or by whom he was cajoled or wooed, the prized invitation was only received by those who he considered deserved one or those he counted as his closest friends. He had his particular favourites, from old and new Hollywood, and he had his aversions (some of whom were extremely famous) and *nothing* anyone could do or say would change his mind. Raquel Welch had incurred his wrath the previous year by shamelessly networking the room during the Oscar transmission, stopping to sit, once in a while, on a producer's knee: 'She'll never be invited again,' said Swifty. And she wasn't.

Robin and I arrived fractionally after five o'clock to be greeted by the irascible gnome himself, flanked by a couple of privileged photographers. Swifty was also highly selective about who should be allowed to snap his gilded throng: *Women's Wear Daily*, of course, the *Hollywood Reporter*, naturally, and perhaps one or two other eminent representatives of the fourth estate were allowed inside. But outside the pavements seethed with *paparazzi* and TV news cameramen.

'Why are you so late?' Swifty hissed in my ear, as we posed together.

'Sorry, darling, the traffic's vile.'

'That's *no* excuse,' he admonished sternly. 'You should know it's always bad on Oscar night.'

Suitably chastened I apologized again. He was just like my father in this way who, when asked to arrive at eight, would always be there ten minutes early. I have always admired the punctuality of that older generation who must find today's life so stressful and hectic, but who still always manage to get where they're going on time.

There are three dining rooms at Spago. The one considered to be the most prestigious looks out on to glittering Sunset Boulevard below so those who were seated in the two at the back were often not pleased.

The tables were covered with white linen cloths sprinkled with little black and gold stars. The centrepiece on each was an amazing concoction of a two-foot-high black polystyrene star studded with tiny gold Oscars, on top of which was perched an arrangement of black and gold plastic ribbon, which looked like rolls of film, topped off with an actual-sized gold Oscar. Swifty devised something different every year, and many guests would shamelessly take one home with them, much to Swifty's extreme displeasure. He rightly considered stealing the table arrangements to be 'the limit'.

'No class,' he grumbled. 'No one would have the nerve to do that in Europe.'

Around the walls hung giant posters of the nominated films, and ten or twelve enormous television screens were strategically placed around the three rooms.

It was imperative to Swifty that everyone was seated by five thirty, and remained glued to the televisions for the entire ceremony. Too much loud conversation was frowned upon, except during commercial breaks. In Swifty's strict code of etiquette any talking was unforgivably rude until the transmission was over, when the socializing was allowed to begin.

Robin and I checked to see at which table we'd been put, and were touched to discover that we were at Swifty's.

'Who the hell's Miss Ciccone? She's sitting next to you,' I asked Robin.

He looked at me in amazement. 'You mean you don't know who that is?'

'Haven't a clue.'

'Well, she's almost the biggest star here tonight,' he said mysteriously.

Just then Swifty clapped his tiny hands and announced that everyone must take their places *immediately* and three hundred of the most popular and influential people in Hollywood scurried to their tables like obedient schoolchildren. At our table three seats reamined unoccupied, those for Miss Ciccone, Miss O'Donnell, and Mr Keshishian.

I sat between Robin and Walter Cronkite, the dignified television news-anchor for over thirty years, and opposite Dennis Hopper and Mica and Ahmet Ertegun, she one of New York's best dressed women, he the big chief of Atlantic Records.

Half an hour into the ceremonies, there was a huge barrage of flashes from outside, like the Battle of the Somme, and Madonna, the current superstar of the planet, made her entrance. In stark contrast to the satins, chiffons, and fairy frocks already *in situ*, she looked deliberately downbeat tonight, although decked out in the latest street-cred fashion: a blue-and-white checked Vivienne Westwood smock, so voluminous that she could have been carrying triplets, and black suede wedgies, all topped off with a black beret perched jauntily over her short, peroxided hair. Deep red lipstick, lady-like pearl earrings and matching choker completed her look. Swifty did his best to disguise his displeasure at her tardiness but failed. However, she seemed not to care in the least, continued to chew her gum and plonked herself next to Robin. '*That's* Miss Ciccone,' he whispered. After she'd sat down and brisk introductions had been made – I received a cursory 'Hi' – she proceeded to blow large pink bubbles throughout most of dinner.

As each course was served, Madonna raised her plate and put her nose as close as possible to its contents. Then she stuck out her tongue and prodded the food with it, sniffed it again and, if it passed these various table tests, she tucked in. Needless to say, the rest of us at the table were absolutely riveted by this unusual culinary ritual.

She talked solely to the people on her right, who were the comedienne Rosie O'Donnell and Alek Keshishian, who had directed *Truth or Dare*, during which film Warren Beatty had shrewdly remarked to her, 'You don't *live*, do you, unless you're on camera?' Robin, no slouch at the conversational stakes, was studiously ignored.

Swifty became so annoyed at what he later described as Madonna's appalling rudeness that, after about twenty minutes, he leapt up, stalked over and whispered something angrily in her ear. Whatever it was, she instantly ceased bubble-blowing, turned to Robin and bestowed upon him a dewy-eyed girlish smile. From then on she chatted happily away to him.

The year before, Madonna had been a guest on David Letterman's chat-show. At the time she'd been dating Warren Beatty while appearing in his movie *Dick Tracy*, which that year had been nominated for several Oscars.

Letterman had asked, 'Now you're dating Warren Beatty, aren't you jealous of some of the women that he's been with, like Diane Keaton, Isabelle Adjani or Joan Collins?'

'Joan Collins, HA!' Madonna had sniffed. '*I'm* not worried. Have you seen *her* lately?'

Although I thought this rather an unpleasant remark, I was long past the stage when any bitchy remark from another actress could upset me. However, I certainly didn't think Madonna was looking too good, particularly for someone of only thirty-three.

Some time later, the room suddenly hushed. The Best Film of 1991 was about to be announced. Everyone stared at the screens while scenes from the five nominated pictures were shown.

As the clip from *Bugsy* came on, Madonna turned to me and asked, 'Did Warren fuck Vivien Leigh?'

'Well, I was engaged to him at the time, so it's hardly likely he would've told *me*,' I replied archly.

'Well, he *says* he did.'

A vision of Madonna and Warren sitting up in bed together, ticking off all the people he'd slept with, suddenly came into my head and I giggled.

Madonna continued, 'Warren's always had this great knack of going with the right actress at the right time. He was living with Diane Keaton when they were making *Reds*, he got *lots* of publicity from that, last year he was with me when we were doin' *Dick Tracy*, and this year Annette Bening's having his baby. He's *truly* an operator. I wonder what he'll do for an encore *next* year?'

There was no time to answer this hypothetical question as the winner was being announced.

'The Oscar for best picture goes to *Silence of the Lambs*.' The whole room erupted in cheers.

After that, Madonna didn't stick around much longer. She chatted a while with Robin and Alan Nevins, Swifty's associate, then swept out – no doubt to blow her bubble-gum into the faces of a more appreciative audience.

Two days later Robin and I were waiting for friends, in a booth at Dominick's, a dark dive, with red-checked tablecloths and candles stuck in Chianti bottles. It had been popular in the sixties and seventies, but was now enjoying such a renaissance that it was often hard to get a table.

Suddenly, Alek Keshishian bounded over and slipped into the seat beside me.

'Hi,' he said. 'Nice to see you guys again. Great party the other night, wasn't it?'

We agreed it had been.

'Wow! What did you do to Madonna?' He looked at Robin. 'She thought you were great.'

'Really.' Robin's eyebrows rose sharply, looking as if they were making a bid to touch his hairline. 'Well, I must admit I liked her, too. She's quite a girl – in spite of her bubble-gum and her rather eccentric gastronomic habits.'

'Ah, take no notice of that, she just *loves* to shock,' laughed Alek. 'But she thought you were real cool.' He looked at me. 'You, too,' he said.

'Me?' I was surprised. 'You're joking.'

'No, really. In fact, she said we should get together with you all one of these nights.'

'That'd be – interesting,' I mused.

'Yeah, well, we'll do it sometime. See you guys.'

As he sauntered off to join his table, I said to Robin: '*Don't* hang by the thumbs, darling. That's pure Hollywood bullshit talk. The next time we meet Ms Ciccone I doubt she'll even remember that we've met.'

The great female movie stars of Hollywood's golden era had enormous personal style. Every one was an original from Gloria Swanson, Clara Bow and Jean Harlow to Marilyn Monroe, Audrey Hepburn, Grace Kelly and Claudette Colbert. All of these women had their own unique individuality, charisma and glamour.

With few exceptions this doesn't hold true of today's female stars which is perhaps why young girls today idolize super-models rather than actresses. As my generation used to emulate Ava Gardner and Rita Hayworth, today's pre-teens go for Kate Moss or Claudia Schiffer. Why? Because the female stars of today simply don't have glamour, and few of them have much off-screen charisma either.

One notable exception is Sharon Stone. She actually looks and behaves like a real movie star, but without any of the negative connotations that that might imply. Witty, well-dressed and sure of herself, Sharon knows *exactly* what she's doing. She also has a splendid sense of self-parody. At a party on Valentino's boat, during the 1995 Cannes Film Festival, she told me; 'I just wore a couple of your beaded dresses from *Dynasty* in my last movie *Casino*.'

'But we must be a different size,' I replied. 'I'm fatter than you!'

'Not in the hips, honey!' She shot back a wry grin.

Sharon will probably continue to act for as long as she wants, then turn to directing or more producing. Not for her to be used, abused and chucked on the slag heap, as has happened to so many stars.

Dressed beautifully for public appearances, Sharon loves clothes and loves talking about them. She told me, 'When I'm on a publicity tour, I'll never be caught in the same dress twice. The public deserve to see me looking different each time.'

What a refreshing change she makes from those stars who delight in looking as battered and unfashionable as possible. It's no surprise to me that in the last poll of the world's ten most popular movie stars, nine were men.

It's been my great good fortune to meet many legends of the silver screen, among whom Claudette Colbert was one of my favourites. In 1994 Carole and Anthony Bamford and Robin and I were asked to lunch with her at her house in Barbados. I was thrilled to be finally meeting this extraordinary lady, one of the all time great actresses, whom I'd admired not only for her comedy technique but for her dazzling glamour and style.

Born Claudette Lily Chauchoin in Paris in 1905, she'd made her stage début on Broadway and in 1927 had started in films. She was considered pretty rather than beautiful, but she possessed sophistication and elegance far beyond her years. She became one of Paramount's biggest grossing actresses and starred in De Mille's *The Sign of the Cross*, in which she so memorably bathed in asses' milk. Then she made an enormous success opposite Clark Gable in the multi-award winning comedy *It Happened One Night*, for which she received the best actress Oscar. Claudette was slightly vain and jokingly called the right side of her face 'the dark side of the moon', as she refused to be shot from that angle. Noel Coward always maintained that she didn't actually have one.

She had starred in more than sixty films, then in 1987, when she was eighty-two, she made a comeback starring opposite Ann-Margret in the television version of Dominick Dunne's controversial novel *The Two Mrs Grenvilles*. Nolan Miller, who designed Ann-Margret's clothes, told me that Claudette possessed the supple body of a woman at least two decades younger. That had been seven years ago. How would she look now?

When we arrived at Bellerive, her beautiful house, her friend Helen O'Hagen, took us out to the terrace where Claudette greeted us all warmly. Her thick grey hair was tied back in a pony-tail with a white bobble band like little girls wear. She was wearing small classic gold earrings, and was perfectly made-up. Behind her crimson-tinted glasses her pale face was almost unlined, making it almost impossible to believe that she was nearly ninety-one.

She beckoned me to sit next to her under a banyan tree, and after drinks were served proceeded to tell an anecdote: 'Once, while I was entertaining some guests here, the monkey dropped its calling card into my hair. So *rude*. I gave *such* a shriek.' She chuckled. 'I rushed into the bathroom leaving my guests sitting there, to scrub away all traces of monkey.' We laughed then she said, 'I saw a movie of yours recently that was shot here in Barbados.'

'You mean *Island in the Sun*?' I said.

'That's right,' she said, 'you were so young it must have been your first picture. Was it?'

'No,' I said. 'It was probably my eighth or ninth and I wasn't that young. I was about twenty-two.'

'Well, you *looked* young and that's always the main thing. I loved that movie. It really captured the spirit of this wonderful island.'

We talked of mutual friends and acquaintances, particularly the much-loved Leonard Gershe, who had instigated this lunch. He'd told me that, since her recent stroke, Claudette hadn't wanted to see anyone except her closest friends.

'Leonard was one of the first people I met in Hollywood,' I told her. 'At Gene Kelly's with his friend Roger Edens.'

'Oh, I *loved* Roger,' said Claudette enthusiastically. 'He was *so* amusing and *so* talented.'

We talked about Billy Wilder, how he was becoming such a media animal again since the musical of *Sunset Boulevard* had become a hit. 'I made one of my best movies with Billy,' she mused. 'He didn't direct it, he wrote it with Charlie Bracket. It was called *Midnight*. You must try and get it on video, it's my favourite.' Then she asked if we'd seen *Tovarich*. 'I made it with Charles Boyer. Billy and Charlie wrote that one too, it was *such* fun to make.'

Although she was irritated with herself for not being able to remember certain things, I was astounded by the breadth of her memory.

She had talked animatedly throughout lunch, and although somewhat hard of hearing, was the kind of ninety-year-old we would all want to be like.

After lunch Helen took us up to the main house, where we admired the pictures in the drawing room. One particularly caught my eye: a red-headed child with amazing cornflower blue eyes. 'That's Deborah Kerr's daughter,' said Helen. 'Claudette painted that.'

A silver-framed photograph of Claudette shaking hands with the Pope looked as though it had been taken when she was in her early fifties. I was astonished when Helen told me that she'd been eighty then. She looked so young, and vital, an inspirational life force.

We returned to the terrace where coffee was being served. Anthony was talking to Claudette, who again called me over. I told her what Valentino had said to me a few years ago about her: '"My *deeah*, Claudette, she come to dinner in my apartment in New York three years ago – she walk into the room wearing a *divine* sable coat. She walk like a young girl. *Perfect* posture, legs to die, *so* elegant, *so* light on the feet, graceful like a gazelle, and so, *so* beautiful."'

Claudette seemed pleased at this, smiling and nodding as though she completely agreed with him.

Then amidst fond farewells, we left, not before my asking her for a signed photograph. My entire childhood autograph collection had gone missing from the Bowmont Drive house, so I'd again started collecting original photographs of the truly great stars from Hollywood's golden era. Claudette said sadly that she could only sign with her left hand but gave me a drawing of herself on a postcard.

As we said goodbye, I knew instinctively that we'd meet again.

Sure enough, six months later and back in Barbados, Carole, Robin, Leonard and I all dined at Claudette's on Beluga caviar in baked potatoes, which she loves as much as I do, and on sirloin steak all flown in from New York. Her grace, charm and tenaciousness, in spite of considerable adversity, was a great inspiration to all of us. I'd always believed that 'That which does not kill you makes you stronger', and Claudette Colbert proved this to be true.

The usual suspects were milling about backstage at the Savoy at the *Evening Standard* Film Awards, waiting to be presented to the Duchess of Kent. It's sad that there are so many fewer stars in Britain than there are in America, but those we have are tremendously supportive of their industry. That night Nigel Hawthorne, Anthony Hopkins, Richard Attenborough and Susan George were at the celebrations.

When I was chatting to Nigel Hawthorne, he asked if Robin and I were going to spend time in the South of France this summer.

'Of *course*, darling and I hope you'll all come down. Besides, I've got another novel to write.'

Ann-Margret, the Swedish-American actress was there too: she was in London to play Belle Watling in a television sequel to *Gone With the Wind*. I'd known of Ann-Margret since Bob Goldstein, head of Fox in London, had shown a singing and dancing test of her to some moguls after a screening. She'd had tremendous potential, was full of zest and vigour and very pretty with her long red hair and sunny smile. She was still all those things, and friendly, though quite shy, so I was surprised when she said, 'Joanie, I want to apologize to you sincerely.'

'Whatever for?' I asked.

'On behalf of all the Swedish people, I want to apologize to you for that *rat* Peter Holm.'

'But you never even met him,' I said.

'I know,' she replied, 'but he gave all Scandinavians such a bad name.'

I burst into hoots of laughter. What a delicious thing to say!

By now I was becoming seriously concerned about the lack of communication that was developing between me and Joni Evans, my Random House editor. Nobody had held a gun to their heads to sign me, and Joni had actually begged Swifty for me, like a man asking for a virgin's hand in marriage. 'I want Joan Collins in my stable of writers so badly I can taste it,' she had gushed. And in those days what Joni wanted, Joni got.

In 1990 I had delivered an outline for my new novel *A Ruling Passion*, which Joni hadn't liked. By September 1991 I'd written a different manuscript, which, some six months later, she also rejected out of hand. I had the distinct feeling that something not quite kosher was going on.

I was anxious to get another novel published. Far more anxious, in fact, to get a book out than I was to receive the half-million bucks that Random House were supposed to pay me on delivery of a complete manuscript.

'Why are they doing this?' I asked Swifty despairingly. 'It's a perfectly good novel which needs an editor on it, as promised. I've written the plot *exactly* as Joni and I planned it, so how can she hate the whole thing? It just doesn't make any sense.'

But unfortunately Swifty was not himself. He had suddenly had a *coup de vieux* and senility seemed to be taking over. Sometimes he was lucid on the phone, sometimes he made little sense. No longer the crisp take-charge dynamo, he seemed weak, frail and indecisive. He even said to me at that time, 'Your tits are too big – you should have 'em lopped off.'

Mary wasn't well either, and soon we received the shattering news that she had terminal cancer. I started to rely on the advice of Alan Nevins, the young man who'd been Mary's secretary, and was now doing much more of the day-to-day work in the Lazar Agency.

Alan knew the importance of continuity to an author, so when I was told that *A Ruling Passion* was not to Joni's liking, he had said, 'Put it aside – you can always go back to it – and start the other book. *That* can be the first book Random House will publish.'

'Even though it's the second one I've written for them?' I asked.

'Sure,' said Alan. 'We'll get the money due to you. What's important is that you get another novel out soon, otherwise you're going to lose your readers.'

He was right and I knew it. So in the spring of 1992 I began my second novel for Random House, *Hell Hath No Fury*.

In 1991 our privacy had been rudely shattered when a sleazy American tabloid printed pictures of Robin and me standing at our bedroom window in France, taken at a distance of nearly half a mile with a powerful telephoto lens. They also got me alone, coming out of the pool when my bikini top had slipped.

I loathed being stalked by an unknown and unseen adversary who had been free to snap me whenever he liked if I was outside working or by the pool.

We were furious, and felt almost violated. How could this *paparazzo* – whom we later found out had staked out Destino for at least three days – be allowed to get away with such a gross invasion of privacy? I don't like lawsuits, but I was in the final tweaking process with my book so I had to take action.

Robin and I brought a suit against the *Globe* for invasion of privacy and damages.

When I know I'm in the right I will *never* give in and I was determined to win. Destino was our sanctuary. It was private. How dare some sleaze-ball snapper stalk us then sell his pictures for thousands of dollars?

The *Globe*'s lawyer fired back with: 'Joan Collins is a public figure, who has often willingly stripped, not only for movie roles, but also for *Playboy*. What difference should it make to her to be seen with one naked breast showing?'

I couldn't believe this self-righteous justification for such a dirty trick.

Neil Papiano, my Californian lawyer, insisted that, 'Even celebrities are entitled to privacy within the sanctity of their own homes.' But the case dragged on for nearly two years. After endless depositions, in which Robin and I were grilled mercilessly, the *Globe* capitulated just before the case was due to be heard and paid a substantial sum.

Since then, some of the amateur – and sleazier – *paparazzi* have stooped to new lows. I watched a grinning amateur on a TV documentary recently bragging about how much 'lolly' newspapers paid him for his snaps of celebrities caught unawares. He then displayed a picture of me wearing a headscarf and carrying a Peter Jones plastic bag. 'This isn't how she's usually photographed so it was a valuable shot,' he said exultantly. 'I made nine thousand quid out of that, and it won't be the last I get of her.'

Some may argue that that's what the famous deserve. That those who seek the limelight must expect their private side to be revealed, but I disagree. A sneaked snap of a star in the street is fair game, but *not* on their property or in their own home, for heaven's sake.

'How'd you like to do an episode of *Roseanne*?' My agent was calling me in Los Angeles where I had been attending two deeply sad events: the funerals of Mary Lazar and my old friend Sammy Cahn.

Roseanne was one of the most popular shows on TV and Roseanne Arnold, the fat, foul-mouthed star, was the epitome of Mrs Average American.

It was January 1993 and I was at Cabrillo. The recession had worsened so I had dropped its price as I really needed to sell it.

'What would I play?' I asked.

'Her cousin,' he said triumphantly.

'Her *what*? You must be kidding! Roseanne and I look about as much alike as Laurel and Hardy.'

'She loves ya,' said my agent succinctly. 'And she don't love too many people. You should do it.'

I asked the opinion of Sue Mengers, who had just left the William Morris Agency.

'I'll give a dinner for you and Roseanne,' said Sue. 'Then you can judge for yourself. I think you'll get along great.'

Sue was as good as her word and, soon afterwards, organized the party. Roseanne and her then husband Tom Arnold, Barry Diller, a Hollywood mogul, the talk-show host Sally-Jessye Raphael, and Robin and I were guests. Roseanne seemed significantly different from her brash TV character. Certainly her voice was strident and somewhat coarse, but I noticed a gentle side to her, which became most apparent when she cuddled up to Tom like a puppy.

'I *have* to sit them next to each other at dinner,' Sue whispered, with a disdainful shrug. 'She's shy.'

'Oh sure, like I'm shy to Woody Allen,' I said sarcastically.

During dinner Barry sat between Roseanne and Sally-Jessye, directing his entire conversation to Roseanne with not a word to the talk-show maven who looked far from pleased. At the end of dinner she said to him frostily, 'You are the rudest man I've ever met.'

He gave her his killer smile and said, 'Yeah, I know.' Barry is known as someone not to be tangled with and, since Roseanne was a great deal more important than Miss Raphael, he obviously couldn't have cared less what the latter thought.

After dinner, we were all treated to a viewing of the tattoo on Tom Arnold's chest.

'Who *is* that?' I asked.

'That's ma darlin'.' He gazed down fondly into Roseanne's pudgy face, which was nestled on his shoulder. 'That's Rosie, ma honey.'

Robin and I exchanged glances.

'But it looks just like Brenda Vaccaro,' I trilled with my usual lack of tact.

Roseanne and Tom looked crestfallen.

'It *does*?' he wailed. 'Gee, I think it looks just like ma Rosie.'

I knew I'd made a gaffe. Sue and Robin shot me despairing looks, and the subject was rapidly changed as Tom quickly rebuttoned his shirt.

That night the Arnolds seemed overly lovey-dovey almost as though they were putting on a performance for everyone's benefit. Since they separated acrimoniously a year later, we could have been right. Tom has probably gone through agony to have 'his darlin's' likeness removed from his chest.

I liked Roseanne, so I decided to do her show. I was curious to get a feel of what making a sitcom would be like, as several producers had approached me touting this idea.

However when I received the *Roseanne* script, I felt like taking to my bed for a week. It was truly dreadful, and I couldn't find one decent comedic line in it. But I'd signed so I was trapped.

I arrived at CBS Studios for the first read-through, which took place on set with all of the actors, the director and producers around a plain wooden table. One of the producers was Tom Arnold and behind us, sitting on high director's chairs, were ranged a dozen other assorted individuals.

'Who are all those people?' I asked to Tom.

'They're our writers,' he said proudly. 'And damn good ones too.'

I glanced over at them. They all wore resolutely hang-dog expressions and the kind of I'm-a-serious-individual gear that many Hollywoodians affect: T-shirt with slogan, baseball cap, jeans and scuffed sneakers. I'd dressed casually in grey flannel pants, shirt and blazer, but Roseanne, in a screaming pink tracksuit and matching fluorescent trainers, looked at me and wailed, 'Gee, Joan, you're *so* dressed up.'

This was dressed up? I smiled, and said, 'Tracksuits aren't my scene, Roseanne, but maybe I'll wear one in the show, if you want me to.' Alexis would rather be put in a strait-jacket, I thought.

At the reading I was surprised to hear shrill peals of laughter emanating about every twelve seconds from the row of assembled writers.

I turned to stare at them, with their dead eyes and fake hilarity. It seemed bizarre that they could greet every fifth line with such merriment because their flat, frightened faces showed little mirth. No doubt their jobs would be on the line if this show wasn't to Madam's liking.

At the end of the reading Roseanne leaned back and stared at everyone long and hard. She pulled no punches and everyone knew it, so they looked suitably nervous.

Finally she announced, nasally, 'This is a piece of crap. Fix it,' and waddled off the set, a few flustered lackeys trailing in her wake.

The assistant director smiled sheepishly at the bemused actors sitting around the table.

'OK, folks, that's it for today. Same time tomorrow. We'll read, then we'll block. Have a nice afternoon, people.'

I rushed home, brought out the Greek worry beads and the Marlboros and called my agent in a panic.

'The show stinks,' I cried. 'Even Roseanne thinks it's crap. Get me *out* of it, *please*.'

'Calm down,' he said. 'I've heard Roseanne's readthroughs are *always* like that. It'll be OK by the time you tape on Friday night.'

'Tomorrow's *Tuesday*,' I said. 'How can I possible learn new lines by Friday?'

'Well, I'm afraid that's the sitcom game for you,' said my agent. 'Don't worry, you'll do fine.'

'I don't want to "do fine". I want to be good and I want to be funny.'
I hung up wearily. Comedy is *far* harder to play than drama: it depends
on such precise timing and technique, and you *must* know your dialogue
inside out. Although *I* knew I could play comedy quite well, American
viewers did not. They still thought of me as Alexis the super-vixen.

That week set a new record. I had the actor's nightmare every night,
and with good reason, because each day the *Roseanne* script changed.
Every morning and evening new pink, yellow and blue pages rained down
on us. I didn't bother to learn any of it because I knew it would only be
changed again the following day.

Roseanne was definitely the boss and, except for a couple of the
actors, everyone in her immediate orbit was frankly terrified of her.
Understandably. Three of the sycophantic sniggering writers had already
been fired, and as Roseanne had demanded slicker, better dialogue, the
remainder were on tenterhooks.

Came Friday morning. Came the dress rehearsal. Came more new
dialogue, this time on lilac pages, which I read with mounting revulsion.

'I can't say this,' I announced to Tom Arnold, who'd just handed
them to me in my dressing room. 'It's unbelievably tacky.'

'We're a tacky show!' he crowed. 'Wait'll you see what I'm gonna give
'em for the warm-up, they're gonna *love* it.' He whipped up his T-shirt,
revealing not only, once again, the huge tattoo of 'Brenda', but also
several angry-looking scars around his middle.

'I'm gonna tell them all about my liposuction.' He smiled proudly.

I was aghast. 'Tom, you can't!'

'They'll *love* it.' He winked. 'They'll eat it up. Now think about this
scene with Rosie, honey. You should do it – it's really cute.'

'Cute? It's about as cute as a lobotomy,' I said.

'Hey, *that*'s good,' he said. 'Why don't we write that in?'

'No,' I yelled. '*This* is bad enough.'

In the final scene Roseanne and I have a knock-down argument cul-
minating in a barrage of insults. My final verbal was to be delivered with
cutting sarcasm: 'Excuse me, Rosie dear, but I can't understand a word
you're saying because of that piece of dead luncheon-meat stuck between
your teeth!'

'I won't say it! I just *won't*,' I said. My agent, who had just arrived, was looking anxious.

'OK, OK,' Tom shrugged good-naturedly. He never seemed to lose his cool. 'We'll get the writers to come up with another line – something blander. But it's a real pity. That luncheon-meat gag was a winner.'

I winced. It was now six o'clock; we taped in front of the audience at seven. This was more than nerve-racking, this was mental terrorism.

In spite of the prominent No Smoking signs, I smoked feverishly until finally, at six forty-five, a runner delivered three turquoise pages for the last part of the scene. Panic-stricken, I attempted to memorize them as the five minutes was called.

I have seldom been more petrified in my life. I hadn't had time to learn the scene thoroughly so I just had to rely on instinct. As soon as Roseanne paused I jumped in with what I *hoped* was the correct line. It was the actor's nightmare come true and the whole thing was sheer, unadulterated hell. But, to my amazement, when the show was finally over, the audience, who screamed and laughed at *everything* whether it was funny or not, cheered themselves hoarse.

'They loved ya,' said Roseanne, as we hugged each other. 'Ya gotta come back – we love ya too.' As everyone congratulated everyone else and said how *fabulous* the show was, I realized that you had to have nerves of steel and balls of brass to do an American sitcom, and although I'd often been accused of having both, I didn't think *this* particular medium was for me.

In June of 1993 Katy turned twenty-one. She looked absolutely gorgeous at her jazzy party at Pizza on the Park, in London, where everyone bopped till they dropped. It had been thirteen years since Ron and I were told that our beloved child probably wouldn't survive the night. How lucky can one be? I thought as I looked at my healthy lovely daughter.

I felt sad that Ron hadn't survived to see this day, and that Katy had had to grow up without a father. I've tried to compensate for that loss as far as I can, because I appreciate how important my own parents' influence has been to me. In this respect I'm old-fashioned and probably politically incorrect, but having brought up three children, I've become aware that they needed both a male and a female figure in their lives. I know (and, no, I haven't forgotten that I've been married four times) that children who have two parents who stay together have a huge advantage over those who don't. Recent statistics have apparently proved this to be so, and although I may not be in a position to preach, I still believe firmly in the importance of the traditional family.

CHAPTER TWENTY-TWO

The ego has landed

When Steven Berkoff, the unique *enfant terrible* of the English theatre, finally raised the money for his film *Decadence* and asked me to appear opposite him, I was ready, willing and able.

They say theatre makes your reputation, films make you rich and television makes you famous. Well, television had certainly done that for me but there was no way this movie would make me rich. Shot in Luxembourg on a low budget and a short schedule, I would play the dual roles of Helen, a snobbish upper-class bitch (just for a change), and the common-as-muck *nouveau-riche* Sybil.

Having worked with Steven when he played the wicked Nazi in *Sins*, I wasn't as intimidated by him as many actors are. However, I wasn't aware that he had such a reputation for being tough, uncompromising and narcissistic. On *Sins* he'd behaved like a pussycat, and we'd developed something of a mutual admiration society. He is a wonderful actor, larger than life, who possesses a fiercely macho sexual charisma in spite of his shaven head and barrel chest.

Steven had recently given a bravura performance as Adolf Hitler in the *War and Remembrance* mini-series, in which he bore an uncanny resemblance to the Führer with his staring eyes and manic attitude.

I adored Steven's writing, his books and plays, and I was equally impressed by his *Decadence* script. It was funny and wickedly salacious, and the dialogue in verse was beautifully written. But it was going to be challenging for me to utter the F word so frequently, not to mention the many scatological references, *and* to make the text sound almost

Shakespearian – which was what Steven wanted. *Decadence* was going to be an art-house film, so it certainly wasn't going to have them queuing up at the Odeons, but I was keen to do it.

However, I made Steven one proviso: that we have at least one week's rehearsal so that I could block and master the long and complicated speeches. Since Steven had performed *Decadence* over a thousand times in the theatre, I thought it was only fair that I should be allowed to rehearse my part at least a dozen.

But, alas, due to budget problems, weather problems and all the other myriad screw-ups that befall movie companies, rehearsal time wasn't possible and I started the first day's shooting stone cold.

In my first scene, gorgeously coiffed and dressed as Helen, I sit alone on a white sofa in a stylized, Syrie Maugham set, and spout a non-stop two-page speech. It's never easy to perform long speeches without having rehearsed them, but having worked on it myself I got through it without a glitch. Steven seemed delighted. So delighted, in fact, that after only two takes, he said, 'I don't need any more, darling, you were brilliant. Go and relax in your dressing room.'

I protested, 'I really feel I need more coverage, Steven. You did that long speech all in one shot so you can't cut in.'

But he insisted it wasn't necessary. 'Perfect. You were perfect,' he purred. 'Now go and have a lie-down, darling.'

After 'relaxing' for two hours, I returned to the set to find Steven doing reverse shots on himself for the same scene from every angle.

'He's now shot himself from every angle except up his bottom,' the costume designer, David Blight, whispered.

'That's so weird,' I murmured. 'He only shot my part of the scene from two angles.'

I sat behind a flat, drinking studio coffee from a styrofoam cup and watching Steven direct himself. Suddenly he stopped in mid-take, rushed over, with a manic grin, and gushed, 'Darling, you were so wonderful in your takes that I felt I had to cover *myself* a bit more.'

'Yes – well – you're the director.'

And the writer *and* the egomaniac, *and* the control freak, I thought, looking at him in disbelief. But I didn't want to make waves. This was

Above: 'Yes you are a real stud, yes you are, yes you are.' Oliver Tobias *is The Stud*, 1977.
(BRIAN ARIS)

Right: With John Gielgud playing my 'Jeeves' in Roald Dahl's 'Neck' in *Tales of the Unexpected*, Norfolk 1978.
(JOAN COLLINS)

Above: With Daddy in the pink in London, 1980.
(JOAN COLLINS)

Opposite: Leonard Rossiter and I celebrate the success of our Cinzano commercials.
(CHRIS BARHAM/DAILY MAIL)

Left: The immortal Leonard Rossiter about to throw Cinzano over me yet again, 1983.
(COLLETT, DICKENSON & PEARCE)

Right: 'Don't you dare die on me, Cecil – don't you *dare*.' One of the more memorable scenes in *Dynasty* when Alexis weds Cecil Colby on his death-bed! 1982.
(METRO MEDIA PRODUCERS)

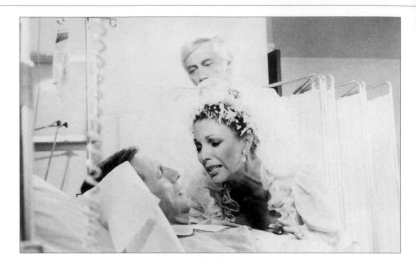

Below: The *Dynasty* set became a mecca for visiting celebrities. Even Michael Jackson came to say hello, Los Angeles 1984.
(JUDY BRYER)

DYNASTY

John Forsythe
Linda Evans
Emma Samms
Gordon Thomson
James Healey
Jack Coleman
Michael Nader
William Beckley

Photo by Jim Globus

Tamkin Color

Above left: At the Carrington Mansion in Warner's Hollywood Studios, the *Dynasty* cast pose prettily for a publicity shot, 1987. (JIM GLOBUS)

Above right: The back of the *Dynasty* cast publicity shot, which was sent to the many fans.

Left: Darling Nolan Miller sees the ravages of the mud fight with Krystal on his exquisite Elizabethan-style creation, Hollywood. (A.B.C.)

Above: Arnie and I present the technical awards at the Oscar ceremony, 1983.

(LONG PHOTOGRAPHY INC.)

Right: As the wicked witch with Ricky Shroeder in *Hansel and Gretel* for which I won best actress from the National Cable TV Association in 1983.

(JOAN COLLINS)

Left: Backstage at
The Royal Albert
Hall after reciting
'Imagine', I curtsy to
my ruler, 1983.
(RICHARD YOUNG/REX
FEATURES LTD)

Above: Getting my
star on Hollywood
Boulevard, Los
Angeles 1983.
(JOHN PASCHAL/DAVID
McGOUGH INC.)

Left: With the
Baywatch hunk David
Hasselhoff in *The
Cartier Affair*,
Hollywood 1984.
(N.B.C.)

Above: On the set of
Sins in the South of
France, 1985.
(EDDIE SANDERSON)

Right: Lauren
Hutton and I
checking each
other out in *Sins*,
Venice 1985.
(EDDIE SANDERSON)

Above: Andy Warhol snaps away for his portrait.
He assured me he would only paint two portraits,
one for him and one for me, New York 1985.
(JUDY BRYER)

Above: Last year,
anyone could have the
portrait as the Andy
Warhol Foundation for
the Visual Arts, Inc.
brought out a postcard.

Left: The day after my
infamous dance with
Prince Charles, this
cartoon appeared in the
Daily Mirror, 1985.
(GRIFFIN)

"Take it from me, Joan, the age gap won't spoil anything."

Above: Judy Bryer and I leaving the office of Peter Holm's attorney with The Swede demonstrating about our divorce terms behind us.
(PHILIP RAMEY PHOTOGRAPHY)

Opposite: Clint Eastwood hosts the Variety Club International award night when they honoured my 'artistic and humanitarian achievements' (whatever they may be), Hollywood 1987.
(PETER C. BORSARI)

Right: David Niven Jr brought me this T-shirt to celebrate the end of my marital fiasco, 1987.
(JOAN COLLINS)

Above: With the amazing Sybil, the Dowager Marchioness of Cholmondeley, at Houghton Hall in 1989. (ROBIN HURLSTONE)

Right: With my two husbands in *Private Lives*. Simon Jones (right) as Elyot and darling Edward Duke as Victor, New York 1992. (T. CHARLES ERICKSON)

Left: Joanne Woodward and Paul Newman visit *Private Lives* backstage at The Broadhurst Theatre, Broadway 1992. (JUDY BRYER)

Right: With Mary and Swifty Lazar at the Spago launch party he threw for my first novel *Prime Time*, Hollywood 1988. (SCOTT DOWNIE PHOTOGRAPHY)

Left: Studying the script of *In the Bleak Midwinter* with Kenneth Branagh, Shepperton Studios 1995.
(JOAN COLLINS)

Opposite: Having finally been allowed into the Royal Enclosure, I spent most of the day in Robert Sangster's box, Ascot 1995.
(THE TIMES)

Right: Steven Berkoff snaps the snappers at the Cannes Film Festival, 1993.
(UNIVERSAL PICTORIAL PRESS AGENCY)

At The Children's Trust,
Tadworth I visit Sarah,
who is just one of
so many children
recovering from a
serious head injury,
England 1996.

only our first day. Contrary to media fabrications, I've never caused trouble on a set. I just hoped that this would be a one-off and that in the future we'd both get something approaching equal screen time.

But this scenario, Steven favouring himself in every scene, was repeated throughout shooting.

Since the movie had been financed largely on my name and I was getting first billing, I protested eventually to the producer, Lance Reynolds, who tried to persuade Steven to shoot more on me, but Steven insisted it wasn't necessary. 'I'm getting exactly what I want,' he said stubbornly. 'Don't interfere.'

Lance admitted he couldn't control him. 'Directing is going to his head,' he said bitterly.

'But, Lance, you've *got* to intervene. This is the first movie he's ever directed, for Christ's sake.'

'Wait.' Lance nodded. 'It's all going to change.'

'Oh, yeah?' I said charmingly.

The following week I thought I'd sprained my wrist, which was swelling and becoming quite painful. Lance and the make-up girl peered at it in my dressing room, and suggested that I should go to hospital and have it examined.

Lance went to Steven in his dressing room and said, 'Joan's got to go to hospital. You'll have to shoot round her.'

'Oh, God! That's *great*!' screeched Steven excitedly. 'Now I'll be able to do more of my close-ups.'

He jumped up, started issuing orders to his 'gofer' and feverishly getting dressed. He was changing his clothes for the umpteenth time when an assistant director, with Lance, popped his head in and announced, 'Joan's still here. She put ice on her wrist and the swelling's gone down. She hasn't had to go to the hospital and she's OK to shoot.'

Steven stared angrily at Lance then screamed, 'What do you *mean* she's here? You *told* me she'd gone to hospital. Shit! Now I can't do my extra close-ups.'

'Sorry, Steven.' Lance shrugged. 'It's not my fault she's recovered.'

Steven is a mountain of insecurities as well as talents, and if he doesn't get his own way he behaves like a monstrous child. But I liked and admired him, recognizing the self-effacing, rather sweet man lurking beneath the melodrama.

But most of the German and French crew loathed him and made no secret of it. He had agreed that Sybil and Les's house should be painted mainly red, but two days before shooting he demanded that it be redone in black, ignoring expostulations from the set designer and the lighting cameraman that it would be impossible to light properly: 'Black is what I want,' he stormed, 'and black is what I'll bloody well get.'

So black is what they gave him. Dense, unforgiving, bible black, for the walls, ceiling and all the furniture. The set looked like the inside of some giant squid's ink sac.

The day before shooting Steven went to view it.

'Oh, my God, what have you done?' he screamed. 'How can we *possibly* shoot in here? It's too bloody *dark*!'

The lighting cameraman explained patiently, 'But this is exactly what you said you wanted.'

Steven, however, insisted that he hadn't wanted it *completely* black, and that they had taken him too literally: 'I just wanted the set a bit darker,' he sulked.

A terrible screaming row ensued, after which most of the European crew decided to walk off the film. It was only Lance's patience and diplomacy that saved the project from becoming an aborted catastrophe.

I told Lance that he should think about getting somebody in to assist Steven: 'He's struggling to do everything by himself and it's just not humanly possible. Christopher Biggins has had so much theatrical experience, I think he'd be an excellent assistant for Steven. You *need* somebody to be on set with him, get out there to help him. Somebody with balls, and Christopher has enormous—'

'Balls,' said Lance. I stared at him coldly.

'Talent,' I said.

We held each other's eyes for a few seconds then burst out laughing.

'Steven's simply taken on too much,' I said. 'No one can direct, write, and play two major roles in a film without *some* sort of back-up.'

'I know, I know,' sighed Lance, 'But he's so selfish, he doesn't want to give anyone any credit except himself.'

Steven's selfishness extended to everybody on the crew. For several days we had to sit endlessly on the restaurant set during Steven's extraordinarily long speech in which his character vomited, broke wind, swore like a football hooligan and spat out his food. In lighting breaks he berated the hapless continuity girl: 'You're distracting me! When I'm shooting I can see you writing things down. All the time you're in my eyeline. Are you doing it deliberately?'

The girl raised her eyes to heaven and the assistant director explained that she *had* to write everything down for continuity. Steven screamed at them both, then asked me accusingly, 'How come you just sit there so calmly? Doesn't all this affect you?'

I put down my magazine and smiled serenely, Grace Kelly personified. 'No, Steven, it doesn't. I've been doing this job for *far* too long to get my knickers in a twist about hanging around. And that girl's only doing her job, so why don't you give her a break?'

'Well, it makes me nervous you being so calm,' he grumbled. Then he sat down, gave me one of his endearing little-boy smiles, and threw me a lavish compliment, which somehow made up for his awful behaviour.

I'd worked on Sybil's big scene with a dialogue coach for weeks. It consisted of a long, iconoclastic monologue about men and the evils they perpetrate on women. The sequence had been pushed down the schedule several times, then pushed further and further back until I was going crazy waiting for it. It was my most demanding scene and needed to be shot from several angles so I was prepared to shoot for at least half a day. The last day of shooting was when it was finally scheduled.

'Right, darling,' said Steven, when I arrived on the set. 'You look lovely.'

'Thank you, darling,' I said.

I was anything but understated in a waist-length flame-coloured curly wig, an inky-dinky black Lycra micro-mini, and black Versace knee-length gold-studded boots. David Blight and I had worked on this outrageous costume for weeks and we felt it personified Sybil's expensive but ghastly taste and her flamboyant character. It would also show up well against the black leather sofa.

'Now we're going to shoot this all in one shot. I want you to say every-thing directly to camera in lovely close-up, daarling.'

'What?' My mouth dropped. 'That's *impossible*, Steven. You can't. This scene's *got* to be shot on and around the black sofa with me strad-dling it and moving around. I've *blocked* it using the black sofa. Where *is* the black sofa?'

'In Luxembourg,' said the prop man laconically.

'*Luxembourg?* Steven, how can you do this to me?' I was trembling with rage and had just realized that the Luxembourg props had been rented and, as we were now shooting in Germany, they had all been left behind.

'Daarling, daarling heart, it doesn't matter. You don't *need* the sofa. You're so good, we'll just do this all in one shot. You'll talk straight to camera in close-up darling. It'll be fabulous – it'll be so strong, I promise you. You'll love it.'

I slammed down my script and stamped my boot, 'Steven, this is my *most* critical and *most* difficult scene. I repeat, you cannot shoot it all in one shot. If you *insist* on doing that you might as well not shoot at all. In fact, I'm leaving.'

I turned to go and he took my arm. 'Calm down, daarling.' Steven loved it when I exploded. He instantly became cool, calm and conde-scending. 'What is it you want, darling, tell me.'

'I want *some* sort of sofa, black, red, green, I don't *care*, and I want *coverage*. Promise, Steven, please promise me you'll shoot me on the sofa after we shoot the close-up?'

'I promise.' He nodded. 'You have my word. All right, darling, we've got lots to do today, so let's *go*.'

I acted my socks off in extreme close-up, and Steven seemed pleased. Then, after two hours of shooting, I excused myself to go to the loo.

'When I come back we'll do coverage with a sofa, right, Steven?' I asked.

'Right, darling. Diva on the divan – lovely, darling.'

When I returned I bumped into the crew in the corridor, all carrying their paraphernalia.

'Why is everybody leaving?' I asked the assistant director.

'Steven says he's got it in the can. We're on the way to another set.'
He shrugged sympathetically. 'Sorry – I know what this scene means to
you, but he won't listen.'

'What?' My face was now as scarlet as my wig, I raced back to the set.
'You *promised* me, Steven. You gave me your *word* you'd shoot my
monologue both ways.'

'Oh, I know I did, daarling.' He put a placatory arm around my shoulder, which I shrugged off. 'But we're running out of *time*. It's almost
noon and we've still got to shoot my vomiting scene.'

'Your vomiting scene!' I gave him a look of withering contempt.
'You're disgusting. You made me a promise and you broke it. I think you
are an unprofessional shit and an outrageous bloody liar.'

I stalked off the set, drove to the hotel, packed and took the evening
plane to London. But not before I had received a full report about how
the crew had had to spend the afternoon. A five-second scene of Steven
throwing up into a lavatory bowl was shot from no less than *four* different angles for a total of *six* hours!

Steven knew I was furious with him, and that my four-minute monologue had only been given a cursory two hours' shooting time, but he also
realized that I'd get over it.

I don't bear grudges so, a month later, when Steven's agent called to
ask if I would go to the Cannes Film Festival in May to help plug
Decadence, I agreed. After all, I was getting a percentage of the film's
profits, not that I seriously believed there would *be* any.

The producers had allowed Steven final cut, which meant that 70
per cent of the movie featured *his* face. I'm not suggesting that the film
would have been any better had the camera been on mine for 70 per
cent of the time, but *Decadence* was *supposed* to have been a *pas de deux*,
not a solo.

In Cannes, Steven and I greeted each other like old friends, and dined
with Lance and my English publicist, Stella Wilson, before our press conference. The media had been called for eleven thirty, and I duly arrived
at the Martinez Hotel at the appointed hour. Banked high at one side of
the swimming pool, hundreds of cameramen from every country in the
world were poised for the best shot. The plan was for me to do the pic-

tures first, then to be joined by Steven and for us to pose together. Afterwards we would go inside and be interviewed by the press.

I strutted the usual stuff for several minutes then beckoned to Steven, who had been lurking behind a palm tree. Sporting designer stubble, a black baseball cap, an ancient T-shirt, and crumpled black jeans, he shuffled over sheepishly to join me and jokingly raised his own camera towards the photographers. A squawk of collective rage issued from their throats.

'Who the fuck is *he*?'

'Piss off, you old fart.'

'Get him outta there.'

'*Va t'en*, we don't want you, we want her.'

Totally embarrassed and disconcerted, Steven gave me a pleading look and a faint smug smile crossed my face. No one had recognized the scruffy actor, and although it was quite amusing to see the great thespian so humbled, I actually felt sorry for him.

I genuinely liked and respected Steven and that respect, I believe, was mutual. Some months later, he sent me another script. 'I've written this specially for you, Joan. It's a take-off on the John Bobbitt case,' he said. 'You play a Hollywood producer who wants to make a movie about this guy who's had his cock cut off by his crazy wife.'

'Sounds like one for the vicar,' I said.

'You'll *love* it. It's juicy and original.'

I read the script which was pornography, almost laughable in its lewdness, and called Steven immediately. 'I couldn't possibly play this. It is so bawdy it makes *Decadence* read like *Pinocchio*.'

'Well, turn it down if you don't like it.' Steven sounded huffy. 'I bet Jerry Hall will do it.'

'I honestly don't think any actress could speak this dialogue and make it believable,' I said sweetly. 'Ask her.' Needless to say, Mrs Jagger refused.

'You owe the IRS a million dollars,' said Larry Turner, my accountant, business manager and lawyer, as calmly as if it were a demand for a thousand.

'*Whaaat?*' I almost fell out of the car. Robin was driving us down-town to Neil Papiano's office. 'What happened?' There was a tight fist of doom in my gut. 'It's not *possible*! I've always paid my taxes. You prepare the forms, I sign them, right?'

Larry sighed. 'Right, but apparently we missed '87.'

'*We missed '87?* We *missed signing my tax returns*, just like *that*? How come?'

'I don't know.' Larry looked dejected. 'But it's probably got some-thing to do with Peter's machinations.'

I sighed. Always the Swede. Was this my everlasting cross to bear? This IRS problem had to be a bad dream. How *could* it have hap-pened? After Peter Holm, I'd continued to trust Larry with my busi-ness affairs. Was there ever going to be *any* end to these financial horror stories?

It took over a year to unravel this mess, at the end of which it came to light that indeed Larry Turner had never filed my 1987 income tax returns at all.

'My mistake,' Larry apologized.

Some mistake.

The IRS are tough cookies who, predictably, were unmoved by my genuine ignorance of the whole thing. Most actors are hopeless with taxes and finances. If we're not working, we're either trying to get a job or learning lines. Filing returns is up to a business manager or accountant, who usually gets paid well for his services.

I soon discovered that fighting the IRS is a no-win situation and even-tually, with penalties and interesting accruing at over $300 a day, I had to write them a cheque for $1,357,432 and 14 cents, which was almost *twice* what I'd owed them seven years previously. I was only able to do it because Cabrillo was finally sold. Oh, happy day indeed. We opened the champagne, praying that nothing would happen during the ninety-day escrow to blow this lucky deal.

Edward Duke's luck, however, was running out. To Robin's and my dev-astation Peter Charlesworth, our mutual agent, called us in September 1993 to say that Edward was suffering from full-blown AIDS. Although we'd suspected it for some time, we hadn't wanted to voice our fears and were amazed when Edward told us, quite stoically, that he had known since 1984 that he had it.

He had been appearing in a Noël Coward play with Susan Hampshire so we hadn't seen him for several months, and soon after we returned from France, Robin invited him to lunch at Wilton's. I was shocked at his appearance: Edward had lost at least three stone, walked with a cane like an old man, and seemed terribly weak. But we had a merry lunch and Robin and I talked of our plan to go to India the next year. Edward said he would love to come too.

Later, Robin said sadly, 'I'm afraid I don't think he's going to be with us next year.'

I was stunned by Edward's rapid disintegration. I'd known many people who had died from AIDS but no one had been as close as Edward, who had been almost like a brother to both Robin and me. We had spent so much time together during *Private Lives*, and he had been one of our first and most regular visitors to Destino. We both adored him.

By Christmas 1993, Edward had entered St Mary's hospital in Paddington, where Robin and I, sometimes with Christopher Biggins, often went to visit him.

The true horror of AIDS was brought home to me in that hospital. Every time we went, skeletal figures would be sitting or standing in the corridors or lurking in the doorways of their rooms. Many had feeding tubes in their noses, and most had lost their hair and flesh. It is the cruellest way to die. Edward had a private room and was being wonderfully taken care of, particularly by Una-Mary Parker.

His funeral was held on 14 January 1994, where he was mourned by his many, many friends. He had been forty years old.

'Don't worry, we're all fine here.'

Judy was trying to sound calm but I could sense her panic.

'What *are* you talking about?' It was a bleak January morning and after a Selfridges signing session for *My Secrets*, my book on beauty and health, Stella and I were off to Birmingham and Manchester for a stimulating round of interviews and more signings.

'The earthquake! Haven't you heard? It's finally the Big One,' gasped Judy. 'I thought we were done for.'

I listened closely as Judy told me some of the horrific details. 'It sounded like a jet crashing,' she said. 'Everything in the house fell down, every cup, every ornament, every book – so much is broken. It's *total* devastation here – and everywhere in the valley too.'

After she'd finished Steve, my driver, turned on the radio and we heard: 'Early eye-witness reports say that LA has been devastated by a major earthquake, at least a 7.5 on the Richter scale. There are many dead, hundreds injured and thousands trapped in buildings.'

I tried calling my sister and friends in LA but all the circuits were down, and a tinny, robotic voice announced, 'Due to a severe earthquakes in the area all communications with Southern California are temporarily suspended.'

The moment Stella and I reached our suite, we turned on the TV. LA looked like a dying city – miles and miles of devastation and reports of people still stuck in lifts and trapped under debris or in their apartments. Then they announced that after-shocks, almost as strong as the original, were occurring. We could actually see – on television eight thousand miles away – the buildings shudder and the earth undulate in that terrifying way I could never forget.

'Let's have a drink,' I said, glad I wasn't there but feeling terrible about all my friends who were.

'We need one.' Stella opened a bottle of champagne. 'By the way, what about *your* house?'

'*My* house? I haven't got a house. Cabrillo's just been sold, remember.'

'Signed, sealed and delivered?' Stella asked.

'Oh, my God. Escrow! You're right!'

Later I managed to get through to my real-estate broker. I could hardly bring myself to ask, 'Has my escrow closed?'

He sounded smug. 'It closed just three days ago. You sure are one lucky individual. If the 'quake had done any damage at all, the buyers could have legally backed out of the deal.'

I let out a huge sigh of relief.

'Cabrillo took the tremor well,' he said. 'It's still standing, though the patio's pretty wrecked, and the roof's sprung a few leaks. Frankly if escrow hadn't closed I think the buyers would've certainly abandoned the whole thing.'

After I hung up Stella winked conspiratorially. 'Who's a clever girl, then?'

'Not so much clever, just bloody lucky,' I said fervently. 'Do you realize that house has been on the market for nearly *five years*? We'd dropped the price to almost rock bottom and finally found a buyer. I certainly *am* lucky. At least this time.'

I had met Placido Domingo several times, and was keen to meet that other great tenor, Luciano Pavarotti. We were staying with the Bamfords, once again, in Barbados, in February 1994, when he came to dine. Benevolent and rotund with Quink black hair and matching beard, he clutched a mobile phone in one hand and his pretty young secretary, Nicolette Mantovani, in the other.

He created a tremendous stir: the sophisticated guests suddenly became starstruck opera groupies. Cameras were produced and everyone wanted to be snapped with this towering legend. I watched Pavarotti admiringly as he patiently posed with everyone and wondered how he managed the same spontaneous grin on each shot. I studied him carefully: when each camera zeroed in on him he inhaled, then as he breathed out a smile would cross his face and a perfect musical note issue from his priceless lungs just as the shutter clicked.

'You should take lessons from him,' Robin told me. 'His charm and patience are *amazing*.'

At dinner I sat beside the great man who bewitched everyone with his exuberant sense of humour. He told me he was on a strict dietary 'regime' and had to be extremely careful what he ate.

'Mmm, me too,' I said. Then I spotted the magnificent chocolate pudding on its way round, and my resolution began to waver. If you're a chocoholic, you can resist temptation as long as it isn't put directly under your nose.

When the butler presented the delicious confection to me, I shook my head, but without much conviction.

'But *of course* you must have some,' boomed Signor Pavarotti, inspecting the pudding with gleaming eyes. 'Look, I will share it with you.' With that he scooped a generous helping on to my plate and grandly waved away his own.

'We share,' he commanded. We did.

Luciano fed me chocolate pud and I fed him back. When we'd finished everything on *my* plate, he ordered some for himself, which we polished off with equal relish.

The aria that wafted across the terrace later was 'Nessun dorma'. Pavarotti's magical voice enchanted everyone on that scented Barbadian night, and I shall always be proud to have shared with him *two* plates of chocolate pudding.

Extract from 'Suzy's Column', *Woman's Wear Daily*, January 1995

Joan Collins, glamorized from top to toe, was in town recently, promoting My Secrets, *her new beauty, exercise and stay-young-forever book, and going to parties in her honor. Blaine and Robert Trump took over Café Mortimer to celebrate Joan's New York arrival, and speaking of arrivals, her arrival at the Trump party was something to see – sexy white suit, glittering jewels and all the other big-time accoutrements of someone whose glamour is her business.*

The party was a blast and what a mix. Just some of the guests were Carolina and Reinaldo Herrera, Cari Modine, CeCe Kieselstein Cord, Paul Wilmot, Ann Jones, Marina Palma, Kenneth Jay Lane, Isaac Mizrahi, Joan Rivers and Oren Lehman, Bob Colacello, Karl Welkner, Richard Levy, Dr Dan Baker and his wife Nina Griscom and Jeffrey Lane. After dinner, Lord and Lady White popped in for a drink. He is, of course, Gordon White, the tycoon who wears his title gracefully. One has not lived until one has heard his take on the Princess of Wales. It was the kind of party where everyone talked at once and everyone listened at once. If you find that hard to follow – well, you had to be there.

I was having too great a time in New York, and plugging my beauty book was getting in the way of it. When I was awoken by Jeffrey pounding on our connecting door at the ungodly hour of six a.m. after the Trumps' party, I yelled, 'I feel like death.'

'So do I,' said Jeffrey. 'Turn on the TV, that should wake you up.'

Eyes closed, I switched on the remote and heard a voice I vaguely recognized. Squinting at the screen I saw a tall, bearded man, swathed in Arabian robes, chasing Maureen O'Hara across the desert.

'Who's that?' I mumbled to myself. 'He's got the strangled enunciation of a failed RADA student.'

Suddenly I recognized him: my first husband, Maxwell Reed himself, starring in some long-forgotten Universal epic.

'If I'd seen this movie, I wouldn't have married him,' I shouted to Jeffrey.

'Pity you didn't,' he called.

Later, I moaned, 'This tour is killing me,' as we rushed at seven thirty to do a morning show, the sort of breathless, primitive television for young, sophomoric Americans

The show was an excruciating ordeal. Every time I tried to plug my book I was interrupted. Do interviewers *really* think celebrities come on their talk shows just to come on their talk shows?

At Brentano's bookshop I was worried that there wouldn't be many people: book signings aren't as popular in America as they are in England. I'd heard a rumour the previous week about a famous movie star doing a signing for his new autobiography at Century City when only *three* people had turned up. God, what a nightmare. It reminded me of another. A well-known writer sat, smiling pleasantly, in front of a desk piled with her books at Harrods. For twenty minutes the crowd of about forty people stared at her, discussing her hair, clothes and make-up in loud voices. No one came near her and she was experiencing the first symptoms of panic. Finally a very old man tottered towards her. Enthusiastically the author picked up her pen but as he reached her the old man wheezed, 'When's it coming out in paperback?'

The following day I woke up in beautiful Disneyworld in Orlando, Florida, where we were staying at a charming hotel designed to look exactly like the one in *Some Like It Hot* where Marilyn Monroe and Co stayed.

The main event of the day at Disneyworld was a cavalcade parade through 'Hollywood Boulevard' in an open car in front of a cheering (or jeering?) crowd. I tried the waving and smiling routine but the Queen Mother bit didn't suit me. A large Mickey Mouse person sat next to me.

'Hello.' I smiled sweetly.

'He' stayed silent.

'How are you?'

Mickey wouldn't answer me and continued to stare at me with that fixed look of surprise he always has, as though someone's got their finger up his rodent tectum.

'Obviously you are not allowed to talk to guests,' I said.

A red-uniformed guard marching beside the automobile glanced at 'Mickey' suspiciously.

'Are you male or female?' I hissed. Mickey fidgeted uncomfortably and I grabbed his/her/its upper arm. 'Umm, muscles,' I said. 'Nice ones, too.'

The over-sized rodent squirmed as I moved my hand down its leg and felt the knee. 'You're a girl,' I crowed. Still no answer but I knew those muscles were feminine.

The procession was headed by ten musicians in blue and white uniforms performing '76 Trombones'. I waved as if I was drowning and smiled as best I could, though my face was aching and the sun was beating down. I worried about Jeffrey, who was gamely traipsing behind the procession. Since he doesn't have any hair and is extremely light-skinned, he would probably look like a lobster by sundown. Every time we caught each other's eye, we got the giggles.

When we arrived at an exact replica of Grauman's Hollywood Chinese Theatre the MC introduced me as 'the legendary Joan Collins' and I blushed violently. Then I was handed a small stick with which, to a fanfare from the trumpeters, I scrawled my name in a large slab of wet cement then pressed my handprint into it. To indifferent applause, 'Mickey' whisked me back into the open car.

You're a girl, aren't you?' I leered and wiggled my ears. 'C'mon, tell me the truth.'

Finally, a deep, resonant voice announced from within the Mouse, 'Actually my name's Hank.'

The red-faced official reprimanded me: 'It's forbidden to make contact with Mickey.'

'Do I get sent to Disney prison?' I asked innocently.

During this tour I realized that America had developed anti-smoking mania: light up in a restaurant or a public place and people looked at you as though you were offering them a plate of steaming horse-shit.

Never one to let anyone get the better of him, George Hamilton had opened a private club in LA in which not only *could* people smoke, but if they weren't smoking they were banished to a special section in social Siberia. It was called, naturally, Hamilton's, and contained a room in which many of George's friends, including Jack Nicholson, Bob Evans and David Niven Jnr, stored their cigars in a special temperature-controlled room like a giant humidor.

I'd just finished working with Robert Wagner and Stephanie Powers in a *Hart to Hart* movie-of-the-week, and George threw an elegant dinner party for me at Hamilton's private upstairs restaurant. It was a great evening, with some of my favourite people, enjoying delicious food, excellent claret, with the rich aroma of cigars in the air. Everyone present was a good old friend: RJ's wife, Jill St John, I'd known since she was a teenager in *The Roman Spring of Mrs Stone*; Alana Stewart who came with George, her ex, Judy Balaban Kantor Franciosa Quine (she got married *again*) was there, as were George and Jolene Schlatter, Suzanne Pleshette, a very funny lady, and her husband Tommy Gallagher, Judy and Max Bryer, Jeffrey Sacha, Nolan Miller, and David and Barbara Niven.

I've never been one for the ephemeral relationships that pass for close friendship in Hollywood. Loyalty is thin on the ground in those parts, and judgemental cynicism flourishes like so many weeds. Sadly, many actors who achieve stardom are so often conned into believing that all those people who cluster around them really do like them. Wrong. Hollywood is a tough company town where the key words are Power, Money and Box-office-clout, and if you don't have one or all of these, many people won't even bother to say hello.

CHAPTER TWENTY-THREE

The wilder shores
of Billy

I first met Billy Wilder at a party at Gene Kelly's house in the late fifties. He was, as usual, the centre of a laughing crowd, both of sycophants and of genuine admirers, none of whom could ever hope to match him wit for wit. His beautiful wife Audrey seemed just as entranced by his sparkling conversation as were the other guests.

Throughout the years I've attended many Hollywood social gatherings where the Wilders were also present, but I never became close to either of them until five or six years ago.

Although Billy hasn't made a film since *Buddy Buddy* in 1981, he still puts in a full day. Every week-day he drives to his Beverly Hills office where he works all morning, takes a lunch break with friends, then works all afternoon. Since the Wilders are extremely popular, very much part of the Hollywood social scene, and invited everywhere, they usually go out several nights a week. Audrey, an elegant beauty, often voted one of America's best-dressed women, loves to sing and it was at a party at Sammy and Tita Cahn's in the seventies that I first heard her perform. She'd been a singer for Tommy Dorsey in the forties and still possessed a great voice. Even after forty years of marriage, the Wilders are a devoted couple, Audrey still doing all the cooking, cleaning and marketing. And it can't be easy living with a genius.

That Billy Wilder *is* a genius there can be no doubt. He has created some of the greatest films ever made and he is also one of the funniest men in the world. His delivery of a one-liner is unsurpassed – even Bob Hope or Jack Benny might have envied it – he has superlative command of language, and is an unmatched raconteur.

Born in Austria in 1906, Billy had been a journalist and often likes to say that he was once a well-paid gigolo, charging money to dance with middle-aged ladies. He left Vienna for Berlin to work in the thriving movie business there, but moved to Paris in 1933, then New York the following year, *en route* for Hollywood. He had twenty dollars to his name, little knowledge of English, but the promise of a writing contract. When he teamed up with the screenwriter and producer Charles Brackett his career took off. The pair wrote the darkly brilliant Lubitsch comedy *Bluebeard's Eighth Wife*, the great classic *Ninotchka*, for Garbo, *Ball of Fire*, which Howard Hawks directed for Barbara Stanwyck, and *Midnight*, with Claudette Colbert and John Barrymore.

In the forties and fifties Billy's career soared to even greater heights as he co-wrote and directed a series of incredibly successful films including *Five Graves to Cairo, Stalag 17, The Lost Weekend*, for which he won his first best director Oscar, *Double Indemnity* and, of course, *Sunset Boulevard*. A recurring theme in his films of this period is a dark cynicism, which often turned off some audiences, so in the mid-fifties he decided to make his movies more widely accessible like the more lighthearted *Sabrina*, with Audrey Hepburn, William Holden and Humphrey Bogart, *The Seven Year Itch*, with Marilyn Monroe, *Love in the Afternoon*, again with Hepburn, and the film which must appear in everybody's top five, *Some Like It Hot*.

One night in the spring of 1995 the Wilders, Robin, Sacha, Leonard Gershe and I dined together at La Dolce Vita, an Italian restaurant in Beverly Hills. It was a chilly evening and Billy was suffering from a slight cold, but he didn't allow it to deter him from going out. The restaurant was an old-fashioned but 'in' spot, frequented by Frank Sinatra and Dean Martin, but which had remained unfamiliar to tourists. It was also one of the last restaurants in LA where smoking was still allowed, and as several of us were smokers, this was another good reason for going there.

'In America you're a pariah these days if you smoke,' said Billy. 'Mind you, it's a disgusting habit.' A reformed smoker himself, he twinkled as he said this.

We started to discuss the merits of European films, and Billy quipped, 'What seems to make foreign films more 'artistic' than ours is that we don't understand the dialogue.'

I remembered that Billy had been a lifelong friend of Dietrich, and asked him to tell us about her.

'Marlene was a worker and a great trouper,' said Billy. 'Many people thought she was difficult, but she wasn't really, she was simply a perfectionist. She just wanted to give the best she could. She was a real *hausfrau* too, she *loved* scrubbing floors. We always remained friends, and when Audrey and I went to Paris in 1987, we knew she wasn't well so we tried to contact her. We'd heard she'd stopped all the long distance and daily conversations she'd been having with everybody from David Niven Jnr to Jean-Pierre Aumont. When we phoned she pretended at first to be the Spanish maid, then the cook, but finally she admitted it was her. She agreed to have dinner with us, so we suggested a restaurant.' He paused for a sip of German beer. 'Marlene didn't seem to like that restaurant so we asked: "Would you prefer we came to the apartment and brought food?" Marlene agreed, then called later with some excuse about having to see a doctor. It was obvious she didn't want to see anyone.'

'But it was pretty obvious she didn't want anyone to see *her*,' said Audrey. 'I always thought she was awful. I remember once at our house she asked me in front of everyone what sign I was. I told her Scorpio. She then declared with great relish that Scorpio and Gemini are a terrible combination. Guess what sign Billy is.'

'Poor thing, though I heard that the press were offering thousands of dollars for photos of her looking wizened and decrepit,' I said.

'God, the press really are revolting,' said Sacha.

Billy looked at him with that twinkle again. 'You've just discovered that, have you? Anyway, I heard that Marlene was a pretty sorry sight in her last years,' he said. 'Nobody saw her. She just lay in her bed until her legs atrophied and then she never got out of bed again.'

'Not even to go to the bathroom?' someone asked.

'Not even,' said Billy. 'My God, can you *imagine* what it must have been like? To have been the greatest glamour goddess of the thirties, forties and fifties, to have kept yourself beautiful by every possible means until your seventies, then to let it all go?' He shook his head. 'Tragic.'

'Did you see that awful picture of her in *Paris-Match*?' asked Robin.

Audrey shuddered. 'That was dreadful. And what an intrusion. They finally got a picture in her bedroom. God, what a sight!'

'I met her once briefly at a party,' I said. 'She wasn't very friendly.'

Billy's brown eyes narrowed. 'You amaze me,' he said sarcastically.

'She never much liked broads,' said Audrey flatly.

'I don't think she even liked her own daughter,' said Billy. 'If you read her book that becomes pretty obvious.'

Marlene Dietrich had died recently and Billy told us that she had called him a few months before, saying she was flat broke. He had sent her a cheque for ten thousand dollars, adding, with his inimitable irony, that he'd sent ten in order not to be *asked* for fifty. 'But she never acknowledged it.' He sniffed. 'I called her but she pretended to be the goddamned maid again. Marlene was always terrible at accents so I said, "Marlene, it's Billy, I know that's you. Did you get the cheque I sent?" She wouldn't admit who she was. But she cashed the cheque, though.'

'What about Bogart?' I asked, changing the subject. 'Is it true he was a real pussycat?' I added provocatively.

Wilder raised his eyebrows. 'A pussycat? Don't believe *those* stories. Bogart was a big bully and incredibly jealous of Audrey Hepburn. On *Sabrina* he used to try to imitate her voice and English accent, but when he started imitating mine I really gave it to him. I told him: "When I look at you, Bogey, beneath the surface of an *apparent* shit, I see the face of a *real* shit." That shut him up.'

Billy chortled and ordered another glass of his favourite German brew. 'Yeah, Bogart was a real pain in the ass,' he mused. 'At the end of every shooting day I'd have a little gathering in my office for drinks, but I never asked Bogart, just as I never asked Chevalier when we were making *Love in the Afternoon*.'

'Why not?' asked Sacha.

'Nobody liked *him* either. He was a bad-tempered son-of-a-bitch and a German collaborator during the war. So, since it was my party, I only invited the people I liked.' He beamed and asked the waiter for some more mashed potatoes. He definitely has a hearty appetite.

'Billy, tell Joan and Robin your story about Peter Sellers,' said Leonard.

'Sellers!' Billy sniffed. 'That guy told me he'd always wanted to work with me. He said he thought I was the greatest comedy director in the world.' He smiled modestly.

'Sellers was screwing around with the script of *Kiss Me Stupid*. He wanted to change *my* script – can you imagine?' Billy looked around the table and we all gave appropriate looks of astonishment.

'He was also screwing all night long with that girl he'd just married, Britt Ekland. I told him he'd been allowed to get away with too much off-the-cuff stuff in those Blake Edwards films and some of it was like amateur night in Dixie. Sellers didn't like my criticism. He didn't want discipline. He didn't understand that Izzy Diamond and I had been working on that *goddamn* script for the better part of two years – then this Limey thespian turns up and tries to tell *us* what to do.'

Leonard chipped in, 'Do you remember how Sellers used to get really annoyed when anybody he didn't know visited the set, but whenever it was *his* friends they could do no wrong?'

'Yes, I remember he did that on *The Optimists* – which Ron produced. It was quite disturbing for everyone,' I said.

Wilder looked at me with an amused but accusing glint. 'Was Sellers a friend of yours?'

'Yes, I mean, no, well, not really – more of a good acquaintance. He was a *sort* of friend, I suppose. Sometimes he was extremely friendly, but he was so confusing because he ran so hot and cold, and was so totally unreliable that I can't really consider him to have been a friend. I don't think he ever knew who he was.'

'I know what he was – a pain in the ass,' said Billy. 'He wasn't happy about being in my movie, and he certainly wasn't happy about Kim Novak or Dean Martin. Then all of a sudden we hear he's in goddamn intensive care at Cedars of Lebanon. Izzy Diamond called me and said, "Sellars will do anything to get out shooting this fucking movie. He's just had a fucking heart-attack." I said, "What d'ya mean, he's had a heart-attack? You've gotta have a heart before you can have an attack."'

Billy grinned his pixie grin. 'I have to say Sellars was brilliant in the parts of the film we did shoot, even though we had to reshoot the whole damn thing with Ray Walston.'

'What happened to all that footage?' asked Robin. Billy shrugged.

'No one knows, it's disappeared – but I'll tell you something. For all his problems, when he was on form Sellars was a brilliant comic, one of the best.'

'Do you think he had a heart-attack because of all that horizontal dancing with Britt?'

Billy's eyebrows rose again. 'Of *course*. He loved poppers and all those crazy things actors do. He brought it on himself, and I also think he was quite angry because Hollywood never really took to him.'

'He queered his pitch with *me* when he didn't show up for dinner we were giving for him at the apartment,' said Audrey, lighting another cigarette. 'I was *real* mad.'

'He did the same thing to me,' I said, '*and* he left me with thirteen at the table.'

Robin and Billy started chatting about pictures, as they always do, while Audrey and I talked fashion as the waiter cleared away our plates. Later on I realized this was a perfect opportunity to ask Billy about Marilyn Monroe.

'Tell me about Marilyn,' I asked. 'Was she *really* as difficult as everybody says?'

'Making a movie with Marilyn was like going to the dentist. Hell at the time, but after it was all over it was wonderful,' Wilder said. 'She was the meanest woman I ever met in this town, but I've never seen *anyone* as fabulous and luminescent on the screen, not Dietrich, not Garbo, not anyone – ever. You know, when I used to look through the camera at her when she was doing a scene, I used to think, this is going to be terrible, we'll probably have to reshoot. But when I saw the rushes, she would be *fantastic*. Something magical used to happen between the time the film was taken out of the camera, processed and then screened. It's still a mystery to me to this day. The only other person this used to happen with was Gary Cooper. Marilyn was a master of delivery. She could read comedy better than anyone else in the world.'

'You told me she had breasts like granite and a brain like Swiss cheese – full of little holes,' said Leonard.

'Yeah, maybe,' said Billy. 'But I'll tell you something, when I finished the two movies with her, and I was asked if I'd ever cast her on a third film, I said, "I'm too old and too rich to go through all that again," but I was lying, I *would* have gone through it all again.'

Leonard suggested it was time to go but Billy said, 'It's early, it's only half past ten.' To most inhabitants of Hollywood, half past ten is seriously late. 'Would you like to come back to the apartment for a drink?' Billy asked.

Leonard asked for the bill, studied it for a moment and then announced he was going to go home.

I asked Billy if Leonard was all right, as he didn't look too well.

'He's fine. He just got a good look at the bill,' said Billy impishly.

The Wilders' large apartment is a treasure trove of wonderfully eclectic objects, furniture and pictures. On every available surface is placed a piece of such originality or beauty that you can only keep your eyes on it for a moment or two before they're drawn away to something even more extraordinary. Two complete walls of the living room are lined with shelves, groaning with books and interspersed with marvellous objects and some smaller pictures. Over in a corner, Billy's battalion of Oscars glitter down seductively. We stayed for over two hours while Billy talked with non-stop enthusiasm. And as we left, Robin, Sacha and I couldn't get over Billy's *joie de vivre* and energy.

'I'm sure it's because he never stops working and he's never lost his passionate interest and curiosity in life,' Robin offered.

'But how many people are like that at eighty-nine?' Sacha asked.

'None I've ever come across,' said Robin.

The Golden Globes are a major event of the movie and television season, second only to the Oscars. For the 1995 event, Nolan designed a divine dress of lilac jersey for me and I arrived with Jeffrey at the Hilton in broad daylight and full make-up at five p.m. How any woman is supposed to look good at this time of day is quite beyond me, but we do our best.

Celebrities minced up a long red carpet while eager newshounds grabbed at them for soundbites. All asked the same question: 'What do you think of the Golden Globes, and why do so many people like them?' I wanted to reply to this by quoting Billy, 'Awards are like haemorrhoids – in the end every arsehole gets one,' but resisted the strong temptation. Joan Rivers, flushed in a red dress, at least asked some amusing and original questions. This little manoeuvre took half an hour, then we entered the main ballroom where thousands pressed close to catch glimpses of the stars, who seemed to be thin on the ground tonight. People had paid $450 a seat for these festivities. We sat with various household names and there was much strategic table-hopping kiss-kissing and 'Hello, darling, you look *great*, I hope you win.'

Dominick Dunne, sitting with friends, told me *I* looked great – in fact, everyone told *everyone* they looked great. Nolan Miller came over to chat while he waited for his date, Sophia Loren. Heather Locklear, this year's hot TV female, stopped by and we posed and reminisced about *Dynasty*. Lots of girly starlets in incredibly short skirts and low-cut dresses slithered past looking for attention, all outshone by Jamie Lee Curtis in a slinky white number.

When the show began a cameraman placed himself in front of me to take a shot for the credits, then focused on Tom Hanks, Arnold Schwarzenegger, Hugh Grant and just about everyone else. Cybill Shepherd and Dudley Moore came on stage to present the first award – she large in a white pant-suit, he tiny in black – and clowned around to a deathly silence. Hollywood is a tough town to work and this was *not* a good beginning to the show.

Called backstage to present, I discovered my lilac gloves were slipping and I was convinced I would slip on the shiny stage. The wardrobe man stuck double-sided Scotch-tape inside the top of my gloves, and I was off. I'd never met Lou Diamond Phillips before, the actor with whom I was co-presenting. We announced the nominees for best mini-series or movies of the week as though we were best friends. John Frankenheimer won for *The Burning Season*. Mr Golden Globe 1995 was John Clark Gable, son of same. He passed me the award, which I handed to John Frankenheimer with a chaste stage kiss.

The high point of the rest of the show was Sophia Loren accepting the Cecil B. De Mille Award. Clips were shown from some of her movies, after which she walked out on to the stage in a Dior dress. From where Jeffrey and I sat we could see the zip was buckling (she should have worn Nolan) but she made a charming speech. Then thankfully the ceremony ended, and we dashed through the back corridors to Trader Vic's.

The dinner had been inedible, so we were starving and consumed spare ribs and Navy grog with alacrity while talking to some rather chatty senior citizens at the next table. Later we limoed off to the Polygram party at the Four Seasons, which was in full swing and where Lew Grade, a sprightly eighty-seven, was still going strong. He had picked up his 'date', Stella Wilson, at three thirty that afternoon, and was holding court, at midnight, chattering energetically to everybody and puffing on his cigar. Many of us could barely stand up, but Lord Lew was so full of life it was almost contagious.

We left the hotel together and, walking to our cars, he asked, 'Do you miss your father?'

'Of course,' I said. 'Even though I didn't see Daddy all the time, just to know he was in London was so important. It was such a loss when he died.'

'You know *why* it happened?' Lew asked. 'Why your father died? He decided that he wanted to stop working. He should *never* have done that, my dear, because the secret of a healthy long life is that you must *always* work, you've *got* to be totally involved, and you have to *love* what you're doing.'

'You're right, I've always thought that,' I said.

'Couch potatoes die young,' he continued. 'If people can't work any more they *must* get involved in something else, whether it's painting, walking the dog, or baking a cake. Because if you don't keep your mind and body involved, you'll just die,' said Lew cheerfully. He took his cigar out of his mouth for a moment and gave me a cheeky kiss. 'Goodbye, dear. Don't forget to keep your nose to the grindstone.'

As Stella and I watched him skip lithely into his limo I reflected that what he'd said was excellent advice. And it was obviously what kept Billy Wilder so vital too.

'We can learn a lot from these fabulous old boys,' I murmured to Stella. 'Both pushing ninety, they certainly set a wonderful example.'

CHAPTER TWENTY-FOUR

Don't look now

Carole Bamford had asked Robin and me to spend ten days with her and some friends in Venice. The cast was made up of Carole's daughter, Alice, with her friend Wellie, both eighteen, Hugo Guinness and Tina Zerbino; the venue was an impressive Venetian *palazzo* that Carole had rented. It was dusk when we arrived but, even though it was September and hot, the evening felt strangely ominous and the *palazzo* was dank and unfriendly. The wonderfully wicked Hugo greeted us, saying laconically, 'I'm sure this joint's haunted.'

We scoffed at this, and had a drink while while the staff scurried about preparing for Hugo's birthday dinner, and dressing the dining table with masses of beautiful white flowers.

The elderly butler, who came with the *palazzo*, kept shaking his head and murmuring, '*Male, male, che male.*' I asked Carole what his problem was.

'Oh, they didn't want us to have the dinner party in the dining-room, something about the family not wanting us to use the room and something to do with that picture.' She gestured to a vast seventeenth-century portrait of an aristocratic-looking woman, whose malevolent, black eyes seemed to follow one everywhere.

That evening, during dinner, I felt an extraordinary freezing draught on my ankles. When I mentioned it, everyone said it was probably some air vent in the floor under the table. I flicked up the white damask table-cloth to look. There was no air vent.

The next morning Robin asked me if I'd laid across his chest during the night and watched him sleep.

'Don't be ridiculous, of course I didn't.'

'Well, *someone* bloody well did,' he said.

We both felt an uneasy sense of foreboding.

At teatime, dozens of gold and silver sugared almonds, which had been on the table the previous night, were found carefully arranged on the floor in the shape of a prone body. Everyone asked everyone else who had played this silly trick, but no one owned up.

The ancient butler muttered in Italian, 'That's where the Contessa's body was found.' He looked terrified.

We looked up at the Contessa's portrait which, if anything, now appeared even more sinister.

'A lot of nonsense,' scoffed Hugo, and changed the subject.

That evening a storm hung directly over the city for more than four hours, which did little to uplift our mood. All the lights in the *palazzo* flickered off and on. Amid the thunder and lightning we set out for dinner at Harry's Bar, feeling our way through the wet, dark streets, in a high state of tension. None of us wanted to admit that we sensed this malevolent Contessa's spirit, yet without question there was *something* in that place, and it didn't like us one bit.

Hugo and Robin said *their* nerves were bad because everyone had ordered white truffles at Harry's Bar and they were splitting the bill between them.

When we returned, Carole's housekeeper and chauffeur, Karen and Sean, were getting ready to leave for the night.

'Where are you staying?' I asked.

'At a hotel nearby,' said Sean.

'Where's the butler and the maids?' asked Carole.

'Oh, they don't live here.' Sean glanced nervously at the dim light bulbs which had continued to flicker. 'In fact, none of them will *stay* in this house after four in the afternoon.'

'Why on earth not?' asked Robin, already knowing the probable answer.

'Because it's haunted. Everyone *says* it's haunted, anyway. Load of rubbish, I think.' With that, Sean and Karen bade us goodnight and left the room.

By now we were all thoroughly wound up, except Tina who remained completely sanguine and trotted off to bed with an airy 'Goodnight, everyone.'

Suddenly there was a terrible noise. 'I'm going to see what that was all about,' said Robin. After a few minutes we all rushed out into the corridor after him where we saw Sean and Karen, riveted to the door of the dining room. Sean was now a trembling wreck, crying, shaking and whispering, 'Can you feel it?'

'Can I feel what?' asked Robin.

'There, over there,' Sean replied.

'Come back into the study,' said Robin, handing Sean a brandy, which he couldn't even swallow.

Then Robin told us what had happened. 'I found Sean kneeling in the dining room, his hands clamped to his head, saying, "Oh, God, oh, my God." I said, "What the hell's going on?" "But don't you feel it?" he said. And I said, "Feel what? What *are* you talking about?"

'He said, "Stand there." I moved about four feet further into the room and suddenly I felt a kind of electrical, tingling force-field. All the hairs stood up on my arms, on the back of my neck, and I said, "My God, I can now." I moved away from the spot and the feeling went. There was the most ghastly presence in that room.'

'I've *got* to get out of here,' said Carole shakily. 'I don't like it.'

'Me too,' I said. 'I'm not spending another night in this place.'

Just like some dreadful low-budget horror film, the wind howled, and the lightning flashed while the lights continued to flicker. But this wasn't some late-night Hammer movie, this was really happening.

Alice and Robin were telephoning hotels to try and find us some rooms for the night, but their request for five rooms at one thirty in the morning was treated by every night porter with understandable hilarity.

We all agreed that we simply couldn't stay there, but Robin and Hugo said they couldn't possibly leave Tina.

I rushed up to our bedroom with Robin, threw a few necessities into an overnight bag, and tried to persuade him to come with us.

'There's something very bad in this house,' I pleaded.

'Yes I know there is,' he said, 'but we *can't* leave Tina. You go. Hugo and I will be fine.'

Such foolish gallantry, I thought as we rushed down the stairs and through the winding corridors. I kissed him goodbye and went out into the *piazza* to join the others. We stood, for a few minutes, undecided, wondering which way to go. Suddenly Robin and Hugo dashed out of the *palazzo*, ashen-faced. 'We're coming with you,' Robin gasped. 'Just wait for us. We've got to go back to wake Tina and get her out.'

After what seemed an eternity they finally emerged, both with an arm round her, and we went off in search of rooms.

Later, Robin told us exactly what had happened, and why they'd *had* to leave.

'While we were in the drawing room, we suddenly noticed a huge bronze jardinière moving across the floor towards us. Something in that place was so furious with us all that it just wanted us out of there. As we were waiting outside Tina's door while she got dressed, a long Sabatier carving knife flew through the air and embedded itself in one of the champagne crates piled next to the door. There was a solid wall only six feet from where the knife was still quivering in the crate – I mean the direction it came from was just a blank wall. It was then that we realized that we probably wouldn't last the night if we stayed, at least not without having our hair turn white, so we grabbed Tina and got the hell out of there.'

We were so tense, none of us could sleep, and in the morning Tina, Robin and I returned to the *palazzo* alone to pack.

I insisted on two maids staying with me while I was packing and asked them in Italian, 'Is there a bad spirit in this *palazzo*?'

They both nodded a little hesitantly, looking at each other with concerned expressions.

'*Si, Signora, una donna cattiva, molto cattiva,*' said one, and they both gave pantomime shivers.

Then Anthony arrived in his jet to whisk us away to safety, like a knight in shining armour. In the plane going to the South of France, Carole told us that several people had told her that they'd heard the *palazzo* was haunted by evil spirits but, like most sensible people, she hadn't taken any notice.

'Well, I certainly believe it now,' she said. 'I never want to go back to Venice, ever.'

'Me neither,' I said.

The postscript to this story is as follows: a few days later, Tina talked to the servants who had told her, 'A Contessa from this family was murdered almost four hundred years ago by her jealous husband who, suspecting her of infidelity, decapitated her with his sword in what is now the dining-room. However, it wasn't true, she hadn't been unfaithful to him, she had loved him. The story goes that she was so angry that he'd unjustly murdered her that she haunts the *palazzo* to this day.' Tina shrugged. 'I don't believe in such things, do you?'

I didn't answer as I have a healthy respect for what happens in the hereafter. But I did go back to Venice. It was a year later with Kenneth Branagh.

I'd never met Kenneth Branagh, who had been the British theatre's golden boy and was now the British cinema's *wunderkind*, but I had greatly admired his work. I also empathized with him for the flak he continually received from the press, which was wholly unjustified. I'd attended the première of *Mary Shelley's Frankenstein*, which he directed and in which he also starred, a much-hyped movie that the media tore to shreds, some before they'd even seen it.

It was announced that Robert de Niro, who played the monster, would fly over for opening night, as would Sylvester Stallone and many other stars, but few turned up. During the performance two seats beside me, which apparently had been for Stallone, remained empty. De Niro attended neither the American nor the British première because he wasn't happy with his performance. I agreed with him: it was the weak link in the movie. But Branagh was excellent, and the film was terrifyingly Gothic.

At the Café Royal party afterwards, there were so many empty seats it looked like an ill-attended wake. Branagh stood forlornly in a corner with an older lady. When I was introduced, I said, 'I enjoyed your film very much. It was exciting and scary and very sexy. Well done.'

Branagh beamed and introduced me to his mother. 'That means a lot to me. As you've probably heard I've been having quite a bit of aggro.'

'I know, I understand what that's like. Try not to let it bother you. They're petty and envious – ignore it.'

'Not that easy.' He grinned again. 'But thanks for the advice.'

I forgot about *Frankenstein* until Peter Charlesworth called several months later. 'Ken Branagh's asked you to play an agent in his new film, *In the Bleak Midwinter*,' he said. 'It's quite a funny script. Except for a couple of drawbacks. Your part's small, but quite good, and they can only pay everyone scale – in fact, everyone gets the same salary.'

'How much?'

'Four hundred quid a week.' Peter, who is fond of a buck, said this quietly. 'You'd better *love* the script for that money.'

'Well, I'll read it. If I *really* like it I don't give a damn *what* I get paid.'

In the Bleak Midwinter was amusing, poignant, and heart-warmingly honest about what actors are really like. My part, the tough agent, Marguerite, with a heart of gold, had some snappy dialogue and a few good scenes, so I accepted happily. The following week, Ken suggested that we dine with the male lead, Michael Maloney, who was to play Joe, the actor I'm supposed to represent, so that we could get to know each other. Since Joe and Marguerite are supposed to have an intimate work-ing relationship this seemed a fine idea: most of the time you arrive on set to shoot with someone you've never even met.

Ken had financed the film himself, which was why it was being made on such a low budget. 'I don't want any of the majors telling me what I can or can't do any more,' he said bitterly. 'When I was making *Frankenstein* they made my life a total *nightmare*. One person would say one thing, then that would be contradicted by someone else. They wanted *complete* control. This way the film will be made the way *I* want it. The world perceives actors as shallow, vain, foolish and narcissistic. I'm going to show everyone with this film that they're not.'

We talked tall tales and giggled a lot and, after several hours, Michael said, 'We should be going. It must be almost midnight.'

Ken glanced at his watch. 'It's two o'clock,' he said. 'We've been here almost six hours!'

Time rushes by when actors start chewing the fat about their favourite subject – the business.

Shooting started in March 1995 but, even on his tiny budget, Ken went out of his way to ensure that all his actors were treated equally well. The main location was an old church near Shepperton where we each had a small dressing room which Props had filled with flowers. We also had a 'green room', supplied with all the newspapers and periodicals, where we could relax, smoke and gossip.

Lunchtime was always a riot. John Sessions who, like Edward Duke, is a brilliant mimic, would enthral us with hysterical stories and impressions of everyone from Dirk Bogarde to Michael Redgrave, while Ken, not to be outdone, gave us his Glenda Jackson and John Gielgud.

Like many actors Ken is a Woody Allen aficionado and he shot *Bleak Midwinter* in black and white. Instead of breaking up a scene into several different shots, he usually did only one 'master' shot, which would be as much as four minutes long, and often consisted of several actors all talking their heads off, desperately trying to remember their lines. Since Ken had written the script, he was a stickler for the correct dialogue, and woe betide the hapless thesp who interposed a word or two.

Unfortunately I had a tendency to do this. 'Cut, cut, that was beautiful, darling, just great, but you said boring instead of tedious.'

'But it means exactly the same thing,' I protested.

'Oh, I know, darling, I know, but let's try it again, shall we? It'll sound much better if you say tedious.'

'I'd like to see Marilyn Monroe try this. We'd all be here for a fortnight,' I muttered to Michael after fourteen takes.

The enormous advantage movie acting has over stage acting is that on film a scene will generally be covered by many different angles and shots. If the master is acceptable at the beginning, but weak at the end, the director can go again, assuring his actors that he's already got part of a decent take in the can, and that the close-ups will cover the rest. Consequently an actor can be more relaxed, knowing that, usually, only the best parts of their performance will be used.

In *Bleak Midwinter* we didn't have this advantage. Ken shot the film like a stage play, but since we didn't rehearse like a play, thus knowing the lines inside-out and upside-down, some of us felt at a disadvantage.

'It's an experiment, darling,' Ken said, when I begged for a bit of coverage after I thought I hadn't done my best in a scene. 'I'm shooting it this way and we'll either sink or swim with it.'

Well, happily, he swam with it. On the whole the film received good reviews and it was also one of the highlights of the Welsh, Belfast and Venice international film festivals.

During shooting Ken had received several offers for the distribution. Soon after it was finished one of the major American independents, Castle Rock, bought it.

'Now you'll all *definitely* see some money.' Ken was delighted as he had been genuinely concerned that his crew and cast should be properly paid, and we all received a percentage.

In September Ken, Michael, David Barron, the associate producer, and I attended the Venice Film Festival where *In the Bleak Midwinter* received the prestigious Osello d'Oro award. After seven spontaneous rounds of applause, plus a standing ovation at the end, Ken and I were mobbed as we walked from the Lido.

'Is this what *Dynasty* was like?' he joked.

As we walked along I reflected how different was this Venice with its cheering crowds from the creepy gloom of the previous year.

Kenneth Branagh, one of the most down-to-earth actors in the business, suffers from the 'tall poppy' syndrome. His early success had caused rampant jealousy among many people, and particularly in the media. He wanted to make an incorrigibly British film along the lines of the early Ealing comedies and he succeeded, but he still received a tremendous amount of criticism for it. Some of the critics *still* called it a 'luvvie film'.

The majority of jobbing actors are hard-working, dedicated, and genuinely love their chosen vocation. But most of the time they're seriously underpaid in a profession which is staggeringly cruel, particularly to women. If one survives one should be given a medal, and to survive *and* make a decent living, one should be given a chestful.

CHAPTER TWENTY-FIVE

Random thoughts or trial and error

When Random House, the most powerful of American publishers, had contracted me for an astronomical $4 million for two steamy novels, they hadn't insisted that I produce the next *Gone With the Wind*.

However, after three years of confusing and contradictory messages, changing their minds as often as Alexis used to change her clothes, my publisher had realized that the celebrity-book market was on the wane, and had decided they wanted their million-dollar advance *back*.

Believing that the best defence is attack, they sued me for it in 1994 and I immediately countersued, insisting, and rightly so, that they owed *me* for what I had contractually fulfilled.

Unable to rely on advice from fast-fading Swifty, my advisor had become Alan Nevins, now a partner in Lazar's Agency.

With each rejection of my literary efforts, Alan had suggested I try again, so I'd spent the past two years writing and rewriting with virtually no input from Joni Evans, my editor, other than a cursory: 'Yes, this is an improvement, very inventive, but it's got a long way to go,' etc., etc., etc. I was banging my tired head against a brick out-house but I was not one to give up.

It was a ridiculous suit. I'd delivered two complete novels in a timely manner. I'd written half a million words, the rough drafts of which filled fifteen large cardboard boxes, and there was no acceptance clause in my contract, meaning that if I *delivered* a complete manuscript of 125,000 words, they *had* to pay me.

My contract we Random House in New York also stated clearly that Random House was required to publish the manuscript within a year after I had delivered. If the contract was terminated all rights would revert to me.

One problem was that, in my eagerness to get a book published in 1992, I *hadn't* asked for the half-million dollars due to me on delivery of the manuscript, and when Random House rejected it, I had agreed with Alan to write another.

It was obvious that Random House were attempting to pull a thick woolly sweater over my eyes. The book business was losing big money, particularly on the sex 'n' shopping novels that had been so popular in the eighties. That's the way the cookie was crumbling but instead of writing off Joan Collins and her advance, Random House chose to sue.

The acceptance clause, which publishers insist on including in most authors' contracts, is the publishing world's most powerful weapon: it allows them not to pay for work they don't like. But it is also grossly unfair, as a writer can work solidly for two years, then if the publisher doesn't like the work, although it's what he commissioned, he simply says, 'Give us our money back,' and the poor writer is screwed.

Swifty, oh, brilliant, super-agent that he was, would *never* allow this clause to appear in any of his clients' contracts, and since he had some pretty important authors, the publishers were impotent. 'If you insist on keeping this clause in we'll go to another house,' was Swifty's maxim. So nine times out of ten the publishers reluctantly agreed to omit it.

Alberto Vitale, Random House's vertically-challenged chief executive officer, was so starstruck that he had *had* to accommodate the super-agent if he wanted to sign any of his celebrity clients. But now Random House were digging in their collective heels, eager to burn Joan publicly at the stake, and with truly appalling cynicism they filed the suit only six weeks after Swifty's demise.

It seemed extraordinary to me, and still does, that publishers of the calibre and power of Random House should stoop to such depths by weaseling out of an honest deal. Didn't Harold Evans, Random House's president (who pretended it had nothing to do with him), and Si Newhouse, whose family not only owned the company but also the vast network of Condé Nast Publishing, have better things to do than to try to claw back a million bucks for books written in good faith?

Apparently not.

I was now in a David and Goliath situation: one small individual fighting for vindication and her rights against a multibillion-dollar monolith. I truly believed that this company deliberately set out not only to destroy me, my reputation and my finances, but also to teach a harsh lesson to *other* authors.

They'd been throwing six- and seven-figure advances around to celebrities and stars for years and now the reality of falling sales had exposed their cupidity.

I'd recently dined with a producer in LA who'd said, 'Swifty got a million dollars from Random House for my autobiography three years ago.'

'How much was your first payment?' I asked.

'A quarter of a million.'

'And how much have you written?'

'Nothing.' He grinned. 'I guess I've just slipped between the cracks.'

Another friend told me, 'Swifty changed the rules of the publishing game so Vitale wanted to break Swifty's system and *you* are now the fall-guy they're using to bust it. It's being planned like a military manoeuvre. They're desperate to stop these big agents and their 'pay or play' contracts which take out the 'satisfactory manuscript' clause. It has *nothing* to do with you – Joan Collins – you're just being used to frighten off any other authors to whom Random House think they've paid too much, *and* those agents who have the temerity to force this clause on them. They hate it.'

Everyone in the book world was fascinated by this case and most thought Random House was insane to consider litigation. The general consensus was that I'd been badly wronged and that Random House were trying this on, because they'd decided my deal now looked far too expensive.

Jeffrey Archer said in *The Times*: 'Random House is taking an enormous risk. I'm puzzled *why* they're suing Joan because if the lose they're defeated for life, and if they win, what celebrated author is ever going to want to sign with them?'

Jeffrey admits to doing over a dozen drafts of a book which was edited by Joni Evans ten years previously. She had told me: 'I went to Jeffrey's house in the Bahamas for a month with his two other editors and we *completely* reconstructed his novel.' So why, apart from a handful of early meetings, hadn't Evans even given me the time of day?

Now let us cut to the chase.

New York City on a chill February morning in 1996. A grim court-house in downtown Manhattan; scuffed chairs and hideous artificial light. In one corner the all-seeing eye of Court TV prepares to beam the events of this trial to the world. When Vitale heard that he was to be filmed on Court TV he was so furious he sent his legal representatives to insist that when he was on the witness stand, Court TV would guarantee a blue dot on his less-than-film-star face – this dot, actually a wavy blank shape blur-ring the face so the audience can't recognize the individual, is usually only used to maintain the witness's privacy. Suddenly Vitale had become a shrinking violet.

Ken Burrows, my lawyer, large and avuncular, married to writer Erica Jong, Don Zakarin, the dynamic counsel Ken brought in to assist him, and Stacy Grossman, Ken's young assistant, were all assembled at one end of a table with me.

At the other end was Robert Callagy, Random House's counsel, elderly, thin-lipped and stooped. He bore an uncanny resemblance to George Bush and his self-righteous manner made him look like an actor playing a Bible-belter in some schlock Western: 'Vengeance is mine saith the Lord.' He had one female assistant.

When Judge Ira Gammerman appeared everyone stood. Known around the court-houses as 'The Rocket Docket' he was famously iras-cible and jumped to swift conclusions. He was smart and inflexible, a no-nonsense sixtyish toughie who was *definitely* the boss in *his* courtroom.

The jury filed in, eleven men and women, all looking like college grad-uates. They seemed bright-eyed and bushy-tailed but their expressions were inscrutable.

Joni Evans was the first witness called by Callagy. I was surprised by her raddled appearance and how much older she looked since last we'd met, probably due to her recent fall from grace. Twenty years earlier, a high flyer of driving ambition, she'd started at Simon and Schuster and had had an affair with Dick Snyder, the chief executive officer, whom she went on to marry. Snyder elevated Joni Evans to be one of the most powerful people in publishing, nicknamed 'The Manhattan Mercenary'. After their famously bitter divorce and when her tenure running her own imprint at Random House was abruptly terminated, Evans dropped out of the major-player league and was now a literary agent at the William Morris Agency.

I found it curious that she needed to testify against me, when it had been Random House who had done her wrong. As an editor she'd been supposed to help me; instead she'd let me flounder.

'A pay-off,' said Ken. 'I've heard that Random House paid her handsomely when they dumped her. A condition of that payment was that she would never do or say anything against them.'

That made sense.

I suspected Evans was going to be a Judas and I was soon proved right. I'd realized at deposition time that this wasn't to be a case about a contract. Instead my literary ability was on trial and I'd been warned to beware.

'Are you *sure* you know what you're doing, taking on those guys? They're as unforgiving as the Mafia,' a friend had warned. But there was no question of *choice*. I was in the right. I'd fulfilled my side of the contract to the letter, and there was *no way* I was giving back my advance.

This bottle blonde on the stand, with her leathery orange skin, now attempted a weak smile in my direction then started ripping my novels to shreds – occasionally glancing in my direction with a smirk.

I sat stoically. I simply couldn't believe her falsehoods. When she was asked, 'Did this book have a beginning, a middle and an end?' she answered smugly, to my astonishment, 'No.'

'The B word's too good for her,' I said to Judy at the break. 'She's the C word – with a capital C.'

'She's worse than Alexis ever was.'

'At least Alexis had a sense of humour and bags of style,' said Jeffrey. 'Her only bags are under her eyes.'

'To lie so blatantly – it's just unforgivable,' I said.

For almost two days Evans trashed me. And, oh, how the tabloids rushed to print the slander: 'Primitive rubbish – flawed – inane – fragmented – gibberish – makes no sense – she can't write.' What also annoyed me during Evans's testimony of lies was the constant assertion by the press that 'celebrities don't write their own books', which, in my case, is absolutely NOT true. And in case you're wondering, dear reader, this is all my own work.

Having admitted to a columnist that I'd spent the advance – 'Half went to taxes and my agent, almost all the rest to my lawyers' – I was castigated in some newspapers as though I'd broken into a Red Cross charity box, and with five bestselling books under my belt, the consensus of media opinion had now become, 'She's no writer.'

To add insult to injury Random House leaked one of the more embarrassing passages – which would have been edited out – and it was printed in practically every paper around the world. My reputation was being ruined.

Every day Judy and Jeffrey sat loyally in the court-house.

'They're destroying me,' I said sadly.

'Don't let the bastards get you down,' said Judy. 'That's your motto, isn't it?'

'It certainly is,' I said, 'but opinion seems to be going against me.'

'It won't be when you get a chance to speak.' Judy was like a rock, and I cherished her unconditional concern.

When Evans had finished her self-serving litany, several expert publishing witnesses were called. Thomas Lipscomb, a highly experienced publisher and editor who apparently knew his stuff, had read both my novels and pronounced them publishable. During his cross-examination, Callagy abruptly interrupted to demand that Lipscomb show him the file he'd brought with him. Glasses slipping to the end of his beaky nose Callagy scanned the offending documents.

'What does "Hail Mary Pass" mean?' he asked suspiciously.

'It's an American football term to describe a despairing and spectacular attempt to score a goal in the final seconds of the game,' said Thomas. 'I wrote this note to myself because I believe that Random House had thrown all caution to the wind in suspending the acceptance clause, and had left themselves with no means whatever to get back their full payment, whether the manuscript was satisfactory or not.'

At this the court erupted and Ken whispered, 'Random House have just given themselves a knock-out blow.'

Then came another expert witness, the jocular Lucianne Goldberg who had ghostwritten a few bestselling novels and, according to several sources including Dominick Dunne, was a fine editor. She had the court in stitches several times.

When asked by the craggy Callagy, 'Why does the heroine have cancer and heart disease simultaneously and then recover?' Goldberg quipped, 'It's a miracle!' to screams of laughter from the court. Then she said, seriously, 'Putting all that stuff right is what editors are *supposed* to do. They just use their blue pencil.'

When asked by my counsel if she thought my novels were publishable, she said, 'Absolutely. All they needed was some cutting and moving things around. All the stuff editors get well paid for.'

Then Rosie Cheetham, British editor and publisher of my bestseller *Too Damned Famous*, described *A Ruling Passion* as 'a fast page-turning read, which required substantial surgery, but which I could have turned into a successful work of commercial fiction.'

Each day, going and coming from the trial, the press greeted me more kindly, but they all asked gleefully, 'What's it like to have your work trashed?

'Will you have to stop writing now?'

I gritted my teeth and smiled bravely.

My hotel suite looked like a conservatory. Flowers, notes, faxes and telephone messages flooded in full of love and encouragement from friends, acquaintances and many fellow writers, all rooting for me.

The second night, during a meeting with my lawyers, I asked if Callagy might call me to the stand tomorrow.

'Highly unlikely,' they said.

'Because I'm sure he'll try to confuse me with what I said in my *Globe* deposition. I don't feel properly prepared. How *can* I remember what I said four years ago?'

'Stop worrying,' said the lawyers. 'We'll prepare you tomorrow night.'

The next day, immediately after the jury had filed in, Callagy barked, 'Call Joan Collins to the stand.'

My heart did the rhumba, and I glared at Ken, who shrugged. Into the witness box unprepared – another actor's nightmare.

Callagy tried basic intimidation techniques, throwing my manuscripts and depositions before me while firing off belligerent questions. When I tried to explain the differences in my *Globe* depositions and why I'd referred to the novel I was having trouble publishing (because of the distress caused me by the *Globe*'s unlawful publication of its photographs) as *The Ruling Passion* when it was actually *Hell Hath No Fury*, I was sternly reprimanded.

'Just answer yes or no, witness,' Judge Gammerman snapped.

I'd admitted in a previous deposition that my memory for dates was poor, yet the questions Callagy asked were a memory test. Example: 'Did Joni Evans tell you your writing was "too Gothic" in 1991?'

Trying to explain that it was *I* who had used the word Gothic about my own work was useless. Both Callagy and the judge insisted on only yes or no answers. I was surprised my lawyers didn't object to such tricky questions that were designed to trip me up on memory.

It was incredibly frustrating. Callagy was a bully, all right, and I thought all the men at Random House were cowards to hide behind his skirts.

I knew that *all* Random House had to go on in this case were these minor differences between my two 1992 depositions, my 1994 deposition, and what I answered now. Who remembered 'he said', 'she said' or 'I said'? Not me. Callagy was trying to fluster me but each time I tried to explain he cut me off with: 'Yes or no, witness?'

I wanted to throttle him.

Then Callagy triumphantly revealed to the jury an enormous blow-up of the release I'd signed in the *Globe* case. 'Did you sign this?'

'Yes,' I said.

'Do you realize you were under *oath* and penalty of *perjury* when you signed?' he spat.

'Yes, but I—'

'Just yes or no, witness.' The judge sounded bored.

'So you say one thing to the *Globe*, when you're trying to get money from them, and then two years later when you're trying to get money from Random House you say something else?'

'No – no, no,' I stammered.

His lips curled in a 'gotcha' sneer.

'Don't you have any shame?' he sneered.

'*Objection*,' Ken yelled.

'Counsellor, counsellor, *please*.' Gammerman banged his gavel as the courtroom erupted again.

'No more questions.' Callagy turned his back on me with a satisfied smirk, the famous plagiarized line from the McCarthy trial ringing in my ears.

I couldn't *believe* what was happening. Callagy had insulted me, calling me a liar *and* a perjurer yet I was *powerless* to explain. This court was a theatre of the absurd.

Trembling with frustration and fury I sat with my lawyers. Young Stacy squeezed my hand. 'Don't worry,' she said.

But I did. I *was* worried. Callagy had made me look utterly stupid and a liar. I tried not to think about the TV camera fixed on me. I tried to dismiss the personal and professional humiliation, and the possibility that I could be ruined, but my emotional tether, stretched to breaking-point after two years of this litigation hell, finally snapped.

I fumbled in my bag for a Kleenex.

'Go into the Judge's chambers,' Stacy whispered, so I dashed in and cried me a river – more tears than I'd shed for years.

Two really sweet courtroom officials bustled around, dispensing water, tissues, coffee and condemnation of Callagy's venom.

'Attacking a witness doesn't go down very well with the jury,' said Belinda, wisely.

'He went too far,' said Barbara.

'I've heard convicted killers treated with more respect than Callagy gave me,' I said. 'It was like being interrogated by the Gestapo. But if there's any justice I *will* win.'

'No Way to Treat a Diva!' shrieked the front-page headlines of the *New York Post* the next day beside a photo of me crying, plus the story of my 'ineptitude' in the courtroom. 'She's no Alexis!' they crowed. 'Alexis would have given as good as she got. Joan is brittle and unconvincing, a frail shadow of her TV roles.'

Frail? Me?

'Just *wait*,' I muttered to Judy, later that night, as more messages of support for me and anger towards Callagy poured in. 'Just *wait* till *I'm* allowed to speak.'

My friend Louise Fennell telephoned from London first thing in the morning. 'Darling, you must get rid of that boring beige. It's so *down*. Wear something red or pink. Be cheerful.'

She was right. I put on a pink silk shirt, and sailed off to day four and Ken's direct examination. At *last* I *myself* would be able to tell the jury *everything* including the *Globe* deposition, in my own words.

Ken started well enough and for ten minutes I was able to articulate how diligently I'd worked and how much I'd written.

Then, as I began to explain the inconsistencies in that *wretched* 1992 deposition, I was interrupted in mid-sentence.

'Objection,' Callagy called.

I could not believe this. It's hard enough for a lawyer to ask *exactly* the correct question without appearing to 'lead' the witness and Ken was doing it right.

'Sustained.' The judge sounded even more bored than he had the previous day.

Ken rephrased the question.

'Objection,' Callagy barked again.

'Sustained,' said the judge.

Ken, by now becoming slightly flustered, went to Don and was heard whispering on Court TV, 'I don't know how the hell to get out of this.'

He then rephrased the question again, but Callagy objected and the judge sustained it.

I felt this was all totally unfair and infuriating. I was being tongue-tied *by my own lawyer*. Callagy, no slouch, knew that I was on a roll of directly explaining events to the jury, so he went flat out to stop me *and he succeeded*! I wanted to scream but, in court, rules are rules.

At five o'clock, we broke for the long weekend and I went to stay with Blaine and Robert Trump in their country house in upstate New York. Friends came to visit, the consensus of their opinions being that my lawyer should *never* have allowed the bombastic Alberto Vitale off the hook.

'He's chairman and chief executive of Random. He *should* have testified, even if he pretended he didn't know anything,' said Robert. 'He's the starstruck fool who got you into all this, after all.'

'He's obviously frightened to get on the stand,' I said.

'Do you mind if I say a mass for you tomorrow?' Liam Neeson asked sympathetically.

'Say as many as you can,' I said. 'I need all the help I can get.'

Legal manoeuvres weren't my scene but books were, so I asked Robert to pick any popular novel from his bookshelf and I read a couple of paragraphs aloud.

Robert grinned. 'That sounds ridiculous.'

'That's what Callagy's been doing in court – reading out excerpts derisively, making me a laughing stock.'

'If Swifty were still alive would this still have happened?' asked Robert.

'No way. He had so much power in publishing and protected his authors to the death. One phone call and Random House would have backed off,' I said.

Monday was still a holiday and the snow was thick on the ground. I spent the entire day reading my nightmarishly confusing depositions.

'I can't remember it at all – there are *hundreds* of pages to memorize.'

'Study them thoroughly tonight,' Ken instructed. 'You're on with Callagy first thing. He's going to do *everything* he can to try and get you.'

I was full of gloom. It was *impossible* to remember who'd said what to whom and when. I was weighed down with dates and conflicting statements.

Another close friend, Sue St Johns, rang, then I spoke to her lawyer husband Dick.

'*Don't* let Callagy rattle you,' he warned. 'Because that's what he's going to attempt to do. If he tries confusing you with dates just tell him you don't *remember*. You're not a computer, for God's sake. You don't have to remember things if you can't. Be strong – be assertive and *look* that jury in the eye.'

I'd hardly glanced at the jury, having been warned by Judge Gammerman not to make eye-contact, but suddenly I thought, Why not? It made sense. They seemed intelligent. I would *make* them understand that *I* was telling the truth and the plaintiffs were misrepresenting *everything*.

I *won't* be persecuted any more, I thought.

Before going to sleep I did some visualization-meditation. The following morning I felt ready to take on the world. How *dare* Random House treat me in this demeaning way? Didn't *they* have any shame?

I wore something old, something new, something borrowed and something blue. The Fabergé good luck rabbit Robin had given me was safely tucked in my bag and I put on all my lucky charms and talismans. I felt in commanding form when I greeted Judy.

'You look totally different,' she said. 'Really powerful and confident.'

'I'm ready for those bastards.' I grinned. 'And I *won't* let 'em get me down this time.'

While Callagy rained questions on me I stared at him coolly and unyieldingly. I'd finally realized that if I only answered what I *could* answer I had a chance of winning this game of trial and error.

Several times I said, 'I can't recall,' which seemed to irritate him. Finally he stalked over close to me holding out my manuscript.

'Counsellor, you're supposed to ask permission of the judge before approaching the witness.' I smiled at him flirtatiously.

Callagy gulped, then stared at me furiously. I continued smiling. I was finally in the driver's seat. A line I'd often said in *Dynasty* came into my head: 'Don't mess with Alexis!'

'Mr Callagy, I'm not a *computer*,' I said. 'How can you possibly expect me to remember all these different dates?'

He tried another tack and I answered, 'You're deliberately switching about and trying to confuse me, aren't you, Mr Callagy?'

He then asked about the number of times my novel's title had been changed.

'Look, I called it *Athena, Atlanta, Hell Hath No Fury*. Sometimes I even called it *Hitler's Mistress*.' The court and jury laughed, and the judge called for order.

The cooler I behaved, the more rattled Callagy became. Eventually, having failed to crack me, the mulish attorney conceded defeat. 'No more questions,' he hissed.

Then Don Zakarin summed up my case, ramming home the salient points.

When he finished, Callagy jumped up and gave the jury a histrionic performance that would have done credit to *Richard III*. His trump card was the 1992 document I'd signed, which he called, melodramatically, 'The Smoking Gun' and he mentioned this no less than *nine* times.

'It's all he's got,' Ken whispered.

Jury time now. The judge instructed the jury that there were only three questions to answer:

(1) Did defendant Joan Collins fail to deliver complete manuscript number one?
(2) Did defendant Joan Collins fail to deliver complete manuscript number two?
(3) Was manuscript number two a revision of manuscript number one?

I'd insisted that each juror be given a copy of both manuscripts and was feeling confident until Don said, 'I can't predict how it's going to go with this jury. You can never predict a jury.'

Judy, Sarah, Lance and I went to the Harbor restaurant, a mile away, where the Teflon Don, the infamous Mafioso John Gotti, had waited for his verdict on a murder charge. This wait was absolute murder for me.

'It'll take them *hours* to reach a verdict – we'll be here all night,' I said. Two hours passed.

I'd just decided to order a glass of wine when our mobile phone rang. Everyone jumped several inches into the air.

'They've reached a verdict!' Belinda said from the court. 'Get down here right away.'

As the jury filed in my heart was beating so wildly I thought it would burst through my rib-cage. I tried to read the jurors' impassive faces.

'If it's "No" on question one, it's in our favour,' whispered Ken.

The foreman, a well-upholstered, bearded man, stood up to read from his piece of paper.

I started to shake uncontrollably. Although my contract was iron-clad, would this jury be swayed by Random's fabrication about my 'unpublishable' writing?

I willed myself not to break down if I lost. I was squeezing Ken's hand tightly when, through the roaring in my ears, I heard the most beautiful word in the world. 'NO!'

I trembled with delight, and bounded over to the jury to shake all of their hands.

I'd won. Justice had been served, and how sweet it was.

Callagy was talking to the press, his face clearly showing his bitter disappointment.

'Every author will make you a heroine now.' Ken grinned.

I realized that, to millions of TV watchers who didn't know the anguish I had gone through, my ordeal had merely been entertainment for the winter-weary.

My reactions to what was the culmination of two of the most harrowing years of my life were described as 'an Oscar-worthy performance' and 'She squeezed a three-act drama out of those vital seconds before the verdict was announced.' Did some people think I was *acting*? Hey, boys, I didn't ask for the cameras to be there.

The jury insisted on meeting me, so Ken and I dashed to their room to be greeted by a standing ovation and eleven beaming faces.

'My God, you can *smile*!' I said. 'You were all so completely stone-faced during the trial it terrified me.'

'We were told to be,' laughed their jolly spokesman, then each juror requested I sign their copies of the manuscripts.

'This looks real good, I can't wait to read it,' said the foreman.

Then we were whisked through the winding stone corridors and out into the freezing New York night where a large crowd had gathered, as well as press and photographers. A cheer went up as I came out of the court-house and I punched the air with my fist raised joyfully in triumph, a gesture I'd never before made in my life.

The questions came thick and fast. 'How does it feel to have defeated one of the most powerful publishing houses in the world?'

'Vindicated,' I said. 'I've been writing for eighteen years. I've had six books published, and five bestsellers, so I'm going onward. I was terribly pleased by the verdict. I'd taken on a giant with money to burn, who didn't care if they ruined my career *and* my livelihood. People advised me not to continue, but I'm not a quitter, and revenge is *so* sweet.'

My lawyers answered the financial questions in which the press were most interested: 'We expect Miss Collins is owed in the vicinity of two million dollars,' said Don.

'Nice work if you can get it,' I said. 'I bet those bastards appeal.'

'If they do, they're fools,' said Don. 'They should swallow their loss and behave like gentlemen.'

'Gentlemen they *definitely* ain't,' I said.

'It just drags it out for them,' said Don. 'But this is a wonderful, famous victory. It's an out-and-out triumph because Random were trying to intimidate all authors by saying, "Don't mess with us or we'll show the world the differences between what you send to us and what we publish."'

'Amen,' I said fervently.

The next day Alberto Vitale told the *New York Times* that his company were 'dismayed by the decision and terribly disappointed but we're reviewing our legal options.'

A month later Random House appealed the unanimous verdict. Don't they have any shame?

The party that night, at Peter and Jane Marino's beautiful apartment, had been planned for several weeks and would have gone ahead even if I'd lost. 'It would either have been a wake or a celebration,' I told Robin, who had flown in that afternoon from London to watch the nail-biting finale on television with Hugo Guinness.

Champagne flowed, jubilant faces gushed congratulations and delight at my victory, my back ached from enthusiastic hugs, and I simply couldn't stop grinning at everyone's exuberant rejoicing.

Many friends were there: Dominick Dunne, who had followed the trial closely and given me wonderful advice, Bob Colacello, Blaine and Robert, Cari Modine, Ann Jones, Kenneth Jay Lane, Marina Palma, Janey Longman, Hugo Guinness, Natasha Richardson and Liam Neeson, Nan Kempner, and those who had been closely by my side every day – Ken and Erica, Judy, Sarah Standing, Lance Reynolds – and, of course, my beloved Robin.

Then, after more congratulations, toasts and some touching speeches, I stood up and raised my glass of champagne to heaven: 'To Swifty, wherever you may be, you *certainly* came through for me.'

So there it is. My Second Act. I hope I'll be fortunate enough that my third will be as enjoyable.

There's a saying in the theatre that 'There are no good third acts.' Cynical, maybe, but not always true and I shall try to prove otherwise. My life continues at its usual accelerated pace, but I prefer it that way. Not for me the slippers and the hearth: there are too many fresh fields and plenty of pastures new.

I started this book around the time Random House sued me and I'm finishing it now while sitting at Destino, looking out at a view of such incomparable loveliness it almost breaks my heart. After this I shall continue writing, for my belief in myself transcends all negativity.

I know I have a lucky life even with my fair share of disaster. I think I've played the cards I've been dealt pretty well. The most important things are that my children are healthy and thriving and that my relationship with Robin continues to flourish.

As Tennessee Williams often used to end his letters to Maria St Just, *En avant!*

Major Television Productions

1959, 1962 & 1966   *The Bob Hope Show* (NBC)

1963   *The Human Jungle* 'Struggle For A Mind' (BBC)

1965   *The Man From U.N.C.L.E* 'The Galatea Affair' (CBS)

1966   *The Virginian* 'Lady From Wichita' (NBC)

1967   *Batman* 'The Siren', 'Ring Around The Riddler', 'The Wail Of The Siren' (ABC)

1967   *Star Trek* 'City On The Edge Of Forever' (NBC)

1970   *Mission Impossible* 'Nicole' (CBS)

1970   *Orson Welles' Great Mysteries* 'The Dinner Party' (Hallmark/NBC)

1971   *The Persuaders* 'Five Miles To Midnight' (ITC)

1973   *Orson Welles' Great Mysteries* 'The Man Who Came To Dinner' (Hallmark/NBC)

1973   *Drive Hard, Drive Fast* (TV movie, NBC)

1974   *Fallen Angels* (TV play, Anglia)

1975   *Ellery Queen Whodunnit* 'The Adventures of Auld Lang Syne' (NBC)

1976   *Space 1999* 'Mission Of The Dariens' (ITC)

1976   *Police Woman* 'Trick Box', 'The Pawn Shop' (NBC/Columbia TV)

1976   *Switch* 'Stung From Behind' (Universal)

1976   *Gibbsville* 'Andrew' (Columbia)

1976   *Baretta* 'Pay or Die' (ABC)

1976   *The Moneychangers* (TV movie/NBC)

1977   *Fantastic Journey* 'Turnabout' (NBC)

1977   *Starsky & Hutch* 'Murder on Playboy Island' (ABC)

1977   *Tales Of The Unexpected* 'Neck' (Anglia)

1979   *Tales Of The Unexpected* 'Georgy Porgy' (Anglia)

1980   *Tales Of The Unexpected* 'A Girl Can't Have Everything' (Anglia)

1981   *Fantasy Island* 'My Fair Pharaoh' (ABC)

1981–89   *Dynasty* (Aaron Spelling Productions/ABC)

1982   *Paper Dolls* (TV movie, ABC)

1982   *The Wild Women of Chastity Gulch* (TV movie, ABC)

1982   *Faerie Tale Theater* 'Hansel & Gretel' (Showtime)

1983   *The Love Boat* 'The Captain's Crush' (ABC)

1983   *The Making Of A Male Model* (*The Look* USA) (TV movie, ABC)

1984   *The Cartier Affair* (TV movie, CBS)

1984   *Her Life As A Man* (TV movie, CBS)

1984   *Blondes versus Brunettes* (ABC)

1984   *The Dean Martin Celebrity Roast Honoring Joan Collins* (NBC)

1985   *Sins*, also Executive Producer (TV mini-series, CBS)

1986   *Monte Carlo* , also Executive Producer (TV mini-series, CBS)

1987   *All Star Party for Joan Collins* (CBS)

1991   *Dynasty – The Reunion* (TV mini-series, Aaron Spelling Productions/ABC)

1991   *Tonight at 8.30* (*Collins Meets Coward* USA) 'Ways And Means', 'Still Life', 'The Astonished Heart', 'Shadow Play', 'Red Peppers', 'Family Album', 'Hands Across The Sea', 'Burned Oak' (TV series, BBC)

1993   *Roseanne* 'First Cousin, Twice Removed' (ABC)

1993   *Next* (*Mama's Back* USA) (TV pilot, BBC)

1995   *Hart To Hart* 'Two Harts In Three Quarter Time' (TV movie, Family Channel)

1995   *Annie: A Royal Adventure* (TV movie, ABC)

Stage Appearances

1946   *A Doll's House* (Arts Theatre, London)

1952   *The Seventh Veil* (Q Theatre, London)
1952   *Jassey* (Q Theatre, London)
1953   *The Praying Mantis* (UK Tour)
1953   *Claudia And David* (Q Theatre, London)
1954   *The Skin Of Our Teeth* (Q Theatre, London)
1979   *The Last Of Mrs Cheyne* (Chichester Festival Theatre)
1981   *The Last Of Mrs Cheyne* (Cambridge Theatre, London)
1990–1   *Private Lives* (Aldwych Theatre, London)
1991–2   *Private Lives* (Broadhurst Theatre, (Broadway, New York/US Tour)

Film Biography
1951   *Lady Godiva Rides Again* (British Lion/London Films)
1952   *The Woman's Angle* (Associated British)
1952   *Judgement Deferred* (Associated British)
1952   *I Believe In You* (Rank Films)
1952   *Decameron Nights* (Eros Films)
1953   *Cosh Boy* (*The Slasher* USA) (Rank Films)
1953   *The Square Ring* (Ealing Studios)
1953   *Turn The Key Softly* (Rank Films)
1953   *Our Girl Friday* (*The Adventures of Sadie* USA) (Renown Pictures)
1954   *The Good Die Young* (United Artists)
1954   *The Land of the Pharaohs* (Warner Bros)
1955   *The Virgin Queen* (Twentieth Century-Fox)
1955   *The Girl In The Red Velvet Swing* (Twentieth Century-Fox)
1956   *The Opposite Sex* (MGM)
1956   *Sea Wife* (*Sea Wife and Biscuit* USA) (Twentieth Century-Fox)
1956   *Island In The Sun* (Twentieth Century-Fox)
1957   *The Wayward Bus* (Twentieth Century-Fox)
1957   *Stopover Tokyo* (Twentieth Century-Fox)
1958   *The Bravados* (Twentieth Century-Fox)
1958   *Rally Round The Flag, Boys* (Twentieth Century-Fox)
1959   *Seven Thieves* (Twentieth Century-Fox)
1962   *Esther And The King* (Twentieth Century-Fox)
1962   *The Road To Hong Kong* (United Artists)
1964   *La Congiuntura* (*One Million Dollars* Europe/*Hard Times For A Princess* USA) (Columbia)
1966   *Warning Shot* (Universal)
1968   *Subterfuge* (Commonwealth United Pictures)
1969   *If It's Tuesday, This Must Be Belgium* (United Artists)
1969   *State of Siege* (*Besieged* (unreleased, USA)/*Lo' Stato De Assedio* (Cinegal, Italy)
1969   *Can Hieronymus Merkin Ever Forget Mercy Humppe And Find True Happiness?* (Universal)
1970   *Three In The Cellar* (*Up In The Cellar* USA) (American International)
1970   *The Executioner* (Columbia)
1971   *Fear In The Night* (*Dynasty of Fear/Honeymoon of Fear* USA)
1971   *Quest For Love* (Rank Films)
1971   *Revenge* (*Inn Of The Frightened People/Terror From Under The Stairs/After Jenny Died/Behind The Cellar Door* USA) (Rank Films)
1972   *Tales From The Crypt* (Cinerama)
1972   *L'Arbitro* (*The Referee/Playing The Field* USA) (Documento Films)
1973   *Tales That Witness Madness* (Paramount)
1973   *Dark Places* (Film International)
1974   *Alfie Darling* (*Oh! Alfie* USA) (EMI)
1974   *Poliziotto Senza Paura* (*Fearless Fuzz/Police At The Service Of A*

Citizen/Fatal Charms USA) (Promer Film)

1975 *The Bawdy Adventures Of Tom Jones* (Universal)

1975 *Call Of The Wolf* (*The Great Adventure* USA) (Pacific International)

1975 *I Don't Want To Be Born* (*The Devil Within Her* USA) (Rank Films)

1977 *Empire Of The Ants* (American International)

1977 *The Big Sleep* (ITC)

1978 *Zero To Sixty* (First Artists)

1978 *The Stud* (Brent Walker)

1979 *The Bitch* (Brent Walker)

1979 *Game For Vultures* (Columbia)

1979 *Sunburn* (Paramount)

1982 *Homework* (Jenson Farley Pictures)

1982 *Nutcracker* (Rank Films)

1994 *Decadence* (Mayfair Entertainment)

1995 *In The Bleak Midwinter* (Castle Rock)

For more information please contact:

Paul Keylock

The Joan Collins Fan Club

16 Bulbecks Walk

South Woodham Ferrers

Chelmsford

Essex

CM3 5ZN

England

Index